Polydrug Abuse

The Results of a
National Collaborative Study

Polydrug Abuse
The Results of a
National Collaborative Study

EDITED BY

Donald R. Wesson

Department of Psychiatry
University of California Medical Center
San Francisco, California

Albert S. Carlin

Department of Psychiatry and Behavioral Sciences
University of Washington
Seattle, Washington

Kenneth M. Adams

Department of Psychiatry
Henry Ford Hospital
Detroit, Michigan

George Beschner

National Institute on Drug Abuse
Rockville, Maryland

ACADEMIC PRESS   New York   San Francisco   London   1978
A Subsidiary of Harcourt Brace Jovanovich, Publishers

ACADEMIC PRESS, INC.
111 Fifth Avenue, New York, New York 10003

United Kingdom Edition published by
ACADEMIC PRESS, INC. (LONDON) LTD.
24/28 Oval Road, London NW1 7DX

Library of Congress Cataloging in Publication Data
Main entry under title:

Polydrug abuse.

    Bibliography: p.
    1. Psychotropic drugs. 2. Medication abuse––United
States. 3. Drug utilization––United States. 4. Drug
abuse surveys––United States. I. Wesson, Donald R.
RM315.P62   614.3'5   78–12620
ISBN 0–12–745250–8

To Phillip Rennick, who taught us a great deal and whose many contributions to neuropsychology were cut short by his death.

Contents

CHAPTER XVII

Conclusions and Recommendations for Future Research   371

Albert S. Carlin, Kenneth M. Adams, George Beschner, and Donald R. Wesson

List of Contributors

Numbers in parentheses indicate the pages on which the authors' contributions begin.

Kenneth M. Adams (1, 223, 263, 359, 371), Department of Psychiatry, Henry Ford Hospital, Detroit, Michigan 48202

A. M. Anch (299), Department of Psychiatry, Baylor College of Medicine and Veterans Administration Hospital, Houston, Texas 77030

Paul A. Attewell (337), Department of Psychiatry, School of Medicine, University of California, San Diego, La Jolla, California 92039

Richard F. Avery* (337), Department of Psychiatry, University of California, San Diego, La Jolla, California 92039

John Benvenuto (211), Department of Psychiatry, New York Medical College, New York, New York 10016

G. James Berry (129), Resource Alternatives Corporation, Denver, Colorado 80206

---

* Gifford Mental Health Clinic, Department of Psychiatry, University of California at San Diego, 3427 Fourth Avenue, San Diego, California 92103

George Beschner (1, 371), National Institute on Drug Abuse, Rockville, Maryland 20857

Reginald G. Bickford[*] (273), Department of Neurosciences, University of California, San Diego, La Jolla, California 92093

G. Nicholas Braucht (129), Department of Psychology, University of Denver, Denver, Colorado 80210

Albert S. Carlin (1, 97, 223, 263, 371), Department of Psychiatry and Behavioral Sciences, University of Washington, Seattle, Washington 98195

B. S. Comstock (299), Baylor College of Medicine, Department of Psychiatry, Houston, Texas 77030

E. G. Comstock (299), Institute of Clinical Toxicology, Houston, Texas 77030

Grace Dammann (59), San Francisco Polydrug Project, San Francisco, California 94117

Edward Farley (1), Polydrug Research and Treatment Center, Bala Cynwyd, Pennsylvania 19004

Charles Gdowski (149), Division of Psychology, Lafayette Clinic, Detroit, Michigan 48207

Igor Grant (223, 263, 273), Department of Psychiatry, University of California, San Diego and Psychiatric Service, Veterans Administration Hospital, La Jolla, California 92093

Charles Harris (263), Department of Psychiatry, University of California Medical Center, San Francisco, California 94143

Leon Gibson Hunt (183), James Dixon Institute for Public Health, Antioch College, Columbia, Maryland 21045

Lewis L. Judd (223, 273, 337), Department of Psychiatry, School of Medicine, University of California, San Diego, La Jolla, California 92093

Ismet Karacan (299), Sleep Disorders Center, Department of Psychiatry, Baylor College of Medicine and Veterans Administration Hospital, Houston, Texas 77030

John Keegan (17, 149), Department of Psychology, Wayne State University, Detroit, Michigan 48202

Michael W. Kirby (129), Resource Alternatives Corporation, Denver, Colorado 80206

David Lachar (149), Division of Psychology, Lafayette Clinic, Detroit, Michigan 48207

John P. Lau (211), Creative Socio-Medics Corporation, Arlington, Virginia 22209

[*] Department of Neurosciences M–008, University of California at San Diego, La Jolla, California 92093

William G. Lee (273), Department of Psychiatry, School of Medicine, University of California, San Diego, La Jolla, California 92093

Constance A. Moore (299), Baylor College of Medicine, Houston, Texas 77030

M. Okawa (299), Baylor College of Medicine, Department of Psychiatry, Houston, Texas 77030

Nancy Ousley (59), Sexual Assault Center, Harborview Medical Center, Seattle, Washington

John Phin (31), Creative Socio-Medics Corporation, Arlington, Virginia 22209

Robert Reed (223), Department of Psychiatry, University of California, San Diego and Psychiatric Service, Veterans Administration Hospital, La Jolla, California 92093

Phillip M. Rennick (223), Lafayette Clinic, Detroit, Michigan 48207

Winifred B. Riney (337), Department of Psychiatry, School of Medicine, University of California, San Diego, La Jolla, California 92093

P. J. Salis (299), Department of Psychiatry, Baylor College of Medicine and Veterans Administration Hospital, Houston, Texas 77030

Kenneth Schooff* (17, 149, 223), Psychiatric Center of Michigan, Detroit, Michigan 48080

David E. Smith (325), Founder and Medical Director, Haight-Ashbury Free Medical Clinic, San Francisco, California 94117

Fred F. Stauss (97), Department of Psychiatry and Behavioral Sciences, University of Washington, Seattle, Washington 98195

Donald R. Wesson (1, 263, 325, 371), Department of Psychiatry, University of California Medical Center, San Francisco, California 94143

R. L. Williams (299), Department of Psychiatry, Baylor College of Medicine, Houston, Texas 77030

* Psychiatric Center of Michigan, 22777 Harper Avenue, St. Clair Shores, Michigan 48080

Foreword

During the past 25 years, considerable attention has been given to the severity of the heroin problem in the United States. Legislative actions, community organization campaigns, and treatment efforts have been initiated primarily in response to "the heroin problem." Yet, at the same time we have been finding that sedatives, hypnotics, stimulants, antidepressants, and antianxiety drugs are being consumed at increasing levels. The term "polydrug" has been coined and has become part of our vocabulary.

Unlike heroin abuse, the use of polydrugs is surrounded by a multiplicity of different issues. Certain drugs have become essential in medical practice. Physicians currently write more than a quarter of a million prescriptions for psychoactive drugs per year. The relationship of physician-prescribed drugs to polydrug abuse is complex and is the subject of several studies. In our society, it is not uncommon for people to be using different drugs to relax, induce sleep, reduce pain, relieve depression, increase energy and alertness, and alter moods. A portion of these individuals on their own initiative increase their drug use beyond the usual therapeutic dosages.

Control over the supply of drugs included under polydrug abuse is difficult as drugs are available through both legal and illegal channels. They are often used in different combinations (sometimes with alcohol or opiates) and the patterns of abuse cut across social, political, economic, and geographic boundaries.

The Drug Abuse Warning Network (DAWN), a nationwide data collection system designed to monitor the trends of problem use of more than 3000 drugs in 24 Standard Metropolitan Statistical Areas (SMSAs are statistical units composed of a relatively large core city and the adjacent geographical area), showed more than 177,000 drug abuse episodes in the period between May 1976 and June 1977. The episodes identified in emergency rooms, crisis centers, and medical examiners' offices included many of the commonly used household and prescription drugs. Diazepam (Valium), the nation's leading prescribed drug, used by an estimated 15% of the American adult population, is mentioned in more emergency room episodes than any single prescription drug. Barbiturates accounted for 19% of the drug-related deaths in 1975.

Recently, drug-use patterns involving combinations of drugs have aroused widespread interest. The reporting system for federally funded drug treatment programs—Client Oriented Data Acquisition Process (CODAP)—have documented different patterns of multiple drug use (regular use of more than one drug) in different states. New York, California, and Illinois, states that have a higher incidence of heroin abuse, report a slightly higher percentage of clients using only one drug. In contrast, Alabama, Arkansas, Idaho, Maine, Minnesota, Utah, Vermont, West Virginia, and Wisconsin report that more than 68% of clients in treatment have been involved in multiple drug patterns.

In 1969, the Federal Government contracted with Texas Christian University's Institute of Behavioral Research to establish and maintain a patient-reporting system from Federally supported drug-abuse treatment programs as a data base for treatment–outcome evaluation research. The reporting system, called the Drug Abuse Reporting Program (DARP), has demonstrated the importance of examining and establishing the drug combinations most frequently observed in a large contemporary sample of drug abusers. The DARP data, concerning the types and frequencies of pretreatment drug abuse, show that a substantial number of patients (18%) experienced patterns of multiple drug use in which at least three nonopiate drugs were used.

The 1976–1977 state plans produced by state agencies that have been delegated the responsibility for coordinating local drug-programming activities, reflect similar drug patterns across the country. For example, in Rhode Island, a state that is not known as a high heroin traffic area, 1600 drug overdose cases were reported by hospitals in 1975, a sharp increase over previous years. The state agency estimated that there were approximately 6400 polydrug abusers in this state in 1976. This is not inconsistent with the findings of many other states.

Polydrugs may be obtained in a variety of ways: by over-the-counter purchases, by prescription, and illegally. In a national survey conducted in 1977, one-fourth of the individuals 18- to 25-years old and one-eighth of adults 26 and older reported non-medical use of psychotherapeutic drugs (sedatives, stimulants, and tranquilizers; see Abelson, Fishburn, and Cisin, 1978).

According to the latest available statistics, two-thirds of the psychoactive prescription drug users are women. Historically, we have found that disenchanted and confused young people experiment with a wide variety of substances, the choice of which is often based on local availability and peer pressure. Recently there has been growing evidence that the elderly also participate in the mass consumption of polydrugs, and investigations are currently under way to examine the nature and impact of this problem. In studies reflecting trends on the use of dangerous drugs, we are seeing new patterns emerging, particularly in regard to barbiturates and amphetamines. In some respects, the chronic and unsupervised use of these drugs can be compared with heroin as a major social problem.

It is, however, impossible to estimate the number of people who are obtaining polydrugs illegally or abusing them. Because it is such a complex problem with patients appearing in different treatment systems, the total impact of polydrug abuse is virtually unknown. There are considerable costs for the individual, the family, and the community in the form of property losses, health and welfare costs, criminal justice activities, and the loss of productivity.

The federal government has attempted to respond to the problem through regulatory, treatment, and educational measures. Government vigilance and regulations have tightened and new commercial drugs are being more thoroughly and reliably tested. Currently, 40% of the treatment slots supported by the National Institute on Drug Abuse are being ultilized to treat nonopiate patients.

Yet, the failure to produce information about the nature and extent of the polydrug problem has been a major deterrent to the development of coherent and consistent policies. In order to allocate properly our resources in the future, it is critical that we define the scope and dimension of the problem and determine what causes individuals to turn to these drugs and what treatment approaches seem to be the most appropriate.

These steps must be taken with a recognition that there are agencies and institutions currently in existence that, with the required knowledge and equipment, could play a more important role in dealing with the polydrug problem.

In 1973, an important step in this direction was taken when the Special Action Office of Drug Abuse Prevention, in the executive office of the President, initiated a national study of polydrug abuse. This book is the report on the findings from that study which was organized to conduct a comprehensive demographic, sociological, psychological, and medical study of polydrug cases. This national study, although restricted to individuals admitted to special inpatient and outpatient units, is the first attempt to reach, treat, and study a large sample of polydrug abusers.

In some respects the methods and procedures used in this study were unique—12 different programs scattered across the country participated in a collaborative effort. A team of professionals working out of hospital settings were able to initiate new outreach and case-finding techniques, bringing people with polydrug problems into clinical settings and evaluating them systematically. A series of standard tests were integrated to form a program test battery that was employed by all participating programs. Due primarily to the devotion and hard work of those involved, this study was successfully completed. It is my hope that this book, a product of the study, will help us to understand better the polydrug problem so that we can be in a better position to develop intervention strategies.

Robert DuPont

Special Assistant to the Administrator of ADAMHA
(Alcohol, Drug Abuse and Mental Health Administration)
Washington, D.C.

Acknowledgments

During the active data collection phase of the polydrug projects, over 100 individuals were employed by the 12 projects. Each of these individuals contributed in their respective way to the data presented here, however, not all of these individuals were involved during the writing phase. As the data collection phase of the project concluded in mid-1975, a smaller group of individuals undertook the task of data analysis and the writing of this book.

The editors would particularly like to acknowledge the role of Edward Farley, who developed the "Philadelphia drug typology," used in several chapters. In addition, he made a major contribution by persistently tracing down and correcting errors present in the early versions of the national data tape.

Peter Bourne reviewed early drafts of much of the material, and added his perspective and recollections concerning the early phases of the project when he was with the Special Action Office on Drug Abuse Prevention during the formative process of the projects.

Initial drafts of the book included a much broader discussion of the psychological data collected on the patients. The analysis of this data was initially under a task force which included John Benvenuto, Miriam Cohen, Betsy Comstock, and Kenneth Schooff. The more the data was analyzed the more apparent it became that the traditional approaches of looking at the MMPI data, using mean profiles and the Current and Past Psychopathology Seek (CAPPS) and Profile of Mood States (POMS) as level of performance tests, not only suffered from a great deal of contamination due to drug use, but that the scales themselves were not really integer or even ordinal scales. The statistical manipulation of such scale data, while frequently reported in the drug abuse literature, were felt by the editors not to be valid approaches. For this and other reasons discussed in Chapter 2 of this volume, we excluded Miriam Cohen's work on comparing average MMPI profiles, Alfred Friedman's work on the CAPPS, and a Donald Wesson's work on the profile of mood states. Nonetheless, the efforts spent by these individuals in analyzing the data were a necessary step in the evolution of this work.

The national data tape was prepared for the project by a private contractor. The tape, found to be less than optimally constructed, was therefore put in a format useful for scientific data processing by Darryl Bertolucci of the Division of Computer Assistance at the Alcohol Drug Abuse and Mental Health Administration. His work was invaluable in making the transition from the contractor to the data analysis group.

A number of agencies and institutions participated in the Polydrug Collaborative Project effort, planning for and generating the data base that was used as the primary data source for this book. The work was supported primarily by grants administered by the Services Research Branch, National Institute on Drug Abuse, Department of Health, Education, and Welfare. The following 12 organizations contributed to the data base and the writing of the book: Addiction Research and Treatment Corporation, New York City, H81 DA 01474; Colorado Dept. of Health, Denver General Hospital, H81 DA 01687; Duke University Medical Center, Durham, N.C., H81 DA 01665; Friends of Psychiatric Research, San Diego, Calif., H81 DA 01467; Howard Medical School, Boston, Mass., H81 DA 01712; Hennepin County Mental Health Agency, Minneapolis, H81 DA 01662; Lafayette Clinic, Detroit, Michigan, H81 DA 01879; Medical College of Virginia, Richmond, Virginia, H81 DA 01468; Mental Health and Mental Authority of Harris County, Houston, Texas, H81 DA 01466; Philadelphia Psychiatric Center, Philadelphia H81 DA 01657; University of Washington, Seattle, H81 DA 01476; and Youth Projects, Incorporated, San Francisco, Calif., H81 DA 01632. Although these grants were supported by NIDA, the interpretations and conclusions presented in this book do not necessarily reflect the position of the National Institute on Drug Abuse.

During the final year of writing, manuscript flow and revisions were coordinated by Ann Lyerla. Her editorial assistance and retyping of successive drafts of manuscripts greatly facilitated the editorial task.

Polydrug Abuse

The Results of a
National Collaborative Study

CHAPTER I

Introduction

George Beschner, Kenneth Adams,
Donald Wesson, Albert Carlin,
and Edward Farley

Polydrug abuse is used to refer to (1) simultaneous or sequential non-medical use of more than one psychoactive drug (Tinklenberg and Berger, 1977) or (2) the abuse of any psychoactive drug singly, in combination, or sequentially which does not include heroin or alcohol as the primary drug. The last definition was used by the Federal government in establishing their "polydrug projects" and is the definition of polydrug used in this book. Included are prescription drugs obtained illicitly, prescription drugs used in dosages beyond those medically prescribed, and over-the-counter drugs used in dosages beyond the amount recommended on the package. It is important to clarify that the term polydrug, as used here, may refer to the abuse of a *single drug* other than heroin or alcohol as well as sequential or simultaneous use of different psychoactive drugs.

When the Special Action Office for Drug Abuse Prevention (SAODAP) was created within the Executive Office of the President on June 17, 1971, primary focus was on the prevention of heroin use and the treatment and rehabilitation of heroin abusers. The legislation which produced

1

Polydrug Abuse:
The Results of a
National Collaborative Study

SAODAP mandated that abuse of other drugs be included as a secondary priority (legislative history of the Drug Abuse Office and Treatment Act of 1972). President Nixon's staff engaged drug abuse as a major issue because of its association with urban crime. "Drug abuse" was considered essentially synonymous with heroin abuse. There was, at that time, considerable evidence of significant abuse of amphetamines and barbiturates, licitly manufactured and medically prescribed, which were being diverted into illicit supply channels.

The Drug Abuse Warning Network (DAWN) is a large scale nationwide data collection system sponsored by the Drug Enforcement Agency (DEA) and the National Institute on Drug Abuse (NIDA). Its purposes include the identification of drugs and substances associated with drug abuse episodes, analysis of patterns and trends in these episodes and the provision of data for program planning, for assessment of health hazards associated with drugs use and for drug control and scheduling.

DAWN measures "mentions" of adverse reactions to drugs observed by emergency room personnel and adverse drug reactions coming to the attention of crises centers. In addition, fatal drug reactions are reported by county medical examiners and coroners. The majority of "mentions" of psychoactive drugs are those that are medicinally prescribed, obtained most often from prescriptions or over-the-counter sales. Prescription tranquilizers, barbiturates, and other sedatives, and alcohol in combination with other substances, accounted for about 40% of all "mentions" compared to 21% of "mentions" for marijuana, hashish, and hallucinogens. Central nervous system stimulants such as methamphetamine methylphenidate (Ritalin) and cocaine account for approximately 20% and "mentions" of narcotic analgesics including heroin account for about 10%. These statistics helped to focus attention on the abuse of nonopiate drugs.

There was also an increasing realization that most heroin abusers also abuse a variety of psychoactive substances, either in combination or in succession.

Multiple drug use patterns complicated simplistic descriptions of drug abusers. Drug abuse was recognized as a complicated phenomenon related to interpersonal needs, psychic and physical problems, and social adaptations. No one substance could be targeted as "brand switching" commonly occurred among individuals. The choice of a particular drug often appeared to be dictated primarily by availability. Differences in the patterns of drug abuse between geographic areas and among different populations became apparent.

Although SAODAP, under the direction of Dr. Jerome Jaffe, continued through 1973 to focus primarily on heroin, an allocation of

$800,000 was made to develop a polydrug abuse study pilot project. The project developed a series of geographically scattered treatment programs implemented by the Research and Demonstration Branch of SAODAP, then directed by Dr. Peter Bourne. He and his assistant, Ann Ramsey, began with initial goals of (1) establishing drug abuse treatment programs with the capacity to attract a cross section of polydrug users in order to collect data concerning the epidemiology and medical and psychological consequences of polydrug abuse; (2) developing a cadre of professionals experienced in treatment and research of polydrug abuse; (3) developing new treatment technology for patients addicted to nonnarcotic drugs; (4) establishing pilot demonstration treatment programs which could be replicated by state and local agencies.

In an effort to reach the most dysfunctional polydrug users, emphasis was given to providing short-term, acute medical care and detoxification services. Initially, small inpatient units were established in institutions with staff already experienced in investigative techniques and drug abuse treatment. Later outpatient units were added to increase the number of subjects and to test different treatment strategies.

While the programs were designed to provide service to the communities in which they existed, their primary function was research. The programs were to collect data concerning the nature of polydrug problems and the population involved, as well as test the efficacy of various treatment approaches. These data were felt to be essential to the subsequent development of federal policy in response to problems of polydrug abuse.

After the first year, Peter Bourne and Ann Ramsey attempted to increase substantially the number of polydrug programs. These efforts were vigorously resisted by the Office of Management and Budget (OMB). OMB was determined to put a ceiling on all federally funded drug abuse treatment, and was particularly averse to having the federal government assume responsibility for a whole new area of drug abuse where the total number of individuals needing treatment might be many times the number of heroin addicts.

With the formation of the National Institute on Drug Abuse (NIDA) in 1974, polydrug project management became part of the Services Research Branch (SRB) of NIDA. Dr. John Benvenuto was assigned by NIDA to be the project officer for the polydrug project. New grant applications were encouraged from institutions within cities where DAWN data indicated substantial nonopiate abuse. Consideration was also given to the need for an appropriate geographic distribution and to the need to reach different populations. Figure I.1 shows the distribution of programs that contributed the data presented in this book.

During the first year the programs were in operation, a central data base

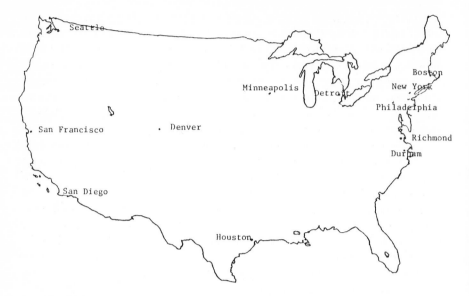

Figure I.1.   Distribution of projects that contributed data presented in this book.

was established using a modified version of the Client Oriented Data Acquisition Program (CODAP)—a form that was already used by other federally funded drug treatment programs. Although these data were not entered into the national CODAP data base, they provided a common basis of comparison to CODAP data. Additional patient information was tabulated from supplemental forms, but the centralized data collected on approximately 800 first-year admissions were not sufficiently detailed to answer many research questions.

Expanded uniform data forms and procedures were added in the poly-drug programs at the beginning of the second year of the project. These included demographic and drug use information and psychometric assessment of psychological functioning. An Intake Form consisting of 27 variables concerning demographic characteristics of the individual socioeconomic indicators, criminal involvement, primary source of income, employment history, family history of substance abuse, past psychiatric treatment, and drug use history was completed by the initial interviewer. Distinctions were made between drugs preferred, current drug usage, and the drug problem resulting in the treatment contact.

The Minnesota Multiphasic Personality Inventory (MMPI) is a well-known psychometric instrument which has been used extensively both as a clinical psychodiagnostic instrument and as a research instrument. The

MMPI is widely used in drug abuse research; however, the analysis of MMPI data is often less than optimal. *Interpretation of composite profiles as if they were generated by individuals* is frequently reported in the drug abuse literature. However, the conclusions drawn are not necessarily valid since the populations are generally heterogeneous in their profile patterns. Many studies compare average profiles of two or more groups. When the individual profiles composing the groups are heterogeneous, real differences are likely to be obscured. Sequential comparisons of scale means using *t* test is likely to reveal a number of statistically significant differences which are artifacts due to the number of tests involved. A method relying on classification of MMPI profiles according to established "code types" is described by Lachar *et al.* in Chapter VII. While this method is less frequently used, the results are more likely to produce interpretable results.

The Current and Past Psychopathology Scales (CAPPS) developed by Endicott and Spitzer (1972) is a 158-item rating scale designed to allow computer-generated diagnoses of psychiatric disorders. Information obtained through a structural interview is integrated into 8 scales which assess current psychopathology and 18 scales which describe historical information and past psychopathology.

The time period covered by the "Current" section of the CAPPS was arbitrarily set by the developers of the instrument at 1 month prior to evaluation. The time period covered by the "Past" section of the CAPPS is age 12 up to the previous month. Several items refer to more specific, delimited time periods, such as work performance which was limited to the period of the last 5 years.

Judgments on most of the individual items of the instrument are made and recorded on a six-point scale of severity that ranged from "1" (no psychopathology or impairment) to "6" (extreme). By means of a principal components varimax rotation factor analysis program, the developers of this instrument derived 8 Summary Scales (factors) from 33 items of the "Current" section, and 18 Summary Scales (factors) from 78 of the 130 items of the "Past" section. The Summary Scale scores are calculated by averaging the ratings on the component individual item scales which have their highest loading on the factor. A number of areas of psychopathology and clusters of symptoms and traits are represented only in the "Past" section. The Summary Role Scale score which is computed only for the "Current" section is the average of the degree of role impairment scores obtained for occupational role, mate role, and parent role. Subjects who are neither a mate nor a parent, or who do not perform an occupational role for nonpsychopathological reasons, are not scored on this Role Summary Scale.

For polydrug patients who were admitted to hospitals for detoxification, the administration of the CAPPS interview was delayed for a period of 4 to 10 days after admission, to ensure that the patient's behavior and responses were not influenced by the toxic state.

The developers of the CAPPS have reported that research workers from a variety of disciplines and with various levels of education have been trained to use it with a degree of reliability satisfactory for research purposes. Interjudge reliability coefficients were determined for four experienced raters, on the 26 Summary Scale scores and the 158 items of the CAPPS, and were found to range from 0.68 to 1.0 for the individual items and from 0.74 to 1.0 for the Summary Scales. At least one research worker representative from each of the 12 local programs participating in this national study attended a training workshop, on the use of the CAPPS and the standardized interview guide, which was conducted by Jean Endicott in New York City. Subsequent to this workshop, the projects continued the training at the local level with standardized training materials in order to assure acceptable levels of rater reliability.

When the CAPPS on polydrug users was computer scored to generate psychiatric diagnosis, a high percentage of the users were classified as schizophrenic. This finding could represent the contaminating effect of drug use or exaggeration of pathology by subjects. The use of the CAPPS as a diagnostic instrument is not reported here; nevertheless, its use in the polydrug project provided useful items and scales reported by Phin in Chapter III the Carlin and Strauss in Chapter V.

When implementation of the expanded uniform patient data collection system began in July of 1974, a contractor responsible for data management and creation of the central data base prepared user manuals for the reporting forms and made field visits to each of the programs to provide on-site training in the use of the forms. The individual case records from each program were coded and sent to the contractor who created and maintained a central data base for future analysis. Overall, admission to programs averaged 120 patients per month.

Following completion of the data collection phase of the project, the data tape, which included data from all programs, was made available to the program's principal investigators, allowing them to pursue analysis of the aggregate data according to their individual interests. Much of the material presented in this volume represents the end product of their efforts.

In addition to the contribution each project made to the national data, principal investigators were encouraged to use their local program data to address research issues. The treatment experience was published through NIDA's Services Research Branch Monograph series (Comstock, Dammann, 1977; Wesson, Jacoby, 1977) and professional journals. This book represents findings of the projects which were not primarily related to the case treatment but to the broader research issues related to polydrug abuse. Those programs which continued into a third year of operation completed the data analysis, the writing of final manuals and reports, and this book.

The organization and selection of papers for this volume reflects an effort on the part of the editors to go beyond the usual descriptive studies amply present in the drug abuse literature. The editors chose a format which first describes the varieties and classification of polydrug abusers, presents an estimation of the magnitude of polydrug abuse, examines certain central nervous system consequences to chronic drug use, and examines the impact of polydrug abuse on physicians and other deliverers of health care.

AN OVERVIEW OF THE POPULATION STUDIED

Most of the individuals studied by the projects were patients seeking treatment. There was, however, a special study which included individuals who were not patients. The majority of "nonpatients" were studied by the Philadelphia program and are described by John Phin in Chapter III. The nonpatients were included because many investigators believed that a substantial population of drug users existed who were not sufficiently dysfunctional, or in sufficient crises, to seek treatment. Many differences between patients and nonpatients did emerge and authors of this book analyzed data from patients and nonpatients separately. One must resist, however, the temptation to consider the nonpatients as a control or matched population to the patient population.

METHODS OF CLASSIFYING POLYDRUG ABUSERS

Faced with as heterogeneous a population as polydrug abusers, methods of categorizing individuals into meaningful conceptual groupings which can contribute understanding to the general phenomena of polydrug use are necessary. Any attempt to classify individuals into meaningful groupings is likely to obscure individual differences on some variables, as well as generate statistically significant but conceptually meaningless group differences. For polydrug users, the most obvious variable on which to classify individuals is their current primary drug of use. Consider, however, the consequences of combining the recreational intravenous barbiturate user in the same category as the user of oral barbiturates who is attempting to self-medicate anxiety. In devising a typology, the important question is whether such a grouping adds anything to the conceptual understanding of the phenomena of polydrug use.

Probably no one classification scheme could be derived that would be adequate for all purposes and, no matter how thoughtfully conceived, be helpful without also producing artifacts. One can, as has been done by Braucht, Kirby and Berry in Chapter VI, devise classifications empirically. A drug typology, based on current drug use and frequency of use, was developed by Ed Farley of the Philadelphia program and has been used in several chapters in this book. The typology, which categorized on the basis of current usage more than three times per week, classified the polydrug sample as shown in Table I.1.

The Domestic Council's *White Paper on Drug Abuse* (1975) emphasized that the abuse of different drugs is not associated with the same degree of risk and devised a high–low risk dichotomy. The dichotomy is discussed in detail in Chapter III. Table I.2 shows the breakdown of patients and nonpatients who used high risk drugs.

Examination of differences between patient and nonpatient polydrug users and examination of subtypes of women supports the findings that polydrug users vary along many characteristics. Users differ in social characteristics and psychopathology, but the salience of the differences depends upon how the subtypes are constructed and whether etiology or treatment needs are under consideration.

A task group was convened specifically to explore the possibility that polydrug abuse produced long-term cerebral dysfunction which persisted beyond detoxification. The tests and clinical training necessary to participate in this study were too time-consuming and expensive for use in all the programs. Investigation of brain damage correlations with polydrug abuse was conducted by staff in three programs (San Diego, Detroit, and Seattle). During the second year, the number of collaborating programs was expanded to seven. The test instruments included Weschler Adult Intelligence Scale (WAIS), the Halstead–Reitan battery, the Indiana–Reitan aphasia screening test, and the MMPI. This collaborative neuropsychological study had principal investigator Dr. Igor Grant and a separate NIDA Project Officer, Dr. Gerald Dubin.

Two major aspects of the central nervous system consequences of abusing nonopiate drugs are described in detail: Chapters X and XII examine the impact of polydrug use on neuropsychological functioning.

Table I.1

PERCENTAGE OF SUBJECTS BY PATIENT–NONPATIENT STATUS FOR EACH
OF THE ELEVEN DRUG USE PATTERNS (N = 1136)

Drug patterns	Patients (N = 832)	Nonpatients (N = 304)	Combined totals
Opiates and sedatives (N = 91)	10.7	1.0	8.1
Opiates and stimulants (N = 51)	6.0	.7	4.5
Opiates alone (N = 129)	14.1	2.6	11.5
Stimulants and sedatives (N = 81)	7.5	6.3	7.1
Sedatives alone (N = 183)	16.9	14.5	16.3
Stimulants alone (N = 132)	10.3	15.5	11.7
Hallucinogens (N = 37)	3.3	3.3	3.3
Combinations (N = 116)	10.1	10.9	10.3
Alcohol and marijuana (N = 75)	3.9	14.1	6.7
Marijuana (N = 128)	6.1	25.7	11.4
Not classified in above categories	10.6	5.6	9.1
Totals	73.0%	27.0%	100%

If drug use produces prolonged or permanent CNS (central nervous system) dysfunction, the implications both for policy and for treatment become a major concern.

Chapter XIII reports an investigation of sleep disturbances in polydrug users. Since many of the drugs utilized by polydrug abusers are specifically marketed to facilitate sedation and sleep, the impact of their chronic use on sleep is a question of major importance.

The questions of incidence and prevalence of polydrug abuse in the United States are addressed by Lau and Benvenuto in Chapter IX and by Hunt in Chapter VIII. These chapters differ markedly in assumptions and methodological style. Benvenuto and Lau, using bold assumptions,

Table I.2

SUBJECTS IN EACH OF THE SIX HIGH-RISK DRUG CATEGORIES BY SEX, NONPATIENT–PATIENT STATUS, AND AGE

	Heroin			Illegal methadone			Other opiates			Barbiturates			Amphetamines			Entire sample totals N (%)
	Daily	Several per week	N using	Daily	Several per week	N using	Daily	Several per week	N using	Daily	Several per week	N using	Daily	Several per week	N using	
Male	58	28	146	35	6	48	57	23	146	124	87	372	71	67	288	426(37)
Female	19	16	55	12	0	18	53	10	98	114	58	245	72	53	195	698(62)
Patients	77	40	179	46	5	62	109	26	206	225	91	440	130	66	299	823(73)
Nonpatients	0	4	22	1	1	4	1	7	38	13	55	178	13	55	185	304(27)
Under 18 years	0	3	10	0	0	1	1	1	21	4	36	96	12	29	74	155(14)
18–20	11	8	34	6	0	9	6	9	35	31	31	132	28	28	125	223(20)
21–25	32	23	83	27	3	33	39	11	76	96	48	210	48	41	162	387(34)
26–30	19	8	48	10	1	16	25	9	59	38	21	90	32	16	80	187(17)
Over 30	15	2	26	4	2	7	39	3	53	69	10	90	23	7	43	175(16)

develop inferences based on the capture–recapture technique to predict the number of polydrug abusers in the United States. Hunt constructs sets of incidence data to demonstrate the major difficulties in extrapolating national incidences from local data.

Judd *et al.* in Chapter XV examine the widespread impact of polydrug abusers on health delivery systems and Smith and Wesson in Chapter XIV explore physicians' attitudes concerning the treatment of drug abusers.

SOCIAL COST

Because the nonopiate abuser is seldom forced to steal or commit other crimes to pay for drugs, the social cost of nonopiate abuse is less obvious than that of heroin abuse and receives less attention. The ultimate cost of nonopiate abuse to society, however, is substantial when all its ramifications are considered. The cost associated with nonopiate abuse can be measured in terms of loss of productivity, industrial and automobile accidents, medical complications, family disruption, and unnecessary use of emergency rooms and psychiatric services. The treatment of physical dependency also expends considerable medical resources.

This study of polydrug abusers attempted to document some of the social cost which accrues in this population. For example, 823 polydrug patients reported a total of 319 auto accidents within the past 2 years. If an increased auto accident rate is actually secondary to driving while intoxicated, a differential pattern of accident rates might be expected for different types of drug users. The data in Table I.3 appears to support this conclusion.

The increased accident rate for marijuana users was unexpected. Complete analysis would, of course, involve knowing the number of miles driven, a variable that was not available in the polydrug data.

Employment difficulties and decrease in work performance are well-known complications in drug abuse. Of 766 polydrug abusers, 259 (34%) self-reported drug abuse as the reason for their unemployment. This self-report is subject to question and probably would represent an upper limit.

VISABILITY OF THE PATIENT POPULATION

Examining polydrug patients in terms of previous treatment system or criminal justice contacts, in addition to referral source, provides a means

Table I.3

AUTO ACCIDENT INVOLVEMENTS DURING PAST 2 YEARS BY POLYDRUG
ABUSE PATIENTS WHO USED ONLY ONE CLASS OF DRUGS[a]

Number of accidents in past 2 years	Opiates alone N = 121		Sedative– hypnotics alone N = 139		Stimu- lants alone N = 85		Marijuana alone N = 50	
	N	(%)	N	(%)	N	(%)	N	(%)
0	97	(80)	109	(78)	64	(75)	24	(48)
1	16	(13)	21	(15)	17	(20)	14	(28)
2	6	(12)	3	(2)	3	(4)	8	(16)
3	2	(2)	5	(4)	1	(1)	2	(4)
4	0	(0)	1	(1)	0	(0)	2	(4)
Total accidents	34		48		26		44	
Total accidents/ population at risk	.28		.34		.31		.88	

[a] X^2 35.8; $df = 12$; $p < .005$.

Table I.4

VISABILITY OF PATIENTS TO MEDICINE, MENTAL HEALTH AGENCIES, DRUG
AND ALCOHOL TREATMENT PROGRAMS, AND CRIMINAL JUSTICE AGENCIES[a]

Known to:	Males N = 496		Females N = 324		Total N = 820	
	N	(%)	N	(%)	N	(%)
Private physician or emergency room	228	(46)	167	(52)	395	(48)
Community mental health	258	(52)	206	(64)	464	(57)
Drug or alcohol treatment programs	275	(52)	162	(50)	419	(51)
Criminal justice system	211	(43)	64	(20)	275	(34)

[a] $X^2 = 35.5$; $df = 3$; $p < .001$.

Table I.5

DISTRIBUTION OF PATIENT BY NUMBER OF SYSTEMS WITH WHICH THEY HAD CONTACT[a]

Number of systems contacted	Males N = 496		Females N = 324		Total N = 820	
	N	(%)	N	(%)	N	(%)
0	45	(9)	38	(12)	83	(10)
1	143	(28)	96	(30)	239	(29)
2	155	(31)	85	(26)	240	(29)
3	111	(22)	87	(27)	198	(24)
4	42	(9)	18	(6)	60	(7)

[a] $X^2 = 6.9$; $df = 4$; p = n.s.

of measuring visability. Table I.4 displays the frequency with which patients had contact with physicians or agencies in which the drug problem was probably known to exist. Female patients had fewer contacts with the criminal justice system, however the similarity of male and female contacts with other systems is remarkable.

Some patients had contacts with several systems. Table I.5 shows the distribution of multiple contacts for males and females. Only 10% of patients had no contact whereas 60% were known to two or more systems. Fifty-one percent of the patients were already identified within the drug and alcohol treatment system. The fact that patients already known to the drug or alcohol treatment system were referred to the polydrug programs probably indicates the inability of the referring program to adequately treat these cases.

PART 1

Classification and Description of the Polydrug Users

EDITORS' INTRODUCTION

We grouped studies that primarily describe or classify the research subjects into the first section. Without an overview of the population, it is difficult to appreciate the complexity of the polydrug phenomena and to put into perspective the strengths and weaknesses of the study.

The first chapter describes the referral base for study subjects. The nonpatient subjects are discussed in detail in the following chapter. The female population is examined first in relationship to conventional stereotypes of female drug users and later with regard to identified subpopulations of female users. Chapters V and VI both focus on development of typologies but are quite different in the methods used to derive them. The final chapter within this section uses the MMPI scales to classify subjects into meaningful subgroups, which could be conceptualized as a psychometrically derived typology.

CHAPTER *II*

Referral Sources and Outreach: Critical Variables in Understanding the Polydrug-Abusing Sample

John Keegan and Kenneth Schooff

As each polydrug treatment program began accepting patients, there was a need to enlist the aid of existing agencies and individuals as sources of patient referrals. Each program worked independently, establishing referral sources suited to its own locale. For example, the Durham, North Carolina program organized special outreach activities toward surfacing the polydrug-abusing housewife. Clergy in the area were contacted and made familiar with the help offered by the program. Efforts were also made to give the center an atmosphere that would be comfortable and familiar to the target group. It was thus important that the program not gain a reputation as a place where "junkies" or other social deviants went for treatment of a drug habit. The unique outreach efforts employed, combined with the physical atmosphere of the program, thus served to engage a particular and hitherto "hidden" drug abuser in treatment.

The Detroit, Michigan polydrug program made special efforts to reach drug users whose problem was of an iatrogenic nature. A symposium was held at a local medical society which offered information to area physicians as to the best way to treat drug abusers from both medical and

Polydrug Abuse:
The Results of a
National Collaborative Study

psychological viewpoints. At the same time, physicians were made aware of a new resource where they could refer patients they felt to have substance abuse problems. In this way, the Detroit program was able to surface a group of prescription medication abusers who had not been treated previously for drug-use problems. The Detroit and Durham projects are but two examples of unique case-finding efforts aimed at substance abusers not previously seen for treatment or previously identified as having substance abuse problems.

Referral sources included drug and alcohol programs, mental health facilities, private physicians, hot lines, hospitals, the criminal justice system, social agencies, and responses to media advertisements. Since characteristics of the polydrug-abusing patient population were found to vary depending upon the referral source, the overall findings of the projects are better understood through an appreciation of the source of patients and an understanding of how referral source influenced patient characteristics. Relationships found between referral source and patient characteristics may also highlight some of the differences among polydrug abusers. It must be stressed that this does not imply that the statistics cited are necessarily representative of what would be found if a random or well-stratified sample of polydrug abusers was canvassed nationally.

DIFFERENTIAL PSYCHOSOCIAL CHARACTERISTICS RELATED TO REFERRAL SOURCE

Analysis Procedure

For the analysis of the outreach and referral data, 800 patients treated in the final year of the collaborative study were used. The 800 cases represented the most complete and accurate file of data available at the time of the analysis.[1] The .05 rejection region was adopted in all statistical tests. All findings reported herein thus meet at least this criterion for significance. Table II.1 illustrates the frequencies and percentages of patients referred from each referral source.

The large percentages of referrals from drug programs, hospitals, and mental health facilities were expected since these are generally the first sources from which drug programs seek referrals. The low percentage of alcohol program referrals probably reflects the mandate of the National Institute on Drug Abuse to exclude individuals from the polydrug projects

[1] Additional cases where accurate data are available have been since added to the data file.

Table II.1

FREQUENCIES AND PERCENTAGES OF CLIENTS FROM FOURTEEN
REFERRAL SOURCES

Source of referral	Absolute frequency	Percentage
Drug program	127	15.9
Alcohol program	12	1.5
Mental health facility	90	11.2
Private physician	54	6.7
Hospital	110	13.7
Hot line or Crisis center	32	4.0
Criminal justice system	64	8.0
Social agency	51	6.4
Friend or relative	139	17.4
Radio	4	0.5
TV	10	1.2
Newspapers and other publications	19	2.4
Prior contract	26	3.2
Other	52	6.5
Missing	10	1.2
	800	100

whose primary drug of abuse was alcohol. The high percentage of referrals from friends and relatives may be a secondary result of prior contacts of friends and relatives with agencies, as well as the result of advertisements in newspapers, on TV, and on radio.

It is a reasonable hypothesis that the patients generated by particular referral sources might have common characteristics and attributes unique to those referral sources. Some of the characteristics associated with referral sources are obvious; for example, one would expect more arrests among those being referred by the criminal justice system. For other referral sources, the patient characteristics are not so apparent. On the other hand, referral sources such as family, friends, media, crisis intervention centers, or social agencies would be expected to refer patients with a wide variety of characteristics.

An effort was thus made to clarify the patient characteristics associated with those referral sources that would be expected to have specific outreach and/or treatment foci. These referral sources included drug and alcohol programs, the criminal justice system, mental health facilities, private physicians, and hospitals.

The conceptual framework of this portion of the analysis considered the referral source to be the independent variable. It is recognized,

however, that the patient characteristics in question probably contributed to a patient's entry into one referral source versus another.

Drug and Alcohol Programs

The referrals from drug and alcohol programs were primarily male and
unemployed (Figures II.1, II.2). Fewer of them have had arrests and
convictions (see Figure II.4) than those from the criminal justice system.
Whether their past treatment helped to keep them out of legal trouble or
whether they were better able to conceal their illegal activities is an open
question. The greater use of heroin and methadone by this group (see
Figure II.8) would suggest that their polydrug use was only one facet of
their total range of drug experiences.

Although these individuals were using substances that would classify
them as polydrug users, it was not always clear whether it was their use of
illegal opiates or of nonopiates that constituted their primary problem.

The motivation for (see Figure II.9) and situation (see Figure II.10) in

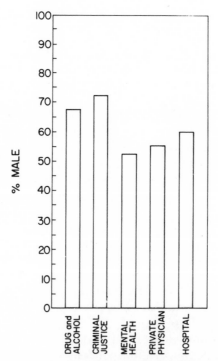

Figure II.1.   Percentage of male polydrug patients by referral source.

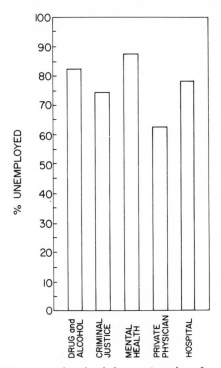

Figure II.2. Unemployed polydrug patients by referral source.

which they originally used substances, suggest that they used drugs initially with friends in order to get high. In many instances, this type of patient did not see himself as needing psychological intervention. Instead, he usually sought help in detoxification or merely wish methadone maintenance. The fact that fewer of these individuals have had previous psychiatric contacts (see Figure II.7) or suicide attempts (see Figure II.6) supports this contention.

In summary, a substantial proportion of the polydrug users referred by drug and alcohol programs had also used heroin and methadone. This population thus does not represent a hitherto unseen group of drug users, but instead makes it clear that many polydrug users had used opiates or were using opiates in combination with other drugs.

Criminal Justice System

Individuals from the criminal justice system (CJS) were primarily single (Figure II.3) males (Figure II.1) with a history of criminal involvement (Figure II.4). They tended to have the earliest first drug experience as well

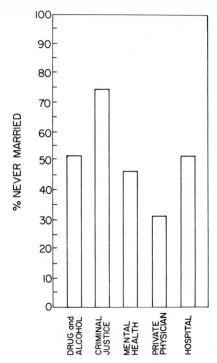

Figure II.3. Percentage of polydrug patients who were never married by referral source.

as being the youngest group to enter treatment (Figure II.5). Substances which are available on the street such as marijuana and hallucinogens were preferred by these patients (Figure II.8). Only 17.2% of these individuals preferred to use heroin. This finding makes it clear that it is difficult at best to make generalizations about their drug preferences.

The less frequent preference for other opiates or synthetics and psychotropic medication (Figure II.8) may also have a variety of explanations. One explanation would be that these medications are not readily available on the street and that they are obtained more often by prescription. Another may be that the substance preference is related to the psychological state of the individual user and the desire to change it in a particular manner.

Mental Health Programs

Those referred from mental health programs appeared similar to those from the drug and alcohol programs and the criminal justice system in

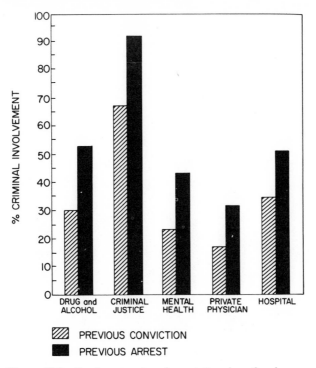

Figure II.4. Previous arrests and convictions by referral source.

that they had difficulty in coping with the demands of everyday life. Only about half were married (Figure II.3) and most remained unemployed (Figure II.2). They began using drugs and entered treatment later than any other group except those from private physicians (Figure II.5). They were second to those referred from private physicians in having the fewest arrests and convictions (Figure II.4), and were approximately equal to those from private physicians in having previously attempted to commit suicide with or without drugs (Figure II.6). As might be anticipated, these patients had had more previous psychiatric treatment (Figure II.7) than any other group.

These patients preferred and used amphetamines, barbiturates, and psychotropics more than individuals from any other referral source. In addition, they were second highest in their preference for other opiates and synthetics such as Darvon or Percodan (Figure II.8). Most patients claimed that their first use of drugs was socially or recreationally motivated. At the same time, there were many who claimed that the first drug used was prescribed for the treatment of a medical disorder (Figure II.9).

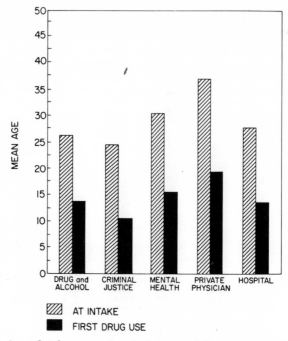

Figure II.5.   Age at first drug use and at admission to polydrug treatment by referral source.

In addition, approximately 36% of the patients were alone at the time of their first drug experience (Figure II.10).

Many important characteristics may be obscured when the data are examined in the aggregate. For example, some patients may have been older and had psychiatric problems prior to any drug experience. For them, drug use may have initially served some appropriate medical or psychiatric purpose. A drug abuse problem may have developed because alternative coping mechanisms were not available. On the other hand, some of the younger patients may have developed psychiatric problems following their experimentation with drugs.

Private Physicians

Those referred from private physicians shared many common features with those referred from mental health programs. Both groups were older at the time of first use and at intake (Figure II.5). Each group was also approximately evenly divided by sex (Figure II.1). As already indicated, both groups showed the least criminal involvement of all groups (Figure

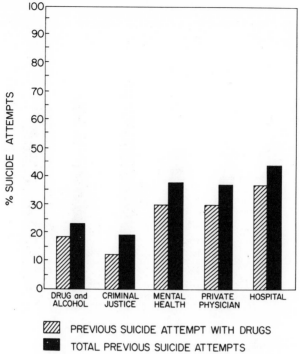

PREVIOUS SUICIDE ATTEMPT WITH DRUGS

TOTAL PREVIOUS SUICIDE ATTEMPTS

Figure II.6. Percentage of polydrug patients who attempted suicide by referral source.

II.4), with those referred from private physicians having even fewer previous arrests and convictions than those referred from mental health programs.

About one-third of both groups also had attempted suicide previously (Figure II.6). Private physician referrals had only slightly less previous psychiatric treatment than those from mental health programs (Figure II.7). The drug preferences of both groups were similar in that each had a low preference for heroin and methadone (Figure II.8). Physicians' prescriptions were indicated as the motivation for first use (Figure II.9) and the lower frequencey of first drug use with others was also about the same (Figure II.10) for both groups.

While the similarities already mentioned are clear, there are also some essential differences when viewed from an aggregate perspective. Physicians' referrals had been or were still married (Figure II.3) and were employed (Figure II.2) more than any other group. Such differences help to distinguish this group from those referred by other sources, including mental health programs.

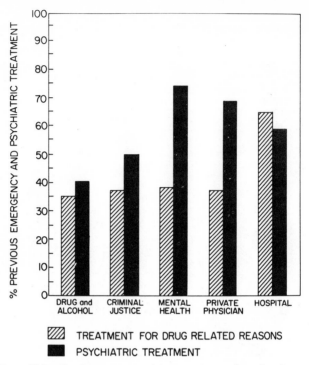

Figure II.7.   Previous emergency room treatment by referral source.

Substance use among these physician-referred patients appears to be in response to physician prescription in response to psychological problems as opposed to drug use for its euphoriant effects. It is noteworthy that these patients showed similarities to 20 patients seen in the Detroit Poly-drug Program who were classified as prescription medication abusers (Schooff & Keegan, 1975). These included patients using substances for the relief of intractable pain, for problems with sleep, and for psychological problems, primarily anxiety and depression. The findings of greater use of synthetic opiates, and psychotropics (Figure II.8) taken together with the self-medicating or prescription motivation for first use (Figure II.9) are in agreement with this assessment. In addition, the greater age at the time of admission and at the age of first drug experience enhance the possibility that this substance abuse problem represents a reaction to some change or crisis in the life of the patient.

   The fact that the majority of substances used by these individuals are available by prescription may have important implications. First, many of these individuals were still using the same substance upon which they first

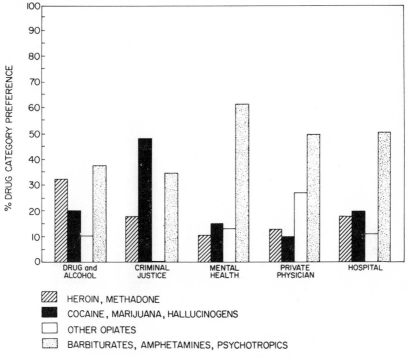

HEROIN, METHADONE
COCAINE, MARIJUANA, HALLUCINOGENS
OTHER OPIATES
BARBITURATES, AMPHETAMINES, PSYCHOTROPICS

Figure II.8. Drug preference by referral source.

became dependent or, second, they were not experimenting with a variety of substances but instead trying to cope with a dependency problem with one particular substance. It is possible that for many of these patients the time between their initial dependency and first treatment is critical. The longer this interval, the greater the likelihood that more substances will be tried. This may help account for the use of street drugs by some of these patients.

The fact that many of the private physicians may also have been psychiatrists, taken together with the initial cause of the problem, may help to explain the similarities between mental health programs and private physician referrals.

Hospitals

It was mentioned earlier that only those referral sources with particular outreach and/or treatment foci would be discussed in terms of patient

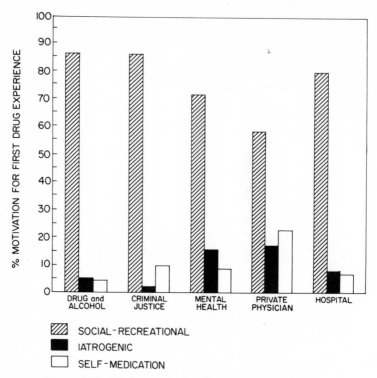

Figure II.9.   Motivation for first drug use by referral source.

characteristics. Hospital referrals pose a special problem in this regard. Patients referred from hospitals show some similarities to patients from the other referral sources while, at the same time, demonstrating an important difference in terms of the acute nature of their problem. One reason for the similarities is that hospitals see patients with the widest range of problems. In this regard, we are assuming that most hospital referrals are an outgrowth of emergency medical treatment. Such patients may thus be anyone who has used a drug and either accidentally or purposely overdosed or had other complications with it.

As is evidenced by Figures II.1 to II.5 and II.8 to II.10, hospital-referred patients appear to be similar to all other groups. This similarity may reflect entry into a hospital setting as the result of an acute medical or psychiatric problem. Potentially any type of drug user may reach a point in the development of his drug abuse problem at which complications requiring general medical attention or an overdose requiring emergency medical attention may arise. One might thus expect most drug abusers to enter the hospital at some time. Figure II.8 shows that patients from the

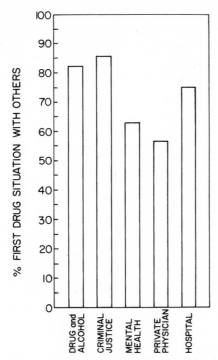

Figure II.10. First drug use with others by referral source.

other four referral sources (i.e., mental health programs, drug and alcohol programs, private physicians, and the criminal justice system),
have about the same percentage, 35.3–37.8%, of previous emergency
room treatment. These patients may thus have been referred to some
type of drug treatment in the past. Moreover, those from the other
referral sources who continue abusing drugs and who have not been seen
for emergency room treatment, probably would need such treatment at
some time in the future. As would be expected, more of those referred by
a hospital have had previous emergency room treatment. This merely
underscores the disruptive nature of their drug problem.

The participation of hospital-referred patients in the polydrug treatment program was probably a direct result of their emergency room
treatment. Figure II.6 shows that those referred by hospitals also had the
highest percentage of previous suicide attempts. The majority of hospital
referrals were thus drug abusers of a variety of types, many of whom had
attempted suicide with drugs and were then seen for a drug overdose in the
hospital emergency room.

The differences among polydrug patients referred from varied sources indicate the heterogeneity of this population and the need to resist the temptation to draw conclusions about the nature of "the polydrug problem." Although tempting, any such characterization would be based on data with such great variability that it is of little value. Generalizations about polydrug abuse must be limited to those which specify sample parameters.

CHAPTER III

Nonpatient Polydrug Users

John Phin

Presumably, there is a population of polydrug users whose drug use does not result in episodes of dysfunction that are of sufficient magnitude for the individuals to seek or require treatment. The programs that participated in the National Polydrug Project offered treatment and/or referral services to attract subjects to the study. This limits the appropriateness of projecting findings to the larger population of polydrug users which includes those users who are not seeking treatment. Comparing the results of the National Polydrug Study to other national data systems, e.g., DARP and CODAP, presents similar difficulties since these systems are also reporting on clients in treatment.

Surveys are another source of information about drug use. While surveys may include drug users who are not seeking treatment, they generally produce incidence, prevalence, and attitudinal information and do not typically address the process by which drug users come to require and request treatment for problems associated with their drug use.

Surveys of drug use that are conducted in schools are also subject to a type of bias. For example, high school and college student survey partici-

31

Polydrug Abuse:
The Results of a
National Collaborative Study

pants have questionable motivational sets that can vary as a function of the method used to encourage the students to "volunteer" for the study.

Glen and Richards (1974) outlined the problems of drug use surveys and identified nonresponse bias as a serious problem. The authors have suggested absenteeism, failure to return questionnaires, and frivolous, inconsistent, or incomplete questionnaire responses (which cause investigators to discard questionnaires) to be factors that may lead to a failure to represent youthful drug use accurately and perhaps to other unknown biases. Dysfunctional drug-using youths may be underrepresented in school surveys to a greater degree because the users may already have withdrawn from school.

This chapter presents results obtained from a sample of drug-using research subjects. They completed the same intake interviews and psychometric evaluations as did project patients *but* these research subjects were neither seeking nor receiving treatment at the time of their participation in the study. This study of a population of drug users not seeking treatment may provide insight into the process by which individuals come to require and request treatment for problems associated with their drug use. It may also be possible to determine if the individuals who are not seeking treatment are earlier in their drug abuse careers and, as such, will become candidates for treatment in the future. Furthermore, it may be possible to determine whether or not the individuals not seeking treatment have psychological or other characteristics that put them at a different level of risk in developing the complications that would bring them to treatment.

METHOD

Subjects

There were 304 subjects in the nonpatient sample. These subjects were specifically invited to participate in the study and received monetary compensation for their participation.

Demographic characteristics of the polydrug patient, polydrug nonpatient, and DARP and CODAP data bases are presented in Table III.1. It is clear that the representation of females and whites in general is substantially higher in both polydrug samples than in the DARP and CODAP samples. The age distributions are relatively comparable, with the notable exception of the overrepresentation of the 18 to 20 age group in the polydrug nonpatient sample. Employment data are generally comparable, with the exception of the DARP sample, which is not dichoto-

Table III.1

DEMOGRAPHIC CHARACTERISTICS OF PATIENTS AND NONPATIENTS

	National Polydrug Study		DARP (Patients, 1969–1973)	CODAP (Admissions, 4–6, 1975)
	Nonpatients (N = 304)	Patients (N = 823)	(N = 38,433)	(N = 48,458)
Sex	%	%	%	%
Male	66.4	60.3	75	74.3
Female	33.6	39.7	25	25.7
Race				
Black	9.2	12.2	44	35.3
White	90.1	83.7	37	52.4
Other	.7	4.0	19	12.3
Age				
under 18	14.9	11.5	11	12.1
18–20	31.6	14.7	17	13.2
21–22	14.5	11.4	16	32.8
23–25	17.4	20.4	18	
26–30	14.5	20.2	17	22.3
31–40	5.4	11.6	15	19.5
over 40	1.4	9.8	6	
Employment				
Unemployed	64.8	75.3	—	76.7
Full Time	15.8	18.5	15	18.4
Part Time	18.8	5.3	—	4.9
School years completed				
9 or fewer	5.6	25.8	11	22.7
10	6.6	12.4	(8 or fewer) 53	
11	17.4	11.8	(9, 10, 11) 36	30.7
12	29.9	30.1	(12 or more)	33.4
13 or more	40.5	19.9		13.2

mous in the same way as the others. In terms of education, the polydrug nonpatient sample stands out as having the highest overall level of education while the polydrug patient sample has the highest proportion of people at the lowest educational level (nine grades or less). The CODAP sample is perhaps more closely comparable to the polydrug patient sample in this respect, while the DARP subjects are similar to the nonpatients.

In general, then, the polydrug samples differ from other national samples in terms of sex representation, racial composition, and age. Minor variances in employment and education also deserve mention.

It may be useful to examine the differences between the polydrug patient and nonpatient samples in an attempt to understand how demographic differences might relate to the more fundamental question of patienthood. Table III.2 presents some relevant variables regarding basic demographic and treatment variables that can help in this process. The differences here suggest that the nonpatient group is younger than the patient group, yet has had more educational experience.[1] The nonpatients were generally employed for 1 of the 2 years prior to the interview which is greater than the 9-month mean for the patients. While the nonpatient group reports their age at first drug experience as 1.5 years earlier than the patient group, it is clear that their immersion in the drug treatment system is lesser in a number of dimensions.

Other life history data show interesting differences between patients and nonpatients. Of the nonpatients, 85.5% had never married (5.6% were married at intake) and 3.5% were living with friends. In the patient sample, 51.6% had never married (22% were married at intake) and 17.5% were living with friends. While these findings may suggest a difference in preferred life-style, they may also reflect age differences and changing social mores. The same considerations would apply to the finding that 91.9% of the nonpatients and 84.5% of the patients were not veterans of the military service.

DRUG HISTORY

To gain some idea of first drug use and current drug preference, the categories of first drug use (other than alcohol and marijuana for procedural reasons) and current preference at evaluation are presented in Figure III.1.

The trend toward early use of drugs more substantial than marijuana

---

[1] It should be noted that 38% of the nonpatients reported some student status at the time of the study.

Table III.2

COMPARISONS OF NATIONAL POLYDRUG STUDY PATIENTS AND NONPATIENTS

	Age[a]	Last school year completed[a]	Months employed in last 2 years[a]	Number of arrests in last 2 years[a]	Number of suicide attempts[a]	Suicide attempts by drug[a]	Number of psychiatric treatments[a]	Age at first drug experience[a]	Emergency room treatments[a]
Nonpatients (mean) (N = 304) SD	22.34 5.62	12.53 2.23	11.69 7.65	.65 1.68	.09 .38	.06 .28	.52 1.08	14.91 3.68	.21 .69
Patients (mean) (N = 823) SD	26.61 9.50	10.94 3.10	8.80 8.44	1.79 4.93	.63 1.42	.47 1.21	1.25 1.82	16.54 7.64	.95 2.50

[a] $t > 3.29$; $df = 1125$; $p < .001$.

35

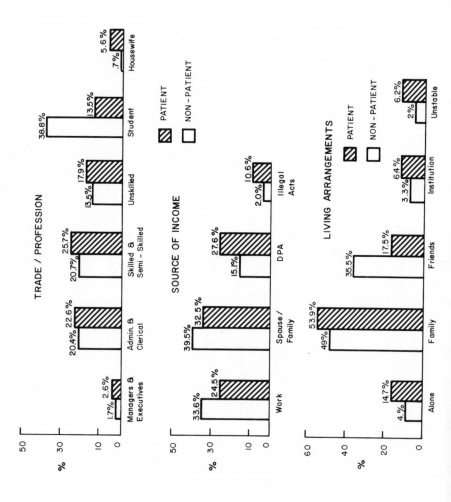

TRADE / PROFESSION

PATIENT
NON - PATIENT

Managers & Executives: 1.7%, 2.6%
Admin. & Clerical: 20.4%, 22.6%
Skilled & Semi - Skilled: 20.7%, 25.7%
Unskilled: 13.5%, 17.9%
Student: 38.8%, 13.5%
Housewife: .7%, 5.6%

SOURCE OF INCOME

PATIENT
NON - PATIENT

Work: 33.6%, 24.5%
Spouse / Family: 39.5%, 32.5%
DPA: 15.1%, 27.6%
Illegal Acts: 2.0%, 10.6%

LIVING ARRANGEMENTS

PATIENT
NON - PATIENT

Alone: 4.%, 14.7%
Family: 49%, 53.9%
Friends: 35.5%, 17.5%
Institution: 3.3%, 6.4%
Unstable: 2%, 6.2%

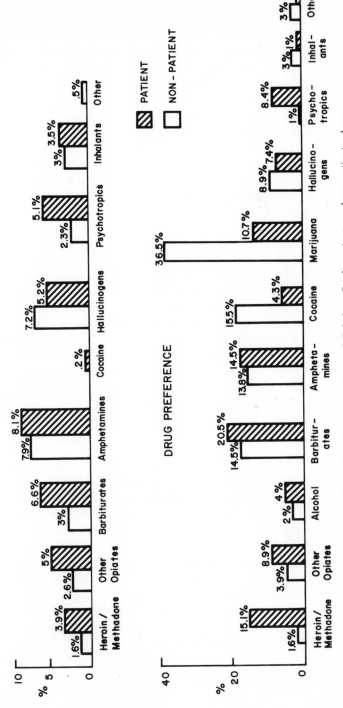

Figure III.1. Distributions of National Polydrug Study patients and nonpatients: demographic and drug use characteristics.

37

and alcohol is reflected in the 2.1 patient-to-nonpatient ratios across most central nervous system depressant classes (i.e., heroin–methadone, other opiates, barbiturates, and psychotropics). Other nondepressant drug types do not show this trend (i.e., amphetamines, hallucinogens).

As noted previously, "primary" opiate–narcotic users were diverted from the Philadelphia program. That factor should be considered when the *Drug Preference Section* in Figure III.1 is examined. It is perhaps not surprising that the nonpatients were more likely to report that they preferred nominally social-recreational substances, that is, marijuana and cocaine, but given the differences in frequency of use in the two National Polydrug Study samples, it is surprising that the nonpatients and patients were relatively close in their reported preference for amphetamines and barbiturates.

Table III.3 presents the frequency of current drug use for patients and nonpatients and reports the portions of the sample using each substance. The two samples differ markedly in their drug use, and higher frequencies of use are present in the patient group, with the exception of marijuana. The relatively high absolute consumption levels of drugs in the nonpatient group, particularly in marijuana and alcohol, are surprising. Beyond the implication that the consumption is social-recreational in character, the results suggest that the nonpatient group is an active group of drug users who represent a distinct and interesting comparison group for the polydrug patients. Multiple drug consumption was typical of both samples with only 15% of the patients and 16.7% of the nonpatients reporting weekly use of only *one* substance.

PROCEDURE

A major effort was made by the Philadelphia program to study available referral resources, in the context of polydrug abuse, to determine the most appropriate treatment service for each research respondent and to make referrals where appropriate. Monetary compensation was used to induce participation in the study.

Signs offering $20 in exchange for information about nonopiate drug use were posted in drug treatment centers, hospital emergency rooms, and also in areas of high pedestrian traffic such as laundromats and shopping centers. Newspaper articles describing the research and mentioning the case incentive were published. After the first wave of subjects, most subjects came to the Philadelphia Center through peer network referrals. Altogether, 91.9% of the Philadelphia nonpatients cited a friend, newspaper article, or street sign as a referral source whereas 30.5% of the patients cited those sources.

Table III.3

FREQUENCY OF USE AND PORTIONS OF SAMPLES USING EACH SUBSTANCE

Substance	Nonpatients (N = 304)			Patients (N = 823)		
	Mean frequency (1.00 = daily use)	N using	% using	Mean frequency (1.00 = daily use)	N using	% using
01 Heroin	.17	22	7.2%	.58	179	21.7%
02 Illegal methadone	.41	4	1.3	.80	62	7.5
03 Other opiates	.19	38	12.5	.62	206	25.0
04 Alcohol	.52	142	46.7	.58	397	48.2
05 Barbiturates	.29	178	58.6	.64	440	53.5
06 Amphetamines	.28	185	60.8	.58	299	36.3
07 Cocaine	.17	119	39.1	.33	135	16.4
08 Marijuana	.82	284	93.4	.71	457	55.5
09 Hallucinogens	.15	141	46.3	.32	190	23.1
10 Psychotropics	.39	62	20.4	.79	304	36.9
11 Inhalants	.20	11	3.6	.46	37	4.5
12 OTC	.61	7	2.3	.64	28	3.4
13 Other	.24	68	22.4	.71	43	5.2

Subjects were screened by telephone before being given an appointment to participate in the study. The criterion for acceptance was use of such drugs as barbiturates, amphetamines, cocaine, hallucinogens, psychotropic medications, inhalants, over-the-counter preparations, phencyclidine (PCP) or, an opiate–narcotic other than heroin or methadone. Subjects had to have used the drug(s) *once a week or more frequently for at least 3 months* prior to participation in the study. In the case of heroin or methadone users, respondents were diverted from the study if they claimed dependency; if they did not believe that they were dependent, they were accepted provided that they met the "polydrug" use criterion. Alcohol and marijuana use was not considered in determining a potential subject's acceptability but use of those substances was recorded if the subject met the "polydrug" criterion.

If the substances used and the rate of use met the criteria for acceptance, the caller was invited to complete the research battery. The battery included the instruments of the National Polydrug Study (Intake, CAPPS, POMS, and MMPI), and local instruments assessing drug usage, family situation, health, alienation, neurological integrity, self-report validity, treatment needs and the referral process, and a thorough medical-physical evaluation which included blood and urine screens. The amount of time needed to complete the battery ranged from 4 to 8 hours depending on the respondent's reading ability, gregariousness, and "mental health."

Whenever possible, the staff member who conducted the telephone screening interview also administered the research battery. Subjects were offered coffee and food. A comfortable and informal atmosphere was established but procedures for protecting the security and confidentiality of information were explained to subjects and were rigorously maintained. When subjects completed the battery, they were given personal cards by their interviewer. Subjects were asked to give the card of their interviewer to any friend or acquaintance who might be interested in the study.

Subjects were never told the exact criteria that had to be met before a caller would be accepted into the study. This procedure was considered to be necessary in light of the financial inducement that was being offered. If an inquiry came from an individual who did not meet the criteria, the caller was told that the Center had seen "enough" people with the caller's drug use pattern, but since the needs of the Center changed from time to time, the caller was encouraged to contact the Center again in several months, "just in case." This procedure was instituted to conceal the criteria and therefore, minimize biased and distorted reports of drug usage.

The reliability and validity of the data obtained from the paid informants has not been formally established but they were asked about their drug use in four different ways at four different times during the interview. If a subject did not tell the same story on those four occasions, the subject was paid and dropped from the study. The few subjects who were dropped do not appear in any tallies or data presentations.

Analysis of the National Polydrug Data

Two orientations toward analysis of the National Polydrug Study data are presented in this chapter. The first is based on a particular statistical procedure called the Automatic Interaction Detector (AID). The procedure is used to identify variables that can effectively differentiate between patients and nonpatients. The second orientation is more conventional and involves attempting to match patients and nonpatients on age, level, and duration of drug use and then examines the matched subsamples for distinguishing characteristics. A variant of the second orientation, controlling age, level, and duration of drug use statistically was to be invoked if matching subsamples could not be developed.

AUTOMATIC INTERACTION DETECTOR (AID)—THE MODEL

Given that some drug users decide to enter a treatment program and others do not, it is important to determine what variables are associated with that decision, and how those variables interact. Further, if the variables were identified and their interaction understood, it is possible that a model could be developed which could predict any one individual's propensity to seek treatment at any given time. Conversely, by isolating specific factors involved in the decision, it may be possible to develop a treatment program that would reduce the importance of these factors relative to those factors that are *not* involved in the decision to seek treatment. In other words, if "problems with living" bring someone to the point of entering a treatment program, perhaps the best treatment would be that which reduced these problems, whether drug use was included or not. Clinically, of course, the idea that drug use per se is not the sole factor involved in a person's entering a drug-treatment program has gained wide acceptance, but few major studies have attempted to identify, through statistically sound methodology, which factors *are* involved in the decision. The present approach has as its goal the discovery of the variables that are involved in the decision to enter treatment in the first place.

The approach is quite simple: First, three mutually exclusive sets of variables were specified—those dealing with personal functioning, social functioning, and drug use. Second, within each dimension, data from the instruments (described in the previous section) were chosen which clearly relate to one of these dimensions and cannot be construed as relating to more than one. Third, through a series of intercorrelations and factor analyses, the variables within each dimension were reduced to approximately 25, a number predetermined by the next step. Fourth, each set of variables was subjected to a computerized technique called the Automatic Interaction Detector (Sonquist, 1970), with patient–nonpatient status as the dependent variable. The process is repeated on each of the resulting groups, with successive splits leading to groups of decreasing size and increasing homogeneity. The goal of subjecting each of the three sets of variables to an AID was to discover, in a retrospective way, which variables within the set are the best predictors of patient–nonpatient status. The fifth step in the process was to evaluate the overall success of each set of variables in predicting the outcome. In order to do so, the results of the three AID analyses were compared on the variable sets' ability to account for the variance in the dependent variable and in their ability to isolate groups composed exclusively of patients or nonpatients.

Step 1: Selection of Variables

All the information contained in the demographic–drug use questionnaire, POMS, CAPPS, and MMPI were considered. Lists were made of scale scores and items that related to the three dimensions, social functioning, personal functioning, and drug use. For example, items assessing adolescent friendship patterns and nonacademic school difficulties were judged as social functioning items while an item dealing with obsessive-compulsive behavior or the schizophrenia scale of the MMPI was judged as personal.

As a result of the selection process, approximately 50 variables were chosen for each of the three dimensions. Items from the POMS, CAPPS, and MMPI, as well as intake forms, were selected.

Step 2: Reduction of the Number of Variables

A frequency distribution was computed for each of the selected variables, and those with the most trivial variance were discarded. Dichotomous variables on which one of the alternatives had a smaller percentage of respondents than the percentage of patients in the Philadelphia sample (i.e., 25.3%) were also discarded. Then an intercorrelation matrix was generated for all of the variables within each set. When the correlation coefficient between variables was found to exceed .60, the list was further reduced by randomly selecting one of the correlated variables. Through this process, each variable set was reduced to approximately 25 variables.

Step 3: "Ransacking" the Data with the AID

The Automatic Interaction Detector is a computerized statistical procedure particularly suited for analysis of nominal, ordinal, and interval variables that interact with each other.

To quote John Sonquist (1970), one of the AID's developers:

> The nature of the measurement process may require the combination of variables into indices representing a single theoretical factor in ways which are not necessarily either linear or additive.
>
> These causal factors may themselves have to be combined into multivariate statistical models which therefore must either take account of interaction explicitly or depend on assumptions which may be unwarranted, and which, if violated, may lead to serious misinterpretations.
>
> The most serious questions about the use of unwarranted additivity assumptions were raised by those psychologists who directly considered the theoretical implications of interactive data. They felt that not only is there a downward bias in the results if additive assumptions are made incorrectly, but serious questions are raised about whether the concept of a main effect is a meaningful one in the presence of significant interaction. It is charged that not even classical experimental methods can solve this problem [pp. 74–75].

The AID was developed to analyze and integrate complex, interactive data with the intention of producing indices and models that are both explanatory and predictive. The mathematics of the program are beyond the scope of this report, and are presented in detail in *Multivariate Model Building* (Sonquist, 1970) and *Searching for Structure* (Sonquist, Baker, & Morgan, 1973). However, a brief overview of the program's function and output is in order. When presented with a set of variables, the AID program assigns codes reflecting "cuts" on each of the predictors. The MMPI scales, for example, were each cut into quintiles and recoded 0 to 4. The program then attempts to split the total sample into two groups on the basis of each MMPI scale progressing from the first to the last. For each variable AID finds the one split that maximizes the difference between the two groups on the dependent variable. Next, it selects the predictor variable (here an MMPI scale) which has the best split and assigns members of the sample to two groups according to their scores on that predictor variable. From a parent group, then, the program creates two subgroups. It then approaches each of the subgroups as it did the original sample, attempting to split a subgroup into two smaller groups on the predictor variables, progressing from first to last consecutively.

The outcome is a "tree," beginning with the total sample (in this case 583 patients and nonpatients), dividing and redividing the groups along "branches" determined by the order of predictors that the program has found to relate to differences in the dependent variable, and ending with small groups (limited to some extent by parameters provided by the researcher) in which the homogeneity of the subsamples is maximized and further splitting is not advantageous. Since, in the current situation, the dependent variable was dichotomous (i.e., a subject is either a patient or a nonpatient), the ideal result of the use of the AID is to isolate subgroups composed exclusively of one or the other type of subject—all patients or all nonpatients.

Step 4: Evaluation of the Three Sets of Variables

After each set of variables was processed by the AID, the final step in building the model was to evaluate the adequacy of each set in "predicting" the outcome variable which is patient–nonpatient status. This was done in two ways: first, by determining the extent to which each set succeeds in accounting for variance in the dependent variable and then comparing the sets on their respective successes. The second involves a consideration of the ability of each set of variables to isolate groups composed of only patients or nonpatients. Both methods of evaluation were employed in the present study.

A third evaluative procedure was added to the model for this report. In this step, a series of 2×2 factorial analyses of variance in which nonpatient–patient status and sex were independent variables and the MMPI scales that were selected by the AID served as the dependent variables. The same ANOVA design was used with the unselected scales to further evaluate the adequacy of the AID procedure. Sex was added as a factor and education as a covariate to examine the influence of those variables.

Only patients with complete records were included in the AID sample. Also, since opiate-dependent individuals had been diverted from the Philadelphia project, daily opiate users were excluded from the AID sample regardless of the completeness of their records. This procedure yielded a sample of 583 cases, 47.5% of whom were nonpatients. Table III.4 shows comparisons of included and excluded subjects including

Table III.4

COMPARISONS OF NATIONAL POLYDRUG SUBJECTS INCLUDED IN AND EXCLUDED FROM AID ANALYSES

	Age[a]	Last school year completed[a]	Months employed in last 2 years[a]	Number of arrests in last 2 years[a]	Number of suicide attempts[b]	Suicide attempts by drug[b]	Number of psyciatric treatments[b]	Age at first drug experience[b]	Emergency room treatments[c]
Included in AID (N = 583)									
Mean	23.85	11.89	10.50	1.05	.41	.28	.91	15.61	.48
SD	7.76	2.60	7.92	2.47	1.15	.89	1.45	5.82	1.09
Excluded in AID (N = 544)									
Mean	27.18	10.80	8.59	1.95	.56	.44	1.22	16.63	1.04
SD	9.65	3.24	8.65	5.65	1.35	1.21	1.90	7.74	1.21

[a] $t > 3.291$; $df = 1125$; $p < .001$.
[b] $t > 1.96$; $df = 1125$; $p < .05$.
[c] N.S.

those subjects excluded because of opiate–narcotic usage or missing instruments.

DERIVED DRUG USE VARIABLES

Five additional drug use scores were derived from the original data for use in the AID analysis of drug use variables. "Frequency of use" was coded as the proportion of daily use for each drug used by the subject, with daily use coded 1.0. The sum of drug use frequencies is the arithmetic sum of these proportions over all drugs used by the subject in the 3-month period preceding testing and mean frequency is that sum divided by the number of drugs used. The drugs themselves were assigned codes which represent their "risk" level, as presented by the recent *White Paper on Drug Abuse* (1975). Alcohol, marijuana, and cocaine were assigned a risk code of 1; hallucinogens, psychotropics, inhalants, and over-the-counter drugs were assigned a risk code of 2; and heroin, illegal methadone, other opiates, amphetamines, and barbiturates were assigned a 3. The mean risk index is a derived score which represents the mean of a subject's risk codes, a score which ranges from 1.0 to 3.0. The drug severity index is the mean of the products of the risk codes multiplied by their respective frequency codes. Finally, the mean age of first use was calculated by summing the age of first use given for each of the drugs that the subject was using during the most recent 3-month period and dividing by the number of drugs used. This variable should not be confused with the age of the first drug experience, which was also included.

RESULTS

Automatic Interaction Detector Analyses

The results of the AID analysis of drug use variables are presented in Figure III.2. In general, if an AID run was entirely successful in differentiating nonpatients and patients, the sequence of variables at the top of the array would end in a group containing 100% nonpatients while the sequence of variables at the bottom would end in a group containing no (0%) nonpatients.

Among the drug use variables, the CAPPS item, "Past Drug Problems," was identified by the AID as best splitting the total sample of 583 subjects. The resulting subgroup of 438 subjects with ratings of "none to moderate"

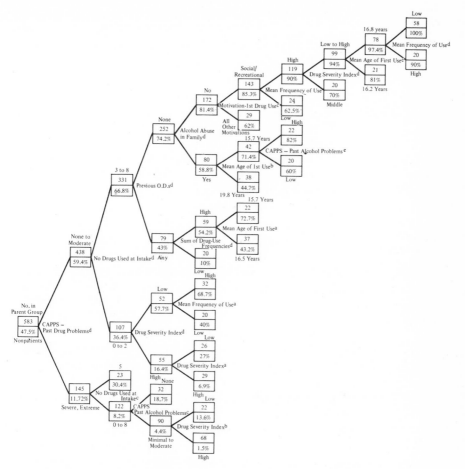

Figure III.2. Drug use variables "predicting" patient–nonpatient status. ($^a p < .05; ^b p < .02;$ $^c p < .01; ^d p < .001; ^e$ N.S.)

is represented in the upper box, and this group contained 260 nonpatients, or 59.4%. The subgroup with ratings of "severe or extreme" is represented by the lower box, and that subgroup contains 145 subjects, of whom 17, or 11.72% are nonpatients. The significance level of the split, obtained from a two-tailed t test, is shown by the notation (a, b, c, or d) at the end of the variable name. By following the successive splits and their resultant subgroups, from the original sample on the left to the smaller subgroups on the right, one can see the increasing homogeneity.

The results shown in Figure III.2 can be reduced to a narrative which describes the progression of variables leading to relatively homogeneous groupings of nonpatients and patients. In effect, the nonpatients presented themselves in a way that led interviewers to rate them as having relatively few problems associated with past drug use, they were multiple drug users with no overdose experience or alcohol abuse problems in their families, and they began using drugs in a social-recreational context. Also noteworthy is the fact that the nonpatients were using drugs at a high frequency across a range of drug risk levels. Beyond that point, the AID made finer differentiations identifying a slightly, but significantly, later starting group with a relatively low mean frequency of use.

On the other hand, the progression of variables leading to relatively homogeneous groupings of patients shows that they tended to be rated as having severe or extreme problems associated with their drug use in the past, that they too were multiple drug users (although some had discontinued drug use by the time they were interviewed), that they were rated as having had problems associated with alcohol use, and that they tended to use relatively high risk substances at a relatively high rate.

Among what might be called a series of marginal differentiations, one can observe a small, primarily nonpatient, group who have had problems associated with alcohol use, who have started drug use relatively young, and who report alcohol abuse in their families. One can also observe that among the subjects with fewer past problems associated with their drug use, the risk level and frequency of use (severity index) was clearly associated with patient status, and that these patients had relatively intense use of one or two substances at intake (again, with some having discontinued use by intake). Table III.5 lists drug use variables that were not selected by this AID analysis.

The results of the AID carried out on personal-functioning variables is presented in Figure III.3. The first predictor variable to split the sample was the CAPPS rating of past depression and anxiety. Again, by following the succession of splits and resulting subgroups, one can identify the variables leading to relatively homogeneous groups of nonpatients and patients. Reducing the results of Figure III.3 to a narrative, the nonpatients were rated as having few problems in the past or in the present with depression or anxiety, and as being relatively intelligent. They endorsed MMPI items that suggest moderate wariness, suspiciousness, and concern for rights and privileges, perhaps befitting their status as paid research informants. They also endorsed few MMPI items that suggest concerns about health and bodily functions. A responsible, easy going, relaxed orientation was indicated by many patients.

The succession of variables that leads toward a relatively homogeneous group of patients (i.e., 62 subjects, 1 nonpatient, no further splits), shows higher ratings of past depression or anxiety, higher self-reported depres-

Table III.5

UNUSED AID VARIABLES

A. Drug-use variables

First drug used by the subject
Situation—first drug experience
Age at first drug experience
Drug preference
Number of emergency room treatments
Drug abuse in the subjects family
Mean risk of drugs used
Current problems with alcohol use (CAPPS item)
Current problems with drug use (CAPPS item)
Toxic psychosis—drug use (CAPPS item)
Delusions–Hallucination: alcohol use (CAPPS item)

B. Personal-functioning variables

Number of suicide attempts
Number of psychiatric treatments
Tension–anxiety (POMS)
Anger–hostility (POMS)
Vigor–activity (POMS)
Fatigue–inertia (POMS)
Somatic concern—functioning (CAPPS scale, current)
Disorganization (CAPPS scale, current)
Reality testing (CAPPS scale, past)
Obsessive-compulsive (CAPPS scale, past)
Memory-orientation (CAPPS scale, past)
Disorganized (CAPPS scale, past)
Phobia (CAPPS scale, past)
MMPI—depression
MMPI—schizophrenia

C. Social-functioning variables

Number of arrests
Social–sexual relations (CAPPS scale, past)
Social isolation (CAPPS item, current)
Suspicion–persecution (CAPPS item, current)
Adolescent friendship pattern (CAPPS item, past)
Efforts to improve (CAPPS item, past)
Adult heterosexual adjustment (CAPPS item, past)
Illegal acts (CAPPS item, past)
Antisocial traits (CAPPS item, past)
Sensitive (CAPPS item, past)
Emotionally distant (CAPPS item, past)
Lacks responsibility (CAPPS item, past)
Suspicious (CAPPS item, past)

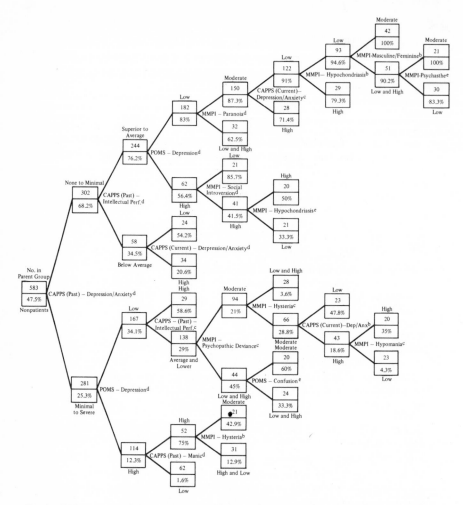

Figure III.3. Personal-functioning variables "predicting" patient–nonpatient status. ([a] $p <$ .05; [b] $p <$ .02; [c] $p <$ .01; [d] $p <$ .001; [e] N.S.)

sion, and a relatively low rating on the CAPPS manic trait, suggesting that these individuals were unwilling or unable to call attention to their discomfort. Among the marginal differentiations, one can observe a group of 23 subjects with 1 (4.3%) nonpatient included. This group endorses items that led to low MMPI-hypomania scores. By tracing the succession of variables that led to this group of subjects, it can be seen that they emerged from groups that were rated higher on depression or anxiety, both in the past and in the present. Given their low self-reported depression (shown in an intervening group), and assuming some perspicacity among interviewer rates, the low hypomania scores may support the contention that individuals within the patient sample have been unable or unwilling to put much energy into calling attention to their discomfort. In this context, drug misusers or self-medicators may be an appropriate descriptor for these individuals.

Along the same line of reasoning, out of a group rated high on intellectual performance, with an intervening group with high self-reported depression, one can observe a small group consisting largely of nonpatients (17 of 21). The members of this subgroup scored low on the MMPI-social introversion scale suggesting that they are able to seek and enjoy the company of others, perhaps as a way of dealing with depression. Table III.5 lists personal-functioning variables that were not selected by this AID analysis.

Figure III.4 presents the results of the AID analysis of social-functioning variables "predicting" nonpatient–patient status. The first variable to split the sample was the CAPPS rating of current problems with reality testing and social disturbance. As before, by following the succession of splits and the resulting subgroups, one can easily identify the variables leading to relatively homogeneous groups of nonpatients and patients. Reducing the results of Figure III.4 to a narrative, one sees that the nonpatients tended to be rated as having fewer problems with reality testing in a social context, and as having had a more adequate adult friendship pattern. For those who had worked, painful relationships had not been a problem and their job performance had been at least adequate. (Beyond that point, statistically insignificant differentiations were made within a parent group of 112 subjects, 97 of whom were nonpatients, on the basis of months employed in the last 2 years and nonacademic school problems.)

Moving in the direction of a homogeneous group of patients, one sees higher ratings for problems with reality testing in a social context and for antisocial traits in childhood. As was the case for nonpatients, the number of jobs held in the last 2 years does not lead to a clear differentiation among the patients, but they were rated as having had more nonacademic school problems and painful relationships in their pasts.

Among the marginal differentiations, one can see that 32 of the 59 nonpatients who had been rated as having had past problems with painful relations, also were rated as having had fewer problems with adolescent sexual adjustments. Given that these nonpatients with more adequate adolescent adjustments were in an intervening group with fewer months of work, it may be that their painful relationships were work related. Table III.6 presents indicators of the success of the three AID variable sets in predicting patient–nonpatient status.

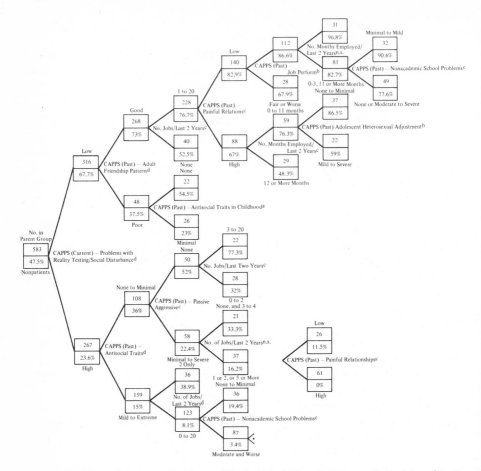

Figure III.4. Social functioning variables "predicting" patient–nonpatient status. ($^a p <$ .05; $^b p <$ .02; $^c p <$ .01; $^d p <$ .001; ^{e} N.S.)

Table III.6

INDICATORS OF THE SUCCESS OF THE THREE AID-VARIABLES
SETS IN PREDICTING NONPATIENT/PATIENT STATUS

Indicator	Drug	Social	Personal
Number of variables used	9	10	14
Number of final subgroups	20	18	21
Number of exclusive subgroups	1	1	2
Number of nonpatients isolated	58	0	63
Number of patients isolated	0	61	0
Percent of variance explained	41.19	36.89	41.76

GENERAL COMMENTS

The preceding presentations have concentrated on the attributes of nonpatients and patients that are clearly associated with their status. On the whole, the nonpatients appear to have had more positive experiences, to have more resources, and to have been able to offset negative attributes with positive ones, for example, depression is offset by extroversion and enjoyment of social contexts. But on the whole, considering the different ways in which the nonpatient and patient samples were generated, it is surprising that there is so much equivocation in the AID results. One might have expected larger and more homogeneous groups. By examining other potential sources of variation, it may be possible to reduce some of the equivocation and, at the same time, confirm the results of the AID analyses.

One obvious potential source of variation that was not controlled in the AID analyses is the sex of the subjects. The reader will also recall that subjects classified as nonpatients may or may not have had treatments in the past for problems associated with drug use or for other "psychological" problems. In the following sections, data will be presented that may clarify some of these issues.

COMPARISON OF NONPATIENTS AND PATIENTS: DERIVED DRUG USE VARIABLES

Means and standard deviations on derived drug use variables for nonpatients and patients by sex are presented in Table III.7. Significant patient–nonpatient differences were found (Table III.8) for mean age severity of first use, mean risk, and sum frequency. Analyses of variance data using patient–nonpatient status and sex as independent variables are presented in Table III.8. "Mean age" of first use was the only variable that showed a status by sex interaction ($F = 18.51$; $df = 1, 1120$; $p < .01$). Consequently, t tests were carried out on that variable. Female patients differed from male patients and male nonpatients and from female nonpatients.

A conclusion that might have been drawn from drug use data presented in the "Subjects" section of this chapter is that drug use was "heavier," more "intense," etc., among subjects in the patient sample. However, Tables III.7 and III.8 present another way of looking at the same data. Here, the opposite conclusion could be drawn. Clarification may come from reviewing the sampling procedures used to generate the patient and nonpatient samples. In order to be accepted into the nonpatient sample,

54

Table III.7

COMPARISON OF NONPATIENTS AND PATIENTS: DERIVED DRUG USE
VARIABLES

	Mean age of first use	Severity	Mean risk	Sum frequency	Mean frequency
Male nonpatients (N = 202)					
Mean	17.55	7.37	1.82	3.28	.80
SD	4.24	5.29	.40	1.87	.38
Female nonpatients (N = 102)					
Mean	16.89	7.44	1.94	3.21	.76
SD	3.24	5.11	.41	1.85	.40
Male patients (N = 496)					
Mean	18.21	6.54	1.93	2.88	.78
SD	7.20	4.85	.63	1.89	.40
Female patients (N = 324)					
Mean	22.19	6.29	2.07	2.64	.82
SD	10.42	4.25	.69	1.69	.38

subjects had to meet specific substance use and frequency of drug use criteria. Obviously, all applicants for drug abuse treatment services are not accepted on an equivalent basis. A large, but undetermined number of patients would not have met the drug use criteria, and in fact, some patients reported no use at the time of testing. The data presented in Tables III.7 and III.8 together with the results of the AID analyses of drug use variables reinforce the notion that drug use per se is not an infallible predictor of problems appropriately associated with drug use. These findings also reinforce the importance of sampling procedures and the need to understand the effects that sampling can have on outcomes. One example from the experience of the Philadelphia Polydrug Program may accentuate the point. One subject (accepted for study because of use of other substances) used LSD three times. Each episode of use was followed by a psychiatric hospitalization. This subject was enrolled in treatment for compulsive, life-threatening LSD abuse. This case is to be contrasted with the 15 (approximately) nonpatients who were seen after 150 to 500 LSD trips with no contact with legal or drug treatment facilities.

Table III.8

ANALYSES OF VARIANCE: DERIVED DRUG USE VARIABLES

A. Mean age of first use

Source	df	MS	F^a
Status	1	1788.87	30.54*
Sex	1	555.09	9.48*
Status × sex	1	1084.23	18.51*
Within groups	1120	58.57	

B. Severity

Source	df	MS	F
Status	1	197.43	8.56*
Sex	1	1.63	.07
Status × sex	1	5.16	.22
Within groups	1120	23.07	

C. Mean risk

Source	df	MS	F
Status	1	2.90	8.11*
Sex	1	3.40	9.52*
Status × sex	1	.02	.06
Within groups	1120	.36	

D. Sum frequency

Source	df	MS	F
Status	1	47.38	14.27*
Sex	1	4.84	1.46
Status × sex	1	1.46	.44
Within groups	1120	3.32	

E. Mean frequency

Source	df	MS	F
Status	1	.08	.53
Sex	1	00	00
Status × sex	1	.32	2.10
Within groups	1120	.15	

$^a F_{.99}$ (1, 1120) = 6.85; $F_{.95}$ (1, 1120) = 3.92
* $p < .01$

DISCUSSION

The AID analysis of drug use variables indicates that for nonpatients drug and alcohol use are not associated with life problems, but that for patients they are. That is an important differentiation, but it relies on an assumption that respondents were rated on the relevant CAPPS items on the basis of experiencing severe problems that were related to drug use and not merely on the basis of frequency of use. The interview staff of the Philadelphia Polydrug Program did rate subjects in that manner. The nonpatients appear to have had fewer problems associated with drug or alcohol use and this in turn may be a function of their relative socioeconomic advantage.

Are the nonpatients merely earlier in their drug abuse careers, and will they become the individuals who will seek treatment in the future? The answer appears to be a qualified no. The nonpatient sample is a younger group who started drug use at an earlier age. Given the common assumptions of stages of psychosocial development, there is an implication that the initiation of drug use served different functions for the members of the nonpatient and patient groups. From the accounts given by the nonpatients, the primary function for them was enhancement of the ongoing peer group process. As noted previously, it is regrettable that there was no sensitive and reliable measure of motivation for initiating and continuing drug use.

In addition, age and duration of drug use were not powerful variables in the substudy of barbiturate and amphetamine users. To whatever extent the MMPI and POMS-depression scales are appropriate measures of personality and emotional adjustments for these samples, they are not strongly affected by age or duration of drug use.

Moreover, most nonpatients who had had previous treatment chose psychotherapy over treatment for drug abuse. Nonpatients interviewed by the Philadelphia Center Polydrug Program staff were questioned about treatment needs. It was the consensus of the interviewer staff that few, if any, nonpatients viewed attaining a drug-free state as an appropriate or meaningful goal of treatment. For them, drug treatment implied discontinuation of drug use. They might turn to psychotherapy if they had problems with living and if their friends were insufficient resources, but psychotherapy did not imply that they could no longer "get high."

Are the nonpatients at a different level of risk in developing the complications that would bring them to treatment? For 105 of the 304 subjects in the nonpatient sample the answer is no, since they already have been involved in treatment. For this population treatment involvement subsumes a wide range of activities ranging from being "forced" to see a psychiatrist as punishment when a parent found marijuana in a subject's closet to lengthy hospitalizations for childhood schizophrenia. Two of the nonpatients said that they entered a methadone maintenance program specifically to obtain methadone. Their heroin use was sufficient for them to convince the program that methadone maintenance was appropriate therapy. They dropped out of the methadone program when the rules covering the dispensing of methadone changed. How likely is it that similar experiences would be encountered in a random sample drawn from the general population of young adults?

The results of the AID analyses and the analyses of variance indicate that not all high rate polydrug abusers are experiencing the economic, social, and personality problems seen in patients seeking or undergoing treatment. Because of the retrospective nature of this investigation it is not possible to elucidate what factors allow the nonpatients to use drugs without experiencing complications or what complex of person and situation precipitates the problems associated with patient status. It appears as if context of drug use and patterns of use, but not substance *per se* are important considerations. However, even differences in these factors probably represent the outcome of social and personality variables.

Even though this investigation could not specify the variables which are causally related to the observed differences, the mere establishment of the differences is important in demonstrating that the polydrug-using population is not homogeneous. The heterogeneity of the polydrug population precludes success of any effort at understanding the problems, mounting prevention programs or providing treatment for "the polydrug abuser." Continuing efforts aimed at developing homogeneous subgroups are required to meaningfully come to grips with the problem of polydrug abuse.

Does drug use put individuals at a different level of risk? The analyses of the derived drug use variables indicate that the nonpatients got "high" at least as frequently as the patients but that they used low and high risk drugs together to a greater extent. One would not conclude that use of low risk drugs counteracts the risks of using high risk drugs, but one might conclude that for the nonpatients, the particular substance is not as important as the effect of the drug and the social context in which the substance is used.

ACKNOWLEDGMENTS

The author wishes to acknowledge the contribution of Donald Wesson, Edward Deaux, Albert Carlin, Mark Morein, Grace Dammann, and David Speck to the conceptualization of this report. Edward Deaux, Harriet Schwartz, and David Speck also contributed to the production of the report.

CHAPTER IV

Female Polydrug Abusers

Grace Dammann and Nancy Ousley

Several studies on prescription rates for mood-modifying drugs indicated that women tended to be the major recipients. In 1969, Balter and Levine reported that 67% of all prescriptions for mood-altering substances were given to women. They found that in 1967 women received 63% of all prescribed barbiturates, 66% of all sedative–hypnotics, 71% of all antidepressants, and 80% of all amphetamines.

In a nationwide study examining prescription drug use trends of 2,552 adults in households, Parry, Balter, Mellinger, Cisin, and Manheimer, found that women reported single use of prescription drugs twice as frequently as men for the year prior to being interviewed (1973). The authors found that the 2:1 (female to male) ratio held when considering what the authors defined as "heavy" use (daily for at least 2 months) in the year prior to being interviewed. The authors further noted that use of drugs in the minor tranquilizer–sedative class accounted for most of the differential use between males and females. Thus, the authors found that more women used prescription drugs than men, both at "occasional" and "heavy" levels, and that the classes of drugs responsible for most of the

59

Polydrug Abuse:
The Results of a
National Collaborative Study

differences in use were minor tranquilizer–sedatives. This pattern of minor tranquilizer–sedative prescription drug use was most marked, in terms of both reported "heavy" use and variance from male use, within the 30- to 44-year-old female age group.

A nationwide survey conducted for NIDA by Response Analysis Corporation of Princeton, New Jersey, compared both medical and nonmedical use of psychoactive drugs for the years 1972, 1974, and 1975/1976. The data indicate a shifting pattern as to which age group is most likely to have used barbiturates, under medical supervision, in the year prior to the interview (Abelson & Fishburne, 1976). This survey concluded that the age bracket in which more persons report medically supervised use of barbiturates, is the 50+ age bracket. Similarly, the Princeton survey suggests that the ratio of female to male use is about 3:2 for 1972 and about 4:3 for 1975/1976.

The Princeton group does not report on the socioeconomic variables associated with the use of barbiturates or minor tranquilizers. The Parry study, however, looked specifically at the stereotype of the "suburban junkie" and found that long-term daily use of prescribed minor tranquilizer–sedatives did not correspond with middle-class status (1973). Using the Hollingshead scoring system, which combines education and occupation, the authors suggested that daily use was found to be most prevalent among lower income, more poorly educated housewives. In all other socioeconomic, educational, and marital status categories, no differences in "heavy" use of sedative–minor tranquilizers were found within the female population.

In an introduction to a series of articles appearing in the *Ladies Home Journal* on patterns of female drug use, Chambers and Schultz (1971a) stated:

> The typical woman who uses drugs to cope with life is not a fast-living rock star, nor a Times Square prostitute . . . nor a devotee of the drop-out-and-turn-on philosophy of Dr. Timothy Leary. She is an adolescent, confused by the stresses of impending adulthood. She is a newly-wed, by turns anxious and depressed. . . . She is a once busy housewife . . . who finds her days increasingly empty. She is, in short, an *average, middle-class American*—one of the folks next door [p. 191].

Their findings, however, suggest that the user of coping drugs is not necessarily "average" or "middle-class." Chambers and Schultz reported that college-educated working women were more apt to report "use" (at least once a month) of minor tranquilizers–sedatives than housewives. Working women, as a group, were also overrepresented as "habitual" users (six times a month, or more) of these substances. College-educated working women, when employing the Hollingshead scoring system to determine social position, would generally (although not necessarily), be found as falling between middle-class and upper-middle-class status.

Working women, the study noted, were also more likely than their housewife counterparts to obtain drugs by means other than prescription, and were more likely to use them in ways other than those recommended by physicians. Finally, working women were more likely to use illicit substances such as marijuana and LSD than their housewife counterparts.

One study examining the relationship between socioeconomic and employment variables and health and psychoactive drug use suggests that desire for paid employment by housewives, and not the role of "housewife," is associated with attitudes toward, and use of, psychoactive medications. Splitting a sample of 465 randomly selected female San Fernando Valley residents into three groups—employed, housewives not seeking employment, and housewives seeking employment—Fidell and Prather found that the group seeking employment had the poorest physical and mental health, the lowest educational levels, the lowest income, and the highest psychotropic drug use.

A study of the patterns of psychotherapeutic drug use among 1104 adults suggests that there are also differences in the drug-using behavior of men and women (Mellinger, Balter, & Manheimer, 1971). They found that the prevalence of psychotherapeutic drug use is greater among women, and the use of over-the-counter substances, alcohol, and marijuana greater among men. They further noted that men, when using prescription drugs, were more likely than women to obtain those drugs through nonprescription sources, such as friends. Within the female population, women in the 18- to 29-year-old age group tended to be the predominant users of psychotherapeutic drugs, regardless of the source (medical or nonmedical) or type (prescription or over-the-counter). Stimulants however, were the drug of choice for the 18- to 29-year-old female age group with minor tranquilizer–sedatives running a close second. When sedative–hypnotics and minor tranquilizers are combined, the use of depressants predominates within this age group of females.

A "household" survey conducted by Chambers and Griffey (1975) supports many of the conclusions of the Mellinger study. Chambers and Griffey found that while men cope with alcohol, women tend to cope with medications. Among those using coping medications, younger persons and men were more likely to use stimulants and older persons and women were more likely to use sedating and tranquilizing drugs. The Chambers and Griffey study also indicates that stimulants appear to be the drug of choice within the younger (18–25) female age group. However, for every drug class, the age group with the greatest likelihood of using drugs were women 35 and older.

The format utilized in both the Mellinger and Parry studies suggests that sampling procedures may have led to underrepresentation of "street" drug users. The data generated by these studies were collected by interviewing respondents who were "selected by rigorous sampling methods in order to form a cross-selection of American adults in households" (Parry et al., 1973).

The restriction to "adults in households" suggests that institutionalized adults were not represented; further, the "household" restriction might exclude persons not living in stable residences from the outset. A footnote to one of the tables on the frequency of use of minor tranquilizer–sedatives within the female population suggests that if represented at all, "street people" constituted a very small portion of the total sample. The footnote reads: "Those few women who were neither employed nor fulltime housewives, e.g., non-working, unmarried students were omitted from our analysis (Parry et al., 1973)."

Finally, the authors, by restricting their sample to adults, excluded a significant female drug-using population (Abelson & Fishburne, 1976; DAWN data, 1975). Although it is not clear what proportion of the female population under 18 years of age use drugs, recent surveys show that their drug use rates are comparable to males of the same age.

According to the 1975 Drug Abuse Warning Network (DAWN) data, persons under 18 years of age represented 30% of the drug mentions and 10 to 20% of the drug overdose mentions (depending on the specific drug type) in the San Francisco Standard Metropolitan Statistical Area.

The Chambers and Schultz study, based on "in-depth interviews with 4,000 New York State Women" (1971) focuses on working women, housewives, and young women in high school and college (1971a, b).

RATIONALE OFFERED FOR SEX-LINKED DIFFERENCES IN DRUG USE PATTERNS

The various authors account for sex differences in the kinds of drugs used, source, and pattern in a number of ways. With regard to drugs of use obtained through prescription routes, the explanations for disproportionate female use are as follows:

Women have a more negative view of themselves than men have of themselves (Bardwick, 1971; Rosenkrantz, Vogel, Bee, Broverman, & Broverman, 1968). Women are "allowed" (even encouraged) to express and experience psychic distress (Copperstock, 1971; Parry *et al.*, 1973; Phillips & Segal, 1969); women make more visits to physicians than men (Anderson & Feldman, 1956); and women are more likely than men to bring their psychic distress to the physician's office (Phillips & Segal, 1969). Some authors have indicated that physicians play an important role in the disproportionate use of prescription drugs by females. It has been said that physicians tend to terminate office visits by giving prescriptions (Muller, 1972); physicians are more willing to give housewives tranquilizers (Brodsky, 1971), and physicians are likely to judge the use of Librium as more appropriate for housewives than for students (Linn, 1971).

Researchers have indicated that physicians who are pessimistic about the outcome of treatment or angry with a patient are more likely to prescribe psychoactive drugs (Shrader, Binstock, & Scott, 1968). In line with these findings, Cooperstock reported on a study in which physicians were interviewed to determine their description of the typical complaining patient—sex not indicated; 72% of the physicians referred spontaneously to a woman. Of these physicians 78% indicated that they wrote more mood-modifying prescriptions for female patients than for male patients (1971).

Finally, advertising for psychoactive drugs perpetuates the sex role stereotyping associated with the use of these drugs. Fidell (1973) conducted a content analysis of a series of randomly selected advertisements in leading medical journals and found that there was a strong tendency to associate psychoactive drugs with females patients, and nonpsychoactive drug advertisements with male patients. The symptoms listed for male and female psychoactive drug users differed significantly, with men usually presenting symptoms that were specific and work related and women complaining of diffuse anxiety, tension, and depression (Fidell, 1973). In all probability, advertising reinforces prescribing practices which, in turn, reinforce female "health-seeking" behavior. Women are encouraged to express distress, are given psychoactive medication when they express or request it, and are thus led to believe they are sick and are reinforced for being sick. The tautology is complete. The responsibility and explanation for its perpetuation rest with the patient, the physician, and the cultural values about sex-appropriate behavior that influence both.

However, men use some psychoactive substances as frequently as women (Mellinger *et al.*, 1971; Parry *et al.*, 1973). A probable explanation for why men are more apt to use psychoactive substances which can be purchased over-the-counter, or are illicit, is that men are less prone to seek medical assistance.

Reports of admission rates to psychiatric institutions and clinical observations suggest that men are less likely to report or display behavior indicating psychic distress and/or are less apt to be reported as exhibiting such behavior (cf. Chesler, 1972; Gove & Tudor, 1973). While substances such as alcohol and marijuana have depressant effects similar to those exhibited by such drugs as Valium and Librium, alcohol and marijuana are not advertised (even though they may be so viewed by consumers) as "medication." Rather, they are.identified as social lubricants and not as adjuncts to a medical or psychological treatment process. The use of alcohol may achieve the same effect as the use of Valium with virtually none of the cost to male identity that would be associated with the use of prescribed psychotropic medication.

DATA ON PSYCHOACTIVE DRUG USE
AND ABUSE

At the national level, data on psychoactive drug abuse are collected through a variety of national reporting systems. Those reporting systems in turn are operated through nationally funded programs designed to treat mental illness (mental health centers), the abuse of drugs (Client Oriented Data Acquisition Program—CODAP) and alcohol (Alcohol Treatment Center Monitoring System—ATCMS), and drug episodes (DAWN). Each system has weaknesses which bias the data it generates.

The treatment data systems are restricted to persons *seeking* treatment, and are therefore not representative of the total drug-using population (see also Chapter III). Table IV.1 gives the age and sex breakdown of persons seeking treatment within the various systems for nonopiate drug abuse problems. The data from the Parry *et al.* 1973 study are also included for comparative purposes.

The data from the DAWN system correlate most closely with the Parry data regarding sex differences and suggest the existence of a large population of sedative-hypnotic and tranquilizer abusers who have not surfaced in other treatment systems. DAWN records data on persons who experience acute drug problems which are collected by crisis centers, county medical examiners' and coroners' offices, and hospital emergency rooms.

Emergency room data, which account for most of the DAWN "mentions," indicate that females represent between 56 and 73% of mentions for acute drug reactions in the sedative-hypnotic tranquilizer class. To understand the nature of the problem there is a need to assess the types of problems the emergency room mentions represent. While the DAWN

Table IV.1

CHARACTERISTICS OF NONOPIATE DRUG USE REPORTED IN NATIONAL DATA BANKS COMPARED WITH U.S. CENSUS DATA

Source	Age				Sex		Race	
	18–29	30–44	45–59	60+	Male	Female	White	Nonwhite
	In percentages							
Use studies								
Parry[a]	16	29	28	27	33	67	—	—
Treatment systems								
DAWN	67	23	8	2	46	54	75	25
Mental health centers	51	39	6	4	75	25	71	29
COADAP	80	17	3	1	68	32	75	25
ATCMS	28	37	29	5	72	28	85	15
U.S. Census (1970)	28	26	25	21	49	51	87	13

[a] Only users at "high" level (daily for at least 2 months).

system attempts a distinction between drug episodes that result from a suicidal gesture, an unintentional overdose, or physical dependence, the data collection methodology (i.e., clerks review of ER report) raises questions of validity.

Investigating the pattern of female emergency room treatment episodes for drug reactions in Dade County, Florida, Peterson (1974) found that the majority of females were white, and, that within the white female population, minor tranquilizers and sedatives accounted for 75% of the overdoses. Further, a fourth of the female population (nearly a third of the white female population) presented multiple substance (alcohol excluded) abuse patterns. In analyzing the data it was learned that 44% of the white females and 60% of the female multiple substance abusers acknowledged that they were attempting to commit suicide.

It may be that national DAWN data on nonopiate abuse are more reflective of psychological distress than of chronic drug abuse or physical dependence upon drugs. The DAWN data for July 1975, for the San Francisco Bay area, shown in Table IV.2, provide additional data to support this speculation. Diazepam (Valium) and secobarbital (Seconal), a tranquilizer and a barbiturate respectively, accounted for the second and fourth most frequently mentioned drugs. The breakdowns for sex and motivation are indicated in Table IV.2.

The data should not be taken as conclusive in that no correlation is made between sex and motivation. More important, motivation in DAWN is determined on the basis of information given the emergency room staff who filled out the DAWN forms.

Thus it appears that while the DAWN system *does* identify females as

Table IV.2

DAWN DATA FROM SAN FRANCISCO SMSA DURING JULY 1975, COMPARING DIAZEPAM (VALIUM) WITH SECOBARBITAL

Characteristics of patients	Diazepam (N = 149)	Secobarbital (N = 26)
	%	%
Sex		
Male	32	29
Female	68	71
Motivation		
Suicidal attempts	78	58
Psychic effects	9	13
Dependence	3	3

the population most frequently treated for overdoses with sedative–hypnotics and tranquilizers, treatment episodes are often attributed to suicide attempts. While the use of a psychoactive substance for a suicide attempt certainly constitutes *misuse* of a drug, it does not generally require drug abuse treatment intervention.

Female nonopiate substance abusers *do* appear for treatment within substance abuse programs (cf. Table IV.1), but only at a rate comparable to the female admission rate to alcohol and heroin treatment programs. What is most surprising is the low rate at which women nonopiate abusers surface for treatment within the mental health system. Women, after all, constitute nearly 52% of the patient population with the community mental health systems (Redick, 1973). There are several possible explanations, none of which are mutually exclusive: (1) women who seek mental health services do not abuse psychoactive substances; (2) women who abuse psychoactive substances do not seek mental health services; or (3) women seeking mental health services may abuse psychoactive substances, but the drug problem is not identified.

In any case, females *do not* appear for treatment for psychoactive drug abuse in any system at a rate resembling the aggregate female use rate reported in the various drug use studies. Because they have not surfaced, they are considered to be "hidden."

The National Commission on Marijuana and Drug Abuse suggested that overuse of barbiturates was America's "hidden drug problem" (1973). Studies examining the prescription and use trends for psychoactive substances indicated that women far exceed men in their use of barbiturates. Thus, the "hidden" drug problem was often identified as the "hidden" female population. While the evidence to support the existence of a specifically middle-class, housewife barbiturate addict population was scant, the media appeal and public response was not.

Methodological Problems

The methodological problems which must be considered when discussing the findings on female polydrug abusers are sampling biases and possible biases resulting from the manner in which the instruments were administered and data elements defined.

The sampling biases resulted from the location and staffing patterns of the various programs. While all the data suffer from the concentration of the treatment projects and patient populations in urban areas, this "urban" setting may influence, to a greater degree, the findings on the characteristics of women abusing nonopiate substances. One prevalence

68 GRACE DAMMANN AND NANCY OUSLEY

study on female patterns of nonopiate drug use indicate that suburban housewives use a disproportionate amount of these drugs (Chambers & Schultz, 1971). The urban location of the projects may well have hindered suburban women from seeking treatment, thereby causing the findings to underrepresent this group. The polydrug programs found that it was particularly difficult to establish the kind of case-finding and referral networks which would "draw" a middle-class population into treatment settings. It was generally a slow process and probable that 2 years was insufficient time to establish the referral networks required.

Some bias in the polydrug programs may have been introduced by the criteria used to define various data elements. The absence of defining objective criteria for defining suicide attempts, for example, could easily have resulted in the skewing of recording in sex-stereotypic directions. Again, the skewing might result from respondent introduced bias. For example, women might be more likely than men to interpret an overdose, retrospectively, as a suicide attempt because it is socially acceptable to express distress. Likewise, male interviewers might be more likely to interpret an overdose by women as a suicide attempt because social science research indicates that women attempt suicide, particularly with drugs, more frequently than men.

The particular schedule offered for determining occupation makes it difficult to assess the socioeconomic level of those women who received treatment in the polydrug programs. The occupational schedule provides for categories such as "housewife" and "none" which prohibit the use of the traditional Hollingshead code in determining socioeconomic status, in that no identifying economic data were collected (particularly for those women labeling themselves as "housewife") on the occupational status of the head of the household. Furthermore, the occupational groupings offered did not include actual status differences which do exist for the female populations. For example, clerical workers and nurses are placed on the same status level.

Finally, certain data elements which are particularly important when considering patterns of drug use among women were omitted. For example, no questions were asked on the standard intake form concerning numbers of children, legal status of those children, or desire—or lack thereof—for employment (lack because of parenting obligations). In addition, no questions were included on gynecological problems or problems of persistent pain. Early studies of female drug use and abuse patterns include speculations about gynecological problems as a causative agent in female nonopiate addiction itself (e.g., Glaser, 1966; 1968).

Another level of bias may result from the absence of criteria to differentiate "use" from "abuse." Admission to the polydrug projects and, hence, inclusion as a subject in the polydrug data were predicated on an assumption of abuse on the part of the would-be client and research subject.

Results

Because of sex-sampling biases likely to exist within the polydrug sample, comparison of male and female data is likely to be misleading. Our analysis, therefore, focuses on defining subpopulations of women who were treated in the polydrug projects. Data are presented for gross comparative purposes, on male patterns of drug use and utilization of community-based treatment systems. The instruments employed for conducting the following analysis include the intake questionnaire, which solicited demographic data.

SUBPOPULATIONS OF
FEMALE POPULATION

Two broad clusters of variables which can be conceptually defined and which overlap at several junctures, describe the female population of polydrug users. Those two clusters consist of: (1) demographic variables describing the current and potential economic status of the patients; (2) variables indicating the interaction of the patients with the health and legal systems for problems resulting from their drug use. These two clusters of variables describe differing patterns of drug use and suggest the need for differential treatment strategies and possible points of intervention.

Table IV.4 shows a breakdown of income source by occupational training. By sorting the population according to primary income source (job, spouse, family, or welfare), a number of differences become apparent (cf. Table IV.3). Such analysis indicates a population diverse as to age, with those indicating support from spouse as the oldest (mean = 35.5 years; SD = 10.9 years) and those receiving family support (mean = 22.2 years; SD = 9.5 years), as the youngest. Mean age of first drug use differs as do the various indices of social productivity such as the number of months employed and jobs held during the past 2 years.

An examination of the variables surrounding first drug use suggests that the history and level of drug use is related to current economic status. The groups vary consistently (Table IV.5) on the history of drug use, with the family-supported group indicating a pattern of youthful drug experimentation. Those in the family-supported group were the youngest when they had their first drug experiences, and those in the spouse-

Table IV.3

FEMALE POPULATION: BY INCOME SOURCE

Characteristic	Job (N = 68)		Spouse (N = 45)		Family (N = 84)		Welfare (N = 103)		
	Mean	SD	Mean	SD	Mean	SD	Mean	SD	
Age at interview	29.5	10.9	35.5	10.9	22.2	9.5	29.9	11.3	$F = 24.78/df = 298***$
Education (years)	12.3	2.2	11.3	3.2	10.6	2.2	10.7	2.6	$F = 7.58/df = 298***$
Months employed in past 2 years: mean number	16.6	7.5	4.6	9.7	6.1	7.2	4.8	6.0	$F = 49.06/df = 299***$

*** $p < .001$.

Table IV.4

FEMALE POPULATION: OCCUPATIONAL TRAINING LEVEL BY INCOME
SOURCE

Occupational training level	Job (N = 68)		Spouse (N = 45)		Family (N = 84)		Welfare (N = 103)	
	N	%	N	%	N	%	N	%
Minor profession	15	22.1	2	4	4	4.8	8	8
Clerical– technical	31	45.6	12	26.7	11	13.1	24	24
Semiskilled– skilled	11	16.2	0	10	11	13.1	18	18
Unskilled–none	8	11.8	7	15.6	20	23.8	32	32
Housewife	0	0	24	53.3	3	3.6	12	12
Student	3	4.4	0	53	35	41.7	6	6

supported group, the oldest. Those in the family-supported group were
more likely to have those experiences in a social context and to explain
their motivation for first use as recreational, while the spouse-supported
women report first use to be physician prescribed or self-medicating.

The groups do not differ in terms of primary drugs of abuse or preferred
drug. However, they do differ greatly in their self-report of drug use in the
2-year period prior to entering treatment (Table IV.6). The family-
supported group reported at least one-time simultaneous use of a wide
variety of drugs while the spouse-supported group indicated a high percentage of use of legally obtainable drugs, such as barbiturates, opiates,
and psychotropic drugs. Of those who report the use of a given substance
in the 2 years prior to entry into treatment, the spouse-supported and
welfare-supported groups are most likely to indicate that their frequency
of use, immediately prior to entering treatment, was daily. Those two
groups were most likely to use barbiturates and opiates on a daily basis
and they were likely to use those drugs along, rather than in a social
setting. Again, as with the context of first drug use, the family-supported
group is apt to use drugs in a social setting. The family-supported group
reports at a consistently highest level that their motivation for use
is "social-recreational" while the spouse-supported group reports
physician-prescribed medication as the reason for use. As motivation for
use differs between the groups, so too does predominant source for the
drugs. The spouse-supported group is most likely to indicate "legal prescription" as the source for psychotropics and barbiturates, while the
family-supported group is most likely to indicate a source other than
prescription.

Table IV.5

FIRST DRUG EXPERIENCE: BY INCOME SOURCE

Characteristic	Job (N = 68)		Spouse (N = 45)		Family (N = 94)		Welfare (N = 103)		
	N	%	N	%	N	%	N	%	
1. Situation									$X^2 = 24.74/df = 3^{***}$
Alone	26	38.2	24	55.8	12	14.6	40	40.4	
With others	42	61.8	19	44.2	70	85.4	59	59.6	
2. Motivation									$X^2 = 33.86/df = 6^{***}$
Prescription	7	10.4	11	26.2	3	6.0	19	19.2	
Self-medication	15	22.4	13	31.0	4	4.8	14	14.1	
Social/recreational	45	67.2	15	35.7	70	84.3	61	61.6	
	Mean	SD	Mean	SD	Mean	SD	Mean	SD	
3. Age	20.2	10.1	24.6	10.6	14.4	6.0	19.49	10	$F = 12.49/df = 294^{***}$

*** $P < .001$.

While sorting the population by income sources revealed marked differences in social and economic backgrounds, there were minor differences among the populations in the *number* of different systems from which they received treatment (Table IV.7). The welfare-supported group was most likely to have received treatment in the drug or alcohol treatment system.

The groups vary according to referral source with welfare- and spouse-supported women more likely to have been referred by mental health programs, welfare- and family-supported persons likely to have come from drug or alcohol programs, and spouse- and job-supported women from private physicians or hospitals.

By Income Source

HOUSEWIFE GROUP

The housewife group ($N = 39$) consists of those women who are currently married, living with their families and supported by their spouses (cf. Tables IV.8, IV.9, and IV.10). The housewife group was as narrowly defined as possible, in order to permit comparisons with the "hidden housewife" stereotype. This group differed significantly from the other women in the sample on indices of age, types of drugs abuse, and rates of entry into the program. The housewife group is significantly older with a mean age of 36.1 as compared with a mean age of 27.4 for the rest of the patient population. Predictably, they differ from the rest of the female population in terms of occupation and employment record during the 2 years prior to admission.

The housewife differs from the nonhousewife population in terms of first drug experiences and current drug use (Table IV.10). The housewife group is more likely to prefer use of CNS (central nervous system) depressant drugs than are the other women and more likely to indicate daily use of barbiturates. Of those who are using CNS depressant drugs, the housewives are more apt to indicate that they secure them through legal prescriptions. The housewife–nonhousewife groups are not distinguished on such sequelae of use as emergency room treatment episodes, overdoses, arrests or traffic accidents resulting from drug use, or drug treatment episodes. In addition, the housewives and others do not differ on possible antecedents such as drug or alcohol abuse by family or spouse, or previous psychiatric treatment episodes, nor do they differ as to their rates of entry into the four major service systems—alcohol and drug abuse programs, mental health, criminal justice, and medicine.

Table IV.6

USE OF DRUGS WITH PAST 2 YEARS: BY INCOME SOURCE

Characteristic	Job (N = 68) N	Job (N = 68) %	Spouse (N = 45) N	Spouse (N = 45) %	Family (N = 84) N	Family (N = 84) %	Welfare (N = 103) N	Welfare (N = 103) %	
1. Use of following drugs in past 2 years.									
A. Barbiturates	41	60.3	32	71.1	60	71.4	71	68.0	$X^2 = 2.55/df = 3$
B. Heroin	14	20.6	4	8.9	22	26.2	32	31.1	$X^2 = 9.11/df = 3*$
C. Amphetamines	32	47.1	15	33.3	50	59.5	52	50.5	$X^2 = 8.28/df = 3*$
D. Opiates	28	41.2	23	51.1	22	26.2	42	40.8	$X^2 = 8.84/df = 3*$
E. Cocaine	22	32.6	5	11.1	25	29.8	18	17.5	$X^2 = 10.77/df = 3**$
F. Alcohol	31	45.6	13	28.9	56	66.7	46	44.7	$X^2 = 18.86/df = 3***$
G. Psychotropics	38	55.9	35	77.8	39	46.4	56	54.4	$X^2 = 11.90/df = 3**$
H. Marijuana	39	57.4	10	22.2	63	75.0	49	47.6	$X^2 = 35.1/df = 3***$
I. Hallucinogens	23	33.8	4	8.9	46	54.8	28	27.2	$X^2 = 31.50/df = 3***$
2. Of those who have used the following drugs in the past 2 years, frequency of use.									
A. Barbiturates									
Daily	15	46.9	25	83.3	14	30.4	43	72.9	$X^2 = 26.12/df = 3***$
Less often	17	53.1	5	16.7	32	69.6	16	27.1	
B. Amphetamines									
Daily	13	52	8	66.7	14	37.8	26	66.7	$X^2 = 5.65/df = 3$
Less often	12	48	4	33.3	23	62.2	13	33.3	
C. Opiates									
Daily	9	50	13	86.7	4	25	25	86.2	$X^2 = 17.89/df = 3***$
Less often	9	50	2	13.3	12	75	4	13.8	
D. Psychotropics									
Daily	17	58.6	29	90.6	23	74.2	40	81.6	$X^2 = 7.62/df = 3$
Less often	12	41.4	3	9.4	8	25.8	9	18.4	

3. Of those currently using the following drugs, social context of use.

A. Barbiturates									
Alone	19	55.9	27	90	19	38.8	36	60	$X^2 = 8.52/df = 3$*
With others	15	44.1	3	10	30	61.2	24	40	
B. Opiates									
Alone	15	83.3	15	83.3	7	36.8	23	71.9	$X^2 = 12.76/df = 3$
With others	3	16.7	3	16.7	12	63.2	9	28.1	
C. Opiates									
Prescription	6	33.3	7	41.2	1	5.0	10	32.3	$X^2 = 32.02/df = 6$***
Self-medicating	9	50.0	7	41.2	1	5.0	13	41.9	
Social-recreational	3	16.7	3	17.6	18	90.0	8	25.8	
D. Amphetamines									
Prescription	2	7.7	2	18.2	2	4.5	5	13.2	$X^2 = 20.99/df = 6$**
Self-medicating	17	65.4	5	45.4	9	20.5	18	47.4	
Social-recreational	7	26.9	4	36.4	33	75.0	15	39.5	

4. Of those using the following drugs, source of the drug.

A. Barbiturates									
1. Legal prescription	15	44.1	24	80	8	20.5	27	45	$X^2 = 24.26/df = 3$***
2. Other	19	55.9	6	20	31	79.5	33	55	
B. Psychotropics									
1. Legal prescription	18	60	31	93.9	18	54.4	35	70	$X^2 = 11.94/df = 3$**
2. Other	12	40	2	6.1	15	45.4	15	30	
C. Opiates									
1. Legal prescription	11	61.1	13	72.2	1	5.3	24	77.4	$X^2 = 24.3/df = 3$***
2. Other	7	38.9	5	27.8	18	94.7	7	22.6	

Table IV.6 continued

75

Table IV.6 (*continued*)

Characteristic	Job (N = 68)		Spouse (N = 45)		Family (N = 84)		Welfare (N = 103)		
	N	%	N	%	N	%	N	%	

5. Of those using the following drugs, motivation for use.

Characteristic	Job N	Job %	Spouse N	Spouse %	Family N	Family %	Welfare N	Welfare %	
A. Barbiturates									
Physician prescribed	6	17.6	8	28.6	1	2.0	15	26.8	$X^2 = 29.34/df = 6$***
Self-medicating	13	38.2	15	53.6	14	28.0	24	42.9	
Social-recreational	15	44.1	5	17.9	35	70.0	17	30.4	
B. Psychotropics									
Physician prescribed	7	24.1	13	40.6	7	20.0	13	27.1	$X^2 = 15.5/df = 6$*
Self-medicating	14	48.3	17	53.1	11	31.4	22	45.8	
Social-recreational	8	27	6	26.3	17	48.6	13	27.1	

* $p < .05$.
** $p < .01$.
*** $p < .001$.

Table IV.7

PREVIOUS TREATMENT HISTORY: BY INCOME SOURCE

Characteristic	Job (N = 68)		Spouse (N = 45)		Family (N = 84)		Welfare (N = 103)		
	N	%	N	%	N	%	N	%	
1. Has received prior treatment in drug or alcohol treatment system.									
Yes	22	32.4	19	42.2	27	32.1	53	51.5	$X^2 = 9.50/df = 3^*$
No	46	67.6	26	57.8	57	67.9	50	48.5	
2. Previous interaction with criminal justice, drug and alcohol abuse, mental health, or emergency room treatment systems: Total number of different systems.									
0	20	29.4	10	22.2	19	22.6	16	15.5	$X^2 = 16.05/df = 12^*$
1	22	32.4	13	28.9	28	33.3	23	22.3	
2	12	17.6	6	13.3	20	23.8	31	30.1	
3	12	17.6	14	31.1	14	16.7	29	28.2	
4	2	2.9	2	4.4	3	3.6	4	3.9	
3. Referral Source:									
Drug abuse program	7	10.6	0	0	14	19.2	18	20.0	$X^2 = 24.16/df = 12^*$
Mental health programs	5	7.6	7	17.5	7	9.6	20	22.2	
Physician or hospital	18	27.3	16	40	14	19.2	16	17.8	
Crisis center	9	13.7	3	7.5	9	12.33	8	8.9	
Other	25	32.8	6	15	29	39.7	28	31.1	

* $p < .05.$
** $p < .01.$
*** $p < .001.$

Table IV.8

AGE AT ADMISSION AND AT FIRST DRUG USE: BY HOUSEWIFE, NONHOUSEWIFE STATUS

Characteristic	Housewives (N = 39)		Non-housewives (N = 285)		
	Mean	SD	Mean	SD	
1. Age at admission	36.1	11.2	27.6	11.1	$T = -4.55/df = 316***$
2. Age at first drug experience	24.8	10.8	17.9	9.3	$T = 3.80/df = 46.28***$

*** $p < .001$.

Table IV.9

OCCUPATIONAL BACKGROUND: BY HOUSEWIFE, NONHOUSEWIFE STATUS

Characteristic	Housewives (N = 39)		Non-housewives (N = 285)		
	N	%	N	%	
1. Occupation					$X^2 = 66.98/df = 5***$
Professional	1	2.6	31	10.9	
Clerical–technical	11	28.2	74	26.0	
Semiskilled–skilled	0	0.0	42	14.7	
Unskilled–none	6	15.4	68	23.9	
Student	0	0.0	45	15.9	
Housewife	21	53.8	20	7.0	
2. Employment in past 2 years					$X^2 = 8.04/df = 1**$
None	23	59.0	101	35.4	
One month or more	16	41.0	184	64.6	

** $p < .01$.
*** $p < .001$.

WOMEN SUPPORTING THEMSELVES BY JOB

As would be expected, those women whose predominant income source is listed as "job" are better educated, have worked longer in the past 2 years (cf. Table IV.3), and show a slightly higher occupational level than the rest of the female population (cf. Table IV.4).

Women indicating "job" as their predominant income source can be divided into those who indicate that they are currently employed and those who are not. The two groups vary on a number of variables, with the "currently employed" group being older ($p < .023$), better educated ($p < .058$), and having been employed for a significantly longer time span in the last 24 months (18.5 as opposed to 11.4 months; $p < .002$). Women, employed at the time of admission, were not as apt to have received drug abuse treatment services ($p < .03$) or to have been arrested or convicted of a drug-related crime ($p < .005$).

Finally, the "currently employed" group was significantly older when they had their first drug experience (21.9 as opposed to 15.6 years; $p < .02$).

WOMEN ON WELFARE

Women supported by welfare had the fewest number of months employed over the past 2 years, with a mean of 4.5. Almost half of the welfare-supported group indicated no employment over the past 2 years. When contrasted with the women supporting themselves by other sources they differ as to vocation with the working group more likely to indicate a "professional" trade than the welfare group, and the welfare-supported group more likely to indicate no trade.

The welfare-supported group, in turn, can be divided into those women who have not worked at all in the 2 years prior to entering treatment ($N = 51$) and those women who have worked at least 1 month in the same time period ($N = 49$). The two groups differ in only one respect: the totally unemployed group is more likely to report daily use of psychotropics ($p < .01$) or opiates ($p < .03$).

Systems' Interaction

The identification of "gatekeepers" is particularly important for the early detection and treatment of women at risk for polydrug abuse. At the point of admission, only 21% of the entire female population had gone untreated by any of the traditional treatment systems. Approximately 90% of the females seen by the polydrug programs had been previously identified by referral or treatment systems. This suggests that prior to admission to the polydrug projects, a large majority of the women had been identified as clients or potential clients (cf. Tables IV.11, IV.12, and IV.13).

Of the Polydrug Project female population, 60% had been treated at least once in the mental health system: 44% had received treatment in

Table IV.10

DRUG EXPERIENCE: BY HOUSEWIFE, NONHOUSEWIFE STATUS

	Housewives (N = 39)		Non-housewives (N = 285)		
Characteristic	N	%	N	%	
1. First drug experience					
Barbiturates	9	23.1	24	22.2	
Other	30	76.9	84	77.8	
2. First drug experience situation:					
Alone	22	56.4	83	30.2	$X^2 = 9.41/df = 1^{**}$
With Others	17	43.6	192	69.8	
3. First drug experience:					
Iatrogenic	9	26.5	33	12.4	$X^2 = 14.31/df = 2^{***}$
Self-medication	11	32.6	39	14.7	
Social-recreational	14	41.2	194	72.9	
4. Drug preference:					
Barbiturates or					
psychotropics	22	56.4	112	39.3	$X^2 = 4.29/df = 1^{*}$
Other	17	43.6	173	60.7	
5. Use of drugs in the past 2 years:					
a. Psychotropics	29	74.4	149	38.7	$X^2 = 6.76/df = 1^{**}$
b. Amphetamines	11	28.2	153	53.7	$X^2 = 8.91/df = 1^{**}$
c. Marijuana	8	20.5	166	58.2	$X^2 = 19.64/df = 1^{***}$
d. Hallucinogens	3	7.7	104	36.5	$X^2 = 11.60/df = 1^{***}$
6. Of those who have used barbiturates in the past 2 years, frequency of use:					
Daily	22	81.5	87	55.1	$X^2 = 5.60/df = 1^{*}$
Less often	5	18.5	71	44.9	
7. Of those who are currently using barbiturates, social context of use.					
Alone	24	53.0	87	88.9	$X^2 = 10.81/df = 1^{**}$
With others	3	46.9	77	8.1	

Table IV.10 (*continued*)

Characteristic	Housewives (N = 39)		Non-housewives (N = 285)		
	N	%	N	%	
8. Of those who are currently using the drugs, source of the drug.					
a. Barbiturates					
Legal prescription	21	36.7	61	80.8	$X^2 = 16.05/df = 1$***
Other	5	63.2	105	19.2	
b. Psychotropics					
Legal prescription	25	92.6	81	92.6	$X^2 = 7.56/df = 1$**
Other	2	7.4	47	36.7	

* $p < .05.$
** $p < .01.$
*** $p < .001.$

emergency rooms for a drug-related problem in the 2 years prior to admission to the polydrug projects; and 42% had received drug abuse treatment within the 2 years prior to admission.

Females who did have contact with treatment providers were likely to have had contact with more than one treatment provider. For example, for those women indicating a prior history of treatment within the drug abuse treatment systems, 70% had also received treatment within the mental health system and 72% had been treated for a drug-related problem in emergency rooms. Of those who indicate a prior history of psychiatric treatment, 53% had been treated for drug-related problems in emergency rooms and 49% had been treated within the drug abuse system in the last 2 years alone. Finally, of those treated within the last 2 years for drug-related problems by emergency room personnel, 70% indicated a history of drug abuse treatment and 74% indicated a prior history of psychiatric treatment.

TREATMENT HISTORY WITH A GIVEN SYSTEM

Psychiatric Treatment

Women who have received psychiatric treatment (N = 196) differ from those who have not (N = 128) on three variables (Table IV.12). The group that has had psychiatric treatment has a greater mean number of suicide attempts (1.1 per person as opposed to .3 per person for the nonpsychiatric group) and a greater mean number of emergency room treatment episodes (1.6 per person as opposed to .8 for the nonpsychiatric group).

Table IV.11

ENTIRE PATIENT POPULATION: PREVIOUS INTERACTION WITH COMMUNITY SERVICE SYSTEMS

	Males		Females		
	(N = 496)	%	(N = 324)	%	
1. Medical community— emergency visits					
Yes	181	36.5	141	43.5	$X^2 = 3.77/df = 1$
No	315	63.5	183	56.5	
2. Community mental health					
Yes	245	49.4	196	60.5	$X^2 = 9.27**/df = 1$
No	251	50.6	128	39.5	
3. Drug abuse or alcohol treatment system					
Yes	205	41.3	137	42.3	$X^2 = .04/df = 1$
No	291	58.7	187	57.7	
4. Criminal justice system—convicted					
Yes	198	39.9	56	17.3	$X^2 = 45.91***/df = 1$
No	298	60.1	268	82.7	
5. Total number of systems					
0	89	17.9	69	21.3	$X^2 = 8.00/df = 4$
1	148	29.8	87	26.9	
2	131	26.4	75	23.1	
3	93	18.8	79	24.4	
4	35	7.1	14	4.3	

* $p < .05$.
** $p < .01$.
*** $p < .001$.

There are a greater mean number of drug-related suicide attempts (.9 per person as opposed to .2 for the nonpsychiatric group).

Emergency Room Treatment

Those women who have been treated for at least one drug-related problem in (N = 141) emergency rooms in the 2 years prior to admission differ from those who have not (N = 183) on several items which, in turn, suggest something about the pattern of emergency room utilization. The group having experienced this form of treatment indicated an average of 2.9 emergency room treatment episodes in the 2 years prior to admission. They differ from the group that has not received treatment on the basis of mean number of suicide attempts (1.4 as opposed to .5), mean number of drug-related suicide attempts (1.0 as opposed to .3), and mean number of psychiatric treatment episodes (1.4 as opposed to .5).

Drug or Alcohol Treatment

Those women who have had at least one drug treatment episode (N = 137) differ from those who have not (N = 187) in several areas. The "known" to treatment group was younger when they had their first drug experience (17.6 as opposed to 20.0 years old). The known to treatment group has a greater mean number of suicide attempts (1.31 as opposed to .5 per person); a greater mean number of psychiatric treatment episodes (1.6 as opposed to 1 per person); and a greater mean number of emergency room treatment episodes (2.3 as opposed to .5).

In addition, those who report at least one drug treatment episode completed less education and have been employed for fewer months in the past 2 years.

History of at Least One Conviction for a Drug-Related Offense

A few differences emerge between those women who have been convicted of a drug-related offense and those who have not. Those who have been convicted have an average of 1.6 convictions in the 2 years prior to admission for drug-related offenses. They report a greater number of emergency room treatment episodes (2.1 as opposed to 1.4 for the nonconvicted group) and more drug-related traffic accidents (.6 as opposed to .2 for the nonconvicted group).

Table IV.12

FEMALE POPULATION: INTERRELATIONSHIP BETWEEN INTERACTION WITH VARIOUS COMMUNITY SERVICE SYSTEMS

1. Those who have had psychiatric treatment prior to admission to the polydrug projects: mean number of interactions with other treatment systems.

	Women who have had prior psychiatric treatment ($N = 196$)	Women who have not had prior psychiatric treatment ($N = 128$)
a. Number of psychiatric treatment episodes	2.18	—
b. Suicide attempts in past 2 years	1.19	.34
c. Drug-related suicide attempts in past 2 years	.92	.22
d. Emergency room episodes in past 2 years	1.57	.76

2. Those who have had drug abuse treatment within the past 2 years: mean number of interactions with other treatment systems.

	Women who have had drug abuse treatment experience ($N = 137$)	Women who have not had drug abuse treatment experience ($N = 187$)	
a. Age at first drug experience	17.16	20.02	$T = -2.61/df = 315^{***}$
b. Psychiatric treatment episodes in lifetime	1.62	1.06	
c. Suicide attempts in past 2 years	1.31	.52	
d. Drug-related suicide attempts in past 2 years	1.01	.37	

	Women who have had emergency room treatment	Women who have not had emergency room treatment	
e. Emergency room treatment episodes in past 2 years	2.31	.47	
f. Years of education	10.71	11.49	$T = 2.52/df = 268.68$***
g. Months of employment	6.17	8.63	$T = 2.61/df = 322$***

3. Those who have had emergency room treatment in the past 2 years: mean number of interactions in other systems.

	Women who have had emergency room treatment (N = 141)	Women who have not had emergency room treatment (N = 183)
a. Emergency room episodes in past 2 years	2.87	—
b. Psychiatric treatment episodes in past 2 years	1.81	.90
c. Suicide attempts in past 2 years	1.36	.46
d. Drug-related suicide attempts in past 2 years	1.10	.30

4. Those who have been convicted for a drug-related crime in the past 2 years: mean number of interactions with other systems.

	Women who have been convicted of a drug-related crime in the past 2 years (N = 56)	Women who have not been convicted of a drug-related crime in the past 2 years (N = 268)
a. Drug-related arrests in the past 2 years	3.09	.27
b. Drug-related convictions in the past 2 years	1.57	—

85

Table IV.12 (continued)

c. Drug-related traffic accidents	.55	.18
d. Emergency room episodes in the past 2 years	2.11	1.07
e. First drug experience	14.91	19.60
f. Years of education	11.38	10.12
		$T = 2.96/df = 74.26$***

* $p < .05$.
** $p < .01$.
*** $p < .001$.

HIDDEN VERSUS NONHIDDEN
FEMALE POPULATIONS

The "hidden" and "visible" female populations were selected by considering the number of major treatment and service systems—criminal justice, drug abuse, mental health, and medicine—with which the women had contact as a result of drug use. For comparative purposes, women who had interacted with three or four of these systems were contrasted with women who had no contact with these systems prior to admission into the polydrug projects (cf. Table IV.13). The "hidden" population did not differ significantly in age or education from the group that received multiple services. Differences that do emerge pertain to drug use patterns and employment variables. The hidden group is more likely to be employed at the time of admission. However, the level of employment for that group, 25.8%, is particularly high. There is no difference between the groups in the mean number of months employed in the 2 years preceding admission, nor are there any differences in occupational status or primary income source.

There is no difference between the groups on first drug-ingested drug experience. The "visible" group is more likely to report that their first drug experience was in a social situation. There are no differences between the populations in terms of current predominant mode of drug use. However, significantly more visible women report having used barbiturates, heroin, and alcohol, within the 2 years prior to admission. The visible group is more likely to report daily use of alcohol.

The Hidden Housewife Group

The "hidden" housewife group, a subcategory of the housewife group, was so defined by their failure to surface for treatment in one of the five community-based systems—(alcohol, drug abuse, mental health, criminal justice, and emergency rooms (cf. Table IV.14). Only nine women were identified as "hidden" housewives. They are slightly older, on the average, than the housewife group with a mean age of 38.8. They were also slightly better educated, with a mean of 12.2 years of education. As indicated by their "hidden" status, these women have not received treatment or service from the major service providers. Four "hidden" women were using barbiturates and five were using psychotropics and opiates on a daily basis. All of those women secured the drugs through legal prescriptions.

A major problem in attempting to provide treatment to the "hidden" population has been the identification of "gatekeepers" or points of access,

Table IV.13

FEMALE POPULATION: BY PREVIOUS TREATMENT INTERACTION

Characteristic	"Hidden" population Interaction with no treatment systems prior to admission to the polydrug projects (N = 69)		"Very visible" population Interaction with at least three of the following systems (N = 93): 1. Emergency rooms 2. Drug or alcohol abuse 3. Mental health treatment systems 4. Criminal justice system		
	N	%	N	%	
1. Current employment status					$X^2 = 6.160/df = 1^*$
Unemployed	49	74.2	83	89.2	
Employed	17	25.8	10	10.8	
2. Occupational classification					$X^2 = 10.45/df = 5$
Professionals	10	15.2	8	8.6	
Clerical	16	24.2	19	20.4	
Semiskilled–skilled	6	9.1	8	8.6	
Housewife	10	15.2	19	20.4	
Student	12	18.2	6	6.5	
None	12	18.2	23	24.7	
3. Major income source					$X^2 = 14.89/df = 5^*$
Job	14	15.2	20	29.9	
Spouse	16	17.4	10	14.9	

	n	%	n	%	X^2
Family	17	18.5	19	28.4	
Welfare	33	35.9	16	23.9	
Illegal activities	10	10.9	0	0.0	
Scholarships	2	2.2	2	3.0	
4. Current living situation					$X^2 = 7.33/df = 3$
Alone	9	13.4	11	12.1	
With family	51	76.1	52	57.1	
With friends	7	7.5	19	20.9	
Institutional–unstable	2	3.0	9	9.9	
5. Drug-related arrests					$X^2 = 28.93/df = 1^{***}$
0	63	91.3	48	51.6	
One or more	6	8.7	45	48.4	
6. Suicide attempts					$X^2 = 35.76/df = 1^{***}$
0	55	79.7	30	32.3	
One or more	14	20.3	63	67.7	
7. Drug-related suicide attempts					$X^2 = 41.77/df = 1^{***}$
0	62	89.9	37	39.8	
One or more	7	10.1	56	60.2	
8. Referral source					$X^2 = 1.03/df = 2$
Drug–alcohol programs	11	16.2	36	14.3	
Mental health	7	10.3	35	13.9	
Private physician–hospitals	11	16.2	56	22.2	
Others	29	42.6	125	49.6	

Table IV.13 (continued)

9. First drug experience situation					$X^2 = 4.07/df = 1^*$
Alone	30	46.9	27	29.7	
With others	34	53.1	64	70.3	
10. Use of drugs in past 2 years					$X^2 = 12.52/df = 1^{***}$
Barbiturate use					
Yes	35	50.7	73	78.5	
No	34	49.3	20	21.5	
Heroin use					$X^2 = 11.46/df = 1^{***}$
Yes	7	10.1	32	34.4	
No	62	89.9	61	65.6	
Alcohol use					$X^2 = 6.97/df = 1^{**}$

* $p < .05$.
** $p < .01$.
*** $p < .001$.

particularly for a more middle-class population. Programs or people who referred the "hidden" population to the projects give some indication of potential referral sources which may be useful in identifying hidden drug users. One-third of the women were referred through private physicians or hospitals, 22.2% through mental health centers, and one-third were referred by friends.

DISCUSSION

A review of the literature concerning women and psychoactive drug use led us to predict that we would find (1) abuse of minor tranquilizers and sedatives varying within the female population as a function of socioeconomic and marital status, with married women of lower income groups more likely to indicate abuse; (2) source of drugs varying for those who abused them on the basis of age, with older women and housewives more likely to secure them through a physician, and younger and/or working women more likely to get them through nonmedical channels.

Women who sought treatment within the polydrug projects were more likely to use barbiturates and sedative–hypnotics on a daily basis than were men, and men were more likely than women to indicate a pattern of "illicit" drug use. Assuming that all persons entering the polydrug projects were drug "abusers," the data of the polydrug projects thus follows the more general data on patterns of drug use. In examining patterns among those women who have used certain classes of drugs, it was found that both spouse-supported and welfare-supported women have a pattern of daily drug use, particularly of opiates, barbiturates, and psychotropics, and the motivation for such use is medication and not recreation. These women tend to use drugs in a solitary setting and secure drugs through prescription sources. The polydrug data thus substantiate general prevalence studies by suggesting that the patterns of drug use and the sources for those drugs vary on the basis of age and employment status, with spouse-supported and welfare-supported women more likely to use drugs for medical or self-medication reasons in a solitary setting and to secure those drugs through traditional medical channels.

For both the welfare-supported and spouse-supported groups there was a self-perceived lack of vocational options. More than half of the spouse-supported group identified themselves as "housewives" alone. An additional 16% listed unskilled or no occupation. Of the welfare-supported group, more than 30% indicated an unskilled or no occupation. An additional 12% indicated their occupation as "housewife." Thus,

Table IV.14

HOUSEWIFE POPULATION: BY PREVIOUS TREATMENT INTERACTION

		Hidden (N = 9)		Not hidden (N = 30)	
		N	%	N	%
1.	Referral source				
	Mental Health	2	22.2	4	13.3
	Physician–hospital	3	33.3	10	33.3
	Friend	3	33.3	4	13.3
	Other	1	11.1	12	40.0
2.	Suicide attempts				
	0	8	88.9	14	46.7
	One or more	1	11.1	16	53.3
3.	Of those using following drugs in the past 2 years, frequency of use				
	a. Barbiturates				
	Daily	4	80.0	18	78.3
	Other	1	20.0	5	21.7
	b. Psychotropics				
	Daily	5	83.3	19	82.6
	Other	1	16.7	4	17.4
	c. Opiates				
	Daily	5	100.0	6	42.9
	Other	0	0.0	8	57.1
	d. Amphetamines				
	Daily	1	16.7	5	50.0
	Other	5	83.3	5	50.0
4.	First drug experience				
	Age (years)		29.44		23.47 $T = -1.48/df = 37$

close to 50% of the welfare-supported group and almost 70% of the spouse-supported group indicated no occupation or employment options. To some extent, the occupational listings may be an artifact of coding biases and/or assumptions (e.g., the interviewers in some instances may simply have coded spouse-supported women as housewives).

In all probability, however, the theme of present and future economic dependence that runs across these two groups is accurate. The broader issue is not so much one of economic dependence per se, as it is one of economic dependence coupled with poor resources to remedy that dependence which combines to offer few options for the woman who wants and/or needs to work. To the extent that she has few employment options, her economic life-style may be seen as static. This pattern of limited employment options coupled with economic need may be either a precipitant to or a result of drug use. In either case, it needs to be addressed as a critical treatment issue by programs attempting to identify and address the needs of female polydrug abusers. Fidell and Prather's study suggests that the desire for employment among housewives was the key variable in determining the level of drug use in general, and the level of minor tranquilizer use in particular (1976). Housewives seeking but not able to find employment differed from unemployed housewives *not* seeking work, and working housewives, in that they used more drugs particularly from the minor tranquilizer class.

Regarding treatment history the men seen by the polydrug programs were more likely (than women) to indicate prior contacts with criminal justice agencies and women were more likely to indicate contact with mental health treatment providers. There were no sex-related differences in the use of emergency rooms or drug and alcohol abuse programs.

Only 21% of the female population had received no treatment prior to admission into the polydrug programs. While the "hidden" population does not differ from the "visible" (treated) population on the basis of educational or occupational background, it is decidedly more "middle-class," more likely to be employed and to support themselves by their employment. However, only 25% of the "hidden" group indicated they were employed at the time of admission. Thus, within the Polydrug Project female subjects, the "hidden" population was small, and the portion of that population which could be considered middle-class was even smaller. Further, only 3% of the female population were "hidden housewives," and less than 2% of the female population were "hidden housewives using physician-prescribed pills (Parry *et al.*, 1973)." Difficulties experienced in outreach efforts and the short history of the participating programs might explain why the "hidden" population was underrepresented in the polydrug treatment effort. Referral data on the "hidden" housewives suggests that they requested help from the same treatment personnel and programs as the housewives who have already received prior treatment for problems related to drug use and abuse. However, the housewife population, as a whole, is more likely to request assistance from programs and persons who are not identified as primary drug and alcohol treatment providers (e.g., mental health programs, physicians and hospitals and friends). These differing referral sources suggest that the housewife population might best be reached through private physicians and hospitals, clinics, and community mental health programs.

Since a number of housewives were referred to the polydrug projects by friends, outreach efforts to reach this population might include contact with traditional women's groups such as the P.T.A. On the basis of a review of data generated by the national reporting system, it was speculated that the female patient population would have used emergency room facilities more frequently than men. They did not. Further, it was speculated that there would be a correlation between the emergency room utilization and suicide attempts. While it is true that women who used emergency rooms had attempted suicide more frequently than women who had not used emergency rooms, the correlation between emergency room utilization and suicide attempts was low. Thus, emergency room utilization was not strongly linked to suicide attempts. Emergency room utilization for the female population reflected a number of overlapping problems such as drug overdose, medical crises secondary to drug use, and medical crises bearing no immediate relation to drug use. For both male and female polydrug abusers, emergency room utilization probably reflects a socioeconomic tendency of lower and lower middle-class income groups to use emergency rooms because of the prohibitive cost of private care.

The treatment history data of the female population suggest that polydrug abuse is a phenomenon that is seen by all major treatment systems and community service providers. The data thus suggest that all treatment systems, particularly community mental health centers, private practitioners, and emergency room personnel should be trained to detect and treat drug problems. This is particularly true of community mental health systems, since 60% of the female patient population had some previous contact with that treatment system.

CONCLUSIONS

The national polydrug data suggest that there is no such person as the "typical" female polydrug abuser and female polydrug users are not likely to fit the "middle-class" stereotype.

The conclusions are important in that they suggest certain recommendations for existing treatment systems. It is important to dispel the notion that the female polydrug user is, typically, a bored, middle-class housewife abusing physician-prescribed pills. While some polydrug abusers fall within this group, the majority do not. The stereotype tends to confound the preparation of appropriate treatment strategies to address the primary and secondary problems of female polydrug abusers. The polydrug data indicate that the female polydrug abuser generally lacks the educational and occupational background and employment history associated with middle-class status. Thus the female drug abuser may require a whole range of treatment intervention modalities—from job training to comprehensive medical care. If a sizable group of middle-class abusers does exist, considerable attention must be paid to the cultural stigma of drug treatment and labeling that contribute to their remaining "hidden." Given the cultural context in which they are purported to use, secure, and maintain their drug "habits," it is important that new intervention and treatment strategies be initiated. Traditional agencies that come into contact with this population must develop the skill to assess drug problems and provide appropriate treatment and referral services.

Both the review of the literature and the analysis of the polydrug data suggest several important areas for further research. As the review of the literature suggests, there have been increasing efforts to assess the nature and extent of drug use among women. This work must continue. Without such studies, it will be extremely difficult. The drug taking behavior of women is a constantly changing phenomenon and thus requires ongoing monitoring.

Currently, there is very little information on the prevalence of psychoactive drug abuse among different subgroups of women outside of the drug treatment systems' generated data.

Some attempt should also be made to identify and study patterns of drug abuse among women seeking treatment in other treatment settings, such as community mental health and crisis centers and health clinics.

Third, as both the literature review and polydrug data indicate, women frequently require emergency services from hospital emergency rooms. At the very least, women served in such settings should be closely monitored to determine the need for referral services.

CHAPTER V

Two Typologies of Polydrug Abusers

Albert S. Carlin and Fred F. Stauss

The societal concern associated with the rapid spread of nonmedical drug use has resulted in numerous attempts to classify types of drug use. These efforts reflect a need to reduce the welter of observations of drug use behavior to a manageable few through abstraction and aggregation. Both program planning and treatment should benefit from the increased understanding generated by the development of useful categories.

This chapter reviews the existing literature and describes two relatively independent classification schemes that stem from both clinical observation and the literature. The review assesses the current literature and clarifies its contributions to the proposed schemata. The presentation of the new classification schemes describes their validity and utility with polydrug patient populations.

Ideally, all classification systems should meet the criteria of validity and utility. Until a typology is verified, it should be considered a hypothesized categorization. Even empirically verified categorizations should be viewed as tentative in the face of other categorizations which may more effectively or simply organize observations. Premature or overly en-

Polydrug Abuse:
The Results of a
National Collaborative Study

thusiastic acceptance of a broad based categorization can result in stereotyping rather than furthering an understanding of the topic. In addition to being valid, the utility of an ideal typology should be realized through increased understanding of the antecedents, consequences, process, or treatment of drug use.

The current literature on classifications of drug users is extensive and variable in quality. Existing classifications generally focus on one of three factors: drug use variables, sociocultural differences, or personality. Utility is usually assessed on these same factors, excluding the categorization variable. Reliability of variables within each of these factors varies from the observable to the highly speculative. Techniques for assessing the validity and utility of classification schemes also vary considerably, ranging from clinical observations to quantifiable empirical analyses.

Most existing typologies stem from the simplest and most obvious differences among drug users. Although valid, these simple typologies have yielded little utility. The growing recognition that the behaviors associated with drug abuse are complex and the result of multiple determinates has led to the creation of more complex typologies. Although validity is not as easily verified, the utility of these typologies appears to be greatly increased.

The most obvious difference among drug users is the selection of different drugs of abuse. Not surprisingly, many investigators have attempted to determine the utility of a classification scheme based on drug choice. Differences in utility have been assessed through both clinical and empirical methods.

The clinical procedure often describes users of a particular drug with only implicit comparisons to users of other drugs or persons who do not use drugs. Milkman and Frosch (1973) suggest that drug choice is related to coping style and that amphetamine users can be described as possessing delusional grandiosity with an inflated sense of self-worth, a tendency to self-dramatize, and a tenuous sense of self, requiring many defenses. Amphetamine users have also been described as self-destructive and philosophical (Robbins, 1970) or as psychopathic, antisocial, and schizophrenic (Ellingwood & Cohen, 1972). Psychedelic use, on the other hand, has been ascribed to those who have a desire to understand themselves, have an absence of a sense of well-being, and are experiencing internal dissatisfaction (Blum & Associates, 1968; Brehm & Back, 1968; Goldstein, Korn, Abel, & Morgan, 1972). Despite providing some insight into users of different drugs the interpretability of these descriptions is limited by the reliance on only implicit comparison groups.

Some investigators have compared users of different drugs through the clinical method. The addition of comparison groups offers a context that allows the descriptive statements to be relative rather than absolute. Distinctions between psychedelic users and amphetamine users were described by Davis and Munoz (1968) in terms of the social distinctions applied to "heads" (psychedelic users) and "freaks" (intravenous amphetamine users) in the Haight Ashbury. Pittel and Hoffer (1973) suggest that psychedelic users who change to amphetamines are more disorganized than those who don't switch, and that amphetamines give disorganized people the motivation and energy to solve their problems constructively, improve ego functioning, and shore up a shaky sense of control. Sharoff (1969) offers a speculative comparison of psychedelic abusers to alcohol, sedative, and narcotic abusers. He suggests that psychedelic users are alienated from American society and use drugs to distort their perceptions so that "they become in reality what they believe they are in their imagination." In contrast, alcohol and sedative abusers, he suggests, have strong conflicts about aggressive and sexual drives, while narcotic users are nonaggressive and use drugs to withdraw from conflicts and from society. Although these comparisons again provide interesting hypotheses, the categorizations should be held as tentative in the absence of data.

Objective differences among users of various drugs have been examined through the use of the MMPI, structured psychiatric interviews, and demographic characteristics. Numerous investigations have pursued differences between users of differing drugs through the MMPI. These investigations have been described in detail by LaChar et al. in Chapter VII of this volume. Typical of these studies are investigations by Toomey (1974) and by Henriques, Arsenian, Cutter, and Saraweera (1972). Toomey compared hallucinogen users with narcotics users and found the former to score higher on the Pa and Sc scales. Henriques, Arsenian, Cutter, and Saraweera compared barbiturate users, amphetamine users, and heroin users and found differences between amphetamine users and barbiturate users on the Ma and Pa scales. Although of potential interest and empirically based, these studies are difficult to interpret. In the study by Toomey, the observed differences cannot be ascribed to drug choice since the groups differed in age and other demographic variables. In addition, the design of both studies precludes establishing any causal relationship between drug use and psychological observations. Even if a clear relationship were established the clinical meaning of differences on single subscales of the MMPI is difficult to interpret.

Hekimian and Gershon (1968) conducted structured interviews with drug users admitted to Bellevue Psychiatric Hospital. They concluded that narcotics users tended to be sociopathic and might be seeking an addiction that requires illegal activities, while users of amphetamines, marijuana, and psychedelics revealed a large incidence of preaddiction psychosis. Limiting their sample to those seeking admission to a psychiatric hospital strongly biases their observations to revealing psychopathology and limits their findings to drug-using psychiatric populations. Furthermore, their statement about the need for illegal activities by heroin users is open to confusion of cause and effect.

The reader's attention is called to Chapter VI by Braucht, Kirby, and Berry which approaches the problem of drug choice in a totally empirical fashion. Using sophisticated statistical techniques they defined clusters of drug use patterns which are associated with a number of demographic and personality differences. In contrast to the other studies that have attempted to categorize drug choice on a univariate categorization and found few differences, Braucht, Kirby, and Berry found pertinent differences through multivariate techniques. This study supports the hypothesis that drug choice is the result of a complex interaction of factors.

In the last several years, individuals have tended to use multiple drugs rather than to rely on a single substance. Although this increased use of multiple drugs has complicated the work of those attempting to investigate users of a particular drug, it has led to attempts to differentiate users on the basis of drug patterns. Similarly to single drug investigations, these studies have found few relevant results. A comparison of multiple and single drug abusers revealed that users of single drugs were more often single, Black, and uneducated, while these two groups did not differ in age, sex, kinds of drugs used, or proportion of addicts versus nonaddicts (Lucas, Grupp, & Schmitt, 1972). A study by Simpson and Sells attempted to define the most common patterns of multiple drug use and generated 28 different basic patterns!

Degree of drug usage, immersion, has been explored as a measure by which drug users can be differentiated. Since many of these studies take only one substance into account, their findings are also confounded by the increased use of multiple drugs. Fisher and Brickman (1973) divided marijuana users into trial users, occasional users, regular users, and heavy users. They found heavier use to be associated with greater use of other drugs. Amphetamine users categorized as casual, moderate, and heavy users were compared along numerous dimensions (Cox & Smart, 1972). Despite the large number of variables examined (age, education, parental occupation, needle use, stimulant effects, other drug use, employment, and MMPI scores) few differences were found. Notable differences included heavy users being more likely to have used the drug by injection and having greater incidence of having seen a psychiatrist prior to beginning drug use. Although these differences are interesting, they are less impressive than the many similarities among subtypes. A possible explanation for the limited findings is the need to make a continuous variable arbitrarily categorical. Such a priori categories may not reflect realistic definitions. More elaborate statistical techniques which allow use of continuous rather than categorical levels of usage and which also allow analysis of more than one substance may lead to more promising results.

Route by which the individual administers the drug to himself has also been used as a variable to differentiate groups of drug users. Levine (1974) has described types of drug users according to their attitudes toward the use of intravenous (iv) needles. The "needle freak" enjoys self-injection and finds the drug itself of only secondary importance. Needle freaks differ from those for whom the needle is secondary to drug use and both of these groups differ from the individual who totally eschews self-injection. Another report compared Navy heroin users in Vietnam who injected heroin with those who "snorted" it (Kolb, Neil, & Gunderson, 1974). Injectors tended to be at lower pay grades and had parents who were less educated and were seen by the subjects to be overly strict or inconsistent disciplinarians. Heroin inhalers did not differ from nondrug using controls or from controls who used drugs other than heroin. These studies on the route of drug administration have demonstrated pertinent differences of socioeconomic factors. However, further research is needed to determine definitely whether that route of administration is not another measure of socioeconomic status or drug immersion.

Few investigators have relied on a purely psychometric approach to categorizing drug abusers. Instead of constructing categories based on either theoretical or clinical observation, psychometric studies collect a large set of data on drug abusers and statistically search for clusters or groupings. One of the benefits of this approach lies in its atheoretical nature which avoids preconceptions of the investigators. A difficulty, on the other hand, stems from the results being limited by the quality and content of the instruments chosen for data gathering.

Two studies are particularly impressive. Rozynko and Stein (1972) administered a battery of psychological tests to 201 drug abusers who were primarily heroin addicts. The test battery included the MMPI, the Motoric Ideational Sensory Test, the socialization scale of the California Personality Inventory, the Hidden Patterns test, the Tennessee Self-Concept Scale, and the Extended Range Vocabulary test. A cluster analysis on these six tests derived 10 subtypes of drug users. The subtypes differed along psychological and demographic dimensions as well as in such factors as drug choice. However, the overall complexity of the measures and of the resultant typologies preclude their direct applications to treatment and diagnosis. Future research aimed at replicating and simplifying the relationships observed among the psychometrically derived types should render them more meaningful to the clinician (Rozynko & Stein, 1972; Stein & Rozynko, 1974). In contrast, Berzins, Ross, English, and Haley obtained results more applicable to treatment. Cluster analyses on the MMPIs of 1500 opiate addicts defined two replicable and homogeneous profiles that accounted for 40% of the subjects. Type 1 (33% of all subjects) showed elevations on the D, Pd, and Ma scales and Type II (7% of the study group) showed a single peak on the Pd scale. The remainder of the population did not cluster. These findings suggest that at least two populations of drug abusers are in treatment at Lexington; a group of disturbed individuals experiencing considerable psychological distress and a group of more sociopathic individuals who are in treatment, perhaps in lieu of incarceration. The large sample size and the nature of the differences make this a very useful study with relevance for the creation of differential treatment modalities.

Numerous investigators have examined the impact of sociocultural membership on drug abuse. Social learning and modeling play an important role in drug selection (Chapter VIII by Hunt, in this volume), perception of drug effects (Carlin, Post, Bakker, and Halpern, 1972), route of administration, and probably the decision to use drugs at all. Levine and Stephens (1972) have defined subcultural addicts as addicts who use drugs as an inherent and meaningful part of a highly organized life style. Subcultural addicts described by these authors include the GI addict, the hippie addict, the street addict, the Chinese addict, and the southern addict. The availability of relatively inexpensive and pure heroin in Southeast Asia led to an epidemic number of servicemen becoming addicted while in Vietnam. However, few of these "GI addicts" maintained heroin use after they returned to the United States (Jaffe, 1975; Levine & Stephens, 1973), presumably because drug use in Vietnam was part of a cultural behavioral context that was not maintained when they returned home. Levine and Stephens have described the "hippie addict" as young, white, and from middle-class origins and whose drug use tends to be focused more toward polydrugs than toward opiates. The street addict is a ghetto dweller in an organized subculture in which drugs play an important role. The street addict favors heroin and cocaine, tends to use drugs intravenously, displays a "cool cat" pattern of behavior (a slightly dated term), relies on deception in his social interactions, and is often criminally involved (Levine & Stephens, 1972; Stephens & Slatin, 1974). The Chinese addicts left their homeland to make their fortune in the United States, only to discover that there were few jobs and that they could not make enough money to return to China. They turned to opium, a drug with a long tradition of use in their homeland. The southern addicts were described by Levine and Stephens (1972) as southern middle-aged white males who became iatrogenically addicted and maintain their addiction through both legal and quasi-legal means.

Although the passage of time has attenuated the current relevance of many of these categories, the descriptions provide an insight into the social and lifestyle variables that affect drug choice and drug use styles. Wesson, Smith, and Lerner (1975) developed a streetwise–nonstreetwise categorization which is a more contemporaneous cultural description that subsumes and updates the street addict, hippie addict, and southern addict described by Levine and Stephens. Streetwise users are able to support themselves through unorthodox means and identify themselves as members of the youth-oriented drug subculture. In contrast the nonstreetwise or straight individual tends to subscribe to more middle-class values. An important contribution of this dichotomy is not only the contemporary definition of the streetwise user, but the recognition of the continued existence of straight abusers. Personality and demographic differences between these two groups were empirically supported.

The sociocultural categorizations tend to be global behavioral descriptions of the context of drug use. Explicit sociocultural categorizations should result in a better undertaking of the environmental factors that influence drug use and attitudes toward it. Although running the risk of becoming dated, emphasis on observable behavior is conducive to empirical validation and exploration.

Global behavioral descriptions have also delineated the pharmacological function drugs serve the user. Separate descriptions have been developed for sedative and for stimulant use. Chambers and Brill (1971) have described three types of barbiturate users. The first type uses the drug regularly for its sedative effect to suppress anxiety and emotional stress. The second type seeks the paradoxical disinhibiting effect resulting from tolerance to high doses. The third type of user employs barbiturates cyclically to counteract the effects of other drugs, particularly stimulants. Similarly, Wesson and Smith (1972) have described four types of people who misuse barbiturates. Chronic users are typically middle-aged persons of higher socio-economic status who obtain the drug from medical sources and use it to suppress anxiety. Episodic users are usually teenagers or young adults who seek a high and who obtain drugs illegally or by occasional prescription. Intravenous users tend to be young adults who have a strong commitment to the drug subculture and who seek the rush of euphoria obtained through injection. The fourth type is similar to Chambers' and Brill's cyclical user.

Shick, Smith, and Wesson (1972) have developed a typology for amphetamine users. They have described four categories: (1) recreational-social use, (2) circumstantial use, (3) self-medication, and (4) high-frequency compulsive use. The recreational-social user takes amphetamines primarily to attain euphoria. The circumstantial-situational user relies on amphetamines for the utilitarian purposes of weight loss or extended alertness. Self-medicators tend to follow a low dose maintenance pattern to obtain the positive effects of calm and confidence or to ameliorate dysphoric states. The compulsive user administers the drug intravenously in high doses for its euphoric effect until the drug is exhausted or maximum tolerance is reached. Chambers and Brill (1971) have proposed two categories of amphetamine abusers: adaptive and escapist abusers. The adaptive abuser initiated drug abuse after a medical situation, has a legal source, uses the drug regularly in a solitary manner, and takes it orally. In contrast, the escapist abuser is a teenager or young adult who started abuse deliberately for its euphoric effects, obtains the drug illegally, uses it in binges or cycles with a social group and takes it intravenously.

The descriptions offered by these authors have intuitive clinical relevance and are based on potentially objective behaviors which allow empirical verification. The similarity of independently derived categories strongly supports the validity of these conjectures. Although the typologies were developed specifically for barbiturates and amphetamines, sufficient commonality exists among the categorizations to allow generalization of these categories without reference to the drug used. Ignoring descriptions specific to a particular drug or to a cultural context results in a continuum describing the function of drug use. This continuum extends from self-medication to social-recreational drug use. Adding a cultural aspect allows a finer differentiation, but the independence of the cultural and functional dimension should be recognized.

This review of the literature suggests that the simple categorization schemes which are basically univariate in nature have made relatively little contribution to a viable typology of drug abusers. Complex multivariate conceptualizations seem at this point to be more fruitful. Greater complexity can be achieved through either statistical sophistication (e.g., Berzins *et al.*, 1974; Chapter VI by Braucht, Kirby, & Berry, in this book; Stein & Ryzenko, 1974) or a priori conceptualizations which are more complex (Chambers & Brill, 1971; Schick *et al.*, 1972; Wesson *et al.*, 1975).

The literature on sociocultural categorizations and on motivation for drug use supported observations of the Seattle polydrug program clinical staff that the streetwise–straight dimension and the social-recreational–self-medication dimension warranted extensive exploration. The remainder of this chapter will be devoted to the further refinement and exploration of these categories.

STREETWISE AND
SELF-MEDICATION DIMENSIONS

The streetwise (–straight) and self-medication (–social-recreational) dimensions were initially clinically derived. Only later were the categories operationally defined and their utility empirically validated. In an effort to communicate a similar intuitive sense of their usefulness, narrative descriptions and brief clinical vignettes describing each category are provided. Once the reader has an intuitive sense of the clinical appropriateness of the categories he can assess for himself not only their ability to account for data, but their utility in the real world of drug misuse.

The streetwise dimension was adopted directly from Wesson et al., (1975). To reiterate briefly, streetwise individuals are able to survive in the drug "underworld" and subscribe to the attitudes and values of this underworld. Streetwise persons are able to acquire drugs outside traditional channels, support themselves through nontraditional means such as dealing in drugs, petty crime, and assorted quasi-legal "hustles," and follow a style of dress and grooming which reflects the youth subculture. Straight individuals subscribe to more traditional middle-class lifestyles. This person is more likely to support himself through employment (him or herself or a family member) and selects a dress style that is less unorthodox. Typically, the drug of abuse is acquired by prescription.

The literature alludes to definitions of self-medication and social-recreational drug use, but does not discuss this dimension independently of other variables. Both clinical observation and abstraction from the work of Chambers and Brill (1971), Shick et al., (1972), and Wesson and Smith (1972) led to a working definition of this dimension. The concept of self-medicating drug use includes those individuals who are pharmacologically treating themselves for psychological distress with self-selected drugs. Self-medicating use is suggested by a pattern of drug use in which the drug is used alone, on a regular basis, and at a relatively fixed or slowly escalating dose. The self-medicating drug user behaves as if he cannot function without the drug and saves amounts of it to ensure that he will not do without if possible. The social-recreational user consumes the drugs in binges with others in a social context. Frequently, dosage during the binges is limited only by amounts available and by toxicity. The social-recreational pattern of use is not limited to occasional users, but may include high-rate daily users.

Combining the two dimensions allows the generation of four categories while still maintaining the distinction between cultural context of drug use and the function served the individual. The four potential categories are illustrated in the following paragraphs by actual case histories.

Type I: The Straight Self-Medicating Individual

William J. is a 50-year-old banker whose daily drug use on entering treatment included 200 mg of phenobarbital, 4 ounces of alcohol, and several Fiornal. Each of the medications was obtained on prescription from several physicians. Despite employment stability the man was frustrated by his occupation, but believed he could not change jobs because of his age. In addition, his wife was terminally ill and he felt great responsibility for her care. He was coping with this stress until he experienced a myocardial infarction which precipitated anxiety not only for his own life, but concern for his wife as well. His physician told him if he avoided all stress he might avoid another infarct. To avoid stress he began use of sedatives, and due to tolerance he began escalating his dose.

Type II: The Straight Social-Recreational Drug User

Ellen K. is a 24-year-old registered nurse who is traditional in social values and outlook. She sought treatment when she realized she had experienced sedative withdrawal while being hospitalized for a fracture following a fall in the shower. One year prior to treatment she began using secobarbital periodically for its disinhibiting effects prior to going to parties or taverns. Over the course of a few weeks her partying usually became more frequent as did her drug usage. Typically, her drug use would be interrupted by the intervention of friends or work pressures prior to the development of actual physical dependence. Several weeks of no drug use would follow. The episode which resulted in physical dependence and injury frightened her and she sought treatment to reinforce her decision to avoid any future sedative use.

Type III: The Streetwise Social-Recreational User

Billy Joe C. was a 26-year-old member of a motorcycle gang who was referred to treatment by his probation officer. His drug use was omnivorous and episodic. Frequently he and his friends would become intoxicated by sedative drugs and then go to taverns and act rowdy; in his words, he and his friends would "pop reds and bust heads." He supported himself through petty crime, hustling, and living off of friends. While under the influence of barbiturates he misperceived the motivation of a bystander in a tavern and "cut the dude." This event led to his being placed on probation and referred for drug abuse treatment. He subscribed to a very sociopathic life-style within which drug use was an acceptable and central feature.

Type IV: The Streetwise Self-Medicating Drug User

Pat R. is a 24-year-old male with a history of extensive use of many drugs. He lived a chaotic life-style with no permanent residence and supported himself through casual labor, petty crime, and the largesse of friends. His style of dress, manner of grooming, argot, and familiarity with the drug scene indicated his allegiance to the drug-oriented youth subculture. Pat contacted the treatment program because he had become dependent on 1000 mg of secobarbital a day and no longer had the resources to maintain his habit. He was hospitalized and detoxified without incident. At this time, although he suffered from anxiety and the lack of social skills, he did·not appear to be psychiatrically disabled. Several months later he returned to the drug program for follow-up. He claimed to have used few drugs in the interim but complained of frightening auditory hallucinations. He was again hospitalized and started on a regimen of phenothiazine drugs. Within a few days the hallucinations no longer plagued him although he found the side effects of the phenothiazines to be very unpleasant. Upon discharge he dropped out of treatment and did not return for renewal of his prescription. Three months later he contacted the drug program again, this time physically dependent on alcohol. He stated that he had stopped using phenothiazines because they made him feel bad. He had begun drinking large amounts of alcohol since it controlled his anxiety and hallucinations as well as the barbiturates, but was not illegal.

The patient vignettes are representative examples of the four categories generated through the simultaneous application of the streetwise and self-medication dichotomies. These cases were chosen on the basis of representativeness rather than ease of assignment since the polydrug clinical staff encountered little difficulty assigning patients to categories. Although each case example used sedative drugs the classification schemata are independent of drug choice and apply equally well to users of other substances. A limitation of the proposed classification schemata is their static description of a dynamic process. They are descriptive of an individual drug abuser's state at a given time rather than a relatively enduring trait.

Not only do the streetwise and self-medication categories possess face validity for the differentiation among drug abusers, they also suggest differential treatment interventions. The streetwise dimension dictates that potential treatment programs should vary in cultural ties. Programs designed for the streetwise drug abuser should be located near recognized youth subculture neighborhoods, and the decor and staff attitude should reflect an atmosphere with which patients could identify. In contrast programs designed for straight drug abusers reflect a more middle-class medically oriented setting. The self-medicating continuum defines not the setting, but the treatment. The self-medicating individual requires a psychiatrically sophisticated approach capable of responding to varying degrees of mental illness. Such approaches may include psychoactive medications used to ameliorate specific symptoms. Interventions aimed at social-recreational drug users are required to be more confrontive, educational, and directly drug related.

Having established an intuitive sense of the qualitative parameters and utility of the proposed dimensions, an empirical verification is still required. The data gathered by the national polydrug study allows this verification.

Method

A procedure was required for assigning subjects to either the streetwise or straight category and to either the self-medication or social-recreational drug use category based on data available from the national polydrug study. Since the existing objective scoring systems required data not available in the national data pool new scoring systems were developed. Bayesian prediction equations were chosen as the method by which subjects would be assigned to the streetwise or straight category and the self-medication or social-recreational categories.

SUBJECTS

Three separate samples of polydrug-abusing patients were used to construct and validate the classification scheme. The largest sample consisted of 141 individuals who applied for drug-related treatment at the Seattle Polydrug Center. This sample included 84 men, who averaged 25.27 years of age, and 57 women, who averaged 28.57 years of age. Additional samples of 42 and 20 patients were drawn from the case files of the San Francisco and Denver polydrug programs, respectively. The San Francisco sample consisted of 24 men and 18 women averaging 30.71 and 27.50 years of age, respectively, and the Denver sample included 15 men and 5 women who averaged 30.20 and 26.20 years of age, respectively. The age differences between centers failed to reach significance.

All subjects misused stimulants, sedatives, or analgesics either singly or in combination. No individual had a primary problem with alcohol or heroin. The definition of misuse was a functional one based on the individual's self-report that drug use was problematic. Problems ranged from physical to psychological to legal.

CONSTRUCTION OF BAYESIAN EQUATIONS

All 141 subjects of the Seattle polydrug sample were subjectively dichotomized on each of the streetwise and self-medication dimensions. The Seattle treatment staff made these judgments by consensus based on life-style and patterns of drug use. These decisions were guided by the criteria presented in Table V.1 and Table V.2. The judgments assigned individuals to one of four possible categories: (1) straight self-medicating drug users, (2) straight recreational users, (3) streetwise recreational users; (4) streetwise self-medicating users.

Of the 141 subjects, 97 were considered to have extreme scores on both dimensions. These 97 subjects were used to develop a Bayesian prediction equation for each of the two typologies. In constructing such an equation, relevant variables were selected empirically. Contingency tables were constructed for each typology to compare the two poles of the typology on demographic variables describing social history, patterns of drug use, and social functioning. Those items that reached statistical

Table V.1

STREETWISE VERSUS NONSTREETWISE SCORING CRITERIA[a]

Criteria	Streetwise	Nonstreetwise
1. Primary means of support	Dealing drugs (+2) Prostitution (+2) Stealing (+2) Friends (+2)	Legitimate employment (−2) Student (−2)
2. Dress	Unconventional (+1)	Conventional (−1)
3. Personal appearance and grooming	Unconventional (+1)	Conventional (−1)
4. Knowledge of street jargon	Yes (+1)	No (−1)
5. Means of funding drug habit	Stealing (+2) Prostitution (+2) Dealing (+2)	Legitimate employment (−2)
6. Ability to purchase drugs from street connections if drugs are not available through usual channels	Yes (+2)	No (−2)
7. Living in a geographic area known as youth drug subculture	Yes (+1)	No (−1)

[a] From Wesson et al., (1975).

Table V.2

SELF-MEDICATION VERSUS RECREATIONAL-SOCIAL USE SCORING
CRITERIA

Criterion	Social-recreational (+1)	Self-medicating (−1)
1. Believes and behaves as if he cannot function without regular use	No	Yes
2. Use pattern is in binges or runs interspersed by periods of 1 or 2 weeks	Yes	No
3. Use pattern includes "blasting," i.e., use of as much drug as can be consumed short of toxicity	Yes	No
4. Client uses the drug alone	No	Yes
5. Client has a group identity. Drug use is in the context of a group of people who identify with his drug use	Yes	No

significance of $p < .10$ were chosen to be included in the equations. Weights, in the form of ratios, were assigned to each variable on the basis of the strength of the relationship of that variable to a given pole of the typology. The product of the individual weights divided by itself plus one results in the probability of being streetwise or the probability of being a self-medicator (depending on the equation)

$$\left[P=\frac{\Pi W_i}{\Pi W_i + 1} , \text{ where } p= \text{ probability and } W_i = \text{ variable weight}\right]$$

For each typology, an individual's score might range from .00 to 1.00.

The initial prediction equations were applied to the original 97 subjects to predict streetwise and self-medication status. Weights of variables were adjusted and variables were eliminated from the equations until 100% accuracy was achieved for the 97 subjects on both typologies. The final set of variables and their associated weights are presented in Tables V.3 and V.4.

ACCURACY OF PREDICTION EQUATION

To test the validity of the equation, the final Bayesian equations were used to predict the streetwise and self-medication status of the remaining 44 subjects of the Seattle sample. In order to determine whether the equation was peculiar to Seattle or whether it could generalize to other regions, it was applied to the patient samples drawn from the San Francisco and Denver polydrug programs. The predictions of the equations were compared to clinical judgments of staff members familiar with the given patient.

Agreement between staff ratings and computed prediction of streetwise status was reached for 41 of the 44 remaining Seattle patients. This level of agreement exceeds chance (sign test, $p < .01$). On the San Francisco and Denver patients, 86% and 90% agreement were attained respectively. Both of these levels of agreement exceed chance (sign test, $p < .01$ for both).

Similar results were obtained for prediction of self-medication. The equation agreed with clinical ratings on 84% of the Seattle sample. Denver and San Francisco clinical ratings agreed with the equation on 85% and 90% of patients, respectively. These levels of agreement exceed chance ($p < .01$, sign test). The consistently high level of predictive

Table V.3

BAYESIAN WEIGHTS FOR CALCULATING THE PROBABILITY OF BEING STREETWISE

Sex Male = 1.87 Female = .37	*Current living situation* Alone = 1 With spouselike person = .44 With friends = 2.66
Referral source Self = .35 Other drug program = 2.08 Health delivery system = 1.64 Criminal justice system = 25 Friend = 2.5	With parents = .5 With relatives = .71 Institutionalized = 1 Unstable = 2.6 *Psychological impairment* None = 10 Minimal = 1
Route of administration Oral = .43 Intravenous = 28 Inhalation = .43	Mild = 1 Moderate = 1 Severe = 1
First use of psychoactive drugs Illicit = 1 Prescription = .04	*Source of income* Work = .33 Other = 1 Spouse = .50
Current source of drugs Legal = .18 Forged prescription = 2 Street buys = 1.5 Over-the-counter = 1 Gift = 2	*Number of arrests* 0 − 1 = 1 2+ = 25

Table V.4

BAYESIAN WEIGHTS FOR CALCULATING THE PROBABILITY OF BEING A
SELF-MEDICATING DRUG USER

Sex Male = .81 Female = 1.28	*Route* Oral = 2.47 Intravenous = .44 Inhalation = .10
Referral source Self = 2.37 Other drug program = .65 Health delivery system = 1.55 Criminal justice system = .07 Friend = .38	*First use of psychoactive drugs* Illicit = 1 Prescription = 6.83 *Current living situation* Alone = 2.9
Current primary drug of abuse Heroin = .25 Opiates (other than heroin) = 1 Alcohol = 1 Barbiturates = 2.07 Amphetamines = .68 Cocaine = 1 Hallucinogens = 1 Tranquilizers = 5.75 Inhalants = .17 Over-the-counter = 1 Other = 1	With spouselike person = 1.34 Other = 1 *Psychological impairment* None = .37 Minimal = .66 Mild = 1 Moderate = 2.5 Severe = 6.5 *Usual setting for drug use* Alone = 3.19 With other = .22

accuracy of the Bayesian equations supports their validity. Cross-validation of the equations in other cities demonstrates that neither equation is limited by geographic locale. These results indicate that the equations can predict the streetwise and self-medication status of patients through the national polydrug data.

ASSIGNMENT TO CATEGORIES

The national data pool contains information on 915 patients. Using the Bayesian equations described previously, streetwise and self-medication probability scores were calculated for each subject. The distributions of both resulting scores are bimodal as can be seen in Figure V.1. The marked bimodal distributions suggest that the data used in each equation cluster together. Despite theoretical independence between the two dimensions and independent variable selection the dimensions were found to be moderately correlated. Streetwise status is associated with social-

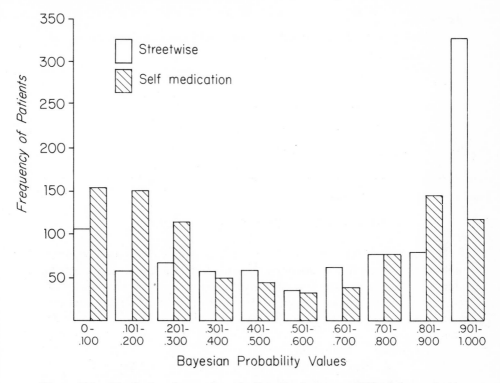

Figure V.1.   Distribution of streetwise and self-medicating scores of 915 polydrug patients.

recreational drug use and self-medication with straightness (Pearson Product Moment $r = .49$; $p < .01$.)

On the basis of the Bayesian equations subjects were assigned to either the streetwise or straight categories and to either the self-medication or social-recreational categories. Patients who had mid-range scores ($.4 < p < .6$) on either continuum were eliminated from further analyses. These subjects were eliminated to sharpen the contrast between categories and to eliminate subjects who were likely to have been erroneously classified. Approximately equal numbers of subjects were eliminated from each dimension; 92 subjects were eliminated from the streetwise dimension and 78 from the self-medication dimension. When the two dimensions are combined in order to create four categories, 751 patients are classifiable on both dimensions. The majority of patients are streetwise social-recreational users (352) followed by straight self-medicators (198), streetwise self-medicators (135), and straight social-recreational users (66). Table V.5 presents the distribution by sex for each category.

Table V.5

DISTRIBUTION OF MALES AND FEMALES AMONG STREETWISE AND
SELF-MEDICATION DIMENSIONS

Dimension	Social-recreational	Self-medicating
Straight:	12 (males)	47 (males)
	54 (females)	151 (females)
Streetwise:	281 (males)	106 (males)
	71 (females)	29 (females)

EMPIRICAL COMPARISONS OF CATEGORIES

Having determined that national polydrug data can be used to assign
patients to these four categories the utility of the dimensions can be
demonstrated. Comparisons of the four groups on demographic and
psychometric data provided an assessment of utility. The selected psychometric measures included the MMPI and the CAPPS. None of the
demographic or psychometric variables used in the assessment entered
into the Bayesian prediction equations.

A 2 × 2 multivariate analysis of variance was selected as the basic
model for assessing utility of the two dimensions. The dichotomized
streetwise–straight and social-recreational–self-medication dimensions
served as blocking factors. The selected dependent variables were clustered a priori into logical analysis sets. The demographic variables were
grouped into three clusters: age-related variables, educational and employment variables, and social and health variables. The MMPI and the
CAPPS served as separate analysis sets of psychometric variables.

DEMOGRAPHIC VARIABLES

The MANOVA on the age variables attained significance for both the
main effects and the interaction (see Table V.6). The univariate analyses
performed on each of the age variables again reached similar levels of
significance for both main effects and interaction. Inspection of the
means presented in Table V.6 reveals that the straight self-medicating
individuals differ most from the others. They began using drugs later in
life, became involved with the drugs that brought them into treatment
later in life, and were older on entry into treatment. On all of the age
variables the self-medicating individuals tended to be older with the

Table V.6

MEANS, **MANOVA**, AND **ANOVA** OF AGE-RELATED VARIABLES FOR THE
SELF-MEDICATION AND STREETWISE DIMENSIONS

	Means			
	Age	First drug age	Problem drug 1 age	Problem drug 2 age
Straight				
Self-medicating (N = 165)	34.39	20.55	25.06	26.27
Social-recreational (N = 62)	22.85	15.52	17.36	18.27
Streetwise				
Self-medicating (N = 127)	26.54	14.80	17.53	19.03
Social-recreational (N = 344)	23.26	13.72	15.34	17.46

MANOVA results

MANOVA
Streetwise versus straight
$F(4,690)$ 18.07
$p<$ .001

Self-medicating versus recreational
$F(4,690)$ 18.22
$p<$ .001

Interaction
$F(4,690)$ 7.96
$p<$ .001

ANOVA results

ANOVA Streetwise versus straight	Age	First drug age	Problem drug 1 age	Problem drug 2 age
$F(1,693)$	23.58	24.11	36.88	32.08
$p<$	.001	.001	.001	.001
Self-medicating versus social				
$F(1,693)$	68.34	20.38	43.64	33.61
$p<$	.001	.001	.001	.001
Interaction				
$F(1,693)$	28.72	12.56	18.50	24.00
$p<$	.001	.001	.001	.001

straight self-medicating group the oldest followed by the streetwise self-medicating group and then the two social-recreational drug use groups.

The multivariate analysis of the education and employment variables yielded significant main effects for both the streetwise and self-medicating dimensions, but not the interaction (see Table V.7). The means and univariate F values delineate the source of the significance. Although

Table V.7

MEANS, **MANOVA**, AND **ANOVA** OF EDUCATION AND EMPLOYMENT
VARIABLES FOR THE SELF-MEDICATION AND STREETWISE DIMENSIONS

		Means	
	Education	Months worked	Jobs held
Straight			
Self-medicating ($N = 198$)	11.62	9.49	1.27
Social-recreational ($N = 66$)	10.88	10.48	1.80
Streetwise			
Self-medicating ($N = 135$)	11.36	7.67	2.05
Social-recreational ($N = 352$)	10.74	8.71	2.59

MANOVA	MANOVA results
Streetwise versus Straight	
$F(3,744)$	9.27
$p<$	.001
Self-medicating versus Recreational	
$F(3,744)$	6.50
$p<$	.001
Interaction	
$F(3,744)$	<1
$p<$	n.s.

ANOVA	ANOVA results		
Streetwise versus Straight	Education	Months worked	Jobs held
$F(1,746)$	2.18	20.74	8.62
$p<$	.148	.001	.003
Self-medicating versus Social			
$F(1,746)$	9.36	2.34	6.32
$p<$	.002	.126	.012
Interaction			
$F(1,746)$	<1	<1	<1
$p<$	n.s.	n.s.	n.s.

none of the groups tended to have completed high school the self-medicating groups were better educated. Similarly, while no group was a paragon of the work ethic, the straight groups completed more months of employment in the 2 years prior to entry into treatment. The number of jobs held in the 2 years prior to treatment is affected by both the street-wise and self-medicating factors. In general, the streetwise subjects tended to have more jobs than the straight subjects, but within each of these dimensions the social-recreational users held more jobs than did the self-medicating subjects. The relationship between months employed and number of jobs held suggests that the streetwise individuals have had a more chaotic job history than the straight individuals and social-recreational drug users have a more chaotic employment history than do self-medicating drug users. Subsequently, the self-medicating straight drug user has the most stable work history and the streetwise social-recreational user the least.

Comparison of the four groups on social and health variables failed to reach significance. No group experienced many traffic accidents, emergency room episodes, suicide attempts, or previous psychiatric episodes. In all likelihood the lack of significance is due to the infrequent occurrence of these events and the resulting trivial distribution.

PSYCHOMETRIC VARIABLES

Although the mean MMPI profiles from each group are similar in configuration, distinct with peaks on scales 2/D, 4/Pd, and 8/Sc, the groups differ significantly on scale elevations. A 2 × 2 MANOVA once again revealed significant main effects on both dimensions, but no in-teraction. As can be seen from Table V.8, self-medicating polydrug patients had significantly higher scores than social-recreational users on scales 1/Hs, 2/D, and 7/Pt. These differences suggest that self-medicating polydrug abusers are more concerned with somatic symptoms and are experiencing poor morale, feelings of inadequacy, and greater tension. Hence, self-medicating polydrug patients appear to be more neurotic than social-recreational polydrug patients.

Table V.8 also indicates that streetwise polydrug abusers are more disturbed than straight polydrug patients independent of self-medication status. The streetwise patients scored significantly higher on scales F, 2/D, 4/Pd, 6/Pa, 7/Pt, 8/Sc, and 9/Ma. Of these scales only 2 and 7 attained significance on both main effects. The pattern of scales on which the streetwise polydrug patient scored significantly higher than the straight polydrug patients suggests that streetwise patients have an impulsive character disorder and are decompensating under acute stress.

Table V.8

MEAN MMPI SCALE T SCORES, MANOVA, AND ANOVAS FOR SELF-MEDICATION AND SOCIAL-RECREATIONAL STREETWISE AND STRAIGHT POLYDRUG PATIENTS

	L	F	K	Hs	D	Hy	Pd	Pa	Pt	Sc	Ma	Si
Straight												
Self-medicating (N = 65)	48.69	70.57	49.54	68.99	72.09	69.83	73.37	67.20	68.97	76.25	66.86	58.31
Social-recreational (N = 24)	47.88	68.92	49.88	57.63	66.88	63.96	76.54	65.25	66.21	73.33	70.17	56.67
Streetwise												
Self-medicating (N = 41)	46.37	78.07	46.17	68.05	80.05	66.51	81.63	72.37	76.10	84.56	71.39	60.73
Social-recreational (N = 129)	48.21	73.05	48.29	63.87	70.05	65.40	78.54	69.07	70.70	79.34	72.91	56.03

MANOVA results

MANOVA

Streetwise versus straight
$F(12,244)$ 2.77
$p <$ .001

Straight
$F(12,244)$ 1.87
$p <$ .039

Interaction
$F(12,244)$ 1.32
$p <$ n.s.

ANOVA results

Univariate Fs

	L	F	K	Hs	D	Hy	Pd	Pa	Pt	Sc	Ma	Si
Streetwise versus straight												
$F(1,255)$	1.12	6.06	3.53	1.12	6.49	<1	8.30	4.95	7.50	6.60	4.07	<1
$p <$	n.s.	.015	.061	n.s.	.011	n.s.	.004	.027	.007	.011	.045	n.s.
Self-medicating versus social												
$F(1,255)$	<1	2.61	1.24	10.75	14.06	2.90	<1	2.01	4.49	2.57	7.47	5.04
$p <$	n.s.	.107	n.s.	.001	.001	.090	n.s.	n.s.	.035	n.s.	n.s.	.026
Interaction												
$F(1,255)$	1.51	<1	<1	2.79	1.08	1.90	2.69	<1	<1	<1	<1	<1
$p <$	n.s.	n.s.	n.s.	.096	n.s.	n.s.	n.s.	n.s.	n.s.	n.s.	n.s.	n.s.

Comparison of the number of MMPI scale T scores greater than 70 for each group assessed the overall relative psychopathology of the groups. Both main effects, but not the interaction, reached significance on a 2 × 2 ANOVA (streetwise, $F = 11.4; df = 1,256; p < .001$; self-medication, $F = 5.32; df = 1,256; p < .02$). The four groups can be ranked from least psychopathology to most: straight social-recreational, straight self-medicating, streetwise social-recreational, streetwise self-medicating (see Table V.8).

The CAPPS provided a second psychometric assignment of psychopathology. Present and past scales were analyzed separately through 2 × 2 MANOVAs similar to those described later. Each of the two main effects and their interaction reached significance for the aggregates of CAPPS scales which describe present and past psychopathology. The results of the MANOVA are presented in Table V.9.

The mean scores of the current psychopathology scales and the associated Fs are presented in Table V.10. Examination of the univariate Fs which reached significance indicates that the same three scales contributed to the significance of the streetwise main effect and the interaction. The significance of the interaction indicates that simultaneous use of both dimensions provides a better understanding of these variables than the streetwise–straight dimension alone. As can be seen from Table V.10 streetwise self-medicators were experiencing the greatest difficulty with both Impulse Control and Reality–Social Disturbance, while the straight social-recreational users were experiencing greatest obsessive symptoms. Four univariate Fs attained significance on the self-medication dimension. Of these, only Reality–Social Disturbance was not unique to this dimension. The three new scales which reached significance were:

Table V.9

MANOVA AND UNIVARIATE ANOVAS FOR PRESENT AND PAST CAPPS SCALES OF SELF-MEDICATING AND SOCIAL–RECREATIONAL STREETWISE AND STRAIGHT POLYDRUG PATIENTS (ONLY SIGNIFICANT VALUES ARE PRESENTED)

MANOVA					
Street(7,378)		Self-medicating(7,378)		Interaction(7,378)	
F	$p <$	F	$p <$	F	$p <$
5.40	.001	3.08	.004	3.08	.004
Street(18,367)		Self-medicating(18,367)			
F	$p <$	F	$p <$	F	$p <$
4.96	.001	3.11	.001	1.63	.05

Table V.10

MEAN CAPPS SCALE SCORES OF STRAIGHT SELF-MEDICATING AND SOCIAL-RECREATIONAL AND STREETWISE SELF-MEDICATING AND SOCIAL-RECREATIONAL PATIENTS AND THEIR ASSOCIATED F VALUES

CAPPS scales	Straight		Streetwise		Street[a]	$p <$	Self-medi-cating[a]	$p <$	Inter-action	$p <$
	Self-medicating (N = 110)	Social-Recreational (N = 32)	Self-Medicating (N = 53)	Social-Recreational (N = 193)						
Present										
Reality testing	1.97	2.12	2.47	2.08	5.95	.015	3.29	.070	6.37	.012
Depression–anxiety	2.89	2.69	3.00	2.60	1		8.57	.004	1	
Impulse	2.23	2.59	3.02	2.66	19.95	.001	1		11.45	.001
Somatic concerns	2.16	1.75	1.96	1.66	1.78		9.86	.002	1	
Disorganization	1.62	1.44	1.74	1.45	1		7.88	.005	1	
Obsessive–compulsive	1.87	2.22	1.89	1.69	4.01	.046	1		5.909	.016
Elation	1.50	1.59	1.68	1.51	1		1		1.99	
Past										
Depression–anxiety	2.61	2.50	2.72	2.37	1		6.19	.013	1	
Impulse	2.21	2.69	3.36	3.08	47.54	.001	1		8.95	.002
Social–sex	3.23	3.16	3.51	3.08	1.37		7.59	.006	1.96	
Reality	1.47	1.53	1.79	1.54	4.91	.027	2.65		1.46	
Dependency	2.27	2.53	2.43	2.21	1		1		4.37	.015
Somatic	2.44	1.97	2.47	2.05	1		18.51	.001	1	
Obsessive–compulsive	1.73	1.59	1.68	1.53	1		2.32		1	
Anger	1.99	2.16	2.40	2.28	5.46	.020	1		1.28	
Manic	1.65	1.88	1.68	1.64	1		1		1.10	
Sex	1.29	1.41	1.53	1.26	1		2.43		2.24	.020

					F	p	F	p	F	p
Memory	1.53	1.44	1.98	1.64	7.48	.007	4.12	.043	1.00	
Disorganization	1.32	1.38	1.60	1.40	3.21	.074	1.48		1	
Organicity	1.18	1.03	1.49	1.21	16.23	.001	14.77	.001	1	
Neurotic child	2.20	2.66	2.85	2.51	3.84	.051	1		9.75	.012
Phobia	1.66	2.50	1.77	1.69	4.31	.039	3.63	.058	13.17	.001
Retardation–stubborn	2.07	2.31	2.36	2.10	1		1		3.88	.026
Hysteric	1.38	1.38	1.24	1.49	1		3.62	.058	1	
Intellectual	3.46	3.53	3.87	3.84	13.94	.001	1		1	

[a] Street here refers to the streetwise–straight contrast and self-medication refers to the self-medication–social-recreational contrast.

Depression–Anxiety, Somatic Concern–Functioning, and Disorganization. Both the MMPI and the present CAPPS indicate that polydrug patients are experiencing considerable psychopathology.

The past scales of the CAPPS should allow a determination of whether the existing disturbance is of recent or long-standing origin. Unfortunately the definition of "past" is so encompassing that it may include present psychopathology. Since the definition of past includes any psychopathology from age 12 to 1 month prior to entry into treatment, conditions originating 2 months prior to entrance into treatment would be included in both past and present scales. To minimize confounding the past with the present, discussions will focus only on new information that is provided by past scales.

Table V.10 lists the means F values of the 18 past CAPPS scales. As can be seen from this table, 7 scales yielded significant Fs for the interaction. On these scales, streetwise self-medicating and straight social-recreational polydrug patients manifested the greatest history of disturbance and the streetwise social-recreational and straight self-medicating polydrug patients the least. Differences found for the Reality–Social Disturbance and the Impulse scales are similar to those found for present psychopathology. Streetwise self-medicators revealed the most Neurotic Childhood and the greatest psychopathology in the areas of Sex and Retardation–Stubborness. Straight social-recreational drug use patients had the most problems with Phobia and Dependency. Straight self-medicating subjects manifested a less disturbed history on all of the scales on which the interaction attained significance.

The univariate Fs which contributed to the significance of the streetwise MANOVA and which were not implicated in the significance of the interaction indicate that streetwise polydrug patients have a history of having more anger, memory difficulties, intellectual failures, disorganization, and problems that could be related to brain damage. Overall, streetwise polydrug patients seem to enter treatment with a history of greater, but still mild, impairment in cognitive functioning. However, the effects of intoxication or withdrawal cannot be differentiated from actual brain damage because of the uncertain time span of the "past."

Six past psychopathology scales contributed to the significance of the self-medication main effect. Two of these scales, Somatic Concerns and Depression–Anxiety, were similar to present problems. Found only on past psychopathology scales, self-medicating polydrug abusers are more likely to have had a history of Hysteria, Social–sexual concerns, as well as problems with Memory and Organic brain damage.

The past scales indicate that the four types of polydrug users differ in the amount of previous cognitive impairment and neurotic concerns.

Scales measuring cognitive impairment indicate that streetwise persons are experiencing more cognitive impairment than straight persons and that streetwise self-medicating patients are experiencing the most impairment. Self-medicating polydrug patients are more likely to be experiencing somatic and depressive problems than social-recreational users while straight social-recreational users are more obsessive and phobic.

SEX AND STREETWISE ORIENTATION

A strong association exists between gender and the streetwise–straight dichotomy; men are most likely to be streetwise and women straight ($x^2 =$ 164.68; $p < .001$). A similar relationship exists for the self-medicating–social-recreational dichotomy in which men are more likely to be social-recreational users and women self-medicators ($x^2 = 45.85; p < .001$). These relationships are not surprising, since sex was used as one of the variables that the Bayesian equations used to assign subjects to the streetwise–straight and self-medication–social-recreational status. The question then arises as to whether the differences found among the four categories are merely the result of sex differences or whether they reflect differences directly relevant to the categories. Put another way, has all of this classification effort resulted in a complex but imperfect gender-detection program? In order to determine the nature of sex differences within each of the four categories the males and females within each category were compared on demographic and psychometric variables.

Within each of the four categories MANOVAs were carried out which compared men and women on (1) age and age-related variables, (2) education and employment variables, (3) MMPI scale scores, (4) CAPPS present scales, (5) CAPPS past scales.

The difference found between men and women for the set of age variables attained significance only within the streetwise social-recreational category ($F = 2.40; df = 4,274; p < .05$). Examination of the associated univariate Fs suggests that differences in age at admission and age at first use of the drug of greatest problematic use contributed most to the overall differences, with women being significantly younger than men. The direction of these differences does not support the contention that age differences found among the categories are merely the result of sex differences. Women polydrug abusers are not older than men polydrug abusers in an absolute sense, but straight users are older than street wise users.

Similarly, the employment and education differences between streetwise and straight users and self-medicating and social-recreational users do not seem to be a function of sex differences. Within the straight social-recreational group men had a better employment history than women ($F = 6.11$; $df = 3.58$; $p < .001$), yet as can be seen from Table V.5 this group was made up predominantly of women. The streetwise social-recreational men tended toward a more active employment history than women, but this relationship fell short of significance ($F = 2.14$; $df = 3,280$; $p < .095$). Thus, although men were more involved in employment activities than women within the categories, the differences between categories cannot be accounted for on the basis of sex differences.

MMPI differences among the categories revealed that self-medicating groups demonstrated greater elevations in D and Pt scales as well as in Hs and Si. Despite greater numbers of women in the straight self-medicating group it is the men within these categories who had MMPI scales significantly higher than women ($F = 192$; $df = 12,50$; $p < .054$) with the D and Pt scales implicated as the major source of the differences. Overall greater psychopathology was associated with streetwise orientation than with straight. Once again, despite male predominance in this category the significant differences associated with sex ($F = 3.37$, $df = 12,123$; $p < .001$) found women to endorse greater disturbance. The associated univariate Fs reveal women to have significantly higher scores for F, Pd, and Si and lower scores for K. Once again, although sex differences exist within some categories they cannot account for the differences between categories.

No significant sex differences were found within categories for the CAPPS present scales although within the straight social-recreational category there was a trend toward a significant difference ($F = 2.04$; $df = 7,34$; $p < .08$). Within this category the univariate Fs suggest women are more disorganized than men. However, this trend could hardly account for the differences found among the categories when sex is disregarded as a variable.

Because of the relatively large number of scales making up the CAPPS past scales and the relatively small Ns within the straight social-recreational and streetwise self-medication categories the sex differences are difficult to evaluate. However, within the straight self-medicating category women tended to be assigned greater scores than men ($F = 1.63$; $df = 18,66$, $p < .08$). Associate univariate Fs suggest that the Depression–Anxiety, Dependency, Manic, and Retarded–Stubborn scales contributed to the overall significance of the MANOVA. Within the streetwise social-recreational category sex differences reached significance ($F = 1.75$; $df = 8,169$; $p < .035$). These scales reached or approached significance on univariate ANOVAs and can be taken to be major contributors to the overall significance: Depression–Anxiety, Somatic Concerns, and Sexual Disturbance. Once again women were seen to have greater difficulties except for sexual disturbance.

The contention that category assignment is primarily based on gender and that differences among categories are merely reflective of sex difference is not supported by data. Indeed, the increased homogeneity of subgroups provided by the classification scheme offers an insight into the relationship between sex role and patterns of polydrug abuse. For example, women whose polydrug abuse patterns are "typical" (i.e., straight self-medicators), endorse less disturbance than men with similar drug use patterns, while women who subscribe to more typically male patterns of drug abuse (e.g., streetwise social-recreational users) endorse more disturbance than men who use drugs in a similar fashion.

The apparent inconsistency within the straight self-medicating category between CAPPS and MMPI measures of psychopathology is of interest. Within all categories women endorsed less psychopathology than men in the MMPI, but were judged more disturbed by others on the CAPPS. This inconsistency offers some support for the contention of Dammann and Ousley (Chapter IV) that women drug abusers may be judged in a biased fashion by clinicians. In any case comparisons of women and men polydrug abusers are suspect unless heterogeneity within sex is taken into account.

SUMMARY

Both the streetwise–straight and self-medication–social-recreational categories have been demonstrated to be applicable to polydrug patients participating in the national polydrug study. The majority of patients were unambiguously assigned to one of the four categories. The accuracy of prediction equations is substantiated by their ability to predict clinical judgments.

Although conceptualized as separate dimensions, a moderate correlation exists between the two categories. Whether this association is an artifact of using overlapping variables or a reflection of the real world cannot be directly ascertained. However, it seems likely that social-recreational drug use is more prevalent among streetwise than among straight persons and that the correlation is not merely measurement error. More powerful evidence of the uniqueness of the dimensions is provided by statistical comparison of groups. Each dimension taps different aspects of demographic characteristics and psychopathology.

The most frequent type of patient encountered in the polydrug treatment programs was the streetwise social-recreational drug user. These individuals began using drugs earlier in life than the others and are among the youngest polydrug patients. They also are less educated and have the most chaotic job history. This most frequent type is quite similar to the least frequent type of polydrug patients, the straight social-recreational users, who are also young, less educated, but who have a somewhat better job history.

The straight self-medicating polydrug patient, the second most frequent type, is the oldest group. Not only are they older on entry into treatment, they also began using drugs at an older age and cannot be considered members of the youth-oriented drug culture. Despite having a better education, their employment history is still marginal and chaotic.

The streetwise self-medicators entered treatment at a relatively older age, despite beginning drug use as early as any other group. Similarly paradoxical, although being better educated, they had the poorest employment history.

The psychometric comparisons indicate that the four groups also differ in psychopathology. MMPI profile configurations of the four groups are similar and should be viewed with caution in the light of problems inherent in generalizing from mean profiles, but differences in relative psychopathology exist. Streetwise polydrug patients are generally more disturbed than straight polydrug patients and present greater characterological problems manifested by impulsive acting out and potential thought disorder. In the context of their differences, streetwise self-medicators are experiencing more neurotic symptoms than the streetwise social-recreational users.

The description of current and past psychopathology from the CAPPS is consistent with the MMPI. Streetwise patients and self-medicating patients each manifest greater psychopathology than their counterparts. Streetwise users present a picture of mixed characterological and thought disorder problems while self-medicating patients are experiencing more neurotic symptoms such as somatic preoccupations and dysphoria. Unfortunately, the established definition of "past" for the CAPPS precludes a reliable statement of the degree to which current difficulties reflect past problems. However, the great differences in types of "past" problems indicate the previous differences among the groups. The finding that straight social-recreational users admit greater phobic behavior, obsessive difficulties, and problems with dependency is in marked contrast to the more pervasive and basic problems admitted to by the streetwise self-medicating polydrug patients.

The CAPPS scales sensitive to cognitive impairment suggest that streetwise and self-medicating polydrug patients were experiencing more chronic difficulties in intellectual, educational, and organizational functioning, and are consistent with the findings of differences in vocational and educational differences. Assessments of cognitive functioning are described in detail by Grant *et al*. (Chapter X in this volume).

Present and past CAPPS scales taken together suggest that streetwise polydrug patients are experiencing long-standing difficulties with socialization as well as cognitive impairment, while straight polydrug patients are experiencing less impairment but more neurotic and interpersonal concerns. Superimposing the self-medication–social-recreational drug use dimension allows further refinement. Both streetwise and straight self-medicating patients are more depressed and more preoccupied with somatic concerns and functioning than the social-recreational drug users.

The marked differences in distribution of men and women within each of the four categories raise the question of whether the observed differences in demographic variables and psychopathology reflect only basic sex differences. For example, differences in vocational achievement or in impulsive acting out might be a function of sex differences rather than truly a function of streetwise–straight orientation. This supposition was not supported by an examination of sex differences within each category. Differences between men and women were not contributory to differences among categories. Indeed, differences between categories within each sex indicate that differences in drug use styles and drug use function cut across gender.

Recognition of systematic differences in psychopathology and social functioning among polydrug abusers indicates the necessity of avoiding blanket characterizations of the nature of the polydrug problem or of the treatment needs. Some polydrug abusers will require treatment aimed at resocialization and termination of drug use, while others might require appropriate psychoactive medication and more traditional mental health treatment. In order to succeed, research, policy, and planning must recognize the heterogeneity of polydrug abuse and avoid single solutions and simple statements.

CHAPTER VI

An Empirical Typology of Multiple Drug Abusers

G. Nicholas Braucht, Michael W. Kirby,
and G. James Berry

The present chapter has three primary aims: (1) to identify major empirical clusters of multiple drug abuse; (2) to develop, on the basis of these empirical clusters, an empirical typology of multiple drug abusers; (3) to describe each cluster and type using the same set of theoretically derived psychosocial variables.

A review of the existing research literature in this area leads us to believe that the simultaneous investigation of these three questions would represent a distinct advance over present research strategies. This is so because nearly all of the current literature reflects one of three approaches: (1) some investigators have attempted to identify distinct patterns of multiple drug use but have provided no information about the distinguishing characteristics of persons using different patterns of drugs (e.g., Simpson & Sells, 1974; Smart & Whitehead, 1972); (2) others have provided systematic descriptions in terms of theoretically articulated sets of psychosocial variables and their relationship to various forms of social deviance, but these investigators have not focused on patterns of multiple drug use (e.g., Braucht, 1972; Jessor, 1976; Jessor, Jessor, & Finney, 1973);

129

Polydrug Abuse:
The Results of a
National Collaborative Study

(3) a third approach is represented by studies concerned with only one pattern of multiple drug abuse, often providing anecdotal or demographic descriptors not based on any identifiable theoretical perspective (e.g., Campbell & Freeland, 1974; Chambers, 1969; Devenyi & Wilson, 1971; Hamburger, 1964; Kirby & Berry, 1975; Ludwig & Levine, 1965). To our knowledge no investigators have attempted to develop a truly empirical typology of multiple drug users.

Against this background of extant research strategies and knowledge, the identification of multiple drug use patterns and multiple drug abusers, together with some kind of theoretically based description of the distinguishing characteristics of these abusers, could be expected to be of heuristic value to public health program planners, to provide information on which to plan treatment programs, and to aid in program evaluation.

Having stated the objectives and *raison d'être* for the present study, the literature would suggest that an optimal investigation of these objectives must possess several key methodological features. To achieve the first objective—identifying major patterns of multiple drug use—three requirements must be met: (1) the reduction of a large potential number of drug use patterns to some manageable number without loss of information, a requirement met by any of several forms of dimensional analysis; (2) the obtaining of a large, maximally heterogeneous sample of persons who are regular users of more than one kind of drug; (3) the assessment of the frequency and chronicity of each kind of drug used for each person in the sample.

The accomplishment of the second major objective follows directly from the achievement of the first objective. One feature of the BC-TRY cluster analytic system is termed "person-typing," which refers to the process of empirically typing subjects on the obtained clusters. This program thus generates an empirical typology of persons; in the present study a typology of multiple drug abusers would be developed based on the particular multiple drug clusters identified.

In order to address the third objective—theoretically based differential description of multiple drug use patterns and multiple drug abusers—a theoretical approach which appears to be promising in accounting for drug abuse must be identified, and appropriate measures derived from the theory selected. In the present study, the theoretical approach adopted is a variant of social learning theory as developed by Jessor and his colleagues (Jessor, Graves, Hanson, & Jessor, 1968; Jessor & Jessor, 1976). This theory has been fruitful in understanding and predicting adolescent deviant behavior, including alcohol and marijuana use. Measures employed in this study consist of a set of sociocultural and personality variables developed by Jessor *et al.* (1968, 1972, 1973, 1975, 1976) and Braucht

(1974), and a scale of recent stressful life events developed by Holmes and his colleagues (Holmes & Rahe, 1967). It should be emphasized that the present study is not intended to be a theory-testing endeavor; rather, as an initial exploratory inquiry, the present study will employ these theory-based variables in a purely descriptive role.

METHOD

In-depth, face-to-face- interviews were conducted with 440 clients receiving treatment in seven drug programs located in the Denver metropolitan area. The largest percentage were patients in the Polydrug Treatment Center ($N = 164$); 100 were patients in the Denver General Hospital Alcohol Detoxification Ward; 102 were patients in two methadone programs; and the remaining 74 were patients in three other Denver drug programs. The anonymity of respondents was assured.

The interview included more than 50 psychosocial scales, demographic questions, and a comprehensive drug questionnaire. Because these measures and the theoretical framework from which they were derived have been described previously (Braucht, 1972; Jessor, Collins, & Jessor, 1972; Jessor et al., 1968; Jessor & Jessor, 1974, 1975), they will not be elaborated upon here. Fifteen drug classes were studied: heroin, illegal methadone, other opiates and synthetics, alcohol, barbiturates, amphetamines, cocaine, marijuana, hallucinogens, codeine, nonnarcotic analgesics, volatile inhalants, major tranquilizers, minor tranquilizers, and methaqualone. Each client was questioned extensively as to current and past drug use history for each of the 15 drug classes. Subsequently, a chronicity/frequency (C/F) index was calculated for each drug class used representing the product of: (1) the number of *months* of recent, regular use of that drug; (2) the number of *times per week* the person used the drug across the time in (1). Thus, for example, a drug used either for 6 months on a daily basis (6×7) or for 3 months on a twice daily basis (3×14) yields a C/F index of 42; a drug used daily for 1 year yields a C/F index (12×7) of 84; and a drug used three times per day across a period of 1 year (12×21) yields a C/F index of 252. It should be noted that, except for alcohol use, the definition of "regular use" was left to the subject. That is, the interviewer did not attempt to impose a predetermined definition for the amount of a drug that constituted a single use of the substance. With regard to alcohol use, the questions asked specifically about drinking to drunkenness, so that drinking to a drunken state constitutes a single usage for this drug.

RESULTS

Cluster Analysis of Chronicity/Frequency Indices

In order to identify the most general groups of drugs defined by the 15 chronicity/frequency (C/F) drug use indices, a full-cycle key cluster analysis was performed (Tryon & Bailey, 1970). Four cluster dimensions were identified involving 11 of the original 15 drugs. The remaining four drugs included (1) heroin, (2) alcohol, (3) major tranquilizers, and (4) the over-the-counter drugs.

Inspection of the mean chronicity/frequency indices across the entire sample for the latter 4 drugs showed that the major tranquilizers and over-the-counter drugs were little used (twelfth and fourteenth ranked of the 15 drugs), while heroin (sixth ranked) and alcohol (second ranked) were used to a considerable degree. For this reason, both heroin and alcohol were included as the fifth and sixth basic drug clusters in addition to the 4 identified by the empirical key cluster analysis. Even though these 2 single substances are not clusters of multiple drugs, of course, it was decided to retain them throughout subsequent analyses in order to provide a comparative perspective against which the 4 true clusters could be viewed.

The resulting 6 drug substance dimensions (patterns of multiple drug use involving 14 of the original 15 drugs) accounted for 99% of the original communality and 92% of the mean square of the original correlation matrix. Thus, these 6 clusters of drugs may be studied as they relate to each other and to other variables with very little loss of information. In the section following, each cluster is described in terms of: (1) the drugs defining the cluster; (2) statistics indicating the strength of association among usage of the drugs defining each cluster.

DRUG CLUSTER ONE: COCAINE, OTHER OPIATES AND SYNTHETICS, METHAQUALONE, AND ILLEGAL METHADONE

The use of the four drug classes comprising this basic drug cluster is highly interrelated—the heavy user of one drug class is very likely to be a heavy user of the other drugs and vice versa. This is evidenced by the domain validity for this first drug cluster of .85 and the cluster score's alpha reliability coefficient of .72. Across the entire sample the average intercorrelation of the C/F drug use scores among these four drugs was +.40.

DRUG CLUSTER TWO: INHALANTS, CODEINE, AND NONNARCOTIC ANALGESICS

The use of inhalants, codeine, and the nonnarcotic analgesics is also strongly related in our sample—persons who use one heavily are likely to be heavy users of the other two. This drug cluster had a domain validity of .82 and an alpha reliability of .68.

DRUG CLUSTER THREE: MARIJUANA, AMPHETAMINES, AND HALLUCINOGENS

As shown by this third cluster's domain validity (.76) and the cluster score's alpha reliability (.57), the degrees of use of marijuana, amphetamines, and hallucinogens are strongly associated with one another—the heavy user of one is likely to be a heavy user of the others.

DRUG CLUSTER FOUR: MINOR TRANQUILIZERS AND BARBITURATES

Although minor tranquilizers and barbiturates are not as strongly interrelated as are the drugs in other clusters, their use is associated to a considerable degree in our sample. This drug cluster's domain validity is .62 and its alpha reliability is .38. Thus, the heavy user of barbiturates is also likely to be a heavy user of the minor tranquilizers and vice versa.

As stated earlier, the chronicity/frequency of neither heroin use nor alcohol use is related to the use of any of the other 13 drugs. Thus, these 2 drugs do not form a multiple drug pattern with one another nor with any other drugs. Because of the significant levels of use of both heroin and alcohol in this sample, however, these 2 drugs are included as the fifth and sixth basic drugs in remaining analyses.

Correlations among the Six Clusters of Drug Use

The correlations among the cluster scores for the six patterns of multiple drug use are presented in Table VI.1, which shows that the six form moderately intercorrelated oblique clusters of multiple drugs.

Relationship between Use of the Six Basic Patterns of Drug Use and Other Drug Use Variables

Table VI.2 presents correlations between the six basic drug cluster scores and scores on four indices of polydrug use: (1) number of drugs (up

Table VI.1

INTERCORRELATION, INTERNAL CONSISTENCY, AND MEAN USE LEVELS OF
THE SIX EMPIRICAL CLUSTERS OF DRUGS

	Drug cluster one	Drug cluster two	Drug cluster three	Drug cluster four	Drug cluster five	Drug cluster six
Drug cluster one Cocaine–other opiates and synthetics–methaqualone–illegal methadone	1.0	.06	.24	.12	.10	.05
Drug cluster two Inhalants–codeine–non-narcotic analgesics	—	1.0	.15	.24	−.04	.00
Drug cluster three Marijuana–amphetamines–hallucinogens	—	—	1.0	.11	.19	.05
Drug cluster four Minor tranquilizers–barbiturates	—	—	—	1.0	−.03	.07
Drug cluster five Heroin	—	—	—	—	1.0	−.06
Drug cluster six Alcohol (to drunkenness)	—	—	—	—	—	1.0
Domain validity of drug type cluster	.85	.82	.76	.62	na	na
Alpha reliability of drug type cluster score	.72	.68	.57	.38	—[a]	—[a]
Mean chronicity–frequency of use	68.8	27.6	293.0	94.8	45.6	188.8

[a] Since the fifth (heroin) and sixth (alcohol) drug clusters each consist of only one drug alpha, reliability estimates are not applicable.

to 15 possible) *ever* used; (2) number of drugs used recently on a *regular* basis; (3) number of drugs used recently on a *daily* basis; (4) extent to which subjects reported the deliberate use of drugs in combinations for the express purpose of achieving some desired effect. Correlations which failed to attain a significance beyond the $p < .01$ level have been omitted from Table VI.2.

From Table VI.2, it may be seen that use of a large number of drugs at one time or another during one's life is significantly related to the C/F indices on four of the six drug patterns—particularly to use of the

Table VI.2

CORRELATIONS BETWEEN THE SIX EMPIRICAL CLUSTERS OF DRUGS AND
FOUR INDICES OF POLYDRUG USE

	Empirical drug clusters					
Polydrug indices	Drug cluster one	Drug cluster two	Drug cluster three	Drug cluster four	Drug cluster five	Drug cluster six
Number of drugs ever used	—	.16	.40	—	.16	−.20
Number of drugs used recently on a regular basis	.37	.27	.66	.23	.15	—
Number of drugs used recently on a daily basis	.96	—	.13	—	—	—
Extent of the use of drugs in combination to achieve an effect	−.14	.17	.60	.30	—	—

marijuana–amphetamines–hallucinogens cluster (positively) and the alcohol use index (negatively). Thus, people using large amounts of the
marijuana–amphetamines–hallucinogens cluster have at least experimented with a wide variety of drugs during their lives, while individuals using a great deal of alcohol tend not to have had experience with a
wide variety of drugs.

Not only have heavy users of the marijuana–amphetamines–hallucinogens drug cluster had experience with a wide variety of drugs at
some time or another during their lives, but they are also currently using
the greatest number of different drugs on a regular basis. The extent of
use of all of the other clusters of drugs except alcohol is also significantly
related to the number of drugs currently used on a regular basis.

It may give some perspective on the preceding relationships to note
that across the present sample, the mean number of drugs ever used is 6.5
drugs (out of a possible 15) and that the average number of different drugs
currently used on a regular basis is 2.8 drugs.

In contrast, the number of drugs currently used on a *daily* basis is
related at an extremely high level to the current use of the drug cluster
consisting of cocaine, other opiates and synthetics, methaqualone, and
illegal methadone. Heavy users of the cluster are currently using a large
number of drugs on a daily basis, as compared with an average of 2.0
drugs used daily across the whole sample.

Finally, Table VI.2 shows that the deliberate, conscious use of multiple
drugs either sequentially or simultaneously in combinations in order to

achieve some desired effect is most strongly related to heavy current use of the marijuana–amphetamines–hallucinogens drug cluster and also related to the minor tranquilizer–barbiturate cluster and the inhalants–codeine–nonnarcotic analgesics cluster. Even though heavy users of cluster including cocaine, other opiates and synthetics, methaqualone, and illegal methadone are using the highest number of different drugs on a daily basis, they actually disclaim the notion of intentionally using drugs in combination, as shown by the significant negative $(-.14)$ correlation in Table VI.2.

Relationships between Use of the Six Types of Drugs and Psychosocial Variables

Table VI.3 presents the correlations between use of the six clusters of drug use and selected psychosocial variables. All entries in Table VI.2 represent correlations significant beyond the .01 level of probability, and absence of an entry indicates that the coefficient of correlation did not reach this level. Some of the psychosocial variables which were assessed have been omitted from Table VI.2 entirely, since they did not correlate at the $p \le .01$ level with use of any of the six drug patterns.

First, Table VI.3 shows that the level of use of the first drug cluster—cocaine, other opiates and synthetics, methaqualone, illegal methadone—is significantly related to only two psychosocial variables. A high level of use of drugs in this first cluster is associated with (1) the

Table VI.3

SIGNIFICANT CORRELATIONS BETWEEN THE SIX DRUG CLUSTERS AND PSYCHOSOCIAL VARIABLES

Psychosocial variables	Drug cluster one	Drug cluster two	Drug cluster three	Drug cluster four	Drug cluster five	Drug cluster six
Age in years	—	—	−.28	.14	—	.25
Need value for conformist goals	—	—	—	−.19	—	—
Attitudes toward deviance	—	—	−.17	—	—	—
Religiosity	—	−.13	−.25	−.17	—	—
Need value for vocational success	—	—	−.16	−.19	—	—
Alienation	—	.18	.25	.17	—	—
Social agent's agreement	—	—	−.17	—	—	—
Life chances disjunctions	—	—	—	.15	—	—

Table VI.3 (*continued*)

Psychosocial variables	Drug cluster one	Drug cluster two	Drug cluster three	Drug cluster four	Drug cluster five	Drug cluster six
Peers' advice salience	—	—	-.17	-.12	—	—
Expectation of vocational success	—	—	—	-.23	—	—
Family advice salience	—	—	-.21	—	—	—
Peers' value for conformance goals	—	—	-.15	-.15	—	—
Internal–external locus of control	—	.16	.14	.24	—	—
Peers' value for vocational success	—	—	-.17	—	—	—
Opportunity to procure drugs	—	—	.19	.20	—	—
Peer support for drug use	.16	—	.42	—	—	—
Positive social function of drugs	—	—	.23	—	—	—
Personal effects function of drugs	—	.17	.24	.24	—	—
Conforming social functions of drugs	—	—	—	—	—	.13
Family value for conformance goals	—	—	—	—	.14	—
Exposure to parental medical drug use	—	—	.28	—	—	—
Family support for drug use	—	—	.32	—	—	—
Family proscription of alcohol use	—	—	.14	—	—	—
Internal negative functions of drug use	—	—	.12	—	—	—
External negative functions of drug use	—	—	.15	—	—	—
Hostility guilt score	—	—	-.15	—	—	—
Peers' sanction likelihood	—	—	-.20	—	—	—
Ease of communication re drugs with family	—	-.14	—	—	—	—
Ease of communication re drugs with peers	—	—	.14	—	—	—
Assaultiveness	—	—	.13	-.24	—	—
Total stress score	.13	—	—	—	—	—
Number of arrests	—	—	—	-.16	.17	.18
Number of convictions	—	—	—	—	—	.29
Socioeconomic status	—	—	—	—	—	-.20
Self-ideal self-discrepancy	—	.14	.19	.19	—	—
Self–others overvaluing others	—	—	—	—	—	.19

presence of a peer subculture which is supportive of such drug use; and (2) a high level of life stresses (the only group of multiple drugs to be significantly related to life stress level).

Second, Table VI.3 shows that the use of the inhalants–codeine–nonnarcotic analgesics cluster of drugs is significantly related to six psychosocial variables. The greater the use of drugs belonging to this second cluster: (1) the less the religiosity; (2) the greater the alienation; (3) the more external the locus of control orientation; (4) the more important the personal effects (escape from problems) functions of such use; (5) the more strained is communication regarding drugs with one's family; (6) the greater the discrepancy between the kind of person one feels he is versus the kind of person one would ideally like to be.

A rough picture suggested by this array of relationships is that use of inhalants, codeine, and nonnarcotic analgesics is associated with a psychosocial syndrome of alienation, lack of values and norms, lack of meaningful channels of communication with one's family, feelings of helplessness and inferiority, and a strong desire to escape from the pressure of personal problems.

Inspection of Table VI.3 shows that the use of the third class of drugs—marijuana, amphetamines, hallucinogens—is related to 25 psychosocial characteristics (presented in the third column of Table VI.3). The general psychosocial condition suggested by this array of significant relationships is one of the use of marijuana, amphetamines, and hallucinogens on the part of youth embedded in family and peer groups who model and support drug use. The use of drugs in this cluster appears to be firmly entrenched in a drug subculture with all of its characteristics as popularly conceived. Use of this cluster not only is associated with the desire to escape from personal problems but also is associated with the function of enhancing social occasions, the only class of drugs that is perceived to serve this social enhancement function.

In contrast, Table VI.3 shows that use of the minor tranquilizers–barbiturates cluster is associated with a pattern of psychosocial characteristics suggestive of older users who are intolerant regarding deviance from conformist ethos, who have pervasive feelings of helplessness in controlling their own destiny and a lack of confidence in their own vocational career success.

The use of heroin is related to only two psychosocial variables: heavy heroin use is associated with having been arrested a large number of times and is also associated with a family ethos which places a high value on the importance of conformist goals.

Finally, Table VI.3 shows that the use of the last basic type of drug, alcohol, is related to older user age, importance attached to using alcohol as a means of conforming to social expectations, elevated levels of criminal arrests and convictions, low socioeconomic status, and a classic sign of depression—the feeling that others think more of one than one thinks of oneself.

Identifying Distinct Types of Drug Abusers

Thus far, six drug clusters have been identified and the patterns of relationships of each cluster to psychosocial characteristics have been described. Next, a typology of drug abusers, rather than drug clusters, was developed empirically by means of proximity cluster analysis (Tryon & Bailey, 1970). Eight quantitatively and qualitatively distinct types of multiple drug abusers were identified. Of the 440 abuser profiles, 418 were classified into one (and only one) of the 8 drug abuser types. The remaining 22 abusers' profiles were unique or too discrepant to be included in any of the 8 types.

Thus, independently of their standing on psychosocial variables, eight distinct types of drug users were identified solely by analysis of their standing on the use of the six basic clusters of drugs. Table VI.4 presents a complete description of each type, in terms of both drug use patterns and psychosocial characteristics. Using drug user types as the independent variable, a set of one-way analyses of variance was performed. Each row of Table VI.4 represents a significant F ratio ($p < .01$), indicating a significant difference among the eight drug user types on that psychosocial characteristic. The plus and minus entries in each row of Table VI.4 describe the results of post-hoc multiple range tests (by the method of least squared differences) that were performed following the significant F test. On any given psychosocial variable, drug user types with a plus sign are relatively high on that characteristic and are significantly higher ($p < .01$) than user types with no table entry (average on that characteristic) who are, in turn, significantly higher ($p < .01$) on that psychosocial variable than user types with a minus sign.

Table VI.4 has been designed to communicate a wealth of significant findings about the characteristics of each type of drug user as directly and completely as possible. The characteristics of each type of drug user are briefly summarized in the following paragraphs.

DRUG USER TYPE ONE:
INFREQUENT EXPERIMENTERS

Comprising the bulk of our sample, the type one user has experimented with more than 6 different drug classes (of 15 possible) during

Table VI.4

DRUG USER TYPES: ONE-WAY ANALYSES OF VARIANCE BY PSYCHOSOCIAL VARIABLES

	Variable							
	Type one[a]	Type two[b]	Type three[c]	Type four[d]	Type five[e]	Type six[f]	Type seven[g]	Type eight[h]
	N = 230	N = 67	N = 17	N = 16	N = 11	N = 8	N = 7	N = 62
% of total sample	55%	16.0%	4.1%	3.8%	2.6%	1.9%	1.7%	14.9%
Chronicity/frequency indices of drug use								
Heroin				+				−
Methadone		−	−	+	−	−	−	
Opiates				+				
Alcohol	−	+						
Barbiturates	−	−	+					−
Amphetamines	−	−	−	−	+	−	−	
Cocaine	−	−	−	+	−	−	−	−
Marijuana	−	−	−		+	−	−	+
Hallucinogens			−	+		−		+
Codeine	−	−	−	−			+	−

140

	1	2	3	4	5	6	7	8
Analgesics	–	+		–	–		–	–
Inhalants	–	+		–	–	–	–	–
Major tranquilizers	–	–	–	+	–	+	–	–
Minor tranquilizers	–		–		+		–	–
Quaaludes	–	+	+	–	–	–	–	–
No. ever used				+			–	–
Used recently and regularly	–			+				–
No. (15) used daily	–			+				–
Sum (1) chronicity/frequency			–	+	+		–	–
Use of drugs in combination			+	+			–	–
Arrests	–		–	–	+	–	+	–
Convictions	–	–	–	–	+	–	+	–
SES		+					–	–
MSGO F3 (depression)					–	–	+	–
Age	Youngest			Youngest		Oldest	Oldest	
Sex: Male		All male						
Female							65%	
Ethnicity		No Blacks	No M-A	No M-A	M-A Few whites	No Blacks 88% white		
Alienation	–	–	–	+		–	–	–

Table VI.4 (continued)

	Variable							
	Type one[a] N = 230	Type two[b] N = 67	Type three[c] N = 17	Type four[d] N = 16	Type five[e] N = 11	Type six[f] N = 8	Type seven[g] N = 7	Type eight[h] N = 62
% of total sample	55%	16.0%	4.1%	3.8%	2.6%	1.9%	1.7%	14.9%
Internal locus of control	+		−			−		
Opportunity to procure drugs	−	−	+	−			−	
Positive social function		+		−	+			+
Conforming social function				−	+	−		
Personal effects function	−			−	+			
Negative (internal) function		−				+		
Assaultiveness			−	+	+	−		+
Peer value for conformance goals	+	+	+	−			+	
Peer value for deviant goals	−	−	−			−	−	+

[a] Infrequent or experimental drug users
[b] Alcoholics
[c] Barbiturates–minor tranquilizers users
[d] Heroin–methadone–opiates–coke–hallucinogens users
[e] Amphetamines–marijuana–major tranquilizers users
[f] Quaaludes–some other users
[g] Codeine–analgesics–inhalants–quaalude users
[h] Marijuana–hallucinogen users

his or her lifetime, has recently used 1.7 drugs on a regular basis, but is unlikely to have used *any* on a daily basis. This type tends not to use drugs in combinations very often—42% have never consciously used drugs in combinations to achieve an effect.

In contrast to the other types of drug users, these infrequent experimenters feel that they themselves are in control of the direction of their lives. In general, they, their families, and their peer groups are relatively conformist in orientation and they enjoy a relatively high socioeconomic status. Finally, the infrequent experimenters tend not to use drugs to escape the press of personal problems.

DRUG USER TYPE TWO: ALCOHOLICS

The alcoholic type of drug user is older, poorer, and has been convicted of crimes more often (11 times) than any other type of drug user. He or she has had experience with fewer drugs during his or her lifetime than any other type of user (on the average, about 3 different drugs). The alcoholic type is currently using 1.9 drugs on a regular basis, and 1.1 drugs (alcohol) on a daily basis. More than any other type, alcoholics tend *not* to use drugs in combinations, at least not intentionally—65% report "never" using drugs in combinations to achieve an effect. Alcoholics are relatively conformance oriented in their own values and beliefs, and while they perceive little support for drug use among their peers, they say that they drink as one means of conforming to their social group. Compared to any other type of drug user, they recognize fewer drawbacks to their own use of drugs.

DRUG USER TYPE THREE: BARBITURATE AND MINOR TRANQUILIZER USERS

The user of barbiturates and minor tranquilizers is likely to be an older, white, middle-class housewife who feels powerless to control the direction of her own life. Relatively conformist in orientation, and with the lowest rate of arrests and convictions, the users of barbiturates and minor tranquilizers were the only type of drug users in our sample who had never had any experience with heroin or methadone. In regard to the conscious use of drugs in combinations to achieve an effect, 31% of these barbiturate–minor tranquilizer users reported "always" using such combinations. Also they report their access to drugs to be easier than any other type of drug user.

DRUG USER TYPE FOUR: NARCOTICS USERS

The users of heroin, illegal methadone, other opiates, cocaine, and in conjunction with these narcotics, hallucinogenic drugs, tend to hold beliefs contrary to the conformist ethos—they are assaultive and tolerant of deviance. The average narcotics user in our sample had been arrested an average of 28 times, but had only been convicted 3 times. Narcotics users feel that their peers devalue vocational success more than does any other type of drug user. Their use of these "hard" drugs is heavy, and 31% of this type of user report "always" using drugs in combinations to achieve an effect. In our sample, 57% of the members of this type were of Mexican–American descent, the only type composed primarily of this ethnic group.

DRUG USER TYPE FIVE: USERS OF AMPHETAMINES, MARIJUANA, AND MAJOR TRANQUILIZERS

Users of amphetamines, marijuana, and the major tranquilizers have used more different drugs during their lives (11 drugs); they have used the widest variety of drugs recently on a regular basis (7 drugs); they have used the most different drugs on a daily basis (3.8 drugs); and they are more likely than any other type of user to be using drugs in combination to achieve an effect—73% of these users reported "always" using such combinations and none reported "never" using combinations.

These heavy, multiple drug users are extremely young, alienated, and assaultive. They are more likely than any other type of user to value drugs as a means of escaping from their personal problems, and they also see drugs functioning for them as social enhancers and as means of conforming to the group. In our sample, no member of this drug user type was of Mexican–American descent.

DRUG USER TYPE SIX: USERS OF METHAQUALONE, MINOR TRANQUILIZERS, AND BARBITURATES

The sixth type of drug user feels himself to be in a highly stressful environment, while at the same time feeling relatively helpless to change the course of his life. Very unlikely to be extroverted or assaultive, he does not view drugs as a means of "going along" with the group. In fact, he feels that his peer group disapproves of drug use. This type of user sees more drawbacks to his own use of drugs—in terms of loss of self-control, self-respect, and loss of friends—than does any other type of drug user.

DRUG USER TYPE SEVEN: USERS OF CODEINE, INHALANTS, ANALGESICS, AND METHAQUALONE

The type seven drug user tends to use alcohol to a state of drunkeness very infrequently, if at all. These users are relatively high in socio-economic status. In our sample, there were no Black members of this drug user type, and all members of this type were male. In general, members of this type hold relatively conformist values and attitudes. Their drug use occurs despite their report that: (1) they find drugs hard to get, and (2) their peers do not support drug use.

DRUG USER TYPE EIGHT: HALLUCINOGENIC USERS

Primarily users of marijuana and the hallucinogenic drugs (the type eight drug user uses more than does any other type), they also are using some amphetamines. These are young, assaultive individuals, and in contrast to members of drug user type five, who use many of the same kinds of drugs, they are not alienated. More than any other type, they report their peers to be supportive of drug use, and they see the primary function of drug use to be as a means of enhancing social occasions.

DISCUSSION

To return to the three primary aims of this study, six basic classes of drugs were identified empirically. In the present sample, four multiple drug clusters were found, while neither the use of heroin nor the use of alcohol was strongly associated with the use of any other drug.

In general, the four multiple drug clusters found here do not corre-spond to patterns previously reported in the single published study ad-dressing the problem of identifying multiple drug abuse patterns (Simpson & Sells, 1974). In this study of 11,380 patients who were in-cluded in the initial 2 years of the NIMH–TCU Drug Abuse Reporting Program (DARP), 28 distinctive patterns were found. The most frequent pattern, representing more than 28% of the patients, was the daily or weekly use of heroin alone. Moreover, daily or weekly use of heroin with cocaine, with marijuana, and with both cocaine and marijuana were also prevalent patterns. These four patterns—each involving heroin—accounted for just over 52% of their patients.

There is, however, a major difference between the Simpson and Sells study and the present one: the requirement for admission to the participant treatment programs. The treatment agencies within DARP were primarily treating opiate addicts, and during the first 2 years, users of other drug classes usually were not admitted unless some level of opiate use was also indicated. Thus, given these selection criteria, the finding of a high prevalence of heroin use, singly and in combination, would be expected. In contrast, the present study utilized subjects from a variety of programs, and while 23% were drawn from an alcohol treatment program and 23% from a heroin treatment program, the majority (54%) were from programs not having these selective admission requirements.

In exploring the second objective—the development of an empirical typology of multiple drug abusers—eight distinctive types were identified. These types were an intriguing finding, since some of the types, such as type one (marijuana–hallucinogen users), conform to previously reported and commonly described types, whereas other types would not be expected on an a priori basis. For example, type five (users of amphetamines, marijuana, and major tranquilizers) and type seven (users of codiene, nonnarcotic analgesics, inhalants, and methaqualone) are types that are not widely described in the literature. The degree to which the types discovered in this study represent general types of multiple drug abusers remains to be seen.

The third objective was to determine the differential association of a coherent set of psychosocial variables with each of the six drug clusters and the eight drug user types. The particular set of psychosocial measures employed in this study are based upon social learning theory as articulated by Jessor and colleagues and have been shown previously to be powerful predictors of adolescent deviant behavior. Because the users of the drugs comprising the third drug cluster (marijuana, amphetamines, and hallucinogens) most closely approximate the subject population on which this theoretical approach has been developed, the strong associations of these psychosocial variables with this drug cluster were not unexpected. Nevertheless, if the underlying theory's explanatory scope were adequate, one would have expected stronger associations with the remaining multiple drug clusters and with the eight drug user types. Tables VI.3 and VI.4 show only those psychosocial variables that were associated with at least one cluster or type. The entire set of psychosocial measures employed was considerably larger than those shown. The general absence of significant relationships between these psychosocial measures and the clusters and user types, as well as the striking differences in the general level of association, raise questions about the utility of this theoretical approach in explaining a wide variety of multiple drug use patterns and users. It may be that alternative theories and their associated constructs will be required to provide sets of descriptive variables which relate to differing drug use patterns and users, as has been implied by several authors (see Bentler & Eichberg, 1975; Braucht, Brakarsh, Follingstad, & Berry, 1973; Lettieri, 1975; McGlothlin, 1975). On the other hand, it may be that merely introducing key moderator variables or the use of alternative analytic strategies such as those suggested by Gorsuch and Butler (1975) and Dunnette (1975) will reveal additional explanatory power now latent in present social learning theory.

It should be stressed that this study represents an exploratory effort. Future research is needed to build upon this step, replicating and extending the present investigation with larger numbers of subjects from differing locales and differing subcultural groups. To provide perspective, a sample of "normals" should be interviewed using the same set of measures employed with drug-abusing groups. There is also a need for further sampling of theories and theoretical constructs in order to provide an arena for the comparative assessment of competing theories in explaining different clusters of multiple drug use.

CHAPTER VII

Dimensions of Polydrug Abuse: An MMPI Study

David Lachar, Kenneth Schooff,
John Keegan, and Charles Gdowski

MMPI investigations of the personality correlates of substance abusers have been prolific. A review of the literature (Dahlstrom, Welsh, & Dahlstrom, 1975) revealed 263 references in which this instrument has been used in research with substance abusers. The data have varied from particular items, special scales, and several clinical scales, to complete mean clinical profiles. The review that follows focuses on studies presenting mean profile data or two-point code frequencies and divides substance abusers into three classifications: alcoholics, narcotic addicts, and polydrug abusers.

CLASSES OF SUBSTANCE ABUSERS

Alcoholics

In 1943, the earliest attempts at an MMPI personality description of substance abusers was presented by Hewitt; neither the validity scales nor

Polydrug Abuse:
The Results of a
National Collaborative Study

scales 9/*Ma* or 0/*Si* were included on the MMPI profile at the time. Hewitt's Alcoholic Anonymous (AA) males generated a normal limits 4-2 mean profile while his female subjects produced a 4-spike profile. Since that initial research, numerous investigators have studied a variety of dimensions: sex differences, hospitalized versus outpatient subjects, alcoholics not in treatment, treatments changes, and prealcoholic personality characters. Although the subject population of this chapter does not include the alcoholic substance abuser, MMPI research on this substance abuse population will also be briefly reviewed. The investigators' research for specific personality characteristics associated with substance abuse began with the alcoholic. Variables considered important in other substance-abusing populations were first investigated in the alcoholic. Further, MMPI descriptions of alcoholics provide a frame of reference against which to view the other populations of drug abusers.

If a two-point code is used to categorize the mean profile of alcoholics, a vast majority of them are of a characterological nature (cf. Lachar, 1974). Scales 2/*D* and 4/*Pd* figure predominantly in the mean profile code types of alcoholics. The 2-4/4-2 code or 4-spike with a moderate elevation on scale 2/*D* has been reported in VA alcoholic patients (Jones, 1971; Miller, Pokorny, & Hanson, 1968; Wilkinson, Prado, Williams, & Schnadt, 1971; Rohan, 1972; Rohan, Tatro, & Rotman, 1969; Sinnett, 1961; Soskin, 1970), in hospitalized male and female alcoholic patients (Hill, Haertzen, & Davis, 1962; Hodo & Fowler, 1976; Hoffman & Nelson, 1971; Jansen & Hoffman, 1973; Kammeier, Hoffman, & Loper, 1973; Kurland, Unger, Shaffer, & Savage, 1967; Mascia, 1969; McGinnis & Ryan, 1965; Overall, 1973; Shaffer, Hanlon, Wolf, Foxwell, & Kurland, 1962; Zelen, Fox, Gould, & Olson, 1966), outpatient male alcoholics (Goss & Morosko, 1969; Rosen, 1960; Zelen *et al*. 1966), and outpatient female alcoholics (Rosen, 1960). Two studies reported 2-spike profiles with moderate elevations on scale 4/*Pd* for hospitalized males (Rae, 1972; Rae & Forbes, 1966). Other investigators have reported mean profiles where scales 2/*D* and 4/*Pd* are the two highest clinical scales but not exceeding 70*T*. Button (1956), Hoyt and Sedlacek (1958), Zelen *et al*. (1966), Kristianson (1970), Curlee (1970), and Hoffman (1973) reported profiles of this type for hospitalized alcoholics. Hampton (1953) reported similar results with male AA members.

A few studies have reported other mean profile code types. Rae's (1972) subgroup of nonabstaining alcoholics generated a 2-spike profile with a moderate elevation on scale 7/*Pt*. Zelen *et al*. (1966) reported a 2-7 code type for outpatient female alcoholics. Members of the Link Society (Swedish equivalent of AA) generated a 2-spike profile with a moderate elevation on scale 8/*Sc* (Kristianson, 1970). Normal limits profiles with scales 4/*Pd* and 9/*Ma* moderately elevated were reported for male alcoholics in a counseling program (Ballard, 1959) and for prealcoholics (Kammeier *et al.*, 1973; Loper, Kammeier, & Hoffman, 1973). Pollack's (1965) sample of male alcoholics not in treatment generated a normal limits 4-8 profile, Dunlap's (1961) remitted female AA alcoholics a normal limits 4-6 profile, while Mathias' (1956) sample of male AA members produced a normal limits profile with moderate elevations on scales 1/*Hs* and 4/*Pd*. Only one study reported a two-point code classification that can be categorized as psychotic (cf. Lachar, 1974b). Kraft and Wijesinghe's (1970) male sample (N = 9) of younger alcoholics (range 19–32 years) generated an 8-7 mean profile. Other research suggests that younger alcoholics are significantly higher on scales *K*, 1,2,4,5,7, and 8 (McGinnis & Ryan, 1965). Older alcoholics were reported significantly lower on scales 4/*Pd* and 7/*Pt* (Hoffmann & Nelson, 1971) and scales 4,7, and 9 (Hoffman, Jansen, & Wefring, 1972).

Hoffman (1973) provided a comparison between state hospital alcoholics in 1959 and 1971. Although some scale differences were obtained, both mean profiles were of the same configuration and no significant differences were formed for two-point code frequencies.

Although the general consensus in the literature concerning the alcoholic is that the 2-4/4-2 code type typifies this substance abuser, mean profiles may mask significant personality differences (cf. Hodo & Fowler, 1976.) Several studies provide detailed two-point code frequencies (Hodo and Fowler, 1976; Hoffman, 1973; Hoyt & Sedlacek, 1958; McLachlan, 1975; Tomsovic, 1968.) Code types of 2-4/4-2 range in frequency from 6.8% to 21%. The 4-9/9-4 code type reports ranging from 8% to 13.7%. Codes of 2-7/7-2 varied in frequency from 2.3% to 13%. It should be noted that McLachlan (1975) and Hodo and Fowler (1976) classified profiles using the two highest scale combinations whether or not they exceeded 70*T* (Gynther, Altman, Warbin, & Sletten, 1972).

Narcotic Addicts

Personality research using the MMPI with narcotic abusers has attempted to delineate stable personality characteristics among these substance abusers. A review of the literature reveals emphases on sex differences, hospitalized versus street addicts, and voluntary versus committed. Since many study samples consisted of imprisoned heroin addicts, nonaddict prisoners were frequently employed to form control groups.

As with other substance-abusing populations, scale 4/*Pd* figures predominantly in the mean profiles of narcotic addicts. In a majority of the published studies, the addicted subjects produced 4/*Pd* spike profiles, with scales 2/*D*, 8/*Sc*, or 9/*Ma* the next highest scale elevation. Although two-point codes of 2-4/4-2, 4-8/8-4, and 4-9/9-4 are similar in that they describe characterological disorders (cf. Lachar, 1974), investigators have attempted to isolate the typical addicts' profile in the hope of describing specific personality characteristics that differentiate these substance abusers from other populations. These studies have attempted to answer the question of whether personality patterns are associated with the use of particular substances or reflect a core "addiction-prone" personality in which the drug of choice is primarily related to situational factors.

Mean profiles in which the 2-4/4-2 or 4-spike and moderate elevation on scale 2 code is present are reported by a number of investigators (Berzins *et al.*, 1971; Gendreau & Gendreau, 1970; Gilbert & Lombardi, 1967; Hill *et al.*, 1962; Hill, Haertzen, & Glaser, 1960; Hill, Haertzen, & Yamuahiro, 1968; Pittell, 1971; Ross & Berzins, 1974; Sheppard, Ricca, Fracchia, & Merlis, 1973; Sutker, 1971; Sutker & Allain, 1973). Except for the Ross and Berzins (1974) sample (voluntary treatment female addict group), all subjects were male heroin addicts, varying in status from voluntary treatment under the Narcotic Addict Rehabilitation Act (NARA), court-committed addicts, street addicts, and prisoner addicts. Other studies have reported composite profiles with peaks on scale 4/*Pd* (moderate elevation on scale 9/*Ma*) or two-point codes of 4-9/9-4 (Belleville, 1956; Gendreau & Gendreau, 1971, 1973; Olson, 1964; Overall, 1973; Regal, 1963; Stoffer, Sapira, & Meketon, 1969; Sutker & Allain, 1973; Sutker & Moan, 1972). Subject populations included male and female addicts (Olson, 1964; Regal, 1963), female prisoner addicts (Stoffer *et al.*, 1969), and female street addicts (Sutker & Moan, 1972), whereas the other four studies reported on male addicts. Status included voluntary and nonvoluntary inpatient treatment, incarcerated addicts, and active, nontreatment addicts. A cautionary note should be added here in terms of generalizability since several of the samples (Belleville, 1956; Gendreau & Gendreau, 1971; Regal, 1963; Stoffer *et al.*, 1969; Sutker & Moan, 1972; consisted of fewer than 30 subjects. Mean profiles in which scale 4/*Pd* was elevated above 70*T* with a moderate elevation of scale 8/*Sc* or with 4-8/8-4 code types were reported for volunteer (NARA), prisoner, and probationer female addicts (Ross & Berzins, 1974), female prisoner addicts (Sutker & Moan, 1972), voluntary inpatient males (Sheppard *et al.*, 1973), male and female voluntary inpatients (Zuckerman, Sola, Masterson, & Angelone, 1975), female addicts (Pittell, 1971), and male, teenage addicts where scales 4/*Pd* and 8/*Sc* were within normal limits (Hill *et al.*, 1960.)

Reports in the literature of significant elevation on scales 2/*D* and 8/*Sc*, but particularly scale 2/D, in the mean profiles of narcotic addicts have focused on the relation between such elevations and subject status of voluntary versus committed treatment. Gendreau and Gendreau (1973) suggested that voluntary patients entered treatment as a result of the subjective discomfort which was being measured by scale 2/D of the MMPI. Sutker and Allain (1973) concluded that street addicts were more psychologically uncomfortable than addict prisoners. However, Sheppard et al. (1973) compared four groups of addicts (outpatient, 4-2 code type; committed, 4'-2 code type; voluntary hospitalization, 4-8 code type; and street addicts on methadone, 4-2 code type) and concluded that the stable personality characteristics elicited overrode any transient effects of street life. The more recently published data of Zuckerman et al. (1975) suggest that elevations on scales 2/D and 8/Sc are likely to decrease after treatment and are not suggestive of enduring personality characteristics. Both male and female addicts generated 4-9/9-4 profiles at the conclusion of their treatment. Prison addicts in Sutker and Allain's (1973) sample who had been drug free for at least 2 years produced a peak on scale 4/Pd with a moderate elevation on scale 9/Ma. The voluntary hospitalized addicts in the Sheppard et al. (1973) sample also generated a 4-9 mean profile when discharged from a 90-day treatment program. The initial two-point code had been 4-8.

Several researchers included two-point code frequencies of their narcotic-abusing samples (Berzins et al., 1971; Hill et al., 1960; Olson, 1964; Sheppard et al., 1972; Zuckerman et al., 1975). Code types of 4-9/9-4 were reported in frequencies ranging from 8% to 30%. The other predominant code type, 2-4/4-2, ranged from a low of 11% to a high of 23%. The reader is referred to Sheppard et al. (1973) and Zuckerman et al. (1975) for more detailed two-point code information.

Polydrug Abusers

Investigations of the personality of the nonopiate substance abuser have evaluated primarily the multiple drug abuser. The subject populations reviewed consistently included subjects who use a combination of drugs regularly. To illustrate this point, when LSD users were compared to nonusers (Smart & Fejer, 1969), the authors reported that in addition to taking hallucinogens, 85% of the subjects frequently took tranquilizers, barbiturates, antidepressants, and stimulants. All of them regularly used marijuana. As a result, it is difficult, if not impossible, to delineate, within these completed studies, personality characteristics related to specific drug usage patterns.

As with alcohol and narcotic abusers, there is marked predominance of scale 4/Pd in the two-point code classification of mean profiles. Significant by its absence is scale 2/D; none of the studies reporting mean profile data on polydrug abusers has scale 2/D as part of the mean two-point code. The subject populations are generally younger with a mean age of 19.2 to 21.3 years. Subject status varies from voluntary hospitalized patients to solicited street abusers not seeking treatment.

Four studies reported mean profile data on illicit LSD use. Subjects were solicited and not seeking treatment. Smart and Fejer (1969) and Keller and Redfering (1973) reported 4-9/9-4 two-point codes. Lynch (1971) reported a 9-4 normal limits profile for a small sample of male and female users ($N = 16$). An 8-9 mean profile code was reported by Smart and Jones (1970).

Most studies reported 4-8/8-4 or a 4-spike with a moderate elevation on scale 8/Sc mean profile. Populations with this code type included male voluntarily hospitalized and nonhospitalized abusers (Burke & Eichberg, 1972; Kendall & Pittell, 1971; Rosecrans & Brignet, 1972; Sanborn, Casey, & Niswander, 1971; Schoolar, White & Cohen, 1972; Zuckerman et al., 1975) and male and female outpatients (Heller & Mordkoff, 1972).

Similar codes have been reported for female outpatients (Schoolar et al. 1972; Burke & Eichberg, 1972) and hospitalized female abusers (Kendall & Pittell, 1971). Casual, moderate (Cox & Smart, 1972), and heavy (Ellingwood, 1967) users of amphetamines also generated codes of this type. Mean profiles with a 4-spike and moderate elevation on scale 9/Ma or 4-9/9-4 code types are reported by Kendall and Pittell (1971) for voluntary, outpatient female abusers and McGuire and Megargee (1974) for incarcerated male abusers. Normal limits profiles with scales 4/Pd and 9/Ma the two highest are reported by Christie and Caldwell (1974) in their solicited polydrug sample and McGuire and Megargee (1974) for occasional and regular users of marijuana.

In addition to the Smart and Jones (1970) data on LSD users, two other studies reported psychotic code classifications (cf. Lachar, 1974b). Heavy users and snorters of amphetamines generated 8-9 mean code types (Cox & Smart, 1972) while hospitalized male polydrug abusers produced an 8-7 mean profile code type (Kendall & Pittell, 1971). Two published articles are of particular interest in that male and female abusers were compared to outpatient psychiatric controls (Schoolar et al., 1972) and inpatient psychiatric controls (Burke & Eichberg, 1972). Hospitalized male abusers were significantly higher on L, F, and all clinical scales except 1/Hs when compared to psychiatric inpatients and higher on all but scales F, 4/Pd, 5/Mf, and 9/Ma when compared to nonhospitalized abusers. Hospitalized female abusers, however, were not significantly different from controls although higher on scales F, 1/Hs, 2/D, and 8/Sc when compared with nonhospitalized abusers (Burke and Eichberg, 1972). The Schoolar et al. (1972) data suggest a similar pattern with male abusers higher on F, 4/Pd, 8/Sc, and 9/Ma and female abusers higher on 4/Pd and 9/Ma. As with narcotic abusers, Zuckerman et al. (1975) provide data that profile changes occur in "soft" drug abusers after a treatment program. From an initial 4-8 code type, the polydrug abusers generated a 9-4 mean profile.

The data comparing the polydrug abusers with psychiatric controls suggest that these abusers admit to as much, if not more, psychopathology. Several studies use the number of scales greater than a certain T score value as a measure of abnormality. McAree, Steffenhagen, and Zheutlin (1969, 1972), using the criteria of two or more scales > 75T reported significant differences between the extensive polydrug abuser and a control and marijuana only group. Greaves' (1971) sample of adolescent and postadolescent abusers ($N = 20$) all produced profiles with at least three scales > 70T.

Two-point code frequencies are reported in several articles (Smart & Jones, 1970; Christie & Caldwell, 1974; Zuckerman et al., 1975; the Christie data used the criterion of the two highest scales > 60T.) Code types of 4-9/9-4 ranged in frequency from 8.4% to 22%. The 8-9/9-8 code type occurred between 8.4% and 21%. Code types of 4-8/8-4 occurred with frequencies ranging from 8.4% to 11%. The only direct comparison of significance between narcotic and polydrug two-point codes is found in the Zuckerman et al. (1975) article. The 2-8/8-2 code type was more frequent in the polydrug group (18.6%) while the 4-9/9-4 code type approached significance in the narcotic group ($p < .10$).

Summary

Several general conclusions concerning these substance abusers are suggested. Alcoholics and narcotic addicts are characterized by mean profiles suggestive of characterological disorders. The most frequent alcoholic mean profile is the 2-4/4-2 code type and as a group alcoholic generated more normal-limits profiles. Mean code types of 2-4/4-2, 4-8/8-4, and 4-9/9-4 characterize narcotic addict profiles. Predominant two-point code frequencies for both groups appear to be 2-4/4-2 and 4-9/9-4.

Polydrug abusers, on the other hand, do not present a clear-cut picture. Several studies that reported psychotic mean profile code types and two-point code frequencies suggests a mixture of characterological and psychotic classifications (cf. Lachar, 1974b).

Further conclusions based on the literature do not appear warranted at this time. A number of variables are known to influence individual MMPI profiles. They include socioeconomic status, sex of informant, subject status, race, age, and education. Very few studies provide descriptive data which cover socioeconomic status, race, age, or education. Gynther (1972), for example, suggests that nonwhite subjects generate significantly different MMPI profiles in the direction of more psychopathology when compared to white informants. Approximately 71% of the alcoholic and polydrug samples and 44% of the narcotic samples reviewed here do not provide racial composition data. Even when specified, separate analyses by race were not typically done. Accordingly, it is difficult to determine whether mean profiles might have been contaminated solely by race. If one assumes, for example, that narcotic-abusing samples contained a substantial percentage of black addicts and if one evaluates these data in light of research that suggests black informants score significantly higher on scales F, 4/Pd, 8/Sc, and 9/Ma (Gynther, 1972), then two-point code frequencies of the narcotic samples could be misleading. Descriptions of socioeconomic status and education of subjects are also disappointingly low.

Attempts to describe personality correlates of a particular kind of substance abuser are further complicated by the age difference of samples. Alcoholic samples tend to be older. McGinnis and Ryan (1965), Hoffman and Nelson (1971), and Hoffman et al. (1972) suggest differences between profiles of alcoholics on the basis of age. Scale 2/D figures predominantly in the profile of the alcoholic, and data from "normal" samples suggest an elevation in scale 2/D with age (Aaronson, 1958; Gynther & Shimkunas, 1965).

The personality description of the heroin addict, based on clinical experience and personality testing, is typically along the lines of psychopathic personality traits. Given the legal status of heroin in the American society, it is difficult to sort out whether MMPI data represent (1) personality characteristics associated with a tendency to abuse heroin, (2) resultant life-style of using heroin, or (3) a life-style necessary to obtain heroin. It would seem necessary that the researcher be aware of these considerations in interpreting his data as when looking at the profiles of the polydrug abuser and attempting to sort out possible drug side effects from personality correlates.

Several studies have attempted to create more homogeneous samples within the polydrug-abusing population by specifying a particular substance of abuse. The LSD, amphetamine, and marijuana studies are examples. Since, however, the drug-taking behavior of the individual is typically complicated with other drugs, drug use patterns may prove beneficial. Frequency of use should be included since MMPI data are apparently sensitive to this variable (cf. Cox & Smart, 1972; Ellingwood, 1967; McGuire & Megargee, 1974).

Finally, a vast majority of MMPI research focuses on mean profiles of substance abusers. The position articulated by Hodo and Fowler (1976) should be taken seriously: several two-point codes of substantial frequency which differ from the mean profile code are noted in these populations. In addition, mean profile analyses of samples defined solely by substance of abuse may obscure patterns of drug use, frequency, chronicity, and motivation for abuse. Certain kinds of two-point codes may also be associated with prognosis or specific treatment success. Needless to say, there is the need for longitudinal MMPI studies with these substance abuse populations.

STUDY SAMPLE

Our analysis of the national polydrug project MMPI data considered for inclusion those polydrug abusers who completed this personality inventory during their initial 10 days of evaluation and treatment and those nonpatient polydrug users whose cooperation was solicited through newspapers and radio spots. These nonpatient study participants were reimbursed for their time; they did not perceive their drug use behavior as problematic and saw no reason to request any assistance.

All available protocols from these two sources were first processed by computer using an automated scoring and interpretation program designed by the senior author; this program is described in detail elsewhere (Lachar, 1974a, 1974b). Inventory responses were transformed into a variety of routine and experimental scale scores as well as a total clinical profile index, or code type, which reflected the pattern of highest clinical scales. Clinical scale raw scores were converted to T-scores using standard K-corrected norms (Hathaway & Briggs, 1957) for subjects 18 years of age and older, and using non-K-corrected age-specific norms for adolescent subjects (Dahlstrom, Welsh, & Dahlstrom, 1972). Adolescent norms were applied since a previous study (Lachar, Klinge, & Griselle, 1976) clearly demonstrated that the inferences drawn from adolescent norm profiles were judged more accurate for adolescents than were those inferences drawn from K-corrected adult norm profiles.

MMPI profiles judged to be technically invalid were excluded from further analysis. Subjects were retained if their obtained profiles included

F scale values under 100*T* and were based on protocols which contained fewer than 30 unanswered inventory items. Subsequent inspection of the ethnic identification of subjects obtaining valid profiles revealed that only 53 (10.4%) were obtained from nonwhite subjects. Since MMPIs of minority subjects may not be comparable to those of whites (Gynther, 1972), a separate parallel analysis had been anticipated for these data. The small number of protocols obtained from minority member subjects, however, severely limited the analysis potential of these data, and these protocols were excluded from all further efforts.

The final study sample contained 454 white subjects which had been evaluated at one of 13 facilities. Patients comprised 62.1% of this sample; the sample of 172 volunteer nonpatients was obtained in the Philadelphia area. Approximately two-thirds ($N = 288$, 63.4%) of this sample was male. Males averaged 23.4 years of age ($SD = 6.1$) and females averaged 25.3 years of age ($SD = 11.2$).

Measures

Each protocol was scored for 32 measures, including 13 standard scales, 13 Wiggins Content Scales, 4 other supplemental scales, profile code-type, and code-type category.

It is not the intent of this chapter to present in-depth didactic material about each measure used. Readers relatively unfamiliar with the MMPI may wish to refer to a general reference such as Carson (1969), Dahlstrom, Welsh, and Dahlstrom (1972), or Lachar (1974b). The 30 scales that were scored are the following:

Standard Profile Scales

L	Denial of common weaknesses, defensiveness
F	Level of pathology, infrequent responses, atypical response sets
K	Subtle defensiveness, effective defenses
1/*Hs*	Somantic concern and complaints
2/*D*	Current mood, depressive symptoms
3/*Hy*	Neurotic defenses, repression and denial, immaturity
4/*Pd*	Acting-out, impulsivity, unmodulated affect, asocial behavior
5/*Mf*	Traditional sex-role interest pattern
6/*Pa*	Interpersonal sensitivity, projection, suspiciousness
7/*Pt*	General discomfort, anxiety, worry, and self-doubt
8/*Sc*	Poor reality testing, social alienation, escape into fantasy

9/*Ma*   Current energy level, restlessness, and irritability
0/*Si*   Social orientation, social skills, social discomfort

Wiggins Content Scales (Wiggins, 1966)

ORG	(Organic symptoms)	Headaches, dizziness, poor concentration
HEA	(Poor health)	Health concerns, gastrointestinal complaints
DEP	(Depression)	Depression, worry
MOR	(Poor morale)	Poor self-confidence, sensitivity
SOC	(Social maladjustment)	Introversion, shyness
HOS	(Manifest hostility)	Hostility, competitiveness
FAM	(Family problems)	Unpleasant home life
AUT	(Authority conflict)	Cynicism, distrust, immorality
FEM	(Feminine interests)	Feminine interest pattern
PHO	(Phobias)	Fearfulness
PSY	(Psychoticism)	Delusions and hallucinations
HYP	(Hypomania)	Excitability, restlessness
REL	(Religious fundamentalism)	Deep religiosity

Supplemental Scales

A (Welsh, 1965)	General emotional upset, tension, inefficiency
R (Welsh, 1965)	Inhibition, reliance on repression and denial
ES (Baron, 1953)	Response to brief psychotherapy, emotional control
AH (MacAndrew, 1965)	Propensity toward substance abuse, probably manifest in current behavior or history

All study profiles were classified into one of 38 code types reflecting highest clinical scales exceeding 69T (see Lachar, 1974a, p. 270) or into one of two profile types if all clinical scales fell below 70T (Lachar, 1974b). In an attempt to reduce these 40 classifications into a smaller number of homogeneous clusters and to allow efficient statistical analysis of code-type frequencies, each code type was also placed within one of five categories that reflected the most probable diagnostic impression associated with each code type: normal limits, neurotic, characterological, psychotic, and unclassified. This classification system is presented in Lachar (1974b) and Lachar *et al*. (1976) and has been used to structure the method of presentation of Table VII.3.

Analysis of Major Sample Dimensions

To determine if any major subject characteristic, aside from drug use variables, was systematically related to MMPI scale variability, an adjusted main effects analysis of variance with subject age, sex, and patient status (patient versus volunteer subject) was conducted for each of the 30 scales. This study sample was divided for this analysis into five age categories: 14–17 ($N = 70$), 18–20 ($N = 106$), 21–24 ($N = 118$), 25–29 ($N = 90$) and > 29 ($N = 70$). The main effects analysis is summarized in Table VII.1. Only 9 of a possible 120 interactions proved significant ($p \leq .05$). As these results may reflect only chance variation, they are cited only when they serve to clarify an obtained significant main effect.

AGE

Although this sample represented quite a restricted range, age was significantly related to 18 MMPI scales. The adjusted age-group means and summary of the post-hoc analysis of those scales obtaining a significant age main effect are presented in Table VII.2. The significantly lower scale values obtained for the 14- to 17-year-old category for scales L, F, 2/D, 4/Pd, 6/Pa, 7/Pt, 8/Sc, 9/Ma, and 0/Si appear to be clearly related to the major effect of applying a different transformation procedure (adolescent norms) to this age group. Although subjects aged 18 to 29 years form a homogeneous grouping on these 30 MMPI variables, differences were clearly indicated on several scales for subjects in the oldest age category (> 29 years). These individuals obtained significantly lower scores on scales F, 6/Pa, 8/Sc, and 9/Ma. Evidence was also obtained for an increase with age in neurotic inhibition (R), defensiveness (K), and depressive symptomatology (2/D). Scale 3/Hy also appears to increase with subject age, although this trend is most clearly manifest among patients (age $\times$ sex $\times$ status, $F (4,434) = 2.57$, $p < .05$). HEA increases with age, but only for females (age $\times$ sex, $F (4,434) = 2.42$, $p < .05$). It also appears that direct admission of psychotic characteristics (PSY), restlessness (HYP), family problems (FAM), authority conflict (AUT), and manifest hostility (HOS) decrease with age, especially within the > 29 years category. The results obtained in the age analysis of the MacAndrew Alcoholism Scale are also of interest, as it suggests that the > 29 years group is different in some way from the remainder of this sample. In summary, the preceding results are consistent with studies of age effects in nondrug abuse samples (Aaronson, 1958; Calden & Hokanson, 1959; Gynther & Shimkunas, 1965).

Table VII.1

ANALYSIS OF MAJOR SUBJECT CHARACTERISTICS' INFLUENCE ON MMPI
SCALE VALUES

Scale	Mean	Main effects		
		Age	Sex	Status
L	47.3	.04	n.s.	n.s.
F	66.1	.001	.05	.001
K	48.8	.04	.04	.001
1/Hs	59.0	n.s.	n.s.	.001
2/D	66.4	.001	.01	.001
3/Hy	62.9	.02	n.s.	.001
4/Pd	71.3	.001	n.s.	.001
5/Mf	—	n.s.	.001	n.s.
6/Pa	63.2	.001	n.s.	.001
7/Pt	64.8	.001	.02	.001
8/Sc	70.3	.001	n.s.	.001
9/Ma	68.2	.001	n.s.	n.s.
0/Si	53.8	.004	.001	.001
ORG	59.4	n.s.	n.s.	.001
HEA	58.1	n.s.	n.s.	.001
DEP	59.3	n.s.	n.s.	.001
MOR	55.4	n.s.	n.s.	.001
SOC	52.3	n.s.	.02	.001
HOS	56.0	.001	n.s.	.003
FAM	66.2	.04	n.s.	.001
AUT	57.1	.02	n.s.	n.s.
FEM	52.2	n.s.	.001	.05
PHO	51.8	n.s.	.006	.001
PSY	61.2	.001	n.s.	.001
HYP	55.9	.005	n.s.	n.s.
RLL	41.8	n.s.	n.s.	.001
A	56.4	n.s.	n.s.	.001
R	47.4	.001	n.s.	n.s.
ES	47.1	n.s.	n.s.	.001
AH	69.6	.001	n.s.	.001

SEX

Except for sex-related differences on the 2 study scales which had been constructed to measure differences in sex-role interest pattern (5/Mf; FEM), only 7 of the remaining 28 scales were found to vary systematically with sex of subject. Male subjects obtained higher scores reflecting greater depression and anxiety [2/D: 67.8T versus 64.0T, $F(1,434) = 6.27$,

Table VII.2

POST-HOC ANALYSIS OF SIGNIFICANT AGE MAIN EFFECTS FOR MMPI SCALES

Scale	$F_{(4,434)}$	p	Mean adjusted age T-scores					Newman–Keuls analysis									
			1 14–17	2 18–20	3 21–24	4 25–29	5 >29	1–2	1–3	1–4	1–5	2–3	2–4	2–5	3–4	3–5	4–5
L	2.61	.03	44.6	47.7	48.1	47.4	47.9	.05	.05	.05	.05	—	—	—	—	—	—
F	6.58	.001	59.3	68.1	68.7	68.2	63.1	.01	.01	.01	—	—	—	.05	—	.05	.05
K	2.52	.04	48.6	47.3	48.3	49.4	51.5	—	—	—	—	—	—	.05	—	—	—
2/D	6.23	.001	59.4	65.2	67.8	67.3	71.7	.05	.01	.01	.01	—	—	.05	—	—	—
3/Hy	2.81	.02	61.0	61.4	62.4	65.3	65.0	—	—	—	—	—	—	—	—	.05	—
4/Pd	7.71	.001	64.5	70.8	74.0	73.4	71.7	.01	.01	.01	.01	—	—	—	—	.05	—
6/Pa	4.87	.001	58.9	64.1	65.8	64.5	60.5	.01	.01	.01	—	—	—	—	—	—	—
7/Pt	7.79	.001	56.9	65.6	67.9	65.4	65.4	.01	.01	.01	.01	—	—	—	—	—	—
8/Sc	13.30	.001	59.0	73.2	74.9	72.3	66.7	.01	.01	.01	.01	—	—	.05	—	.01	.05
9/Ma	11.36	.001	62.2	69.4	71.5	70.8	63.7	.01	.01	.01	—	—	—	.01	—	.01	.01
0/Si	3.94	.004	49.4	55.0	54.9	53.5	55.2	.01	.01	.01	.01	—	—	—	—	—	—
HOS	4.67	.001	57.3	58.8	56.0	54.6	52.2	—	—	—	.01	—	.05	.01	—	.05	—
FAM	2.57	.04	69.6	65.7	66.9	66.0	62.2	—	—	—	.05	—	—	—	—	—	—
AUT	3.03	.02	57.0	58.8	58.3	56.3	53.7	—	—	—	.05	—	—	.01	—	.05	—
PSY	8.98	.001	64.2	62.6	63.0	60.8	53.3	—	—	—	.01	—	—	.01	—	.01	.01
HYP	3.83	.005	56.2	57.2	56.5	56.4	52.2	—	—	—	.01	—	—	.01	—	.01	.01
R	4.88	.001	45.5	45.8	46.8	48.3	51.8	—	—	—	.01	—	—	.01	—	.01	.01
AH	6.37	.001	71.1	71.6	71.5	68.8	62.8	—	—	—	.01	—	—	.01	—	.01	.01

$p < .01$; 7/Pt: 65.9T versus 62.9T, F (1,434) = 5.07, $p < .02$; PHO: 53.7T versus 48.8T, F (1,434) = 7.66, $p < .006$]; 0/Si and SOC obtained inconsistent results, in which female subjects scored significantly higher on the former and male subjects higher on the latter. The statistically significant sex main effect on scales F and K represent minor differences of a quarter of a standard deviation or less.

PATIENT STATUS

Twenty-four MMPI scales significantly separated patients from volunteer subjects. All but two of these main effects were significant at $p < .001$, with patients and volunteers separated by an average of 6.9T. Patients consistently scored in the more deviant direction on those scales which measure symptomatic status. Patients admitted to more somatic concern and specific physical symptoms, which may reflect poor adjustment to self-medication, anxiety correlates, or the defense mechanism of somatization [1/Hs: 62.7T versus 53.0T, F (1,434) = 52.82, $p < .001$; ORG: 63.7T versus 52.5T, F (1,434) = 61.49, $p < .001$; HEA: 60.9T versus 53.6T, F (1,434) = 37.96, $p < .001$]; 1/Hs, in addition, obtained a greater patient status effect for male subjects [sex × status, F (1,434) = 3.74, $p < .05$]. Patients clearly described themselves as experiencing more psychological discomfort than nonpatient volunteers as manifested by depression and pessimism [2/D: 70.9T versus 59.0T, F (1,434) = 61.77, $p < .001$; DEP: 63.2T versus 53.0T, F (1,434) = 60.83, $p < .001$], poor self-image [MOR: 58.2T versus 50.8T, F (1,434) = 40.89, $p < .001$] and anxiety, tension, and rumination [7/Pt: 68.3T versus 59.1T, F (1,434) = 48.79, $p < .001$; PHO: 53.7T versus 48.8T, F (1,434) = 24.63, $p < .001$; A: 59.3T versus 51.6T, F (1,434) = 45.77, $p < .001$]. Patients, in comparison with volunteer subjects, described themselves as more prone to use repression and denial to excess [3/Hy: 65.7T versus 58.3T, F (1,434) = 45.20, $p < .001$], as more likely to experience phenomena associated with poor reality testing [6/Pa: 65.6T versus 59.4T, F (1,434) = 28.2, $p < .001$; 8/Sc: 73.8T versus 64.4T, F (1,434) = 36.70, $p < .001$; PSY: 62.8T versus 58.5T, F (1,434) = 12.64, $p < .001$] and as more likely to evidence poor impulse control and poorly modulated hostility [4/Pd: 74.3T versus 66.5T, F (1,434) = 42.69, $p < .001$; HOS: 57.2T versus 54.1T, F (1,434) = 8.73, $p < .003$; FAM: 68.3T versus 62.6T, F (1,434) = 16.61, $p < .001$]. Patients are more likely to describe themselves as more introverted [0/Si: 55.7T versus 50.7T, F (1,434) = 23.06, $p < .001$; SOC: 54.0T versus 49.3T, F (1,434) = 16.77, $p < .001$], to be seen as generally more disturbed [F: 68.1T versus 62.8T, F (1,434) = 14.67, $p < .001$; ES: 44.1T versus 52.1T, F (1,434) = 51.44, $p < .001$], and obtain higher MacAndrew Alcoholism Scale scores [AH: 72.7T versus

64.4T, F (1,434) = 42.82, p < .001]. Although patients admit to more religious beliefs, this difference is prominent only for female subjects [REL: sex × status, F (1,434) = 4.24, p < .04].

Status differences in sex role interest pattern were only demonstrable for male subjects [5/Mf: sex × status, F (1,434) = 5.82, p < .02; FEM: sex × status, F (1,434) = 5.53, p < .02]. Male volunteers obtained higher scores than male patients (5/Mf: 69.8T versus 66.1T; FEM: 58.3T versus 54.4T), while no significant differences were demonstrated for female subjects (5/Mf: 45.3T versus 46.4T; FEM: 45.4T versus 46.3T). These scales for males are positively related to educational level, since more educated men ascribe to more "traditionally feminine" interests, such as theater and art. In this polydrug sample, scale 5/Mf correlated .30 (p < .001) with years of education for males, but only −.09 (n.s.) with years of education for females. The same relationship was obtained for FEM [males = .15 (p < .01), females = −.09 (n.s.)]. The interpretation of these two scale differences as reflecting an artifact of educational level is supported by the examination of the educational level of male patient and volunteer groups. Male volunteers obtained 1.5 years more education than male patients (12.8 years versus 11.3 years, t = 4.64, df = 283, p < .001).

Code-Type Category

An analysis of code-type category frequency by sex, age, and patient status was conducted using the chi-square statistic for all study profiles except for the few (N = 18) profiles that were placed in the "unclassified" category.

AGE

A significant relation between code-type category and age was obtained [$\chi^2(12)$ = 42.42, p < .001] for the total sample. "Normal" codes were more often obtained by adolescents, "neurotic" codes were more often obtained by the oldest (> 29) subjects, and "psychotic" codes were less often obtained by adolescents and decreased in frequency with age for adult subjects. No differences in frequency of "characterological" codes were obtained across age classifications. Analysis of age effects for "Patient Status by Sex" groupings revealed a significant relation for patients [males: N = 174, $\chi^2(12)$ = 23.03, p < .03; females: N = 97, $\chi^2(12)$ = 30.68, p < .003] but not for volunteers [males: N = 104, $\chi^2(12)$ = 16.14, p > .10; females: N = 61, $\chi^2(12)$ = 12.12, p > .10]. For both patient analyses the results were quite consistent with the results obtained for the total sample. Two exceptions were noted: among males, adolescent as well as the oldest patients tended to have more "neurotic" codes, and female adolescent patients did not obtain less "psychotic" codes as did the male adolescent patients.

SEX

Analysis of code-type category frequency revealed no difference in code-type category distribution between male and female subjects [$\chi^2(3)$ = 3.72, p > .10]. Further analysis of possible sex effects within each "Patient Status by Age" sample also resulted in no significant sex effects.

PATIENT STATUS

As presented in Table VII.3, the pattern obtained in individual scale analysis is clearly mirrored in classification of total profile shape [$\chi^2(3)$ = 35.34, p < .0001]. Volunteers obtained proportionately more profiles without scales in the clinical range (32.6% versus 13.8%); patients, in

Table VII.3

MMPI CODE-TYPE DISTRIBUTION FOR THE TOTAL WHITE POLYDRUG SAMPLE BY SEX AND PATIENT STATUS

| | "Characterological" Codes | | | | | | | |
| | Patient | | | | Nonpatient | | | |
Code[a]	M	F	T	%	M	F	T	%[b]
4 Spike	5	2	7	2.5	9	3	12	7.0**
9 Spike	10	2	12	4.3	18	4	22	12.8***
1-4/4-1	1	1	2	.7	0	1	1	.6
2-4/4-2	16	10	26	9.2	3	1	4	2.3***
3-4/4-3	5	4	9	3.2	0	1	1	.6*
4-6/6-4	4	3	7	2.5	0	2	2	1.2
4-7/7-4	2	0	2	.7	3	1	4	2.3
4-8/8-4	11	5	16	5.7	8	2	10	5.8
4-9/9-4	13	8	21	7.4	10	5	15	8.7
	67	35	102	36.2	51	20	71	41.3

[a] Rules defining code types and code-type groupings are presented in Lachar (1974b), and Lachar *et al.* (1976).

[b] Significance of difference between patient and nonpatient samples.

* $p \leq .10$

** $p \leq .05$

*** $p \leq .01$

Table VII.3 (*continued*)

| | "Neurotic" Codes | | | | | | | |
| | Patient | | | | Nonpatient | | | |
Code[a]	M	F	T	%	M	F	T	%[b]
1 Spike	1	0	1	.4	0	0	0	0.0
2 Spike	6	2	8	2.8	2	0	2	1.2
3 Spike	0	1	1	.4	1	1	2	1.2
7 Spike	1	0	1	.4	0	0	0	0.0
1-2/2-1	4	2	6	2.1	0	0	0	0.0*
1-3/3-1	6	3	9	3.2	0	2	2	1.2
2-3/3-2	4	2	6	2.1	1	1	2	1.2
2-7/7-2	7	4	11	3.9	4	0	4	2.3
2-0/0-2	1	0	1	.4	0	0	0	0.0
	30	14	44	15.7	8	4	12	7.0**

| | "Psychotic" Codes | | | | | | | |
| | Patient | | | | Nonpatient | | | |
Code[a]	M	F	T	%	M	F	T	%[b]
8 Spike	0	1	1	.4	0	0	0	0.0
1-8/8-1	4	2	6	2.1	0	0	0	0.0*
2-8/8-2	19	6	25	8.9	2	2	4	2.3***
3-8/8-3	1	1	2	.7	0	0	0	0.0
6-8/8-6	6	7	13	4.6	1	1	2	1.2**
6-9/9-6	0	3	3	1.1	1	3	4	2.3
7-8/8-7	14	4	18	6.4	5	1	6	3.5
7-9/9-7	0	1	1	.4	0	0	0	0.0
8-9/9-8	10	7	17	6.0	5	5	10	5.8
	54	32	86	30.6	14	12	26	15.1***

[a] Rules defining code types and code-type groupings are presented in Lachar (1974b), and Lachar *et al.* (1976).
[b] Significance of difference between patient and nonpatient samples.
* $p \leq .10$
** $p \leq .05$
*** $p \leq .01$

contrast, obtained more profiles associated with neurotic (15.7% versus 7.0%) and psychotic (30.6% versus 15.1%) diagnoses. No significant difference in frequency was obtained for characterological-code profiles (patients 36.2%; volunteers 41.3%). Analysis of patient–volunteer differences for "Sex by Age" groups revealed no pattern inconsistent with the overall analysis.

Table VII.3 (*continued*)

	"Normal" Codes							
	Patient				Nonpatient			
Code[a]	M	F	T	%	M	F	T	%[b]
Para. 15	17	12	29	10.3	23	13	36	20.9***
Para. 16	6	4	10	3.5	8	12	20	11.6***
	23	16	39	13.8	31	25	56	32.6***

	"Unclassified" Codes							
	Patient				Nonpatient			
Code	M	F	T	%	M	F	T	%[b]
6 Spike	2	1	3	1.1	1	3	4	2.3
0 Spike	0	2	2	.7	0	1	1	.6
1-9/9-1	4	0	4	1.4	0	0	0	0.0
2-6/6-2	1	0	1	.4	0	0	0	0.0
2-9/9-2	0	0	0	0.0	2	0	2	1.2
3-9/9-3	0	1	1	.4	0	0	0	0.0
	7	4	11	3.9	3	4	7	4.1

[a] Rules defining code types and code-type groupings are presented in Lachar (1974a), and Lachar *et al.* (1976).

[b] Significance of difference between patient and nonpatient samples.

* $p \leqslant .10$

** $p \leqslant .05$

*** $p \leqslant .01$

Additional Patient Status Analyses

The importance of patient status was evaluated in three additional analyses. Table VII.4 documents the higher expressed pathology for patient subjects on all but scale 9/*Ma* of the clinical scales. Patients obtained more code types which include scales 1/*Hs* [9.9% versus 1.7%, χ^2 (1) = 10.50, $p < .01$]; 2/*D* [29.8% versus 10.5%, $\chi^2(1) = 17.78$, $p < .001$]; 3/*Hy* [9.9% versus 2.9%, χ^2 (1) = 7.26, $p < .01$], and 8/*Sc* [34.8% versus 18.6%, χ^2 (1) = 10.40, $p < .01$]. Analysis of the relative frequency of individual code types, presented in Table VII.3, indicated that volunteers more often obtained the classifications of 4-spike ($p < .01$), 9-spike, and the two within-normal-limits classifications ($p < .05$). Patients more often obtained code types 3-4/4-3, 1-8/8-1, 1-2/2-1 [$p < .10$]; 6-8/8-6 ($p < .05$); 2-4/4-2 and 2-8/8-2 ($p < .01$).

Table VII.4

PERCENTAGE OF STUDY PATIENTS (N = 282) AND VOLUNTEERS (N = 172)
OBTAINING MMPI PROFILE SCALES WITHIN THREE T-VALUE RANGES

| | T-Value range | | | | | |
| | % less than 70T | | % 70T–79T | | % more than 79T | |
Scale	Patient	Volunteer	Patient	Volunteer	Patient	Volunteer
L	97.9	99.4	2.1	.6	0.0	0.0
F	58.5	70.3	15.2	18.0	26.2	11.6
K	96.5	99.4	3.5	.6	0.0	0.0
1/Hs	66.0	92.4	17.0	4.7	17.0	2.9
2/D	46.8	79.1	22.0	11.6	31.0	9.3
3/Hy	64.2	90.1	19.5	7.0	16.3	2.9
4/Pd	36.2	59.9	29.8	25.6	34.0	14.5
6/Pa	64.5	80.8	22.3	12.8	13.1	6.4
7/Pt	57.1	83.1	22.7	11.0	20.2	5.8
8/Sc	46.1	68.0	20.2	16.3	33.7	15.7
9/Ma	57.4	59.3	22.3	25.6	20.2	15.1
0/Si	88.3	96.5	11.0	3.5	0.7	0.0

All analyses of MMPI data suggest substantial differences between patients and paid volunteers. Patients expressed more responses reflecting psychological discomfort, ineffective defense mechanisms, and deficient internal control and reality testing. Other nonpsychometric variables also support the position that these paid volunteers were drawn from a different population. Aside from the difference in education already noted, volunteers also differed in preferred drug of use. Volunteers more often preferred marijuana [32.3% versus 17.1%, $\chi^2 = 10.31, df = 1, p < .01$] and cocaine [15.9% versus 4.1%, $\chi^2 = 16.55, df = 1, p < .001$] and less often preferred the opiates [3.7% versus 23.0%, $\chi^2 = 24.49, df = 1, p < .001$] and the psychotropics [1.8% versus 9.7%, $\chi^2 = 9.37, df = 1, p < .01$].

The preceding analysis clearly brings into doubt the degree of generalizability that can be assumed about study results of the psychological status of polydrug users when data have been drawn solely from treatment facilities or when the group of users is composed solely of paid volunteers. Certainly, all polydrug users not volunteering for treatment do *not* display the level of psychological disability presented by our polydrug patient sample. On the other hand, the relative stability and character of the volunteer sample may well represent the other extreme of the adjustment continuum in the polydrug population.

It is our contention, therefore, that no estimate of actual incidence of pathology in the total polydrug use population can be derived from this analysis. Rather, the emphases in the remainder of this chapter will be to compare polydrug abusers who seek assistance for this condition with other patient populations, as well as to evaluate the relation between MMPI variables and the number and type of drugs used.

Comparisons with Other Patient Populations

Table VII.5 compares the two-point code type frequency for polydrug patients with the code type frequency for a large, representative sample of psychiatric outpatients ($N = 12,000$) (Webb, 1970) and general medical patients ($N = 50,000$) (Swenson, Pearson, & Osborne, 1973). This presentation clearly demonstrates the dissimilarity between polydrug and gen-

Table VII.5

TWO-POINT CODE-TYPE FREQUENCY FOR POLYDRUG PATIENTS, PSYCHIATRIC OUTPATIENTS, AND GENERAL MEDICAL PATIENTS

Code type	Male			Female		
	Study	Psychiatric	Medical	Study	Psychiatric	Medical
1-2/2-1	2.2	3.8	7.7	2.0	1.7	4.5
1-3/3-1	3.3	3.7	11.2	3.0	5.2	13.0
2-3/3-2	2.2	3.1	2.7	2.0	5.8	3.0
2-7/7-2	3.9	8.6	3.0	4.0	6.4	2.6
2-0/0-2	.6	1.8	2.1	0.0	5.1	2.7
1-8/8-1	2.2	1.3	.5	2.0	.9	.4
2-8/8-2	10.5	6.7	.5	5.9	4.9	.7
3-8/8-3	.6	.5	.1	1.0	1.6	.2
6-8/8-6	3.3	2.0	.2	6.9	3.9	.4
6-9/9-6	0.0	1.0	.3	3.0	1.6	.4
7-8/8-7	7.7	6.9	.7	4.0	4.5	.7
7-9/9-7	0.0	.7	.3	1.0	.6	.2
8-9/9-8	5.5	2.6	.3	6.9	2.4	.4
1-4/4-1	.6	.8	1.2	1.0	.5	.6
2-4/4-2	8.8	6.0	1.3	9.9	7.5	1.3
3-4/4-3	2.8	5.2	1.5	4.0	7.8	1.3
4-6/6-4	2.2	1.7	.5	3.0	5.1	.6
4-7/7-4	1.1	2.7	.4	0.0	2.3	.3
4-8/8-4	6.1	5.2	.4	5.0	8.7	.7
4-9/9-4	7.2	5.8	1.2	7.9	6.7	.8
1-9/9-1	2.2	.7	.8	0.0	.3	.6
2-6/6-2	.6	.7	.5	0.0	1.7	.8
3-9/9-3	0.0	1.3	.6	1.0	1.9	.5

eral medical patients. General medical patients are most characterized by elevations of the neurotic triad (scales 1, 2, and 3), while the polydrug patients are more similar to psychiatric outpatients, who obtain a significant proportion of code types frequently associated with psychotic and characterological diagnoses. Polydrug patients, however, differ from this psychiatric sample in obtaining a smaller proportion of codes 2-7/7-2 and 3-4/4-3 and a greater proportion of codes 2-4/4-2, 4-9/9-4, 2-8/8-2, 8-9/9-8, and 6-8/8-6. That is, they are less likely to display multiple neurotic traits reflecting an internalized conflict or a chronic problem in impulse regulation. Polydrug patients are more likely to manifest depressive symptoms associated with acting-out of impulses (2-4/4-2), as well as stimulation-seeking associated with sociopathic characteristics (4-9/9-4); both of these codes are frequently associated with a history of drug abuse. Codes 2-8/8-2, 6-8/8-6, and 8-9/9-8 are all associated with psychotic diagnoses and suggest a common core of social alienation and a tendency to escape from conflict into fantasy. Depression, oversensitivity to social cues, and agitation are also associated characteristics.

Frequency and Variety of Drug Usage and Personality Characteristics

These polydrug patients currently used, on an average, drugs from 3.0 different categories on at least a weekly basis. (Drug categories are listed in Table VII.6.) Only 16.8% of this sample was currently using drugs from one category and 35.2% was using drugs from more than three different categories each week. Analysis of the relation between frequency of categories of drugs used weekly and personality characteristics clearly suggested that increasing diversity of drug usage was associated with greater admission of pathology on the MMPI. A significant relationship with number of drug categories involved in weekly use was obtained for 10 of the 13 clinical profile scales: F (.25), K (−.12), 4/Pd (.23), 8/Sc (.22), 6/Pa (.20), 9/Ma (.20), 7/Pt (.18), 3/Hy (.17), 2/D (.16), and 1/Hs (.16). A significant relationship with variety of drugs used weekly was obtained for 10 of the 13 Wiggins Content Scales: Dep (.24), FAM (.22), PSY (.21), ORG (.23), HEA (.18), HOS (.16), MOR (.16), HYP (.15), PHO (.12), and AUT (.12). A significant relationship was also obtained for A (.20), AH (.15), and ES (−.16). These data suggest that patients who used more different types of drugs each week were more open in admitting to personal problems (F, K). It is not clear, however, if higher levels of psychological disturbance led to experimentation with a more varied number of drugs, or whether experimentation with a variety of, perhaps

Table VII.6

NUMBER AND PATTERN OF DRUGS USED WEEKLY FOR SEVEN DRUG PREFERENCE GROUPS

Drug preference	N	Mean age	Mean use	Percent of weekly use by drug category						
				Opiates	Barbiturate	Amphetamine	Cocaine	Marijuana	Hallucinogen	Psychotropic
Opiates	62	25.7	3.1	74.2	45.2	16.1	9.7	45.2	1.6	35.5
Barbiturate	61	25.2	2.9	19.7	73.8	14.8	1.6	49.2	11.5	23.0
Amphetamine	38	25.6	3.4	15.8	31.6	86.8	13.2	57.9	13.2	23.7
Cocaine	11	19.9	2.7	0.0	45.5	9.1	54.5	90.9	9.1	0.0
Marijuana	46	22.1	2.6	8.7	21.7	17.4	2.2	65.2	8.7	4.3
Hallucinogen	25	18.9	3.1	12.0	25.0	28.0	8.0	84.0	56.0	12.0
Psychotropic	26	31.4	3.0	23.1	38.5	11.5	3.8	19.2	3.8	80.8

incompatible and symptom-inappropriate, substances led to an increasing number of side effects and continuation of psychological disturbance. The relation between drug usage and the historical items on the Family Problems Scale would support the former, while this relationship with scales reflecting somatic complaints (1/Hs, ORG, HEA) would support the latter interpretation.

The relationship between code-type category and variety of drugs used weekly support the positive relationship between pathology expressed and number of drugs used. Patients obtaining normal-limits profiles used drugs from an average of 2.39 different categories each week (15.1% used drugs from more than three categories weekly), while patients obtaining psychotic profiles used drugs from an average of 3.43 categories each week (44.9% used drugs from more than three categories weekly). Patients obtaining neurotic (M = 2.60 drugs, 23.4% > 3 drugs) and characterological profiles (M = 3.01 drugs, 36.3% > 3 drugs) obtained intermediate levels of variety of drug usage.

Drug Preference and Personality Characteristics

Polydrug patients were separated into seven independent samples by major category of preferred drug to explore the relationship between personality characteristics and drug use pattern. Table VII.6 presents some of the characteristics of each of these seven drug preference groups. The majority (95.4%) of the patient sample was classified by this system. Drug preference had been selected because it did not reflect fluctuating factors such as current cost and supply of each drug and it facilitated selection of independent samples, whose construction would have otherwise necessitated a more complex analysis of drug use pattern data.

Drug preference was clearly related to the pattern of actual current weekly use. Patients who preferred opiates (heroin, methadone, other opiates, and synthetics) predominantly (74.2%) used opiates, although half of this group also used barbiturates and marijuana, and 35.5% used psychotropics. Patients who preferred the barbiturates (and other sedatives) also used them weekly (73.8%), while half of this group also used marijuana. Patients who preferred amphetamines used amphetamines each week (86.8%) as well as marijuana (57.9%) and barbiturates (31.6%). Patients who preferred cocaine used, on a weekly basis, marijuana more often (90.9%) and barbiturates about as much (45.5%) as they did cocaine (54.5%). This disparity between preference and actual use may relate to the relative cost and supply of this drug. The patients who preferred marijuana (hashish, THC) used drugs from the least number of drug categories and expressed predominant weekly use in only one drug category, marijuana (65.2%). Patients who preferred hallucinogens used marijuana weekly (84.0%), while half of these patients (56.0%) took hallucinogens on a weekly basis. Patients who preferred the psychotropics (antidepressants, tranquilizers, and antipsychotics) used them on a weekly basis (80.8%) and often used barbiturates (38.5%).

Inventory Scales

Because the drug preference groups clearly differed in mean age, and previous analysis indicated that several scales systematically related to patient age, analysis of possible differences in scale values between preference groups was computed using inventory scale values adjusted for this age relationship (one-way ANOVA, age as covariate). Table VII.7 presents the results of this analysis for 29 scales (scale 5/Mf was omitted because of its different scoring and interpretation for males and females). Fifteen of the MMPI scales were found to vary with drug preference group placement. Post-hoc analysis (Newman–Keuls procedure; Winer, 1962) as the primary statistic, Duncan Multiple Range test (Edwards, 1960) added as a secondary, more liberal, analysis (since the former statistic yielded no significant comparisons for scales 4/Pd and 0/Si) clearly defined differences, as well as similarities, between these groups. Table VII.7 excludes those group comparisons that did not obtain any significant scale differences. The youngest groups with preferences for cocaine, marijuana, and hallucinogen, did not differ from each other on any of 29 scales, and form a homogeneous cluster. Two other homogeneous clusters were formed by the combination of preference groups (1) opiate, barbiturate, and amphetamine and (2) opiate, barbiturate, marijuana, and hallucinogen.

Patients who preferred psychotropic medications clearly described themselves in more deviant terms than all other preference groups, giving the impression that this group consisted of self-medicating psychiatric patients. Psychotropic patients admitted to more somatic concern and complaints (1/Hs, 3/Hy, ORG, HEA), evidenced less effective ego defenses (ES), displayed more dysphoria and a more negative self-concept (2/D, DEP, MOR), obtained more evidence of anxiety (7/Pt, A), social withdrawal (0/Si), and social alienation–defective reality testing (8/Sc). Patients who preferred psychotropic drugs differed from the cocaine–marijuana–hallucinogen cluster on all 15 of the significant scales.

Patients who preferred amphetamines obtained more deviant scale values than patients in the cocaine–marijuana–hallucinogen cluster. Depression (2/D, DEP), anxiety (7/Pt, A), social withdrawal (0/Si), and neurotic defenses of repression and denial (3/Hy) appear to be differ-

Table VII.7

ANALYSIS OF AGE-ADJUSTED SCALE VALUES FOR SEVEN PATIENT DRUG PREFERENCE GROUPS

Scale	F (6,261)	P	Adjusted preference-group mean scores						
			Opiate (1)	Barbiturate (2)	Amphetamine (3)	Cocaine (4)	Marijuana (5)	Hallucinogen (6)	Psychotropic (7)
F	2.86	.01	67.0	70.1	70.0	59.4	63.6	63.0	74.0
1/Hs	4.20	.001	64.0	62.8	65.6	53.0	58.2	57.3	73.4
2/D	3.60	.002	73.7	72.4	74.5	64.7	63.7	66.0	79.8
3/Hy	4.35	.001	66.8	64.9	70.5	60.9	60.8	62.2	72.2
4/Pd	2.89	.01	76.0	76.2	75.8	69.9	69.1	69.7	78.2
6/Pa	2.88	.01	66.5	65.0	66.7	61.2	61.0	63.0	72.6
7/Pt	4.08	.001	67.7	69.5	72.0	62.5	63.2	63.3	78.8
8/Sc	3.56	.002	72.5	75.1	76.4	67.0	66.5	69.1	85.3
0/Si	2.59	.02	54.6	56.3	60.1	51.9	53.4	52.1	60.4
ORG	3.75	.001	61.7	65.4	66.3	54.9	58.4	60.8	74.1
HEA	5.19	.001	61.8	59.2	62.4	53.9	57.2	57.1	72.5
DEP	5.19	.001	64.0	65.3	66.8	56.2	57.3	58.1	73.0
MOR	2.74	.01	58.4	58.3	60.2	56.5	54.3	55.3	65.7
A	3.01	.007	59.2	60.1	62.2	57.7	55.3	56.2	66.4
ES	3.60	.002	45.0	42.4	42.9	50.6	48.0	46.2	35.9

Post-hoc analysis[a]

Scale	1-4	1-5	1-7	2-4	2-5	2-6	2-7	3-4	3-5	3-6	3-7	4-7	5-7	6-7
F	—	—	—	.05*	—	—	—	.05*	—	—	—	.01	.05	.05
1/Hs	.05	—	.05	.05*	—	—	.05	.05	—	—	.05	.01	.01	.01
2/D	—	.05*	—	—	—	—	—	.05*	.05*	—	—	.01	.01	.05
3/Hy	—	—	—	—	—	—	.05*	.05	.05	.05	—	.01	.01	.01
4/Pd	—	—	—	—	—	—	.05*	—	—	—	—	.05*	.05*	.05*
6/Pa	—	—	.05	—	—	—	.05*	.05	.05*	.05*	—	.01	.01	.05
7/Pt	—	—	.05	—	—	—	.05*	—	.05*	.05*	—	.01	.01	.01
8/Sc	—	—	.05	—	—	—	.05*	.05*	.05*	—	—	.05*	.05*	.05*
0/Si	—	—	—	.05*	—	—	.05*	.05*	.05*	.05*	—	.05*	.05*	.05*
ORG	—	—	.05	.05*	—	—	.05*	.05*	—	—	—	.01	.01	.01
HEA	.05*	—	.01	—	—	—	.01	.05*	—	—	.01	.01	.01	.01
DEP	.05*	—	.05	.05*	.05*	.05*	.05*	.05	.05*	.05*	—	.01	.01	.01
MOR	—	—	.05*	—	—	—	.05*	—	—	—	—	.05	.01	.01
A	—	—	.05*	—	—	—	.05*	—	.05*	—	—	.05	.01	.05
ES	—	—	.05	.05*	—	—	.05	.05*	—	—	.05	.01	.01	.01

[a] Each group comparison made using Newman–Keuls procedure, except for those marked with * which indicates significance of Duncan Range Test (Newman–Keuls, n.s.)

entiating characteristics. Patients who preferred barbiturates described themselves as more depressed (DEP) than patients who stated a preference for cocaine, marijuana, or hallucinogens. Patients who expressed a preference for opiates differed in some degree, excluding the psychotropic category, with only the cocaine group expressing more physical concern and symptomatology (1/Hs, HEA) and depression (DEP).

Three clusters emerge from this analysis. One cluster consists of patients who prefer psychotropic drugs and present sufficient symptomatology to warrant their prescription. A second cluster consists of opiate, barbiturate, and amphetamine groups. In this cluster organic complaints, depression, and social alienation–escape into fantasy appear to be the most salient features. The third cluster consists of nonphysiologically addictive substances: marijuana, hallucinogens, and cocaine. The patients in these groups describe themselves in the most benign terms, receiving borderline mean elevations only on scales 4/Pd, 8/Sc, and 9/Ma, suggesting a mild characterological adjustment. This third drug preference cluster was predominant in the volunteer sample, which also added support for the impression of a relatively mild level of psychological disturbance.

Code-Type Category

The distribution of code-type category frequencies across preference groups presented in Table VII.8 is consistent with the previous individual scale analysis. Normal limits [X^2 (6) = 14.76, $p < .05$] and neurotic code [X^2 (6) = 13.07, $p < .05$] profiles were not uniformly distributed. Also, patients who preferred opiates [X^2 (3) = 8.75, $p < .05$] and psychotropic drugs [X^2 (3) = 12.50, $p < .01$] differed significantly from the code-type category distribution for the total sample. Patients who preferred opiates obtained fewer normal and more characterological code profiles; patients who preferred barbiturates obtained fewer neurotic codes. Patients indicating a preference for cocaine, marijuana, or hallucinogens obtained more normal limits profiles than expected. Patients who preferred psychotropic drugs differed the most from the remainder of the polydrug patient sample: this patient group obtained more neurotic code and fewer normal and characterological profiles than expected.

DISCUSSION

The analyses presented in this chapter clearly support the hypothesis that the polydrug use population is not homogeneous in terms of ob-

Table VII.8

CODE-TYPE CATEGORY FREQUENCIES OBTAINED AND EXPECTED FOR SEVEN
POLYDRUG PATIENT DRUG PREFERENCE GROUPS

	Code-type category							
	Normal		Neurotic		Psychotic		Characterological	
Drug preference	O/E	(χ^2)	O/E	(χ^2)	O/E	(χ^2)	O/E	(χ^2)
Opiate	2/7.9	(4.41)	11/8.8	(.55)	14/18.2	(.97)	30/22.1	(2.82)
Barbiturate	9/8.4	(.04)	5/9.4	(2.06)	21/19.5	(.12)	26/23.7	(.22)
Amphetamine	4/5.2	(.28)	6/5.9	(.00)	15/12.1	(.70)	13/14.7	(.20)
Cocaine	3/1.5	(1.50)	1/1.7	(.29)	4/3.5	(.07)	3/4.3	(.39)
Marijuana	11/5.8	(4.66)	4/6.5	(.96)	13/13.4	(.01)	14/16.3	(.32)
Hallucinogen	6/3.4	(1.99)	3/3.9	(.21)	7/8.0	(.13)	9/9.7	(.32)
Psychotropic	1/3.6	(1.88)	10/4.0	(9.00)	9/8.3	(.06)	6/10.1	(1.66)
Total	36	(13.8%)	40	(15.4%)	83	(31.9%)	101	(38.8%)

tained self-description on instruments such as the MMPI. Studies that combine paid subjects with self-identified patients, minor tranquilizer addicts, and chronic LSD users, etc., may well obscure the relationships that exist between personality traits and motivation for treatment, history, and pattern of drug use.

Polydrug users who seek assistance in modifying their drug use pattern describe themselves as more uncomfortable, impulsive, worried, and withdrawn compared to polydrug users who did not wish to change their drug use pattern. Polydrug users who become self-identified patients apparently are less able to tolerate the drugs they employ, experience undesirable psychological and somatic effects, and maintain a life-style with less environmental supports. Narcotic addicts who volunteered for treatment presented more pathology on the MMPI than did narcotic addicts who did not volunteer for treatment (Gendreau & Gendreau, 1973). Chronic LSD users who did not present themselves for treatment described themselves as much more symptom-free, although in characterological terms, compared to LSD users treated as a result of bad drug experiences (Ungerleider, Fisher, Fuller, & Caldwell, 1968). The percentage of clinical scales > 70T obtained by Christie and Caldwell (1974) in a volunteer participant marijuana–polydrug sample closely parallels that obtained by our volunteer sample, as presented in Table VII.4. Zuckerman et al.'s (1975) study of treatment effects for both narcotic and polydrug abusers indicated that most of the MMPI clinical scales decreased after treatment in a therapeutic community, resulting in a 4-9/9-4 configuration in 63% of the subjects. Similar changes in profile pattern following treatment have also been documented for alcoholics (Lanyon, Primo, Terrell, & Wenar, 1972; Rohan, 1972; Rohan, Tatro, & Rotman, 1969; Vega, 1971).

A clear relationship exists within this patient sample between expressed psychopathology and number of different types of drugs used on a regular basis. This finding is even more notable when one considers that all patients had a history of polydrug use and therefore represented a restricted range of potential frequency of drug categories. Those patients who use the largest variety of drugs described themselves in the most pathological terms. Perhaps these patients' problems are such that the use of one class of drugs does not result in the desired change in psychological state. On the other hand, increased undesirable side effects and drug interactions are expected as the number of drug types used is increased. As Tables VII.6 and VII.7 suggest, expressed psychopathology and variety of drug use increase with patient age in this sample.

The analysis presented in Table VII.7 clearly supports the need for further attempts at definition of homogeneous subclusters within the polydrug population. Drug preference and drug use pattern clearly result in patient groups that differ on MMPI variables. There is some literature support for the results obtained in that marijuana-only users have presented relatively healthy self-descriptions in comparison with users of marijuana plus other drugs (Harmatz, Shader, & Saltzman, 1972; McAree *et al.*, 1969, 1972).

A brief look at the relation between drug preference and source of treatment referral in our patient sample assists in the clarification of both MMPI results and drug use motivation. The patients who described themselves in the most benign terms on the MMPI (hallucinogen–marijuana–cocaine) were most likely to have been referred by a friend or relative, or by the criminal justice system as an alternative to incarceration. The patients who described themselves as the most pathological, in contrast, were more likely referred by mental health facilities or by telephone hot lines or crisis centers.

Table VII.5 graphically displays the similarities between polydrug patients and psychiatric patients. The differences obtained between the polydrug patient sample and a large representative psychiatric sample (Webb, 1970) reveal the expected relative differences in frequencies of characteristic code types. Polydrug abusers frequently display a core personality characterized by insufficient internal control and social alienation. The literature presents support for the similarity between polydrug patients and psychiatric patients as well as an indication of relatively greater psychopathology in the former (Burke & Eichberg, 1972; Schoolar *et al.*, 1972).

Wesson, Smith, and Lerner (1975) in their discussion of a typology of polydrug patients, related their impression of the need for differential treatment of polydrug patient subgroups. Our data also suggest the need for such treatment. Patients placed within the cocaine–marijuana–hallucinogen cluster demonstrate relatively little psychological discomfort and may well be primarily motivated toward drug use to expand self-stimulation experiences. Patients who obtain essentially symptom-free profiles, although experiencing their drug use as problematic, should be readily amenable to behavioral and group approaches to habit change. Patients, such as those found in the psychotropics cluster, who evidence high levels of psychological discomfort and alienation following detoxification must, however, be viewed in a different manner. It seems very likely that polydrug use for these individuals represents an essentially unsuccessful attempt at self-medication. An approach which is most likely to be successful for these patients would include modification (versus termination) of drugs taken and symptom-specific clinical supports.

It is important to avoid a tendency to attribute all significant pathology demonstrated on the MMPI profile directly to drug effects: reflection of drug-related experiences or the effects of withdrawal, nontherapeutic drug levels, or undesirable drug interactions. A delay in inventory administration until detoxification and relative stabilization has been accomplished, and perhaps, retesting will clarify the degree to which currently demonstrated problems are autonomous from drug use. It is possible that indices of depression, tension, social withdrawal, and alienation, and perhaps defective reality testing were present before, and contributed to, drug use patterns.

The Zuckerman *et al*. (1975) study represents a first attempt at studying the important issues of effectiveness of treatment and the use of the MMPI and documents that this inventory can predict the success of specific treatment approaches. Additional effort in identifying subclusters of polydrug abusers and comparing their relative success in various treatment approaches will advance the development of a truly effective treatment program.

PART 2

Epidemiology

One of the early goals of the polydrug projects was to develop information that would allow conclusions to be made regarding the incidence and/or prevalence of nonopiate abuse. This type of extrapolation about particular drug problems allows for more informed policy decisions and resource allocation; and, as such, it represents a major NIDA activity.

Although there is an abundance of numerical data that bear on the nonopiate problem (i.e., survey, DAWN, CODAP, and state and local data), all samples have important sampling limitations, structural or procedural weaknesses, and restrictions on their generalizability. This does not mean that these data are not useful, but the limits on their nature in assessing national trends must be kept in mind.

In all data banks of this nature, there is a "trade-off" between precision and cost. At some points, cost per data element would exceed the utility of the information gained. So although it may be possible to construct a scientifically perfect data base, the price would probably leave little resource left over to implement the conclusions.

These chapters portray two approaches to the nonopiate incidence–prevalence problem. Dr. Leon Hunt was asked to examine the polydrug data and offer his conclusions. His report, which focuses on incidence, is the first chapter of this section. Using distinctive methods to examine the "temporal spread" of drug abuse over several drug categories, Dr. Hunt examines data from a number of cities in the United States. In an attempt to develop a model which will allow reliable estimations of abuse trends, he compares his findings with known factors in a very thorough and careful way. The actual process by which he reasons in this first chapter, is as important as the content conclusions regarding nonopiate incidence.

Using a different tack, John Lau and Dr. John Benvenuto (the former Polydrug Project officer at NIDA), consider both incidence and prevalence questions in the second paper. Using data from highly disparate sources, they attempt to predict the number of polydrug users in the United States. Their use of Bayesian methods on such data is interesting and stretches the data from their various sources to the logical limits. While emphasizing the imprecision of such an approach, the authors point to the potential power of their method if more precise and comparable data in this area could be subjected to a more thorough analysis.

A final point deserves emphasis. The authors, editors, and their consultants all had some reservations concerning the validity of the underlying assumptions in certain aspects of these methods. They are not intended to be examples of flawless methods. However, we all felt strongly that these methods deserve exposition and consideration. In the absence of a definitive and continuing polydrug research effort, these data represent the best national estimates available.

CHAPTER VIII

Incidence of First Use of Nonopiate Drugs: Inferences from Current Data

Leon Gibson Hunt

Misuse of psychotropic drugs has become increasingly common in the United States during the last decade, so much so that conventional wisdom now assumes drug abuse to be a universal problem. Its universality is true only in the aggregate: *some* drug is misused by every important part of the general population, but when the patterns and extent of use of a particular drug are examined, they are found to be highly specific. A given drug often becomes popular in a certain population group in a restricted locale at a definite time. It may spread to other related groups in other places, perhaps following a distinct sequence and a predictable course, or it may appear in several places simultaneously. But in either case, no psychotropic drug has yet achieved the ubiquity of alcohol or tobacco.

This specificity of time and place suggests that it is misleading to conceptualize drug abuse as a homogeneous phenomenon at the national level, or even within large cities. Just as it is meaningless to speak of "the heroin problem," since heroin use is a local phenomenon varying in extent and intensity in different places at different times (Hunt, 1974a), it

183

Polydrug Abuse:
The Results of a
National Collaborative Study

is useless to try to deal with "the amphetamine" or "methaqualone" problems. Abuse of nonopiate drugs involves heterogeneous populations using the drugs in a variety of use patterns. What is more useful is to try to trace the spread of individual drugs in particular populations, to define when, where, and among whom a given substance begins to be abused. Thus, we are concerned with observing *changes* in patterns of use, since without an understanding of emerging differences in pattern of use, no program of prevention, treatment, or even suppression through law enforcement can be sufficiently focused to have much impact on the misuse of an individual substance.

Spreading use of a drug in a given population is best described by incidence of first use, the number (either total or per thousand of population) of individuals who first use a particular drug during a given period of time. For example, 10 new cases of cocaine use per 1000 of population in Washington, D.C., during 1975 is a measure of the population rate of incidence of new cocaine use at a given place and time. Incidence of first use is an explicit measure of the spread of use of a drug because it is a record of the rate at which *new* individuals are becoming involved with the drug.

This usage of incidence differs from the one commonly encountered in drug abuse literature as in "incidence and prevalence surveys." Typically "incidence" has been used to refer to *incidents* or episodes of drug use, whether or not they were the user's first encounter with the substance. Such a usage is very close to the definition of active prevalence, because it measures the number of individuals using a drug within some past interval of time, such as the last month or year.

The confusion results from applying terminology originally developed for acute infectious diseases to a continuing condition such as drug use, which may be chronic but is nearly always sporadic. When a person contracts influenza, his case contributes to an incidence count that is measuring the short-term spread of the disease. But each time a drug user begins an episode of drug taking (however it be defined), the event may not express the spreading of that drug because it usually only represents reemergence of a habit which had become inactive. For example, when heroin is in short supply, addicts typically substitute hydromorphone (Dilaudid) or some other synthetic opiate, or they may switch to another class of drug such as sedative–hypnotic and remain inactive (as heroin users) until heroin is once more available. Their resumption of heroin use does not indicate the spread of the drug, but only reactivation of the market. Because of this ambiguity, we shall restrict the following discussion to incidence of *first* use, and attempt to employ it as a tool in analyzing the diffusion of drug use among different subpopulations.

SAMPLING PROBLEMS: THE SELECTIVITY
OF INCIDENCE DATA

Samples of data on drug users that contain information on first use are always biased since they are seldom either random or probability samples (in the statistical sense of equal or known probability of an individual's inclusion). The data upon which incidence is measured usually come from drug treatment programs, criminal justice referral systems (such as the Treatment Alternatives to Street Crime), mental hospitals or mental health centers, or from special population surveys. All such samples are nonrandom and unrepresentative of the general population. For instance, the location of a drug treatment program in a suburb biases its intake against inner city drug users and in favor of suburban users. Drug-free treatment may fail to attract committed addicts. Data from the criminal justice system do not describe users unless they have been arrested.

Such selectivity is both a handicap and an advantage. While preventing us from drawing any conclusions about the general population's pattern of incidence, it documents that spread of use is often quite different among different groups. Clearly we cannot project data obtained on selected populations to the general population, or even to a comparable population in a different geographic locale; however, we can specify how new drug use is spreading within certain small populations.

In subsequent parts of this chapter, we shall be dealing with such selective samples of first-use data. It is important to remember that, although they are true records of incidence of first use for some populations, the particular group is never very specifically defined in the general population. Indeed the definition is always operational, such as incidence of first use for clients of a particular drug treatment program, whoever they may be.

INTERPRETATION OF INCIDENCE DATA:
ITS RELATIONSHIP TO DRUG ABUSE

Incidence of first-use data are often plotted on a graph showing the number of new cases occurring in each year. Such curves may exhibit sharp peaks, periods during which the number of new cases of use increases rapidly. These peaks have been called epidemics by some investigators (Hughes, Crawford, & Jaffe, 1971) and artifacts of the data by others (Richman & Abbey, 1976).

There is a large and ingenious literature devoted to manufacturing false epidemics from constant incidence by employing peculiar and restrictive mathematical assumptions. These include:

1. Random clustering of year of first use among users who have forgotten when they started and guess in response to first-use queries.
2. Artificial peaks resulting from the opening of new treatment programs which select some onset cohorts and exclude others.
3. Selective admission of young recent new users all of whom exhibit recent onset of use.

Although it is possible to create "pseudoepidemics" by such perverse sampling, no serious researcher disputes that rapid outbreaks of new drug use actually do occur, and in some instances, the outbreaks are corroborated by strong empirical evidence. For example, independent samples of incidence data from the same population may all show similar peaks, even though their biases are completely different (Hunt, 1977). Various mathematical tests have also been devised and applied to incidence data to account for biasing effects. They too demonstrate that use has spread more rapidly during certain periods (Hunt, 1977).

The more interesting question is what first-use incidence tells us about spread of new drug use within a population. Peaks in new use resulting from *contagious transmission*, the spontaneous spreading of a new drug by nonmedical means among groups of closely associated susceptibles, have been documented (Hunt, 1973). While peaks are indicative of abuse with illicit drugs such as heroin, peaks may or may not represent misuse of licit psychotropic drugs. The epidemic character of an incidence curve for illicit drugs is therefore empirical evidence of both illegal supply and inappropriate introduction to use of the substance. Peaks with licitly available drugs may represent either widespread prescriptive use, or illicit supply and nonmedical use.

Such a quantifiable parameter is valuable because the concept of "drug abuse" is imprecise. Overdose and dependence are generally viewed as hallmarks of an abused drug, because they are among the most serious and dramatic consequences. They are not, however, good measures of the extent of abuse. Overdose occurs in less than 20% of all nonmedical users during a year and is unevenly distributed among durgs (Hunt, 1977). Overdoses which present for treatment depend mainly on the toxic properties of a substance. For example, opiates and cocaine cause widely differing rates of overdose. Opiates have typically ranked second after diazepam in DAWN reports, while cocaine is twentieth or lower (Drug Enforcement Administration, 1975).

Another measure of a drug's potential for abuse is its commonness of use or popularity in a population of known abusers, such as dysfunctional abusers in treatment (Hunt & Chamber, 1976). We shall see that commonness of use is closely related to contagious spread, so that drugs which display epidemic incidence of first-use patterns are also those which are most often used by abusers in treatment. They are, however, not necessarily the most physically addictive substances or those most subject to overdose.

EMPIRICAL FIRST-USE DATA FROM TREATMENT PROGRAMS

Incidence analysis has been primarily a tool for drug abuse workers—treatment and prevention program planners and administrators—since it shows where, when, and among whom the use of any given drug may be spreading (Hunt, 1974b). Beyond these practical applications, it has a more general scientific interest as incidence analysis can provide partial empirical evidence to some questions about drug use:

1. Is there empirical evidence that some psychotropic drugs are misused more than others?
2. Have other psychotropic drugs besides heroin spread geographically from coastal high population density centers to isolated, less dense interior locales?
3. Are there distinctive demography-dependent patterns in onset of drug use?
4. Is there a typical progression of use from one type of drug to another?

Answers to all these questions are tentative at best. Samples of drug users are generally limited in size and geographical extent and they are generally restricted to treatment populations. As a result, the samples are subject to the various biases previously discussed.

Data used in the analyses of these questions come mainly from two sources: the National Institute on Drug Abuse Polydrug Projects, and the Drug Enforcement Administration's (DEA) treatment sample taken July–September 1975 (Hunt & Chambers, 1976a). Each has special and differing characteristics.

The Polydrug Project (PD) sample used in this analysis consists of the 800 patients whose characteristics are described throughout this book. The DEA sample, in contrast, represents interviews with 935 clients from various drug treatment programs in nine cities (Miami; Greensboro, N.C.; Washington, D.C.; Atlantic City; Kansas City, Missouri; Des Moines; Phoenix; and San Francisco). Of these clients 80% described themselves as primarily heroin users at the time of interview (summer, 1975) although virtually all had used other psychotropic drugs; 77% are male. Age distributions vary greatly from program to program. Thus, the samples encompass groups with currently different drug use behaviors, nonheroin versus heroin. This contrast will prove valuable in studying some of the questions posed at the beginning of this section.

Both samples contain a "current client" bias, the Polydrug Project samples because its clinics were newly instituted specifically for its purposes, and the DEA sample because it was limited to currently active clients. The effects of this currency bias on historical incidence patterns is uncertain. However, it probably underrepresents older onset groups since many of these users have died, emigrated, stopped using drugs, or already have been treated. The bias is stronger with earlier cohorts, and it is believed to be negligible for recent onset years (Hunt & Chambers, 1976a).

WHICH DRUGS ARE MOST ABUSED?

Since nearly everyone uses psychotropic substances at some time, the typical survey results showing percentage "ever used" is scarcely relevant to the question of abuse, nor is current use, or even frequent use, unless it is specifically nonmedical.

One way (employed by the DEA interview sample) of defining misuse is to ask a user which substances he has used frequently, under nonmedical circumstances, over a prolonged interval. This approach equates frequent nonmedical use with misuse.

Alternatively, incidence analysis, as interpreted in the preceding discussion, provides neutral empirical evidence of misuse if it reveals patterns of contagious transmission.

Comparing these two criteria of misuse in the DEA sample yields the results shown in Table VIII.1.

Here the most commonly misused drugs are also those which most often exhibit incidence of first-use patterns which have a contagious appearance (examples of incidence data for cocaine, methaqualone, and amphetamines are given in Figures VIII.1, VIII.2, and VIII.3).

The consistency of these DEA study results is further corroborated by users' data on their source of the drug at first use (Table VIII.2).

Again, the drugs most often misused—cocaine, methaqualone, phencyclidine, amphetamines—according to the other criteria—are lowest in legitimate medical sources here. Only propoxyphene (Darvon com-

Table VIII.1

COMPARISON OF TWO ESTIMATES OF DRUG MISUSE

Drug[a]	Percentage of total sample reporting nonmedical use of drug (N = 926 users)		Frequency of contagious spread (N = 16 subpopulations)[b]	
	%	Rank	%	Rank
Cocaine	80	1	88	1
Methaqualone	46	3	63	2
Amphetamines	62	2	50	3
Phencyclidine	34	6	50	3
Propoxyphene	38	5	38	4
Hydromorphone	40	4	25	5

[a] Barbiturates and marijuana were not included in this study. Methaqualone data may approximate the frequency of misuse of barbiturates but not their onset pattern.

[b] Subgroups of treatment populations who display different onset histories for one or more drugs.

pounds) and hydromorphone (Dilaudid) show any significant medical sources. Since these users are primarily heroin addicts and both drugs are well-known heroin substitutes, such use may reflect addicts' attempts to allay withdrawal or to detoxify themselves in periods of heroin shortage.

The utility of incidence analysis is clear from these comparisons. Contagious incidence patterns are consistent with other indications of abuse as commonness of self-admitted misuse and illicit source. The latter are difficult and expensive to obtain, except through detailed interviews by skilled subculture workers, while incidences of first-use data are routinely available from standard treatment records. Incidence analysis therefore provides a less expensive and perhaps a more objective approach to studying the emergence of problem drugs.

The Polydrug Project sample is quite different from DEA data. Apart from the demographic and drug preference differences mentioned previously, some Polydrug Project use data are collapsed into broad drug classes. Methaqualone for example is classified as a barbiturate-sedative. The effect of this categorization on incidence of first use is interesting in itself. Since a particular form of a drug tends to be transmitted separately, date of first use for a class (such as barbiturates–sedatives) may represent first use of *different* drugs. Since all members of a class are not available at the same time, the result is to create irregularities in the incidence sequence, local peaks which may represent entirely different drugs. Compare, for example, heroin incidence and barbiturate incidence from Den-

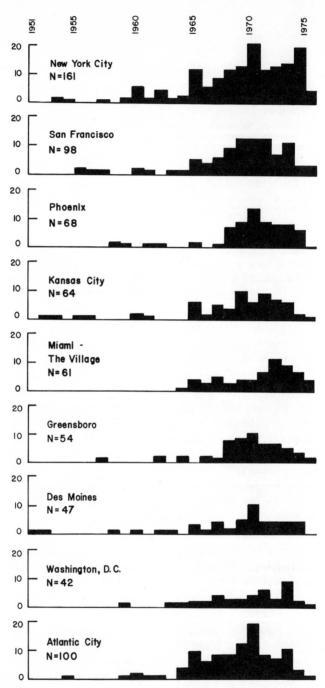

Figure VIII.1. Incidence of first use of cocaine (DEA sample, data through September 1975). Only cities where the sample size was greater than 30 are included.

190

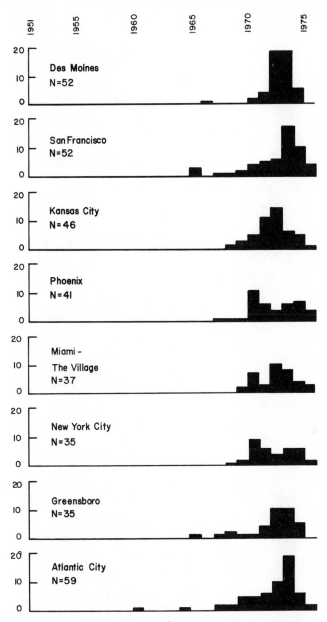

Figure VIII.2. Incidence of first use of methaqualone (DEA sample, data through September 1975).

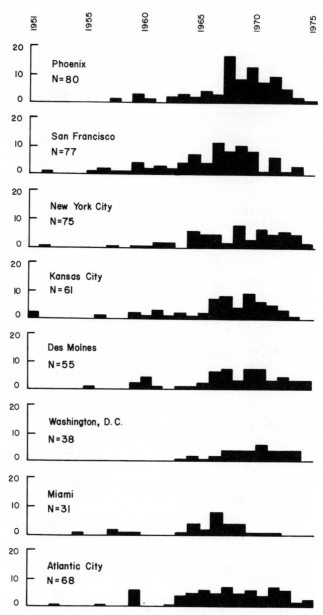

Figure VIII.3. Incidence of first use of amphetamines (DEA sample, data through September 1975).

Table VIII.2

USERS' DATA ON SOURCE OF DRUG AT FIRST USE

Drug	Source (%); N = 926			
	Friends, peers	Medical source	Drug dealers	Other sources
Cocaine	66	—	30	4
Methaqualone	57	10	30	5
Amphetamine	63	9	23	5
Phencyclidine	75	1	17	7
Propoxyphene	48	21	19	21
Hydromorphone	47	20	23	10

ver (Figure VIII.4). While there certainly has been rapid growth of barbiturate use during 1970–1973, it is not nearly as clear as the sharp heroin peak in 1970–1971, although the heroin sample is much smaller (see also psychotropics, Figure VIII.8).

Frequency of misuse of the various drugs in the Polydrug Project sample is somewhat different from the DEA data (Table VIII.3).

The differences are not, however, as great as they may seem. If marijuana is eliminated (it was not included in the DEA sample), and if barbiturates–sedatives in the Polydrug Project sample are equated to methaqualone in the DEA sample, then the only significant difference is the rank of cocaine, here reported used by only 28% of the sample. This contrast is striking. The DEA sample consists of about 80% self-described heroin abusers and 80% of the sample report using cocaine. In the Polydrug sample, 13% prefer heroin and 11% methadone or other opiates, and 28% mention cocaine use. The coincidences of use of opiates

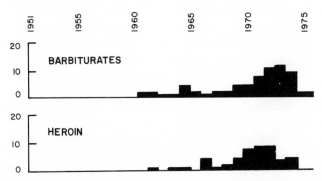

Figure VIII.4. Observed years of first use of barbiturates versus heroin in Denver polydrug sample.

Table VIII.3

FREQUENCY OF ABUSE OF DRUGS IN THE POLYDRUG SAMPLE[a]

Drug	Percentage of total sample reporting nonmedical use of drug (N = 820).		Frequency of contagious spread	
	%	Rank	Frequency	Rank
Barbiturates/sedatives	67	1	7 of 13	1
Marijuana	63	2	5 of 13	2
Amphetamines	52	3	4 of 13	3
Psychotropics	45	4	5 of 13	2
Hallucinogens	39	5	[b]	
Alcohol	54	6	[b]	
Cocaine	28	7	[b]	
Heroin	36	8	[b]	
Other opiates	37	9	[b]	
Illegal methadone	12	10	[b]	

[a] These are not preferences but drugs reported as abused, as some individuals abuse more than one drug.

[b] Sample too small to be meaningful.

and cocaine in the same individual is 45.8%. We may speculate that this association may be the result of access to an illicit market that can supply both heroin and cocaine. Otherwise, it is difficult to explain, since the drugs are so different in their effects. The use of cocaine might otherwise seem to be more commonly linked to the use of amphetamines or other stimulants.

Contagious transmission is not quite as sharp a criterion for distinguishing heavily abused drugs here, perhaps owing to the categorical definition of the drugs, although most of the commoner ones show such incidence patterns (Figures VIII.5, VIII.6, VIII.7, VIII.8). The results are consistent for the first four—barbiturates, marijuana, amphetamines, and psychotropics—which are misused by more than half the sample.

The total evidence from both samples is suggestive that widespread misuse of a drug is often the consequence of contagious spread among peers and associates, rather than through iatrogenic introduction or deliberate marketing by dealers (at least among treated drug abusers). The process is analogous to the diffusion of cultural traits familiar to anthropologists or the spread of information. The consistent correlations among contagious incidence patterns, illicit sources, and frequency of misuse are striking, although these data are both biased and of limited extent.

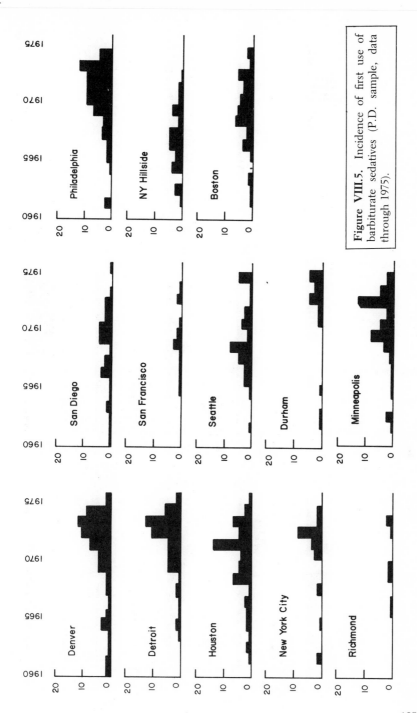

Figure VIII.5. Incidence of first use of barbiturate sedatives (P.D. sample, data through 1975).

195

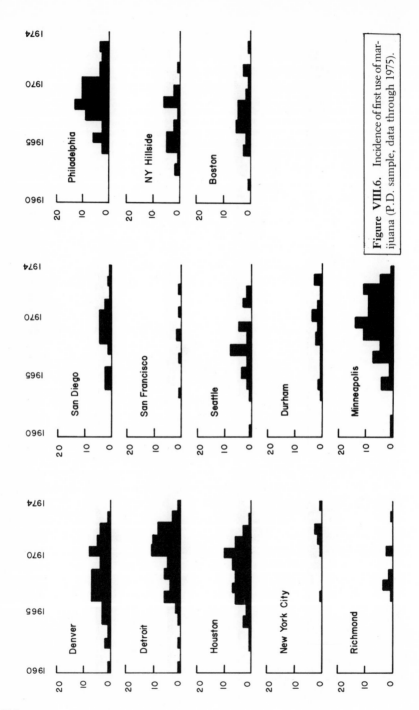

Figure VIII.6. Incidence of first use of marijuana (P.D. sample, data through 1975).

196

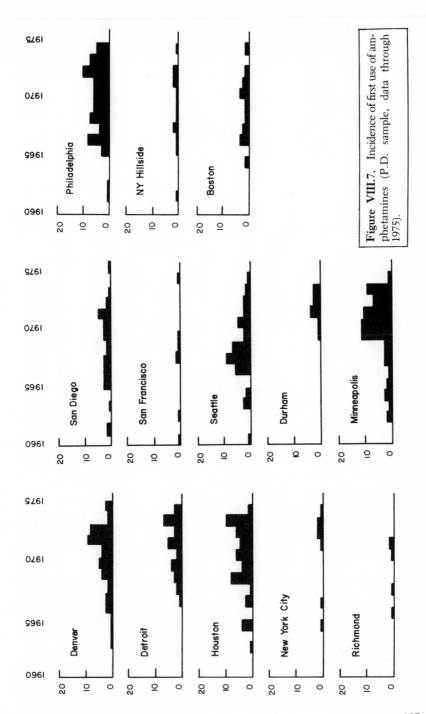

Figure VIII.7. Incidence of first use of amphetamines (P.D. sample, data through 1975).

197

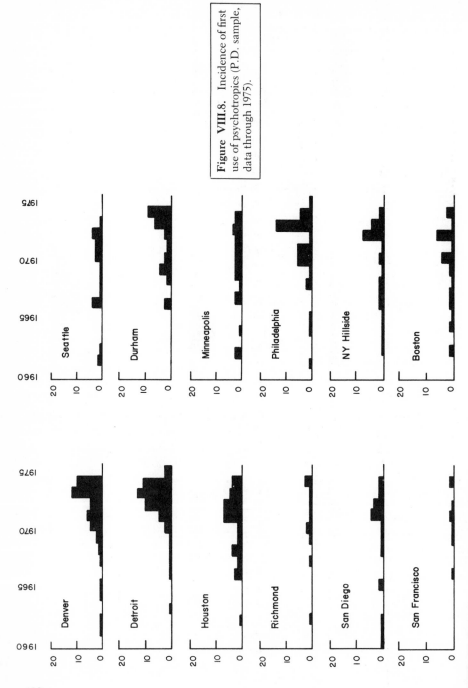

Figure VIII.8. Incidence of first use of psychotropics (P.D. sample, data through 1975).

HISTORIES OF MISUSE: TEMPORAL
SEQUENCES AND MICRO-DEMOGRAPHIC
DIFFERENCES IN PEAK ONSET

Peak incidence of new use of heroin has spread from coastal areas of high population density to smaller interior cities and regions of lower population density in much the same fashion as some cultural innovation spreads (Hunt, 1974a). Heroin differs from misused but otherwise legal psychoactive drugs, however, in its distribution system, illicit market structure, and general availability (although in these respects it might be supposed similar to cocaine). Heroin and cocaine, for example, are never present in quantity in a community unless they are brought there for the purpose of illicit use, whereas a major primary distribution of pharmaceutical drugs such as amphetamines and barbiturates, is already accomplished by the drug industry. We do not argue that all illegal diversion of licit drugs occurs locally, near the site of consumption, since there is a separate illicit distribution system for these drugs too. However, the critical difference remains. For example, the legal U.S. market was simultaneously saturated with methaqualone starting in the late 1960s, whereas nothing comparable occurred for heroin and cocaine at a single period in time.

Thus there should be differences in the appearances of epochs of heavy new use which reflect the peculiarities of drug availability. These onset patterns are, however, complex functions of other variables besides availability, such as changing attitudes of users in various demographic categories (e.g., heroin did not generally emerge as a white middle-class problem drug until after 1970, even though it had been available in many places much earlier). Thus availability is only one condition (although a limiting one) that determines the history of onset of use.

The effects of sudden availability followed by rapid contagious spread are well illustrated by the onset of methaqualone use (Figure VIII.2). It generally spread rapidly everywhere after 1970, and 1972–1973 are the apparent peak years of new use in crude incidence records. There is little indication that city size or location had much to do with the sudden appearance of methaqualone.

In contrast, new cocaine use (Figure VIII.1) had been going on much longer, apparently first achieving some popularity on the northeast and west coasts in 1965 (note the similarity of the onset data for New York City, Atlantic City, and San Francisco). In Phoenix, Greensboro, and Des Moines, peak use seems to have been distinctly later, around 1970. But in other cities, such as Miami and Washington, D.C., incidence sequences are inconsistent and vary from program to program. The same is even more striking for amphetamine onset data from Miami (Figure VIII.3).

Since the characteristics of users in different treatment programs may vary, we might expect these dissimilar onset patterns to be a partial consequence of the clients themselves, rather than just drug availability. A program containing mostly older clients will exhibit earlier onset histories, one with younger clients, later ones.

Such age-dependence of onset is well established for heroin and marijuana (see Figure VIII.12) and undoubtedly characterizes other drugs (see Hunt, 1977). But even though there is a typical age at onset distribution, it cannot influence the shape of an incidence curve if use is restricted by availability, as with methaqualone.

If age plays such an important role in onset histories for a program, should not other demographic or individual characteristics of clients modify incidence patterns also? Drug preference is such a characteristic. Figures VIII.9 and VIII.10 show two samples (DEA data) of Des Moines, Iowa, users: Figure VIII.9 containing 65% self-described heroin addicts, while Figure VIII.10 has only 22% heroin users. Note that amphetamines exhibit epidemic incidence in the second group, but not in the first.

Drug preference may also be correlated with race, so that both variables are reflections of separate and different transmission of use patterns which are illustrated by onset data. Figure VIII.11 shows first use of cocaine clients for Daytop Village, New York City (DEA sample). The later nonheroin users are all white except for one Puerto Rican, whereas two-thirds of the earlier onset primary heroin users are blacks.

All incidence data are influenced by age, race, and sex of the sample, and further conditioned by drug availability. Thus in making assertions about the general spread of new use of a drug, all these contingencies must be weighed. Obviously, most conclusions are true for only a small segment of the general population with age, race, sex, and locale similar to those represented in the sample.

THE PROGRESSION HYPOTHESIS: INFERENCES FROM INCIDENCE ANALYSIS

Among the most venerable rubrics in drug abuse lore is the progression principle, which states that drug misuse typically begins with alcohol or "soft drugs" such as marijuana and evolves through progressively more serious substances to the ultimate hard drugs—heroin and the opiates. Thousands of prevention initiatives—lectures, drug education courses,

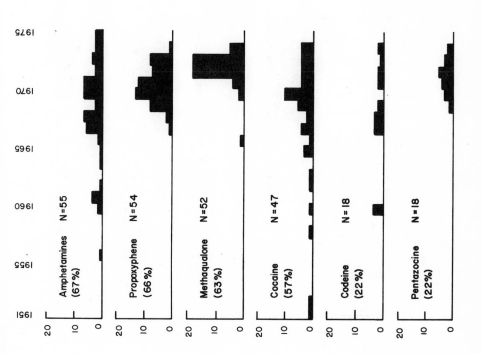

Figure VIII.9. Incidence of first use (in Des Moines, Iowa) for a 65% heroin-using population (DEA sample; interviews, $N = 82$; data through August 1975).

201

202

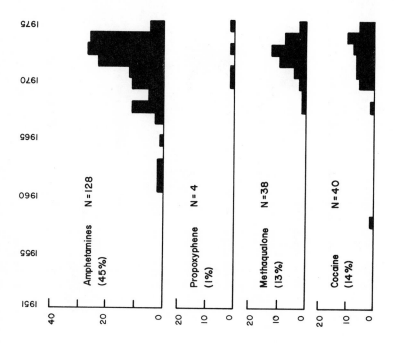

Figure VIII.10. Incidence of first use (in Des Moines, Iowa) for a 22% heroin-using population (program records, $N = 283$; data through August 1975).

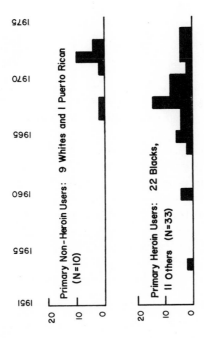

Figure VIII.11. Incidence of first use of cocaine in primary nonheroin versus heroin users in Daytop Village, New York City (DEA sample, data through August 1975).

pamphlets, TV, films, etc.—have used the progression idea as if it were fact: "Marijuana today; heroin tomorrow." The generality and persistence of this notion makes it worthy of detailed investigation.

There are a variety of quantitative approaches which may shed light on the question. First, we may ask whether some drugs are typically used earlier than others. The simplest answer is a comparison of age at onset distribution for users of different substances. For instance, it has been shown that the typical age of first use of marijuana is much earlier than that of heroin. Figure VIII.12 shows the modal age of first use of marijuana to be about 14, whereas that of heroin is 18.

The difference does not prove that marijuana use always precedes heroin use, much less that it leads to it. Obviously there is no guarantee that any of the marijuana users in Figure VIII.12 have ultimately turned to heroin, or that any of the heroin users had earlier used marijuana. Figure VIII.12 shows only that among individuals who use either or both drugs, marijuana use *typically* precedes heroin. However, the implication of possible progression remains: since we know that most heroin users use or have used many other drugs, among them marijuana, there is a suggestion of marijuana's temporal precedence in the data of Figure VIII.12.

However, other data from the DEA sample raise a basic question about the whole idea of progression apart from the drugs involved. They show that virtually all individuals who describe themselves as "primarily heroin abusers" also continue to use other drugs for various purposes. Table VIII.4 is a subsample of the DEA data showing numerical frequencies (not percent) of usage patterns (Hunt & Chambers, 1976a).

"Primary" use is equivalent to preference. "Substitute" is as a replacement for the primary drug—here dominantly heroin. "Concurrent" means use along with the primary drug, for example, those who take a mixture of cocaine and heroin together ("speedballers"). "Independent" means that the drug is used entirely separately from the primary drug, perhaps for entirely different effects.

Here the primary amphetamine users are not opiate users at all, while the others are nearly all heroin addicts. Aside from the users' obvious substitutional use of hydromorphone, propoxyphene, and pentazocine, the most striking fact in Table VIII.4 is the extensive independent use of all these drugs by heroin addicts. It is not clear how much of the independent use predates heroin dependence, but it is known that much is contemporary. Thus, many of these "primary heroin addicts" are really multiple drug users in that they use various psychoactive substances independently within short intervals of time.

Their behavior does not match the progression hypothesis in its most simplistic form. Rather than an evolution in choice of drugs, here is

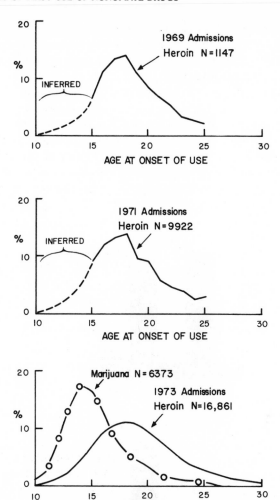

Figure VIII.12. Age at onset of heroin and marijuana use (sample of clients admitted to federal treatment programs). Source: for data of 1969, 1971: SAODAP Monthly Management Report, 1973; for 1973 NIDA Quarterly Statistical Brochure, 1974.

evidence of a current continuum of use of quite different drugs for different effects. This can be seen in Figure VIII.13 (DEA sample data from Des Moines, Iowa), which compares preferential heroin and marijuana users' reasons for using propoxyphene. For heroin users, propoxyphene is both a substitute for heroin and an independent choice; for marijuana users, it obviously provides an entirely different kind of psychotropic experience.

These data argue that much drug use is not sequential at all, but rather cumulative. A user does not progress from marijuana to harder drugs, but rather from some initial drug experience to an ever-widening and more eclectic taste for many drugs.

There remains the question of progression to a drug of preference. Conceivably a user could employ many drugs for differing purposes and still have evolved toward a preference for heroin or the opiates. To examine this question, the Polydrug Project sample provides a comparison between the first drug used and current drug of preference (Table VIII.5). All the significant categories of drugs have increased in popularity except alcohol and marijuana, which have decreased sharply, supply-

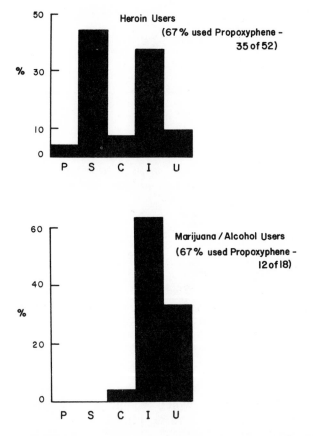

Figure VIII.13.   Nonmedical uses of propoxyphene by primary drug use (P = primary; S = substitute; C = concurrent; I = independent; U = unknown).

Table VIII.4

NUMERICAL FREQUENCIES OF USAGE PATTERNS (DEA SAMPLE)

	Primary	Substitute	Concurrent	Independent
Cocaine	—	1	17	79
Amphetamines	27	—	—	51
Methaqualone	2	—	—	45
Phencyclidine	1	—	—	44
Hydromorphone	3	21	1	25
Propoxyphene	1	8	1	17
Pentazocine	2	5	1	11
Phenmetrazine	—	—	1	9

ing the gains made by the other drugs. Surely these increases might be regarded as evidence of progression.

If the increases are interpreted in this way, then cocaine, barbiturates, heroin, and the opiates and amphetamines show the greatest relative gains, most of their recruits coming from alcohol and marijuana. However, note that about 40% of these users did not progress at all, because they started with some drug other than alcohol or marijuana. Moreover, cocaine and barbiturates show relatively greater gains than heroin and the opiates as current drugs of preference.

This analysis is quite naive, however, since it does not really show that current preference is a terminal state for a user, and indeed the DEA data cited previously clearly cast doubt on any final preference, in the sense

Table VIII.5

DISTRIBUTION OF FIRST DRUG USED AND DRUG OF CURRENT PREFERENCE FROM POLYDRUG SAMPLE

Drug	a. First used (%) (N = 806)	b. Current preference (%) (N = 791)	$\dfrac{b}{a}$
Heroin and opiates	9.0	25.0	2.8
Alcohol	33	4.2	0.1
Barbiturates	6.7	21	3.1
Amphetamines	8.3	15	1.8
Cocaine	.2	4.4	22.0
Marijuana	27	11	.4
Hallucinogens	5.3	7.7	1.5
Psychotropics	5.2	8.7	1.7
Inhalants	3.6	1.0	.3
Nonprescription	1.4	.4	.3
Other	.5	1.0	2.0

that the drug has become either a permanent or an exclusive choice. Aside from the permanency of preference for experienced users, there is also no guarantee that all those newer users represented in the Polydrug Project sample might have reached any stable preference (even if it existed).

We conclude that onset data do not support the progression hypotheses. Earlier modal onset age of marijuana use (from CODAP data) does not imply evolution to heroin use, but is consistent with changes to preferences for a large group of other drugs—cocaine, barbiturates, opiates, etc.

DEA data demonstrate that the use of these drugs may be concurrent with or independent of one another (during the same period of time) so that preference does not mean exclusivity. The likely condition seems to be a cumulative growth in taste for many kinds of drugs rather than progression to a single class.

CONCLUSIONS

Relationship of These Results to Prevalence in the General Population

The preceding analyses demonstrate that onset of use of a drug is highly specific to kinds of individuals, places, and times. It is therefore equally true that overall levels of use—active prevalence—must be just as contingent, and also constantly changing, as new use spreads to different demographic groups, locales, etc. Active prevalence of use of a given drug in any population aggregate, even a small city, is the sum of all these differing patterns of growth, and it is further altered by death, emigration, immigration, and remission and successful treatment among users.

Although we are unable to infer prevalence from the preceding onset data, several qualitative conclusions are possible. First, active prevalence needs to be defined: prevalence of what? From the public point of view the users of greatest interest are abusers or misusers (because of both treatment needs and public safety). An operational definition of this category of use has proved particularly difficult in past work. The theory of contagious transmission, however, provides a solution to the problem of defining abuse. There is suggestive evidence (see earlier discussion) that drugs which behave contagiously are being abused, at least by the groups that display such incidence patterns. We therefore equate contagious spread and active abuse, then note whether the incidence sequences suggest growing or declining abuse, that is, changes in prevalence.

This approach to prevalence of abuse is piecemeal, of course, because of the highly local nature of the incidence records. However, when data are consistent, as in the cases of methaqualone and the barbiturates, the conclusion of rapidly growing prevalence of abuse is warranted, although we do not know its absolute magnitude. For other drugs such as cocaine and the amphetamines, the results are not so unanimous. In some places their abuse is growing, in others it is not. Incidence patterns show interesting differences: cocaine use seems to be spreading in New York City, Phoenix, and Miami, but not in Washington, D.C., which otherwise resembles these cities in having extensive heroin use. In general, new use of amphetamines appears to be declining (Figures VIII.5, VIII.9), hence active prevalence of abuse is probably stable or decreasing.

A DEFINITIVE INCIDENCE STUDY

These results are, of course, both incomplete and biased, and do not characterize nonopiate use in the general population, but only misuse in small demographic segments. They do, however, raise the question of whether an overall characterization is possible, or what its meaning would be if it were made, since spatiotemporal–demographic differences are so sharp.

A definitive incidence study would treat each different group separately, by showing the patterns of spread of distinct types of use (e.g., nonmedically supervised abuse) for given drugs in each population component which had experienced different onset patterns. Probably no truly random sampling is possible in actual practice.

As an approximation, we rely on the traditional sampling mechanisms afforded by hospitals, mental health centers, treatment programs, police and criminal justice system data. We do so with full understanding that the samples from these sources are biased and that they do not represent the general population. However, any drug use of public health significance will probably emerge in at least one of the agencies.

Global treatment of onset phenomena are not meaningful, since it is what happens at a particular time and place that matters. Changes in national survey data may convey only the most rudimentary notions of local happenings in critical areas. The sin of globality was committed in the early 1970s by federal administrators responsible for monitoring heroin use. By now they understand that what is true of New York City or Washington, D.C., may not be true elsewhere in the nation. In spite of their limitations, routine incidence analyses are still the best intelligence for detecting emergent drug problems.

CHAPTER IX

Three National Estimates of Prevalence of Nonopiate Drug Abuse

John P. Lau and John Benvenuto

A growing body of statistical evidence has been developing which suggests that the prevalence of nonopiate drug abuse is becoming a problem of major dimensions in the United States (Chambers & Moldestad, 1970; Glen & Richards, 1974; Parry *et al.*, 1973).

Prevalence estimation in the drug abuse field is in a stage of development which renders it an "emerging science" at best. Because most drug use is private behavior and may also involve illicit behavior, subjects have varying degrees of motivation for concealing their drug use. Traditional random sampling survey techniques are complicated by this, as well as by the fact that samples of street-wise users (defined further in Chapter V) are difficult to randomize. Indirect methods of estimating prevalence such as by determining the prevalence of serum hepatitis, which forms an important facet of heroin prevalence estimates, is not applicable to drugs taken orally. In an attempt to devise prevalence estimates, we utilized several different methods. Our estimates involved two strategies: (1) The alcoholism method in which a prevalence estimate was made by examination of the overlap between alcohol abuse and other drug abuse; (2) the

Polydrug Abuse:
The Results of a
National Collaborative Study

comparison survey method, which attempts to interpret existing surveys of drug use patterns to yield data concerning the prevalence of abuse.

THE "ALCOHOLISM" METHOD

From an analysis of the data collected from the Polydrug Project, 39% of the persons evaluated by these units were found to have a secondary problem with the abuse of alcohol. This finding is generally consistent with the findings of Cahalan, Cisin, and Crossley (1969) who surveyed alcohol use throughout the overall population of the United States. It is also consistent with the observations of Whitehead and Smart (1972). Data reported to the National Institute on Alcohol Abuse and Alcoholism (NIAAA) from its nationwide network of alcoholism treatment centers indicated that 14% of persons admitted to alcoholism treatment had secondary problems with the nonopiate drugs. Again, this finding is consistent with reports in the literature of 15% by Devenyi and Wilson and 20% by Freed (Devenyi & Wilson, 1971; Freed, 1973).

The cross-utilization of these drugs suggested the development of a conditional probability model. Figure IX.1 depicts these relationships graphically and presents the equations for relationship. It is designated as the "Alcoholism method" because it depends on the cross-involvement of nonopiate abusers with alcohol abuse.

This relationship between the prevalences of drug and alcohol abuse involves the following logical assumptions:

1. There exists a group of people who abuse alcohol (circle "A").
2. There also exists a group of people who abuse nonopiate or psychoactive drugs (circle "PD").

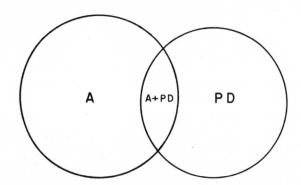

Figure IX.1. Alcoholism method.

3. Finally, there is a portion of each group that also abuses the other substance (overlapping area "A + PD").

This conditional probability model results in the following equation:

$$\cdot P(PD) = P(A) \cdot \frac{[P(PD\,|A)]}{P(A\,|PD)}$$

where $P(PD)$ is the prevalence of nonopiate drug abuse

$P(A)$ is the prevalence of alcohol abuse
$P(PD|A)$ is the percentage of alcoholics who are also nonopiate drug abusers.
$P(A|PD)$ is the percentage of nonopiate drug abusers who are also alcoholics or alcohol abusers.

Probably the best current estimate for the prevalence of alcohol abuse $P(A)$ in the United States is the one derived by Efron et al. (1974) of approximately 5.5 million persons. Using this estimate as the value of $P(A)$, 13.7% as the value of $P(PD\,|A)$, and 38.7% as the value of $P(A\,|PD)$ in the formula yields an estimate of 1.9 million persons as nonopiate drug abusers in the United States:

$$P(PD) - \frac{P(A) \cdot P(PD\,|A)}{P(A|PD)}$$

$$= \frac{(5.5 \times 10^6) \cdot (0.137)}{(0.387)}$$

$$= 1.9 \text{ million persons}$$

Clearly, this estimate of 1.9 million nonopiate drug abusers is dependent upon the accuracy of three critical values—$P(A)$, $P(PD|A)$, and $P(A|PD)$—from which it is computed. The estimate for $P(PD|A)$ was derived from a sample of more than 14,000 persons, but is probably a conservative estimate since underreporting on secondary drugs of abuse is not an unusual problem in systems such as the one used by NIAAA. The estimate for $P(A|PD)$ is derived from a sample of more than 2000 patients and is probably accurate because of conscious efforts to check for secondary alcohol abuse in clients being admitted. The estimate of 5.5 million alcoholics is questionable, however, and is possibly the most conservative, since estimates of the number of alcoholics have run as high as 10 million persons. The authors believe, therefore, that the calculated estimate of 1.9 million nonopiate drug abusers is conservative.

COMPARISON SURVEY METHOD

Two additional prevalence estimates were made using data from two national surveys. The first survey was a study of the national patterns of psychotherapeutic drug use conducted and reported by Parry *et al.* (Parry, Balter, Mellinger, Cisin, and Manheimer, 1973). The second was performed by a nationwide polling and opinion survey firm under contract to the Special Action Office for Drug Abuse Prevention (SAODAP). The results of that survey were reported in an unpublished paper (Green, 1974). Parry *et al.* in their survey reported that 8% of the adult American population used psychotherapeutic drugs daily for at least 2 months during the year preceding the survey (i.e., 1970), although not necessarily at dosages beyond those normally prescribed. The "household" sampling technique probably did not represent the streetwise drug users. Projection of Parry's data to the total United States population would indicate that 12.8 million Americans were using these substances at that level in 1970. Although the Parry survey did not address the question of misuse or abuse among these users, Cohen (1974), at the Institute for Defense Analysis, reanalyzed survey data from five states (i.e., New Jersey, Florida, Arizona, Indiana, and South Carolina) collected by the Research Planning Corporation (RPC), and found that 14.2% of persons using these substances used them in a regular, nonmedical way (see Table IX.1). Assuming that this same proportion was true for Parry's data, it would yield that an estimate of 1.8 million Americans were regular, nonmedical users of the psychoactive drugs. While this estimate of prevalence is close to that obtained with the alcoholism method, several as-

Table IX.1

MEDICAL AND NONMEDICAL USE OF LICIT DRUGS[a,b]

	Any use (%)	Percentage of any use which is nonmedical	Percentage of any use which is regular and nonmedical
Minor tranquilizers	9.1	26	18
Sedatives	5.7	11	5
Stimulants	3.1	42	23
Legally obtained (prescribed) opiates	1.4	50	7
Weighted average	—	25.9	14.2

[a] Percent of total population 14 years or older using in a 6-month period.
[b] Based on a composite survey of New Jersey, Indiana, Florida, Arizona, and South Carolina.

sumptions are involved. First is the application of Cohen's findings to Parry's data, and the second is the equivalence of regular, nonmedical use with abuse. These assumptions are admittedly heroic and in the direction of inflating the abuse estimates derived from using them. However, two additional considerations, both acting in the direction of depressing abuse estimates, appear to offset the effects of the two assumptions. First, household surveys such as the one conducted by Parry *et al.* usually underestimate "street" drug use, since the "street" population is almost never reached in household interviews. Second, some of the persons who reported "medium" or "low" levels of use of these drugs could also be abusers. We believe the resulting estimate of 1.8 million abusers of nonopiate drugs is probably conservative.

There remains, then, the analysis of the survey reported by Green as a third estimator, albeit not a totally independent (in the mathematical sense) one. As will be explained, it was necessary to use some of Parry's findings to interpret the data from this survey, so we shall not proclaim it as a completely independent third estimation.

In April and May of 1974, a series of 17 questions were appended to the national opinion surveys routinely conducted by the Roper organization during those months. The first 9 questions were administered to the panel polled in April ($N = 1984$), while the remaining 8 were administered to the panel polled in May ($N = 2000$). The questions probed the occurrence of what could be termed "negative life events" during the 12-month period preceding the survey for the individuals polled. Further, if a positive response was elicited to a question about the occurrence of any of these negative life events, a subsequent question probing the use of psychoactive substances in the 12-hour period immediately preceding the negative life events was asked. Each respondent who answered positively to both the occurrence of the negative life event and the use of a psychoactive substance within 12 hours was further asked to rate subjectively the relationship between the two (i.e., major role, minor role, no role, didn't know).

There are two alternative approaches that could have been used in the Roper survey to elicit the information sought. One could have first probed drug use and then probed the concurrent occurrence of a negative life event, or one could have first probed the occurrence of the life event and then probed concurrent drug use. The latter approach—the one employed in this survey—is more likely to evoke honest responses because it is couched in less threatening terms.

The interpretation of the survey results can be approached in different ways. One way would be to compare the survey results to what one would have expected to find if the relationship between the occurrence of a negative life event and the concurrent (within 12 hours) use of psychoactive drugs were the result of a mere random coincidence. This would then allow some rational assessment of the observed coincidences for each event.

In order to compute the expected frequency of coincidence of the two events, one must use a conditional probability approach for this study. The equation for this is as follows:

Expected frequency of coincidence occurrences $= P(D|E) \cdot P(E)$

where $P(D|E)$ is the probability of drug use (D) occurring with 12 hours, given the person has experienced a negative life event (E); and $P(E)$ is the simple probability of the negative life event occurring. Now if we assume that the two events are independent[1] of each other (i.e., not related), then we have the following:

$$P(D|E) = P(D)$$

where $P(D)$ is the simple probability of drug use occurring within 12 hours of the negative life event on a sheerly random basis. In other words, the expected frequency of coincidence of the two events on a sheerly random basis is merely the product of the simple probability of each occurring in the manner described.

By using the frequency of appearance of each negative life event as it occurred in the survey, $P(E)$ may be approximated; that is, because the survey probed first the occurrence of the life event, its frequency of appearance in the data may be taken to be the approximate frequency with which it occurs in the population in any 12-month period.

It is possible to approximate $P(D)$ from the work of Parry et al. in their survey of national trends in the use of psychoactive drugs. In that work, Parry found the following levels of psychoactive drug use (excluding alcohol) to have occurred in a 12-month period (1970) in the United States:

No use—78% of the population
High use—8%
Medium use—7%
Low use—6%

High use means daily use for either 2 to 5 months or 6 to 12 months as was noted earlier. Medium use was undefined, but, for this analysis, we

---

[1] This assumption is a mathematical one and does not imply that the two events are always either related or unrelated in real life.

assume it to be daily use for 1 month. Low use was also undefined and we assume it to be daily use for a week. We must now convert these use levels to probabilities that drug use at each level would have occurred on any given day [i.e., $P(D)$]:

Level	%	$P(D)$
No use	78	0
High use	8	.5
Medium use	7	.08
Low use	6	.02

We then compute a weighted average $P(D)$ for all use levels combined:

$$P(D) \text{ average} = \overline{P(D)} = \frac{(78 \cdot 0) + (8 \cdot 0.5) + (7 \cdot 0.08) + (6 \cdot 0.02)}{100}$$

$$= 0.047$$

Thus we can compute the expected occurrences for each event and compare the ratios of the observed to the expected occurrences (eliminating alcohol and opiates) for each event (Figure IX.2).

The observed coincidences exceed the expected coincidences by sub-

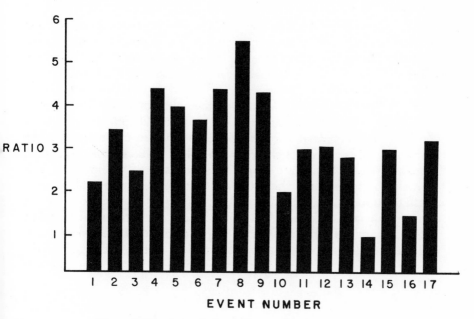

Figure IX.2.   Ratio of observed to expected occurrences.

stantial margins for almost every negative life event. The average of the observed frequencies is:

$$1.4\% \pm 0.4\%$$

Since the adult population in the United States was approximately 150 million persons at the time of the survey, this would lead to a prevalence estimate for nonopiate drug abuse of 2.1 million persons. Again, this must be viewed as a conservative estimate because of the underreporting of "street" drug use in household surveys.

DISCUSSION

Because prevalence estimation in the drug abuse field is still largely an emerging science, it is imperative that both the methods employed and the assumptions made be painstakingly detailed. With regard to the "Alcoholism Method" two critical assumptions were made: (1) that the degrees of secondary substance abuse noted in our data are generally true in alcohol- and nonopiate-abusing populations; and (2) that the prevalence estimate of 5.5 million alcoholics in the United States is reasonably correct.

The assumptions made in using the data from the two national surveys can be characterized as more heroic. (1) The equivalence of regular, nonmedical drug use with abuse; (2) the application of Cohen's findings to Parry's data; (3) the mathematical independence of the two events of drug use and a negative life event.

Despite these assumptions we believe the nature of most of the assumptions would be to make the estimate conservative. Despite these assumptions and the somewhat stringent definition of abuse used in the "Alcoholism method," we conclude that nearly 2 million adult Americans abuse a variety of nonopiate drugs. This estimate of 2 million persons is approximately four times the estimated number of heroin addicts (estimated to be about 500,000 in 1970). The social cost attendant to the abuse of the nonopiate substances probably exceeds that attributed to opiate abuse, although the manifestations of this social cost are probably less visible and dramatic. Nonetheless, any problem that has an impact on the lives of 2 million Americans and their families is one that warrants attention.

PART 3

Central Nervous System Consequences of Polydrug Abuse

EDITORS' INTRODUCTION

This section considers central nervous system function in polydrug users. The first two chapters describe the results of the Collaborative Neuropsychological Study of Polydrug Users (CNSP), which employed the Halstead–Reitan Battery (HRB) to assess brain functions in a sample of 151 polydrug users and comparison groups of psychiatric patients and nonpatient controls. The third chapter presents findings of a related but independent study by the San Diego Project, in which both EEG and HRB assessments were employed.

The evaluation of brain dysfunction—sometimes called organicity to distinguish it from "functional" disorders, such as schizophrenia—is a complex task. Four strategies are commonly used:

1. The *clinical neurological examination* is not particularly sensitive to milder forms of cerebral dysfunction, even when performed by an experienced neurologist. The neurological examination is highly specific, how-

ever, in the sense that the unequivocal presence of a neurological sign allows us to infer with confidence that CNS (central nervous system) pathology exists.

2. *X-ray examinations* of the brain are designed to demonstrate the anatomical integrity of brain tissue. Until recently, angiography and pneumoencephalography were the most sensitive and commonly used of these tools. Both are painful procedures with definite morbidity, and in general are not suitable for research subjects. Computer assisted tomography (commonly called CAT scan or EMI scan) is the best available noninvasive method of demonstrating brain anatomy *in vivo*. Unfortunately, the CAT was not readily available in 1974.

3. The *EEG* measures the electrical activity of the brain. It is a noninvasive procedure which is especially sensitive to abnormal electrical discharges, such as those that occur in epilepsy. Asymmetry and slowing are common correlates of other forms of brain pathology, as well. Computer assisted analytic methods, such as compressed spectral array (CSA) analysis are showing promise in increasing the EEG's sensitivity as shown by Judd *et al.* in Chapter XII. Additional techniques which show promise but have not as yet been applied to investigations of polydrug users include averaged evoked cortical potentials and the far field technique for studying brain stem integrity.

4. The *neuropsychological examination* assesses brain function by measuring performance. While there are many neuropsychological test instruments, the Halstead–Reitan battery has undergone the most extensive reliability and validity studies in a variety of patient populations.

Because of the temporal and economic constraints on the CNSP, Grant *et al.* favored the neuropsychological approach as being likely to yield more information which might be of practical value to clinicians who, in their treatment planning, would need to take into account the possibility that their patients' adaptive abilities might be compromised by organicity. Additionally, the results of three pilot studies (Grant, Mohns, Miller, 1976), including two emerging out of the polydrug effort (Adams, Rennick, Schoof, & Keegan, 1975; Grant & Judd, 1976) suggested the presence of neuropsychological impairment in polydrug users.

All evaluation procedures have limitations, and the neuropsychological method is no exception. For example, subjects must be willing to cooperate to their maximum capability with testing in order for the results to be meaningful. In the CNSP, the investigators attempted to create a favorable motivational set in several ways: (1) participation was voluntary, and this was stressed to all subjects; (2) the nature and purposes of testing were explained, to generate curiosity especially among polydrug users, many of whom seemed genuinely interested in the possible effects of drugs on their health; (3) all subjects were paid ($20–$30) for their participation; (4) neuropsychological examiners attended an in-service workshop before the study began. In addition to learning technical skills, all examiners were taught the importance of securing subject cooperation and methods helpful in ensuring proper motivation. As a result, a few protocols ($N = 15$) had to be dropped because examiners raised questions about issues such as negativism, hostility, or lack of effort. The protocols which remained in the study ($N = 276$) appear to reflect genuine effort on the part of subjects to do well on the testing.

The sample for the first two chapters in this part consisted of 151 polydrug users (89 men, 62 women, average age = 25.5, mean education = 11.3); 66 psychiatric patients (35 men, 31 women, average age = 28.8, mean education = 13.5); and 59 nonpatients, nondrug using controls (25 men, 34 women, average age = 26.1, mean education = 12.8).

Grant *et al.*, in Chapter X, "Neuropsychological Effects of Polydrug Abuse," examine in detail the relationships between the use of drugs of abuse and impairment. Wesson *et al.*, in Chapter XI, "Neuro-psychological Impairment and Psychopathology," explore the potential confounding contribution of psychopathology to impairment.

Chapter XII, "Comparison of Results from Serially Collected Neuro-psychological and EEG Data" by Judd, Grant, Bickford, and Lee examines the prevalence and correlates of cerebral dysfunction as inferred from both EEG and HRB. With the exception of a few subjects who also were part of the CNSP, the population studied here was distinct from that on which the first two chapters in this part are based.

CHAPTER X

Neuropsychological Effects of Polydrug Abuse

Igor Grant, Kenneth M. Adams,
Albert S. Carlin, Phillip M. Rennick,
Lewis L. Judd, Kenneth Schooff,
and Robert Reed

INTRODUCTION

Research in psychopharmacology, neuroendocrinology, and biochemistry has produced insights about responses of nervous system tissue to drugs under controlled conditions. However, the generalizability of such knowledge of chronic use to the complex biomedical and biosocial conditions found in drug abuse is limited. Drug actions and reactions occur in drug abusers which involve dosages and exposure rates not encountered during usual prescription use. The impurities and dosage variation in street drugs cloud the issue further.

Without question, univariate attempts to specify neural mechanisms of human behavior in naturalistic environments may be seen as premature. Thus, approaches to research on the association between extensive polydrug use and cerebral impairment should be based on multivariate empiricism. Studies designed to determine whether such a relationship exists should be unencumbered by specific theories of drug use behavior and unfettered by allegiance to particular models of brain function. Multiple measurements in both drug and neuropsychological domains seem indicated to do justice to their individual complexity and to docu-

223

ment fully their possible interplay in a multifaceted psychosocial environment.

With these assumptions in mind, it may be useful to consider previous evidence on the effects of nonmedical drug use in neuropsychological adaptation.

Few studies deal with more than one drug of abuse, and as such, they do not apply directly to the polydrug user. Since most drug users take different drugs for different effects—singly or in combination—it is no longer meaningful to characterize North American drug users as "marijuana users" or "stimulant users."

The investigations cited here have used common neuropsychological measures. The Halstead–Reitan Neuropsychological Test Battery (Reitan & Davison, 1974) is a widely used and well-standardized series of tests which are sensitive to diverse effects of cerebral dysfunction. Validity and reliability studies using this battery have established its ability to discriminate between brain-damaged and nonbrain-damaged cases across a variety of neurological conditions. The empirical base of the battery and its wide-range sampling of adaptive abilities make it the instrument of choice for research on the question of cerebral dysfunction in drug abusers.

Several investigations of the impact marijuana use may have on neuropsychological functioning have been carried out utilizing the entire, or parts of, the Halstead–Reitan battery. Reed (1974) found no differences between 10 moderate and 10 heavy marijuana users, while Grant, Rochford, Fleming, and Stunkard (1973) found no neuropsychological differences between medical students who used marijuana moderately and those who used none. Carlin and Trupin (1977) also found that persons who smoked marijuana several times a week for 2 years did not differ from a group of nonusers matched for age and intelligence. Native Jamaicans who smoked marijuana heavily for a number of years did not differ from nonusers (Rubin & Comitas, 1972). The overall negative findings, although impressive in consistency, must be viewed critically. Reed (1974), Grant *et al.* (1973), and Carlin and Trupin (1977), all studied relatively young, psychologically healthy persons whose exposure to marijuana spanned less than 10 years, and who were of above average intelligence. Cannabis use may not have a similar insignificant impact in less gifted populations or with individuals with underlying psychopathology. Furthermore, the appropriateness of the child's version of the Category Test used by Rubin and Comitas with adult Jamaicans is questionable.

LSD's effects on neuropsychological functioning has also been examined by a number of investigators. Acord (1972) examined psychiatric patients who used LSD at least once, and found impaired abstracting ability. However, the methodological shortcomings of this investigation render it of little substantive value. An elaboration of this study, which used control groups (Acord & Barker, 1973), found persons who claimed use of LSD at least once more impaired than those who denied such use. Again, methodological inadequacies attenuate the findings of increased impairment among users since definitional criteria of LSD use are somewhat liberal, discussion of subject selection is unclear, and sample size is small. Cohen and Edwards (1969) found that individuals with greater than 50 LSD experiences, when compared to controls matched for sex, age, and education, manifested visual spatial dysfunction. McGlothlin, Arnold, and Freedman (1969) compared the Halstead–Reitan performance of LSD users with a matched sample of marijuana users and found the LSD users to do worse on only one subtest—the Category Test. Wright and Hogan (1972) found no differences between LSD users and controls. Acord (1972) and Acord and Barker (1973) used psychiatric patients as subjects while other investigators used nonpatients. Hence, the results are not generalizable across investigations. In addition, no investigation attempted to assess the use of other drugs by these subjects and so could not rule out their influence in creating the observed impairments.

Only one study has relied on the Halstead–Reitan test battery to assess the impact of opiate abuse (Fields & Fullerton, 1974). These authors found that young Vietnam veteran heroin addicts did not differ from a matched sample of medical patients, but that both of these groups differed from a sample of brain-damaged patients. Again, however, the degree of drug dependence or extent of differential drug use was not well documented.

The neuropsychological impact of stimulant drugs has not been assessed through application of the Halstead–Reitan test battery, but many such investigations have been carried out with respect to central nervous system depressants. In early work, Isbell, Altschul and Kornetsky (1950) and Kornetsky (1951) used a variety of psychological tests, EEGs, and neurological examinations to study the impact of "chronic" sedative abuse by addicting prisoners to barbiturate drugs. Impairment was found during acute intoxication, but cleared during and after withdrawal. Hill and Bellville (1953) and Wikler, Fraser, Isbell, & Pescor (1955) employed similar methodologies in studying barbiturate addiction of moderate duration and short-term chronic intoxication. Adams et al. (1975) and Grant and Judd (1976) employed the Halstead–Reitan battery in the assessment of polydrug abusers. Grant and Judd found 45% of a sample of 66 multiple substance abusers to be impaired on entry into treatment, and 27% of 30 subjects to remain impaired on retest 5 months later. They were able to show an association between heavy use of sedatives and alcohol, and impairment. Adams *et al.* compared the performance of polydrug abuse patients with that of medical patients, nonpatients, and neurological patients and found drug abusers to be most similar to neurological patients. Although the polydrug sample in the Adams *et al.* study was not classified by drug use, 20 of 51 subjects noted barbiturates as their primary drug problem and an additional 5 listed barbiturate drugs as a secondary problem.

Although some controversy exists as to the mechanisms involved, alcohol has long been known to be associated with organic impairment as, for example, in the Wernicke–Korsakoff syndrome. Fitzhugh, Fitzhugh, and Reitan (1960) found impaired adaptive abilities among a group of hospitalized alcoholics despite average or better scores on standard measures of intelligence. This study was repeated on a group of younger alcoholics and once again significant impairment was found (Fitzhugh *et al.*, 1965). Goldstein and Shelley (1971) and Jones and Parsons (1971, 1972) found that alcoholics demonstrated impaired abstracting ability and that visual-spatial and temporal-spatial integration were particularly deficient.

As is evident from the literature review, the neuropsychological impact of many drugs of abuse has been studied by many investigators. Marijuana consistently is seen not to impair neuropsychological functioning while alcohol abuse and sedative abuse in the context of multiple drug use seem to be associated with impairment. Little work has been done with respect to the impact of chronic stimulant and chronic narcotic use on human neuropsychological functioning. Inconsistent results were found on the effects of LSD on neuropsychological functioning despite extensive study.

A number of consistent difficulties exist with these studies which preclude ready generalization from the data. Often, sample size is small and selection criteria either unclear or inappropriate on included patients who may have had additional reasons for impairment other than drug use [e.g., Acord (1972) and Acord and Barker (1973), whose LSD-using groups were psychiatric patients who used LSD "at least once"].[1] Multiple drug use obscures attempts to distinguish the contributory role of any single substance to observed impairment, and most studies do not take varying degrees of immersion into account but rely instead on "all-or-none" classification.

Study subjects differed between and within studies in length and inten-

---

[1] See the following chapter which discusses the relationship between psychopathology and neuropsychological functioning.

sity of drug use. As a result of these difficulties most of the preceding findings, although based on reliable and valid measurements of neuro-psychological functioning, are suggestive rather than conclusive.

The review of the literature and the difficulties inherent in many of the previous studies suggest the rudiments of the ideal design necessary to investigating the impact of drug abuse on neuropsychological function-ing. Drug use metrics must reflect both amount, route of administration and intensity of consumption, and data analysis must rely on multivariate techniques for an understanding of the interplay of these substances. Subject selection should include nonpatient, non-drug-using individuals and a comparison group of non-drug-using psychiatric patients as well as the drug-abusing study group. The inclusion of non-drug-abusing psy-chiatric patients will allow an examination of the contribution of psychopathology to any observed impairment. Premorbid and early de-velopmental data must be gathered, despite the limitations of its retrospec-tive nature, to allow differentiation of drug effects from developmental and medical factors which could contribute to impairment. Measures of and screening for acute intoxication are necessary to ensure that rela-tively enduring drug effects, and not intoxication, are being studied.

The Neuropsychological Test Battery: Background and Description of the Measures

The Halstead–Reitan test battery in its present form reflects the influ-ence of the two investigators for whom it is named. Ward C. Halstead served as a professor of medical psychology at the University of Chicago over a 35-year career. His principal interest during this time was the development of ways to measure the highest functions of the human brain. Devoted initially to the concept of biological intelligence, his work expanded into a programmatic inquiry regarding perception, language, and complex problem solving.

His best achievements were in pursuit of these brain quantification objectives. He developed a core battery of 10 tests that were designed to discriminate brain-damaged from nonbrain-damaged adults. In *Brain and Intelligence*, Halstead (1947) presented a theoretical rationale for the results and provided additional supporting analyses which were notable in that era for their sophistication.

Ralph M. Reitan was one of Halstead's students and later became his most important research collaborator. Reitan drew from Halstead's core concept of a battery of tests which provide reliable separation between brain-damaged and normal subjects. He improved the standardization of the original tests and added new components which assessed sensory efficiency, perceptual motor skill, and personality. More important, he demonstrated the viability of his test interpretation approach over an entire spectrum of neurological conditions (Klove, 1974). Brain dysfunction, or cerebral dysfunction, matured as a concept from a highly subjective judgment based on unreliable "soft signs" of a neurological disorder to a quantifiable formation of patterns on objective tests.

Reitan concurrently refined the interpretative use of the tests and advocated blind interpretation of clinical test results as a safeguard against bias resulting from knowledge about extralaboratory data.

Current use of the battery by trained workers in psychology, medicine, and education reflects this history of conceptual and practical battery development. Other investigators have added to the basic battery additional measures which provide additional information about the status of brain-related abilities (Matthews, 1974).

Interpretation of the test battery has likewise grown to be a complex task, involving at least four major modes of data interpretation: (1) level of performance, (2) pathognomic signs, (3) relational patterns, and (4) comparison of left–right body performances. These methods of interpretation are complementary. Clinical judgments and predictions regarding the status of the subject's brain emerge solely from the neuropsychological test data. Statements about the existence, locus, and type of lesion or dysfunction may be made by interpreters.

The primary mode of inference rests on the comparison of individual test results with normative samples with carefully selected performance level "cut points," by which performances are classified as normal or impaired. Increasing demand for trained clinical neuropsychologists and for more information about the interpretative process has fostered attempts to make clinical rules objective and tangible in the form of computer algorhythms (Adams et al., 1975; Russell et al., 1973).

Despite the complexity in test interpretation and application, the Halstead–Reitan battery retains its empirical emphasis. It is the only formalized series of tests with satisfactory validity and reliability over a spectrum of neurological problems. Moreover, this approach has not become identified with particular theories of brain function and thus has typically been employed to describe or generate ideas about brain–behavior linkages rather than confirm particular modes of brain function.

This freedom from preconception about brain mechanisms has made the Halstead–Reitan approach particularly useful in studies that map unknown relationships or interaction between brain and environment. Criticism of these techniques typically ignores the purposeful empiricism and implies that the approach is overly simple or atheoretical. At worst, the validity and reliability studies are criticized for unspecified faults while alternative measures are proposed whose superiority in measurement is far from demonstrated (Smith, 1975).

An individual's neuropsychological deficit, then, is a tangible concept measured by individual test scores as well as composite profile analysis. The clinician's assessment of the results is made in a way that limits potential confounding factors. Impairment may be seen to correlate with slow, disordered, or inappropriate responses by the subject to adaptive demands outside the laboratory. Key problem-solving, abstracting, and judgment faculties may be inadequate to meet everyday demands in living, or the deficits may lower the optimal or expected level of adjustment to life stress.

These difficulties may exist even when basic sensory thresholds, simple motor responses, and uncomplicated personal interactions are unremarkable. The inference of cerebral dysfunction arises from inefficient performance on more sophisticated sensory challenges, perceptual motor integration tasks, and complex problem situations. It is the ability to recognize and respond to new or changing environments that is sampled and analyzed in the neuropsychological laboratory. The application of the behavior sample to the environment depends upon the standardization of the behavior sample (test battery), the skill and impartiality of the interpreter, and the knowledge that the whole process does have something to do with the brain.

Tests Comprising the Halstead–Reitan Neuropsychological Test Battery

THE HALSTEAD BATTERY

Category Test

The Category Test is a relatively complex test of concept formation and abstracting ability and is considered one of the best indicators in the battery of the general condition of the cerebral hemispheres. The subject must note similarities and differences in the stimulus material (slides projected on a screen), must postulate hypotheses that seem reasonable with respect to recurring patterns (e.g., numbers of objects, position of odd items), and must test these hypotheses. Feedback is provided after each response as to its correctness (bell or buzzer). Not only must the subject learn and retain concepts, but he must also shift from one concept to another as required by changes in stimuli.

Tactual Performance Test

The Tactual Performance Test utilizes a modification of the Seguin–Goddard Form Board and requires much from the subject: tactile form discrimination, kinesthesis, coordination of movement of the upper extremities, manual dexterity, and visualization and reproduction of the spatial configuration of the shapes in terms of their spatial interrelationships on the board. The blindfolded subject first places the blocks in the holes on the board with his preferred hand, next with his other hand, and third with both hands. Each effort is timed. Finally, the blocks and board are put away, the subject removes his blindfold and is asked to draw a diagram of the board showing the blocks in their proper places. The drawing is scored according to how many blocks were reproduced correctly (memory) and, of those, how many were placed in the correct positions on the board (localization). These two scores plus total time for right, left, and both hands are the scores obtained from this test. The localization component has been shown to be a good indicator of the overall condition of the brain.

Rhythm Test

The Rhythm Test is a subtest of the Seashore Tests of Musical Talent. The subject must differentiate between pairs of rhythmic beats which are sometimes the same and sometimes different. This test requires alertness, sustained attention, and the ability to perceive and compare rhythmic patterns.

Speech Sounds Perception Test

The Speech Sounds Perception Test consists of a standardized set of nonsense words played from a taped recording. The subject must underline the syllable spoken, selecting from four alternatives printed from each item on the test form. The subject must maintain attention, must perceive the spoken stimulus through hearing, and must relate this perception through vision to the correct configuration of letters on the test form.

Tapping Test

Finger tapping speed is almost purely dependent on motor speed. The subject, using only his index finger, is given a number of trials, first with his preferred hand, then with his nonpreferred hand. The actual speed is important, as is the comparison of right and left hands. Lesions affecting the motor areas of the brain will cause decrements in tapping performance. Three other procedures, Critical Flicker Frequency (two parts) and Time Sense Memory, were in Halstead's original battery, but were subsequently dropped by Reitan because of their low discriminative power.

Halstead Impairment Index

The Halsted Impairment Index is computed by determining what proportion of the seven tests fall above the criterion level. Tests contributing to this index are: Category Test, Tactual Performance Test (total time, memory, and localization), Rhythm Test, Speech–Sounds Perception Test, and the Finger Oscillation Test. Achievement of an index of .3 to .4 confers a borderline to mildly impaired status on a subject; .5 to .6 represents mild to moderate impairment; and .7 or above indicates moderate to severe impairment.

TRAIL MAKING TEST

The Trail Making Test consists of two parts, A and B. Part A consists of 25 circles distributed over a white sheet of paper and numbered from 1 to 25. The subject connects the circles with a pencil line as quickly as possible, beginning with 1 and proceeding in sequence. Part B consists of 25 circles numbered from 1 to 13 and lettered from A to L. The subject connects the circles with a pencil line as quickly as possible, beginning with 1 and proceeding in sequence. The scores are the number of seconds required to finish each part. This test seems to require immediate recognition of the symbolic significance of numbers and letters, ability to scan a page continuously to identify the next number or letter in sequence, flexibility in integrating the numerical and alphabetical series, and completion of these requirements under pressure of time.

APHASIA EXAMINATION

The Aphasia Examination is Reitan's modification of the Halstead–Wepman Aphasia Screening Test. This test samples the subject's ability to name common objects, spell, identify individual numbers and letters, read, write, calculate, enunciate, understand spoken language, identify body parts, and differentiate between right and left. The test also requires a subject to copy certain shapes (e.g., square, triangle, cross, key) and thereby provides information regarding possible constructional dyspraxia.

SENSORY PERCEPTUAL EXAMINATIONS

Sensory Perception

The procedure followed in the Sensory Perception examination attempts to determine the accuracy with which the subject can perceive bilateral simultaneously applied sensory stimulation after it has been determined that his perception of unilateral stimulation on each side is essentially intact. This procedure is used for tactile, auditory, and visual sensory modalities in separate tests.

Tactile Finger Recognition

The Tactile Finger Recognition procedure tests the ability of the subject to identify individual fingers on both hands as a result of tactile stimulation of each finger.

Finger-tip Number Writing Perception Test

The Finger-tip Number Writing Perception Test procedure requires the subject to report numbers written on the tips of each finger without the subject being able to see them.

Tactile Form Recognition Test

The Tactile Form Recognition Test requires the subject to identify through touch alone, pennies, nickels, and dimes in each hand tested separately, and also with coins placed in both hands simultaneously.

An additional procedure makes use of flat, plastic shapes (cross, square, triangle, circle) which, when placed in the subject's hand, must be matched against a set of stimulus figures that are visually exposed to the subject.

LATERAL DOMINANCE EXAMINATION

The procedures followed in the Lateral Dominance Examination are used to obtain information regarding handedness, footedness, and eyedness. The ABC Vision Test is used to provide information regarding ocular dominance. Further right–left comparisons are made by measure of strength of grip in each hand. This measurement is made with the Smedley Hand Dynamometer.

WECHSLER ADULT INTELLIGENCE SCALE

The WAIS intelligence test is well known and is used in the standard manner. Scores result in verbal, performance, and full-scale intelligence quotients. Large discrepancies between verbal and performance IQ or among various subtest scores may be of diagnostic significance when viewed with other data.

MINNESOTA MULTIPHASIC PERSONALITY INVENTORY

The MMPI is used as a personality measure. Subjects obtain scores on 10 personality and 4 validity scales. The validity and content scales are described in Chapter VII by Lachar *et al*.

METHOD

The study plan called for the neuropsychological evaluation of a group of polydrug abuse patients, a group of psychiatric patients who denied drug use, and a group of nonpatients with minimal drug use experience. Evaluations were to be carried out initially and then repeated after 3 months.

Subjects

POLYDRUG GROUP

The polydrug group consisted of 151 patients who were admitted to one of eight polydrug centers for treatment of problems related to misuse of drugs other than heroin or alcohol. The eight programs, located in Denver, Detroit, Houston, New York, Richmond, San Diego, San Francisco, and Seattle, attempted to enroll all consecutive admissions during the period of November 1974 to April 1975.

PSYCHIATRIC GROUP

In the light of previous research, which has suggested that individuals with severe psychopathology are sometimes judged to be impaired, and because polydrug patients often appeared to be experiencing profound psychopathology, we included a group of non-drug-abusing psychiatric patients. This group was composed of 66 individuals currently in treatment at inpatient or day hospital facilities, but who could not be considered chronically ill by the criterion of having been prescribed antipsychotic or antidepressant drugs or lithium more or less continually for 5 or more years. Five of the polydrug units collaborating in the study had access to such psychiatric patients who met the inclusion–exclusion criteria, discussed in the following paragraphs, and who matched polydrug users for age, education, and sex.

NONPATIENT GROUP

A nonpatient minimal drug-using group was constituted of 59 volunteers, from service organizations, hospital blue collar jobs, and other services, who were selected on the basis of demographic similarity to the polydrug group.

Inclusion–Exclusion Criteria

Previous diagnosis of neurological illness or experience with special neurological tests, such as pneumoencephalogram, cerebral angiogram, or brain scan, which would indicate suspicion of neurological illness or positive history of brain injury or surgery, were exclusionary criteria. Nonpatients and psychiatric patients were acceptable as subjects if:

1. They had not consumed more than two fifths of hard liquor (or equivalent amounts of beer or wine) per week for 4 consecutive weeks.
2. They had not regularly smoked marijuana more than twice a week during the year preceding the study (i.e., more than 100 occasions of use).
3. They had not ingested hallucinogenic substances on more than a total of 50 occasions.
4. They had not used amphetamines or other stimulants on more than 20 occasions in the year prior to the study.
5. They had not inhaled fumes from volatile substances such as paint, glue, or gasoline in an effort to produce intoxication on more than 10 occasions in their entire lives.
6. They had never engaged in intravenous drug use.

Psychiatric and nonpatient group members were excluded if their total sedative-hypnotic used exceeded 50 tablets, or capsules in the year preceding the study. Potential psychiatric group members were allowed greater use of benzodiazepines than potential nonpatient group members. Nonpatient controls could not have been hospitalized for psychiatric illness in the year preceding the study, nor have ever taken any antipsychotic or antidepressant medication. The demographic characteristics of the three groups are presented in Table X.1.

Follow-up Testing

The 3-month follow-up testing was completed on 71% of the subjects; 93 of 151 polydrug users (61%), 51 of 66 psychiatric patients (77%), and 51 of 59 nonpatients (86%). A comparison of those who completed the study with those who dropped out revealed significant differences on only 1 of 15 variables presented in Table X.1. Polydrug dropouts were significantly less well educated than those completing the follow-up (10.7 years versus 11.6 < .01). They also scored slightly higher on the PD scale of the MMPI.

Drug Use and Medical History

In order to establish a measure of extent of drug use that was sufficiently detailed to avoid the problems found in previous studies, an exhaustive drug use questionnaire was administered by trained, experienced interviewers. The Drug Use Inventory allowed the gathering of detailed, historical information about alcohol and drug use for a period of 10 years prior to the first neuropsychological evaluation. Type of drugs used, route of administration, quantities used, and periods of heaviest use were elicited. The drug use experiences for the subjects are displayed in Table X.2. Drug dosages were converted to standard units of equivalence in pentobarbital, dextroamphetamine, morphine, and ethanol as appropriate. There is a moderate tendency for increased use of any one substance to be related to increased use of other substances except for antipsychotics. The intercorrelation of drug use is presented in Table X.3.

A medical history questionnaire which emphasized events that would raise a suspicion of neurological dysfunction and which covered the subject's life from the prenatal period to the present was also administered. Included were such content areas as prenatal trauma, learning difficulties, febrile convulsions, and head injury.

At follow-up, all subjects were interviewed regarding interim drug use and health events. Table X.2 presents the interim drug use of all subjects. The overall reduction of drug use by the polydrug patients is notable. Analysis of interim medical history indicated few events which would

Table X.1

DEMOGRAPHIC CHARACTERISTICS OF STUDY POPULATION AT INITIAL (I) AND 3-MONTH FOLLOW-UP (F) TESTING[a]

	Polydrug users		Psychiatric patients		Nonpatient subjects		Combined groups	
	I	F	I	F	I	F	I	F
Numbers	151	93	66	51	59	51	276	195
Age	25.5	26.1	28.8	29.5	26.1	25.9	26.5	27.0
SD	8.0	8.1	6.5	6.5	7.2	7.1	7.6	7.6
Education (Grades completed)	11.3	11.6	13.5	13.7	12.8	12.8	12.1	12.5
SD	2.1	2.2	2.4	2.5	2.2	2.1	2.4	2.4
Sex								
Male	89(59%)	55(59%)	35(53%)	28(55%)	25(42%)	24(47%)	149(54%)	107(55%)
Female	62(41%)	38(41%)	31(47%)	23(45%)	34(58%)	27(53%)	127(46%)	88(45%)
Race								
White	122(81%)	75(81%)	57(86%)	44(86%)	50(85%)	47(92%)	229(83%)	166(85%)
Nonwhite	29(19%)	18(19%)	9(14%)	7(14%)	9(15%)	4(8%)	47(17%)	29(15%)
Handedness								
Right	142(94%)	87(94%)	62(94%)	49(96%)	48(81%)	42(82%)	252(91%)	178(91%)
Left	8(5%)	5(5%)	4(6%)	2(4%)	11(19%)	9(18%)	23(8%)	16(8%)
Both	1(1%)	1(1%)	0(0%)	0(0%)	0(0%)	0(0%)	1(1%)	1(1%)

[a] Reprinted with permission from the American Medical Association (Archives of General Psychiatry © 1978).

Table X.2

DRUG EXPERIENCE OF SUBJECTS[a,b]

	Average weekly use during preceding 10 years			Peak amount used during week of heaviest use			Average weekly use during 3-month follow-up		
	Polydrug	Psychiatric	Nonpatient	Polydrug	Psychiatric	Nonpatient	Polydrug	Psychiatric	Nonpatient
Ethanol (gm pure ethanol)	318	65	72	1458	235	324	199	62	110
CNS depressants (gm pentobarbital)	1.1	0.2	0	2.8	0.2	0	0.5	0	0
CNS stimulants (g dextroamphetamine)	0.14	0.04	0.05	0.37	0.2	0.1	0.02	0	0
Heroin (mg morphine)	1.1	0	0	58	0	0	0.2	0	0
Other opiates (mg morphine)	1.5	0	0	132.5	0	0	5.3	0	<1.0
Marijuana (joints)	39.7	0.5	0.9	78.9	1.6	6.1	7.6	0.4	0.6
Hashish (pipes)	2.5	<1.0	<1.0	2.9	<1.0	<1.0	<1.0	<1.0	<1.0
Hallucinogens (hits—occasions)	0.1	0	0	5.2	0	0	<0.1	0	<0.1
Cocaine (lines)	0.6	0.3	0	5.5	0.9	0	<0.1	<0.1	0
Unclassified substances (occasions)	<1.0	0	0	20.3	0	0	0	<1.0	0
Cigarettes (packs)	6.0	2.0	2.0	—	—	—	—	—	—

[a] Quantities of drugs consumed were calculated as follows. For alcohol, milliliters of ethanol were calculated on the basis of the ethanol content of beer (7%), wine (12%), and spirits (40%). For sedatives, all drugs were converted to pentobarbital equivalents: 100 mg of pentobarbital = 30 mg of phenobarbital, 100 mg of secobarbital, 100 mg of amobarbital, 30 mg of flurazepam, 30 mg of methyprylon, 250 mg of ethchlorvynol, 300 mg of methaqualone, and 500 mg of chloral hydrate. For stimulants, it was calculated that 10 mg of dextroamphetamine = 15 mg of methylphenidate and 5 mg of methamphetamine. For intravenously administered stimulants, each injection was judged to equal 10 mg of dextroamphetamine. For opiates, it was calculated that 10 mg of morphine = 5 mg of heroin (1 spoon = 70 mg of heroin), 120 mg of codeine, 130 mg of propoxyphene, and 10 mg of methadone.
[b] Reprinted with permission from the American Medical Association (Archives of General Psychiatry © 1978).

237

Table X.3

RELATIONSHIPS BETWEEN USE OF VARIOUS CLASSES OF DRUGS BASED ON
A 10-YEAR HISTORY[a,b]

	Depressant	Stimulant	Marijuana	Opiate	Hallucinogens	Ethanol
Stimulant	.473	—	—	—	—	—
Marijuana	.419	.395	—	—	—	—
Opiate	.345	.296	.355	—	—	—
Hallucinogen	.315	.352	.467	.286	—	—
Ethanol	.325	.343	.453	.290	.251	—
Antipsychotic	—[a]	−.102	−.119	—[a]	—[a]	—[a]

[a] Correlations which were not significant ($p < .05$) are omitted.

[b] Reprinted with permission of the American Medical Association (Archives of General Psychiatry © 1978).

place subjects at increased risk for neuropsychological impairment; the most common complaints of headache, faintness, and numbness were reported almost exclusively by the polydrug group.

A comparison of those who completed the follow-up with those who did not revealed no significant differences on medical information or lifetime drug use, although there was a tendency for dropouts to have used more CNS depressants.

Screening for Acute Drug Effects

Three separate screening procedures were used in order to ensure that subjects evaluated were not experiencing acute drug effects or abstinence syndrome during the study. A Drug Interference Scale which assessed six behavioral indices (motor activity, coordination, orientation, nystagmus, thought pattern, and mood related to intoxication or abstinence syndrome) was completed for each subject by the examiner prior to testing. In addition, examiners made clinical judgments regarding the subject's intoxication. If either procedure indicated that the subject was intoxicated the examination could be deferred. Finally, each subject was required to give a urine sample midway through the examination. The urine sample was screened for barbiturates, opiates, and amphetamines. These procedures were carried out during both initial and follow-up testing.

Neuropsychological Evaluation and Rating of Neuropsychological Deficit

Prior to the beginning of the study, 12 neuropsychological examiners from the eight participating centers were intensively trained in the administration of the HRB by core staff at a 10-day workshop. Continued standard administration was assured by periodic site visits by a member of the training staff.

Initial neuropsychological evaluations of the polydrug patients were carried out on each qualifying sequential admission 21 to 30 days after admission. The delay was employed to allow subjects time to detoxify and recover from abstinence effects. Members of the psychiatric control group were tested at a time of clinical convenience, provided they were not so psychotic that they could not cooperate with testing. If the psychiatric controls were receiving psychoactive medication, consultation with their physicians ensured that they were stabilized on their medications. Normal controls were tested at a time of personal convenience.

All subjects were told that they were participating in an investigation of the neuropsychological impact of various drugs, that their participation was voluntary, that a 3-month follow-up was anticipated, and that they would be paid for their time. Their written consent to participate was obtained.

All examiners first carried out the assessments for acute intoxication, then administered the Halstead–Reitan test battery. Following this, a urine sample was collected and the drug use questionnaire, medical screening questionnaire, and MMPI were administered.

All of the data were sent to the coordinating center in San Diego where they were screened for inconsistencies and obvious scoring errors prior to inclusion in the data pool. At this time, an experienced clinician rated each protocol using the inferential methods described earlier. Each protocol was assigned to one of six categories: (1) better than average performance; (2) average performance; (3) borderline-atypical, but not clearly deficient performance; (4) mildly impaired performance; (5) moderately impaired performance; (6) severely impaired performance. In the analysis of results the first three categories were grouped as neuropsychologically unimpaired and the last three became the impaired group. The central data base was prepared for computer analysis by Dr. Kenneth Adams in Toronto and is described in part in his chapter on data management (Chapter XVI).

A Second Measure of Deficit, Halstead's Impairment Index

Halstead's Impairment Index is the number of Halstead's seven tests which are abnormal by his criteria, divided by seven. An impairment index of 0 means all test results fall into the normal range and an impairment index of 1.0 would mean all tests fall into the impaired range. The previously described clinician's rating considered the seven Halstead tests, the impairment index, and a number of other measures not included in the original Halstead battery. The correlation between clinician's rating and the impairment index was ($r = 0.91$).

RESULTS

Drug Immersion and Cerebral Dysfunction—Initial Testing

Polydrug and psychiatric control groups were found to have a greater proportion of impaired subjects than the nonpatient controls. The blind classifications by the clinician placed 37% of polydrug patients, 26% of psychiatric patients, and 8% of the normal patients in mild, moderate, or severe impairment categories. To further assess the relationship between drug use and neuropsychological performance, a 3 × 2 multivariate analysis of variance (MANOVA) was employed with group membership (polydrug, psychiatric, nonpatient) and neuropsychological performance (impaired, unimpaired) as independent variables. Two sets of dependent variables were used: one set of seven cumulative (10 years) drug use estimates (alcohol, marijuana, sedatives, stimulants, hallucinogens, opiates, and antipsychotics), and another set of peak use estimates for the same substances. Because of the skewed distribution of these data, a logarithmic transformation ($\log_{10}[1 + x]$) was employed to reduce distorted variance and bring in outliers.

The group membership main effect was significant ($p < .001$) for both multivariate and all univariate F ratios, confirming the effective selection of the groups on drug use criteria. Results were very similar for both cumulative and peak data. There was no two-way interaction between group membership and test performance factors. The test performance main effect was significant ($p < .01$) for both cumulative and peak variable sets. Significant univariate tests were observed for two of the seven drug categories. Central nervous system (CNS) depressants (cumulative use, $p < .003$; peak use, $p < .002$) and opiates (cumulative use $p < .01$; peak use, $p < .007$) were thus implicated in the main effect. Further statistical analysis showed that these findings persisted even when age and education are individually or collectively covaried out. Table X.4 shows these results. Therefore, we concluded that increased experience with CNS depressants and/or opiates was related to neuropsychological impairment within the parameters of the study.

Table X.4

MULTIVARIATE ANALYSIS OF VARIANCE ON CUMULATIVE AND PEAK DRUG USE SHOWING NEUROPSYCHOLOGICAL EFFECT[a]

	Cumulative drug use	Cumulative drug use minus age	Cumulative drug use minus age, education	Peak drug use	Peak drug use minus age	Peak drug use minus age, education
Neuropsychological effect p less than	.01	.035	.043	.006	.014	.047
Multivariate F	2.89	2.30	2.30	3.12	2.37	2.16
df	(6,266)	(6,265)	(6,264)	(6,266)	(6,265)	(6,264)
			Univariate F ratios (p less than):			
Ethanol	.855	.646	.566	.376	.383	.405
Depressants	.003	.011	.051	.002	.004	.026
Stimulants	.115	.144	.078	.680	.587	.446
Opiates	.010	.015	.008	.007	.010	.009
Hallucinogens	.628	.256	.377	.822	.590	.979
Marijuana	.453	.827	.846	.956	.469	.656

[a] Reprinted with permission, *Drug and Alcohol Dependence*, 2, 91–108, 1978 © Elseiven, Sequoia, S.A.

241

We next focused on the individual neuropsychological test scores.
(Test and retest averaged performance figures for each neuropsychological subtest are listed by group in Tables X.5 and X.6.) To
reduce the large number of variables to workable summary dimensions,
we chose factor analysis. In choosing the variables for inclusion in the
matrix, we specified two conditions. First, variables had to have a nontri-
vial but not necessarily normal distribution to avoid spuriously high or
low correlations. Second, where tests were represented by several scores,
only one summary score was selected to avoid false factor extraction by
virtue of excessive methodological variance. For example, the Category
Test has seven subtest scores and a total score—each of which provides
different clinical information. However, only the total score was included
in the factor analysis to avoid a "Category Test Factor" from emerging.
The final variable selection reflected a balance of cognitive, perceptual,
and motor skills.

Factor analysis software employed was from version 6.01 of the Statistical Package for the Social Sciences (SPSS). Eigenvalues generated from
the four-factor principal axis solution exceeded Kaiser's criterion of 1.0
and the rotated solution accounted for 61% of the variance in the matrix.

The rotated factor loadings are presented in Table X.7. The absolute
magnitude of these loadings allows the reader to understand which tests
contribute most to the emergence of the factor. In general, we judged
loadings of .5 or larger to guide us in evaluating the results. With approximately 10 subjects for each variable, this seemed suitably conservative
—especially in the light of the amount of variance explained.

Factor 1 is essentially a general verbal intelligence factor which is
education related. This comes closest to an overall "G" or general ability
factor found in major studies of psychometrically defined intelligence.
Factor 2 is a nonverbal factor loading principally on tests of visual-motor,
tactile-motor, and perceptual skills. This is an age-correlated factor composed of tests traditionally thought to be most sensitive to cerebral dysfunction. Factor 3 appears to capture tests of simple language perception and
psychomotor speed. It seems more closely related to attentional factors
than specific abilities, and is also keyed in a pathological direction in
relation to the other factors that are positively keyed (i.e., higher is
better). Factor 4 loads heavily on one particular test of motor strength,
but is of limited interpretability because of the likelihood of error variance
inclusion and its small role in the entire solution.

This solution is not unexpected and, in fact, is typical of factor analytic
solutions involving such variables.

In order to examine the differences in ability structure which might
exist between the groups, factor scores were computed for each subject
on all four factors. Briefly, factor scores are numerical products of each

subject and the weights provided by the factor analysis. The sum of these products is the factor score for a particular subject and factor. The factor scores, then, are new summary variables. A MANOVA analysis using group membership (polydrug, psychiatric, and nonpatient) as the independent variables, and the four factor scores as dependent variables was significant ($p < .05$) with factors 1, 2, and 4 implicated in the main effect. These results are summarized in Figure X.1.

A more detailed analysis of the intergroup differences revealed that polydrug users were significantly impaired ($p < .05$) on Factor 1 in reference to the other two groups. Further, both patient groups were inferior to the nonpatient controls ($p < .05$) on Factor 2. A later reanalysis of these factors with age and education covaried out resulted in the same overall multivariate significance, but the Factor 1 differences disappeared.

Equally as important, separate factor analyses of the neuropsychological test results from the groups showed clear *qualitative* differences in ability structures. Whereas in the matrices, control groups were quite similar to each other (as well as to the whole sample), the polydrug group showed a different order of factor extration (nonverbal, perceptual-motor factor first) more reminiscent of organic brain-damage samples.

Figure X.2 compares factor loadings for subjects judged by the clinician to be impaired and unimpaired. The overall MANOVA is significant ($p < .001$) and each of the first three factors shows large differences on the factor scores. Interestingly, the largest difference is obtained on Factor 2 which has the biggest grouping of tests commonly thought to be sensitive to cerebral dysfunction. The overall view of the factor results is that the groups do have differing ability structures. Polydrug users were deficient on Factor 1, which taps school-related verbal skill and intelligence as well as left hemisphere measures in the neuropsychological sense. Both patient groups—polydrug and psychiatric—were deficient on Factor 2. This factor contained the measures most sensitive to cerebral dysfunction. As discussed later, there are qualitative differences which suggest different *kinds* of impairment in the two groups. Finally, we combined the polydrug and psychiatric groups to examine the relationship between cumulative experience with seven major classes of drugs (alcohol, marijuana, sedatives, stimulants, hallucinogens, opiates, and antipsychotics), and neuropsychological performance as measured by the four factors. A significant canonical correlation (.58) was found between drug variables as a set and the four neuropsychological factors. Substantial canonical variate coefficients for the drug set were: CNS depressants, $-.45$; marijuana, $+.83$. Substantial coefficients for the neuropsychological set were: Factor 2, .50; Factor 4, .78. This lends some

Table X.5

INITIAL EVALUATION: CNSP–ANOVA–INITIAL NEUROPSYCHOLOGICAL RESULTS FOR THREE GROUPS

Test	Polydrug N = 151		Psychiatric N = 66		Nonpatients N = 59		F for df = 2 and 273	p =	Newman–Keuls at p = .05
	Mean	SD	Mean	SD	Mean	SD			
WAIS									
FSIQ	103.5	11.7	108.3	13.9	113.1	12.1	13.44	.00	3>2>1
VIQ	104.0	13.0	111.0	14.0	113.0	13.0	14.73	.00	2, 3>1
PIQ	103.0	12.0	103.0	14.0	111.0	11.0	11.10	.00	3>2, 1
Info	10.14	2.68	12.09	2.67	11.94	3.12	15.45	.00	2, 3>1
Comp	11.21	3.64	12.77	3.72	13.25	3.03	8.88	.00	3, 2>1
Arith	9.37	2.88	10.98	3.21	11.73	3.56	14.30	.00	3, 2>1
Sims	11.28	2.64	12.86	3.01	12.74	2.27	11.09	.00	2, 3>1
Digsp	10.21	2.52	10.76	3.22	10.75	2.81	1.30	n.s.	n.s.
Vocab	10.62	2.81	12.24	3.11	12.45	3.10	11.86	.00	3, 2>1
Dig sym	10.03	2.69	10.06	2.74	12.41	2.82	17.44	.00	3>2, 1
Pic com	10.17	2.07	10.50	2.53	11.00	1.90	3.18	.04	3>1
Blocks	10.43	2.89	10.95	2.95	11.80	2.40	5.04	.007	3>1
Piccar	10.26	2.68	9.47	2.40	11.12	2.31	6.58	.002	3>1>2
Obj assmb	10.35	2.92	10.45	3.38	11.36	2.91	2.40	n.s.	n.s.

244

Halstead battery

						F	p	
Category	48.13	24.89	45.98	26.36	35.66	19.25	5.73	.004	1, 2>3
TPT dom	6.30	3.08	7.23	3.73	4.97	2.34	8.29	.00	2>1>3
TPT n dom	4.79	2.80	5.35	3.07	3.72	1.58	5.83	.004	2, 1>3
TPT both	2.93	2.18	3.40	1.96	2.24	.96	5.52	.005	2, 1>3
TPT tot	14.15	7.07	15.80	7.58	11.28	4.81	6.87	.001	2, 1>3
TPT mem	7.77	1.48	7.71	1.58	8.33	1.04	3.80	.02	3>1, 2
TPT loc	4.40	2.29	4.26	2.30	5.47	2.10	5.64	.004	3>1, 2
Speech	7.01	5.61	4.60	3.08	4.93	3.00	8.22	.00	1>3, 2
Rhythm	3.62	2.84	4.15	3.60	2.47	2.22	5.37	.005	2, 1>3
Tap dom	50.86	6.35	48.21	7.91	50.46	5.24	3.83	.02	1>2
Tap n dom	45.81	6.59	43.92	7.06	47.37	4.82	4.62	.01	3, 1>2
Imp index	.32	.26	.34	.26	.16	.15	10.81	.00	2, 1>3
R. finger agnosia	.73	1.13	.73	1.60	.34	.96	2.34	n.s.	n.s.
L. finger agnosia	.90	1.53	.67	1.64	.31	.84	3.70	.03	1>3
R. graphesthesia	1.17	1.64	1.22	1.83	.95	1.15	.50	n.s.	n.s.
L. graphesthesia	.85	1.32	.60	1.25	.95	1.46	1.18	n.s.	n.s.
R. form rec time	10.73	4.25	11.40	3.35	10.33	3.45	1.21	n.s.	n.s.
R. form rec errors	.27	.53	.25	.47	.31	.65	.18	n.s.	n.s.
L. form rec time	9.87	3.48	10.35	3.29	8.95	2.47	2.94	n.s.	n.s.
L. form rec errors	.12	.35	.07	.27	.15	.41	.76	n.s.	n.s.
Aphasia tot error	2.73	3.20	2.11	2.29	1.82	2.19	2.56	n.s.	n.s.
Constr dysprx	1.47	.60	1.35	.48	1.35	.48	1.36	n.s.	n.s.
Trails A	28.41	12.01	31.15	11.34	24.10	6.46	6.51	.002	2, 1>3
Trails B	69.32	33.39	83.97	44.42	59.67	20.78	7.93	.001	2>1, 3
R. pegs time	68.17	14.02	71.39	25.93	61.09	12.03	5.54	.005	2, 1>3
L. pegs time	72.66	14.56	77.57	25.27	63.95	13.16	9.25	.00	2, 1>3
Grip right hand	43.36	14.10	38.36	11.98	38.63	13.41	4.38	.01	1>2, 3
Grip left hand	38.77	13.56	34.78	12.34	35.56	13.34	2.53	n.s.	n.s.

Table X.6

FOLLOW-UP EVALUATION: CNSP–ANOVA–FOLLOW-UP NEUROPSYCHOLOGICAL RESULTS FOR THREE GROUPS

Test	Polydrug N = 93		Psychiatric N = 51		Nonpatients N = 51		F for df = 2 and 192	p =	Newman–Keuls at p = .05
	Mean	SD	Mean	SD	Mean	SD			
WAIS									
FSIQ	107.0	12.5	113.0	15.7	120.2	9.5	17.82	.00	3>2>1
VIQ	106.0	13.3	114.1	14.2	118.1	11.0	17.63	.00	3, 2>1
PIQ	108.2	14.0	110.0	17.8	120.2	10.6	12.52	.00	3>2, 1
Info	10.46	2.71	12.80	2.97	12.59	2.62	15.99	.00	2, 3>1
Comp	11.45	3.40	13.55	3.81	13.78	2.98	10.32	.00	3, 2>1
Arith	9.97	3.14	11.33	3.07	12.29	3.03	9.90	.00	3, 2>1
Sims	11.73	2.55	15.33	2.78	13.55	2.04	11.53	.00	3, 2>1
Dig sp	10.56	2.88	10.88	2.83	12.51	2.69	8.20	.00	3>2, 1
Vocab	10.74	2.82	12.88	2.99	12.76	2.70	13.12	.00	2, 3>1
Dig sym	10.89	3.10	10.90	3.81	13.37	3.05	10.67	.00	3>2, 1
Pic com	10.89	2.75	11.65	2.58	12.20	1.60	4.91	.008	3>1
Blocks	11.11	3.11	11.69	3.07	12.88	2.53	5.94	.003	3>2, 1
Piccar	10.82	2.74	10.61	3.21	12.59	2.08	8.76	.00	3>1, 2
Obj assmb	11.76	3.01	11.69	3.46	13.57	2.88	6.60	.002	3>1, 2

Halstead battery

Category	33.13	23.43	24.84	19.71	18.65	14.66	8.41	.00	1>2, 3
TPT dom	5.12	2.80	6.31	3.04	4.12	1.96	8.15	.00	2>1>3
TPT n dom	3.65	2.23	4.64	2.89	3.21	1.31	5.39	.005	2>1, 3
TPT both	2.35	1.61	3.12	2.41	1.91	.82	6.26	.003	2>1, 3
TPT tot	10.99	6.13	13.97	7.41	8.81	3.63	9.11	.00	2>1>3
TPT mem	8.24	1.33	7.76	1.62	8.47	1.06	3.51	.03	3>2
TPT loc	5.10	2.57	4.84	2.37	6.28	1.90	5.27	.006	3>1, 2
Speech	6.09	5.13	4.96	2.90	4.00	1.93	4.53	.01	1>3
Rhythm	3.52	3.02	3.16	2.60	2.30	2.26	3.11	.05	1>3
Tap dom	51.75	5.94	49.55	7.57	50.51	6.01	1.99	n.s.	n.s.
Tap n dom	46.59	6.10	45.18	6.83	48.06	4.57	2.86	.06	3>2
Imp ind	.26	.26	.25	.25	.10	.15	8.43	.00	1, 2>3
R. finger agnosia	.75	1.28	.71	1.90	.32	.62	1.77	n.s.	n.s.
L. finger agnosia	.62	1.01	.82	2.14	.46	1.09	.84	n.s.	n.s.
R. graphesthesia	1.02	1.37	.67	1.41	.88	1.22	1.15	n.s.	n.s.
L. graphesthesia	.87	1.43	.78	1.79	.76	1.27	.11	n.s.	n.s.
R. form rec time	9.34	2.77	9.27	1.80	9.34	2.17	.01	n.s.	n.s.
R. form rec errors	.26	.53	.14	.35	.04	.20	4.59	.01	1>3
L. form rec time	8.71	1.89	8.90	1.42	8.60	1.92	.37	n.s.	n.s.
L. form rec errors	.15	.39	.06	.24	.04	.20	2.58	n.s.	n.s.
Aphasia tot errors	3.02	3.36	2.04	2.20	1.14	1.56	8.52	.00	1>2, 3
Construct dysprx	1.50	.56	1.41	.50	1.22	.42	5.08	.007	1>3
Trails A	25.80	10.02	28.46	15.45	20.71	5.27	6.82	.002	2, 1>3
Trails B	73.54	62.22	72.52	40.83	48.37	14.58	4.93	.008	1, 2>3
R. pegs time	69.33	53.96	69.42	24.42	57.27	10.19	1.64	n.s.	n.s.
L. pegs time	73.27	56.61	75.94	37.53	16.42	9.61	1.56	n.s.	n.s.
Grip right hand	40.97	14.49	36.12	12.47	38.39	14.63	2.00	n.s.	n.s.
Grip left hand	36.57	14.20	31.98	12.07	35.90	13.64	1.95	n.s.	n.s.

Table X.7

VARIMAX ROTATED FACTOR MATRIX FOR INITIAL TESTING (ALL SUBJECTS)[a]

	Factor 1	Factor 2	Factor 3	Factor 4
WAIS				
Information	83	13	20	−01
Comprehension	66	28	−17	−04
Arithmetic	73	19	−21	08
Similarities	73	25	−22	01
Digit span	34	01	−39	−02
Vocabulary	81	14	−30	−06
Digit symbol	33	34	−31	−11
Picture completion	53	41	−13	16
Block design	46	53	−09	16
Picture arrangement	39	47	−17	10
Object assembly	39	64	01	13
Halstead Battery				
Category errors	−41	−42	31	−12
Tactual perf (time)	−17	−73	23	−19
Tactual perf (mem)	12	63	−24	08
Tactual perf (loc)	10	58	−11	05
Speech (errors)	−44	−19	67	−01
Rhythm (errors)	−17	−15	54	−04
Tapping (dominant)	03	26	−28	46
Aphasia tests				
Total errors	−40	−32	59	04
Drawings	−31	−51	29	−04
Extinction	−12	−22	10	−16
Finger agnosia	−07	−46	19	09
Graphesthesia (errors)	−15	−40	00	−07
Trails B	−14	−51	55	−14
Pegboard (dominant)	−12	−55	21	−07
Grip (dominant)	−04	02	17	98

[a] Reprinted with permission, American Medical Association (Archives of General Psychiatry, © 1978).

further support to results presented earlier that depressants might be implicated in impaired neuropsychological performance. At the same time, an unexpected reverse effect emerges for marijuana.

Medical Risk Factors and Neuropsychological Performance

It is possible that "premorbid" factors such as birth trauma, childhood illness involving the brain, learning disability, or head injury, all could

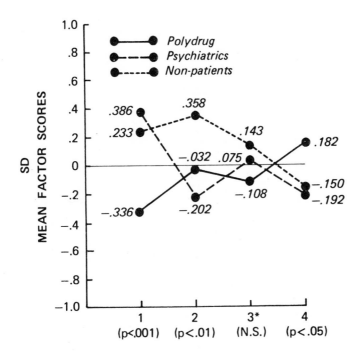

Figure X.1 Mean factor scores by groups at initial testing. (*Tosimplify the figure, factor 3 has been reversed.)

contribute to neuropsychological impairment among polydrug users. To examine the extent of this potential premorbid contribution we computed a medical risk score based on the number of items from Table X.8 which each subject endorsed. The average number of positive items for poly-drug users is 4.4 ± 2.5; for psychiatrics, 2.8 ± 2.0; and for controls, 1.2 ± 1.2 (overall F significant at $p < .05$). The three groups differ significantly from each other (Neuman–Keuls, $p < .05$), with the polydrug group well beyond the others.

While both patient groups reported more medical events, there is no correlation between risk score and neuropsychological deficit as summarized by Halstead's impairment index. To explore the possibility of a relationship between these factors in a more comprehensive way, we selected the four medical risk variables (learning difficulties, head injury, mother's pregnancy, general anesthesia) having the highest correlation with the impairment index. These values were input to a multiple regression program using the impairment index itself as a dependent variable. In all, these medical risk variables accounted for 20% of the variance in the impairment index.

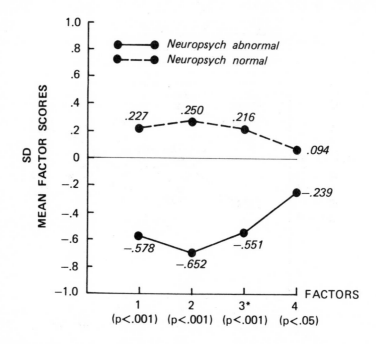

Figure X.2. Mean factor scores by normal versus abnormal clinical neuropsychological rating. (*To simplify the figure, factor 3 has been reversed.)

Some theorists have thought that the reason why CNS depressants and opiates are found to relate to behavioral impairment is that users acquire mild cerebral dysfunction as a result of neurological insult during their perinatal or early developmental period, and then try to cope with their deficit through self-medication. To test this notion we generated correlations between the initial six medical items from Table X.8 (which, by definition, had to precede drug use), and cumulative use of depressants and opiates. Only one chance correlation emerged as significant (depressants and learning disability, $r = -.16$). There is little here to suggest that early medical events are contributing to the drug use–impairment relationship.

Acute Toxicity and Neuropsychological Performance

Although our clinical Drug Interference Scale identified no polydrug user as being behaviorally toxic at the time of testing, urinalysis on 234 of 277 subjects revealed barbiturates, amphetamines, minor tranquilizers,

Table X.8

FREQUENCY OF OCCURRENCE FOR SELECTED MEDICAL SCREENING ITEMS AMONG THE THREE STUDY GROUPS[a]

Event	All subjects (%) N = 276	Psychiatric (%) N = 66	Normal (%) N = 59	Polydrug (%) N = 151	Chi square	
Pregnancy trouble at subject's birth	12	15	12	10	n.s.	
Subject premature	8	6	5	10	n.s.	
Subject required postnatal observation	9	8	7	10	n.s.	
Subject hospitalized before age of 6	37	32	30	26	n.s.	
Febrile convulsions (without other disease)	1	1	0	2	n.s.	
Learning difficulties in school	10	12	5	10	n.s.	
Traumatic head injury	27	20	10	35	15.05	p .001
Posttraumatic amnesia	17	10	11	19	n.s.	
Nontraumatic unconsciousness	34	14	12	51	43.5	p .001
Diagnostic brain tests performed	40	50	7	48	32.6	p .001
History of neurological disease	1	0	0	2	n.s.	
Epilepsy	0	0	0	0	n.s.	
Overdose requiring hospitalization	28	15	0	44	47.2	p .001
Severe headaches	30	25	7	42	24.2	p .001
Frequent muscular weakness	15	10	0	24	19.7	p .001
Numbness of extremities	30	28	3	42	29.1	p .001
Frequent faintness or dizziness	30	29	5	40	22.6	p .001
General anesthesia	67	70	67	65	n.s.	

[a] Reprinted with permission, Drug and Alcoholism Dependence, 2, 91–108, 1977 © Elseiven, Sequoia, S.A.

251

or opiates in 13% of the subjects. The distribution of the positive urine results amont the three groups shows that differentially impaired performance among the three groups was not due to increased acute toxicity in any one of the groups. The relationship between urine toxicology and blind ratings of neuropsychological performance just fails to reach significance ($\chi^2 = 2.63$, $p < .10$). Among the 68 polydrug subjects who gave blood samples for drug screening at the time of testing, the incidence of positive results for any substance was 15%. There was no link here between positive blood findings and neuropsychological impairment.

THREE-MONTH FOLLOW-UP
EVALUATION RESULTS

Drug Immersion and Neuropsychological Performance

Of the 91 polydrug users who completed follow-up testing 34% were judged to be neuropsychologically impaired at follow-up. Of the 51 psychiatric patients retested, 27% were judged impaired, while 4% of 51 controls were found impaired at the retest. The overall *drop* in the proportion of records judged abnormal was sligly higher for the polydrug group than for the two comparison groups (5% for polydrug users, 1% for psychiatrics, and 0% for controls).

In an effort to examine more closely the changes which occurred in each group, a clinician examined initial and follow-up protocol *pairs* for each subject and rated them as "significantly improved," "unchanged," or

Table X.9

NEUROPSYCHOLOGICAL (NP) PERFORMANCE CHANGE OVER 3 MONTHS[a]

Group	Initial NP status clinical rating	Substantial improvement N (%)	Follow-up NP status unchanged N (%)	Substantial worsening N (%)
Polydrug	Unimpaired	5 (9)	48 (85)	3 (5)
	Impaired	9 (25)	25 (69)	2 (6)
Psychiatric	Unimpared	6 (15)	25 (64)	8 (21)
	Impaired	5 (39)	7 (54)	1 (8)
Nonpatients	Unimpaired	5 (10)	43 (88)	1 (2)
	Impaired	0 (0)	2 (100)	0 (0)

[a] Reprinted with permission, American Medical Association (Archives of General Psychiatry, © 1978)

"significantly worsened." Table X.9 presents neuropsychological performance change for all groups as a function of initial neuropsychological
status. Among controls who were judged unimpaired at initial testing
there is a 10% rate of improvement and a 2% rate of worsening. We
regard these changes to be the result of relatively random error in testing
or interpretation, since no historical information suggests other causes
for this change. For purposes of discussion, these rates will be considered
baselines against which changes in other groups can be studied. Among
polydrug users who were originally judged unimpaired, the improvement
rate of 9% appears to be no different from that observed among unimpaired controls. On the other hand, the improvement rate of 25% among
polydrug users initially judged impaired exceeds chance expectation. The
rates of deterioration among polydrug users initially classified as unimpaired or impaired were not significantly higher than the rate found for
controls.

We should note that the global categories of unimpaired and impaired
neuropsychological performance are obviously quite broad, and "significant improvement" or "significant worsening" could occur without
change in global category assignment.

Of 14 polydrug users rated as "significantly improved," 6 also crossed
over from the impaired to the unimpaired category, while 2 of 5 rated as
"significantly worsened" changed from unimpaired to impaired.

These changes among the polydrug group are in marked contrast to the
findings for the psychiatric group. Of the psychiatric patients who were
categorized as unimpaired at initial testing, 21% underwent "significant
worsening" and an even greater proportion, initially judged impaired,
showed "significant improvement" (39%). Of the 11 psychiatrics rated as
improved, 2 crossed from impaired to unimpaired categories in the judgment of the neuropsychological clinician, while 3 of 9 subjects rated as
worsening changed from unimpaired to impaired. The large flux among
psychiatric patients suggests that transient influences (perhaps degree of
psychotic disorganization or amount of medications prescribed) might be
affecting neuropsychological performance in this group, but not in the
polydrug group.

The multivariate analytic approach described earlier for the initial
testing was again utilized to explore possible drug use effects. Group
membership and neuropsychological status (unimpaired, impaired) at
follow-up formed independent variables in this 3×2 MANOVA, while
10-year cumulative experiences with the seven major classes of drugs
constituted dependent variables. The overall MANOVA is significant ($p
< .05$) and neuropsychological impairment is again related to cumulative
drug use ($p < .021$). Univariate ANOVAs indicate that depressants and
opiates are once again the drugs contributing to the relationship ($p <
.024, p < .028$ respectively). When age and education differences among

groups are controlled by covariance procedures, the overall MANOVA falls just short of significance ($p < .057$).

An analogous multivariate procedure substituting interim drug use (only) as the dependent variable did not reach significance. In all likelihood, the large number of zero values for interim drug use (reflecting markedly reduced reported drug intake by polydrug users) contributed to this result (Table X.4).

To assess the stability of the previously described neuropsychological factor matrix and to determine whether group differences on factor scores persist, we repeated the factor analysis, using follow-up test results. The same overall factor structure emerged, and the differences detailed earlier were replicated. Polydrug subjects remained significantly ($p < .05$) less efficient on verbal fluency, abstraction, and problem-solving measures which defined Factor 1 in both analyses. Similarly, both polydrug and psychiatric patients showed significantly ($p < .05$) poorer performances on the same complex of spatial and tactile tasks found on Factor 2 in the first analysis. The distribution of factor scores supported the notion that the ability structures defined in the initial analyses within the three groups did not change qualitatively between first and second evaluations.

We then studied the relationship of life history of drug use and neuropsychological performance at follow-up as measured by the four factors defined by the follow-up testing. The initial findings were replicated. The canonical correlation between cumulative drug use and the follow-up neuropsychological data set being .54. The contribution of depressants was reduced and that of marijuana increased. This may be a reflection of the tendency for the heavier depressant user to drop out of the study during the interim.

Interim Medical Risk and Follow-up Neuropsychological Performance

In general, there were few reports of medical symptoms or injury during the interim period. Few events that would be expected to have neuropsychological effects were endorsed by any subjects. Two polydrug users reported head injuries, but these individuals were not subsequently rated as neuropsychologically impaired. One polydrug subject reported onset of epilepsy, and was found to be impaired.

Acute Toxicity and Follow-up Neuropsychological Performance

At initial testing we noted that the 13% of the polydrug users who showed traces of drugs in their urine tended to manifest impairment more often than those whose urine did not contain drugs, but that this association fell just short of statistical significance. At follow-up, traces of drugs (antipsychotics, antidepressants, and lithium were not counted) were found in 42% of 91 polydrug users, 4% of 43 psychiatric patients, and 0% of 47 controls. The relationship between a urine positive for drugs and neuropsychological impairment reaches statistical significance ($\chi^2 = 13.13$, $p < .001$) for the follow-up group. Thus, it appears that acute toxicity accounts for some (but not the majority) of cases of neuropsychological deficit.

Dropouts versus Completers

The comparison of subjects who did not complete the study with those who did revealed no significant demographic differences. The proportion of persons judged to be neuropsychologically impaired at initial testing is comparable for the two groups as are the medical risk summary scores. Polydrug dropouts tended to report more lifetime experience with depressants and less lifetime exposure to marijuana than did completers, but this trend is not statistically significant. These results suggest that there were no biases in the follow-up data from differences between the completers and the dropouts.

DISCUSSION

In order to comprehend the meaning of the Collaborative Study's findings we must address several methodological and theoretical issues. Are the neuropsychological findings real? To this we can reply with an unequivocal yes. By paying careful attention to standardized test administration and by examining individuals who were unquestionably very heavy multiple drug users we are able to replicate the results of several preliminary investigations (Adams et al., 1975; Grant et al., 1976; Grant & Judd, 1976). The rate of impairment we found corresponds closely to that reported in these earlier studies, leaving little doubt that somewhat less than half of the polydrug users will, in their first weeks after entry into treatment, exhibit neuropsychological deficit that will range in severity from mild to severe.

Given that these are real findings what do they mean? How certain can we be that neuropsychological deficit reflects organic mental disturbance rather than some deviant property of our polydrug sample?

The power of this neuropsychological battery to discriminate between brain-damaged and nonbrain-damaged persons is well documented (Chapman & Wolff, 1959; Halstead, 1947; Klove, 1963; Matthews &

Booker, 1972; Reitan, 1955; Vega & Parsons, 1967; Wheeler, Burke, & Reitan, 1963). The three variables which can introduce potential difficulties in interpreting neuropsychological results are age, education, and mental illness. The first of these presents little difficulty to our study since all of our subjects were youthful (mean age 26), and previous investigations have indicated no important deterioration in neuropsychological abilities up to age 45 (Reitan, 1955, 1967). Although we did find a small age relatedness in certain of our performance measures, this clearly cannot explain the large amount of deficit among the polydrug users (who were, on the average, the youngest of our three groups). Our polydrug users were, however, less well educated than psychiatric patients and non-patients. This presents a more serious difficulty since some of our tests are education-correlated (for a discussion of education effects on the Halstead–Reitan performance, see Matarazzo, Wiens, and Matarazzo, 1974; Prigatano and Parsons, 1976; Vega and Parsons, 1967). Nevertheless, when appropriate statistical corrections for education were introduced into MANOVAs the polydrug users still remained remarkably inferior to nonpatients on performance measures while registering some improvement in academic-language skills. This suggests that poor education accounts for some, but not the majority of the polydrug users' deficiencies. It should also be remembered that, for some, lowered educational attainment might, in itself, be the result of subtle neurological dysfunction rather than psychosocially determined educational deprivation. Since our study did not examine subjects prior to the time they dropped out of school, we can only speculate that a proportion of them might have done so because of mild cerebral disturbance.

The mental illness dimension represents our most difficult confounding variable, and it was in anticipation of this that we included a psychiatric comparison group. The results are discussed in the following chapter.

We can now turn to the major findings of the CNSP. Neuropsychological impairment not only occurred with considerable frequency among polydrug users but was also correlated with long-term and high-density use of CNS depressants (sedatives, hypnotics, and opiates). Thus, the CNSP has replicated previously described association of deficit with sedative–hypnotic immersion (Adams *et al.*, 1975; Grant and Judd, 1976; Judd and Grant, 1975). We have also noted that positive history of premorbid medical and developmental events which might conceivably produce impairment prior to establishment of drug misuse was not related to subsequent use of any drug, and in fact, was inversely correlated with later history of sedative–hypnotic use. This suggests that persons with cerebral dysfunction are not selectively drifting into sedative–hypnotic use (indeed, they might be avoiding these drugs). If this inference is correct, then the possibility that the correlation between these drugs and impairment may reflect a causal–consequent relationship becomes more plausible. It is unlikely that acute barbiturate toxicity or short-term abstinence delirium accounts for the findings. In the first place, subjects were not tested until their third week of treatment, at which time most of them reported no use of these agents. This self-report was confirmed by the low rate of positive finding of drugs of abuse in the urine (13%) and blood (15%) and by the lack of a significant statistical association between a positive urine and impairment. Additionally, as reported by Judd *et al.* in Chapter XII, several subjects who appeared to be experiencing the tail end of an abstinence syndrome as evidenced by dysrhythmia III on their EEG, were not impaired neuropsychologically. Thus, it would seem that clinically unrecognized abstinence is not necessarily contributing to impairment. We cannot exclude the possibility that we might be observing an intermediate duration organicity similar to that which has been described for recovering alcoholics. For example, Bennett, Mowery, and Forte (1960) found that symptoms which might be organically determined, such as amnesic episodes and emotional lability, improved after prolonged abstinence and were paralleled by improvements in the EEG. Smith and Layden's (1972) shorter follow-up (6 weeks) also found that the reaction speed and abstract thinking abilities of alcoholics improved during hospitalization. It is possible that prolonged heavy sedative–hypnotic abuse produces a similar subclinical organic mental disorder which gradually improves. If this sort of phenomenon is contributing to the impairment which we have found, then recovery must be relatively slow, exceeding our 3-month follow-up.

Our discovery that extensive opiate use was related to impairment came as a surprise, since the three studies which addressed this issue previously all reached the conclusion that heroin addicts showed no neuropsychological deficit (Brown & Partington, 1942; Fields & Fullerton, 1974; Pfeffer & Ruble, 1948).

The first two studies that were performed in the 1940s employed neuropsychological techniques which are difficult to compare with ours. Also, although the exact pattern of substance use was not defined, it is likely that our drug users have consumed a greater variety and density of chemicals than were available (or popular) in the 1940s. It is possible that multiple drug immersion in some way facilitated the emergence of opiate-related impairment in our polydrug users. Length of abstinence is yet another variable. Brown and Partington's addicts were drug free for 6 months, whereas ours had reduced or discontinued illicit drug use for a maximum of 3 months. If the model of slowly improving intermediate duration organicity applies to opiates, then it is possible that we were testing subjects at different points in their recovery curves. Since Fields and Fullerton used the Halstead–Reitan battery, our disagreement with their findings is more difficult to understand. There are some differences in subjects which may be of importance. Although comparable in age, our polydrug users are less well educated than Fields and Fullerton's heroin addicts. For those aspects of the testing where education is important (especially verbal measures), our polydrug users might be expected to be at a slight disadvantage. At the same time, we have concerns about the neuropsychological intactness of the Fields and Fullerton medical control group. Their mean category score of 49 errors and TPT (total time) of 14.25 minutes suggests that they were not performing at an optimal level, even though their mean impairment index of .26 is well within the normal range. By way of comparison, our nonpatient controls registered a category score of 36 errors, TPT (total time) of 11.28 minutes, and an impairment index of .16. Age, education, and IQ are comparable. Thus, it is possible that Fields and Fullerton's inability to discriminate between groups resulted from a combination of selecting narcotic addicts who were unusually intact and non-drug-using controls who were performing more poorly than expected. Method of inferring deficit is also of importance. In the CNSP, blind clinical review of total protocols for each subject was used. Our reasoning for adding this level of analysis to the more traditional comparisons of groups on the basis of mean scores is consistent with the arguments of Reitan and Boll (1973). These authors noted that brain damage is not a unitary phenomenon and that differing patterns of deficient abilities can contribute to this judgment in different subjects. Thus, simpler statistical comparisons of central tendencies of a large number of individual test results might result in unusually strong abilities of some impaired subjects canceling out deficient performance of others. For this reason, it would be of interest to reevaluate the Fields and Fullerton subjects using a clinical approach.

Since the CNSP was not designed to be a neuropsychological investigation of heroin addicts (indeed, the relatively high degree of experience which our supposedly nonopiate drug users reported with opiates was an unexpected happenstance), our findings in relation to opiates deserve to be viewed cautiously and skeptically. At the same time, since the neuropsychological effect did express itself strongly on follow-up as well as on initial testing it cannot be dismissed out of hand. It would seem prudent to pursue our findings as potential clues to possible opiate neurotoxicity through careful longitudinal neuropsychological observations of heroin addicts who are on abstinence and maintenance programs. If our results find support, it will be necessary to determine whether neuropsychological deficit is related to opiate-use life-style (e.g., intravenous introduction of nonspecific foreign matter; frequent episodes of uncon-sciousness with compromised respiration) or to direct lasting neurophar-macological properties of opiates per se. If the latter seems probable, the public health implications are considerable. As an example, the safety of treatment programs which utilize maintenance opiates might be open to question.

While the CNSP raises concern for the potential deleterious effects of some drugs, its results also suggest the possibility of cautious optimism regarding the neurological safety of certain other agents, some of which have, in the past, been suspected of causing brain damage. Recently, both the medical community and legislative bodies have expressed con-cern regarding the dangers of CNS stimulants and questioned whether their medical use should be almost entirely banned for this reason. While we cannot dispute that central stimulants can easily produce easy depen-dence and profound behavioral aberration, we find no evidence that these drugs impair brain function. Indeed, stimulant use tends to relate to superior neuropsychological performance. In particular, we do not find confirmation for the suggestions of Citron (1970) or Rumbaugh, Bergeran, and Scanlon (1971) that cerebrovascular accidents are related to stimulant abuse. Our subjects are, of course, still relatively young, and it is possible that, with continued heavy use, some might suffer cerebrovascular disor-der.

We also found no relationship between neuropsychological impair-ment and marijuana or hallucinogen use. For marijuana the trend was in the opposite direction. We would view our results concerning marijuana as supportive of a general consensus among previous controlled investiga-tions that this agent is not neurotoxic, at least in the short run (i.e., approximately 10 years of regular use), and when employed in the man-ner which prevails in the United States. Because our polydrug users were not, in general, heavy hallucinogen consumers, we must regard our negative findings here much more cautiously.

We believe that the results of the CNSP suggests directions for both further research and clinical practice. The research implications are methodological and substantive. As concerns method, future clinical studies must address the reality that heavy consumption of any particular substance of interest (other than alcohol or tobacco) almost invariably occurs in the context of *multiple substance use*. Thus, for the North American experience, at least, it is hopeless to classify persons simply as "heavy sedative users" or "heavy stimulant users" with the expectation that one might find some effect or correlate of that particular agent. Instead, clinical studies must be designed in a manner that will permit simultaneous examination of a large number of pertinent data sets including, but not limited to, multiple drug use, life-style, medical and de-velopmental antecedents, intercurrent injuries, acute toxicity, psy-chopathology (schizophrenic diagnosis), and demographic variables.

The results of the CNSP also suggest that the next step in an effort to delineate brain–drug abuse relationships is a prospective study. A long-term follow-up of the current polydrug sample would be useful in deter-mining whether neuropsychological deficit is stable or whether it fluctuates with drug use changes. Does long-term abstinence from sedatives and opiates yield neuropsychological improvement? Do previously unim-paired persons become impaired with increased use of these agents? Valuable as such a follow-up would be, the interpretability of its results would be limited by our lack of precise knowledge regarding pre-drug-use neurological status. Perhaps people with mild and subclinical cerebral dysfunction drift into drug abuse in an effort to cope. Only a prospective investigation of youths judged to be at risk to become drug abusers can settle this question. Such an approach might also determine to what extent the apparently severe psychopathology of polydrug users is an antecedent or consequence of drug immersion.

The CNSP also offers clues to the clinician. The drug abuse counselor treating polydrug users can expect one-third or more of his clients to be experiencing the deleterious effects of cerebral dysfunction at the outset of treatment. Such clients are often inattentive, distractable, forgetful, labile in affect, concrete in thinking, and generally impaired in their intellectual abilities. Such clients will tolerate some therapeutic tech-niques poorly. Strong confrontations might engender powerful affects which could lead to further cognitive disorganization. Brain-damaged persons might fail to grasp the subtleties of many therapy modalities. Since at some level such persons sense that they are functioning defec-tively, their self-esteem tends to be fragile and vulnerable to easy devalua-tion.

We would suggest that all polydrug users entering treatment undergo neuropsychological evaluation (in addition to other assessment). Those found to have deficits may require simple, unambiguous, and structured treatment plans, coupled with solid supportive relationships. Repeat evaluations some months later (presuming drug consumption abates) can help clarify the nature and permanence of the deficit. On the basis of these evaluations clients may be guided toward activities which build on cognitive strengths and minimize weaknesses.

The preceding discussion should not be interpreted to suggest that polydrug users should be treated like persons with severe dementia. Rather, our hope is that the findings of the CNSP will alert clinicians to potential cognitive deficits in their clients that may pose barriers to intervention if not recognized, defined, and managed with sensitivity.

ACKNOWLEDGMENTS

This study was supported by National Institute on Drug Abuse grants to the following principal investigators and institutions:

DA01467   Lewis L. Judd (Friends of Psychiatric Research of San Diego)
DA01687   G. James Berry (Alcohol and Drug Abuse Division, Department of Health, Denver, Colorado)
DA01476   Albert S. Carlin (University of Washington, Seattle)
DA01466   Eric Comstock (Institute of Clinical Toxicology, Houston, Texas)
DA01468   James L. Mathis (Medical College of Virginia)
DA01474   Beny J. Prim (Addictions Research and Treatment Corporation, New York)
DA01454   Kenneth Schooff (Lafayette Clinic, Detroit, Michigan)
DA01632   Donald R. Wesson (San Francisco Polydrug Unit)

The authors express their indebtedness to the following NIDA officers for their interest and assistance in the initiation and implementation of this project: Dr. Gerry Dubin, Dr. John Benvenuto, Mr. George Beschner.

The following persons were instrumental in implementing this study at polydrug units: Betsy Comstock (Houston); Eugenia Gullick (Richmond); the Reverend Ernest L. Boston, Athan Karras (New York); David Smith (San Francisco); Richard Avery (San Diego).

The authors greatly appreciate the efforts of the central coordinating staff in San Diego: Robert Reed, Dobie Higley, Jan Janesheski, Emiliano Jacuzzi.

CHAPTER XI

Neuropsychological Impairment and Psychopathology

Donald R. Wesson, Igor Grant,
Albert S. Carlin, Kenneth Adams,
and Charles Harris

The possible influence of psychopathology on neuropsychological test performance confounds the interpretation of neuropsychological testing. An exploration of the effects of psychopathology on neuropsychological results is the concern of this chapter. We are not referring to the psychiatrically ill person who is so disturbed that he cannot cooperate with testing (e.g., the floridly psychotic person with severe retardation or mutism). Rather, our concern is the possible interfering role of a major psychiatric disorder which still permits a person to remain functional in routine activities, as might be the case with patients with a history of inpatient psychiatric treatment or polydrug users who often manifest significant psychiatric illness.

The Collaborative Neuropsychological Study included a group of individuals who were not drug abusers but who had either been hospitalized for psychiatric reasons or were currently attending a psychiatric day care center or were in outpatient psychotherapy. These are referred to here as the "psychiatric group." Excluded were individuals who were in psychotherapy for growth purposes or individuals in psychiatric treatment

263

Polydrug Abuse:
The Results of a
National Collaborative Study

due to situation life stresses. In an effort to exclude individuals whose performance might have been altered by prolonged exposure to phenothiazines or antidepressants, subjects were included only if they had less than a 5-year history of prescription drug use. It would have been preferable if patients had never received any psychotropic medication to ensure that any observed impairment would not be the result of acute or long-term medication effects. In actuality most psychiatric patients were receiving varying amounts of psychotropic agents under the supervision of their psychiatrists at the time of testing. Those who were taking medication, however, must have been receiving the same dosage for at least 3 weeks. In theory, decrement of performance observed in the psychiatric patient group could be the result of functional psychopathology, undiagnosed organicity, or prescription medications. These patients, however, were carefully screened to eliminate individuals with a history of drug abuse or clinical evidence of organicity. The inclusion–exclusion criteria for subjects are described in detail in Chapter X by Grant *et al*.

METHOD

We used both the MMPI and clinical psychiatric interview to provide estimates of psychopathology. Subjects in all groups completed the MMPI at initial neuropsychological testing and 3 months later. Diagnoses in addition to drug dependency were based on clinical psychiatric interviews according to the Diagnosis and Statistical Manual of the American Psychiatric Association (DSM II, 1968) and were available for 101 polydrug users. Initial MMPIs were available for all 276 subjects. Follow-up MMPIs were available for 93 polydrug users, 51 psychiatric patients, and 51 nonpatient controls. Not all polydrug users were assigned psychiatric diagnoses since not all polydrug study units were staffed with personnel qualified to do clinical psychiatric interviews. Missing psychiatric diagnoses also resulted in one center from a flood which destroyed a number of records.

For psychiatric patients, clinical diagnoses were supplied by the treating psychiatrist and were available for 48 patients. Completed MMPIs were available on 66 psychiatric patients. At the initial interview, historical data on lifetime experience with various prescribed psychotropic medications were collected. This permitted an estimated total exposure to antipsychotic drugs, antidepressants, lithium, hypnotics, and minor tranquilizers for each subject.

The 59 nonpatient controls did not undergo psychiatric interviewing so that only MMPI information is available.

LITERATURE REVIEW

The first controlled investigation of the interaction of psychopathology and neuropsychological performance was by Watson and associates (1968). They were unable to distinguish a group of VA patients diagnosed as schizophrenic from a group diagnosed as "organic," using the Halstead–Reitan battery. Subsequently, other studies presented evidence that not all schizophrenics yield "organic" performances on these neuro-psychological tests. Rather, it appears that the "chronic" or "process" schizophrenic is most likely to do poorly (Klonoff et al., 1970; Lacks, Golbert, Harrow, & Levine, 1970; Levine and Feirstein, 1972). Whether this represents a concurrent validity problem for the neuropsychological test procedure when used on patients with schizophrenia or whether some chronic schizophrenics are, in fact, "organic" on the basis of either their disease or their antipsychotic medications remains to be clarified. It is also possible that both schizophrenia and organicity decrease the level of performance on the test battery but that there are qualitative differences. This inference was suggested by the factor analytic studies of neuropsychological abilities in the previous chapter.

Although there have been a number of investigations on the neuro-psychological correlates of drug use, these studies generally have not adequately considered the potential confounding effect of psycho-pathology. For example, McGlothlin et al. (1969) tested 16 LSD users (mean LSD exposure was 75 times) and 16 nonusers and found LSD users performed more poorly on the Halstead–Reitan category test, a measure of abstracting ability. Subjects in both groups were in psychotherapy, although "subjects exhibiting serious psychopathology were excluded." The psychiatric information is not sufficiently detailed to allow assessment of the contribution of psychopathology to test results.

Acord and Barker (1973) compared users of hallucinogens with nonus-ers and found users performed poorly on the localization subtest of the TPT and the category test. The subjects were reported as having "no evidence of psychopathology other than character and behavior disorder with drug abuse as a symptom." Kolansky and Moore (1972) in studying marijuana use by adolescents reported frequent, mild organicity in marijuana users; however, most of these subjects were also psychiatric patients. When alcoholics are compared with nonalcoholics, findings seem relatively consistent in suggesting impaired problem-solving psychomotor dexterity and speed (Goldstein & Shelly, 1971) and significant difficulties in visual-spatial abstraction ability and temporal or spatial integration (Fitzhugh et al., 1960, 1965; Jones & Parsons, 1971, 1972). Once again, it is unclear whether alcoholics who perform in the impaired range are any more disturbed psychiatrically than their unimpaired counterparts.

Judd and Grant (1975) and Grant et al. (1976) did attempt to explore the potential contributions of psychiatric disorder to observed neuropsychological deficit in two groups of polydrug users. In each case they split their subject pool into "more deviant" and "less deviant" subgroups on the basis of the MMPI. Although it is not specified in their articles, the authors divided the sample by rank, ordering the MMPI profiles (on the basis of global clinical judgment) and then creating two groups. Since this method of assessing psychopathology is somewhat crude, it is still possible that real contributions of psychopathology to neuropsychological performance were missed.

The present Collaborative Neuropsychological Study of Polydrug Users (CNSP) represents the first opportunity to examine qualitatively the influence of emotional factors on neuropsychological test results.

RESULTS

Factor analysis of the neuropsychological test results reported in the previous chapter for each group, showed that the impairment of polydrug users involved both verbal and perceptual-motor skills, whereas that of psychiatric patients was primarily perceptual-motor in nature. The verbal differences were somewhat reduced when the effects of differences in education were removed by covariant analysis. Increase in age, decreased education, and the presence of certain medical risk factors all correlated significantly with impairment in all groups. For polydrug users, extensive use of central nervous system depressants and opiates and evidence of acute intoxication obtained through urine screening also related to impairment. These latter factors were absent in psychiatric patients, suggesting that other variables must be contributing to impairment in that group. In an effort to understand the correlates of impairment better, we turned to an examination of psychopathology and its relationship to neuropsychological performance in all groups.

MMPI and Neuropsychological Correlates

The mean T scores obtained by the three groups on the validity and scales scores at initial and 3-month follow-up of the MMPI, are shown in Tables XI.1 and XI.2.

Initial MMPIs of individuals who returned for follow-up examination were compared with dropouts and no significant differences in average scales scores were found.

Although psychiatric patients and polydrug users deviate significantly from the nonpatient group, they are not much different from each other at initial or 3-month follow-up testing.

Mean profile analysis, however, is a crude method of comparison and the large standard deviation in all groups suggests considerable heterogeneity.

At follow-up MMPI examination, polydrug users have made significant reduction in mean profile (Table XI.3) whereas psychiatric patients showed no significant mean profile change.

The relationship between change in impairment rating and change in MMPI scales was highly significant for those whose impairment rating

Table XI.1

MEAN PROFILES OF INITIAL MMPI BY GROUP

Test	Polydrug N = 151 Mean	SD	Psychiatric N = 66 Mean	SD	Nonpatients N = 59 Mean	SD	F for df = 2 and 273	p =	Neuman–Keuls at p = .05
MMPI scales									
L	42	8	46	9	46	10	1	n.s.	n.s.
F	73	18	73	21	54	9	27	.001	2,1 > 3
K	48	8	50	10	54	10	9	.001	3,2 > 1
Hs	65	13	58	15	49	7	34	.001	1 > 2 > 3
D	72	16	76	21	51	9	41	.001	2,1 > 3
Hy	66	11	64	13	52	6	35	.001	1,2 > 3
Pd	78	12	74	17	56	9	54	.001	1,2 > 3
Mf	59	13	60	18	51	12	7	.001	2,1 > 3
Pa	68	13	67	15	53	10	25	.001	1,2 > 3
Pt	72	14	72	21	54	10	30	.001	2,1 > 3
Sc	79	19	81	21	55	8	39	.001	2,1 > 3
Ma	72	13	66	19	58	10	22	.001	1 > 2 > 3
Si	57	11	60	12	53	9	7	.001	2,1 > 3

Table XI.2

MEAN PROFILES OF MMPI OBTAINED AT 3-MONTH FOLLOW-UP

Test	Polydrug N = 93 Mean	SD	Psychiatric N = 51 Mean	SD	Nonpatients N = 51 Mean	SD	F for df = 2 and 192	p =	Neuman–Keuls at p = .05
MMPI scales									
L	50	10	49	10	46	7	2	n.s.	n.s.
F	71	20	71	20	50	˙6	27	.001	2,1 > 3
K	50	4	51	8	55	11	5	.006	3 > 2,1
Hs	59	13	57	13	46	6	19	.001	1,2 > 3
D	66	13	73	19	49	7	44	.001	2 > 1 > 3
Hy	62	10	63	10	52	8	22	.001	2,1 > 3
Pd	74	11	71	14	52	10	57	.001	1,2 > 3
Mf	59	12	59	18	53	12	4	.03	1,2 > 3
Pa	64	13	65	15	53	7	16	.001	2,1 > 3
Ps	67	12	70	17	51	8	20	.001	2,1 > 3
Sc	73	14	77	22	52	8	30	.001	2,1 > 3
Ma	70	13	62	12	58	11	19	.001	1,2 > 3
Si	54	9	60	13	51	9	9	.001	2,1 > 3

Table XI.3

COMPARISON OF FOLLOW-UP MMPI WITH INITIAL MMPI VALUES (PAIRED SAMPLES, N = 89) POLYDRUG PATIENTS

Scale	First MMPI Mean	SD	Follow-up MMPI Mean	SD	Difference Mean	Significance[a] t	p
L	48	9.1	50	10	+2	−1.9	n.s.
F	74	19	71	20	−3	1.3	n.s.
K	48	9.0	50	8.6	+2	−2.0	.05
Hs	66	14	59	13	−7.0	4.6	.001
D	74	14	66	13	−8	4.8	.001
Hy	68	10	62	9.9	−6	4.0	.001
Pd	78	12	74	11	−4	3.8	.05
Mf	59	14	59	13	0	0.2	n.s.
Pa	70	13	64	17	−6	3.9	.001
Pt	73	12	67	13	−6	4.3	.001
Sc	81	18	74	19	−7	4.1	.001
Ma	73	13	70	13	−3	2.4	.01
Si	58	11	54	9.1	−4	3.4	.001

[a] Two-tail probability calculated with SPSS paired t-test; df = 88.

improved (Table XI.4), but was not for the 16 individuals whose impairment rating worsened (Table XI.5). Comparisons of significance testing alone may be misleading as the magnitude of change observed in some MMPI scales was comparable to that observed in the group whose N.P. functioning improved. (e.g., F scale). This suggests the failure to achieve significance in the group that worsened could be primarily due to the smaller N.

Diagnosis and Neuropsychological Correlates

As shown in Table XI.6, the clinical diagnoses of the psychiatric and polydrug group were significantly different.

When the initial impairment rating for the psychiatric groups is examined by psychiatric diagnosis, the impairment is disproportionately clustered in those with the clinical diagnosis of schizophrenia (Table XI.7; $p < .05$). This effect was still apparent at follow-up testing ($p < .05$).

We conclude that neuropsychological impairment has a higher than expected occurrence in the group diagnosed as schizophrenic. Causality is not established; however, future neuropsychological studies should

Table XI.4

COMPARISON OF AVERAGE FOLLOW-UP MMPI VALUES WITH INITIAL
AVERAGE MMPI VALUES FOR INDIVIDUALS WITH DECREASED IMPAIRMENT
RATING ON FOLLOW-UP (PAIRED SAMPLES, N = 47)

	First MMPI		Follow-up MMPI		Differences	Significance[a]	
Scale	Mean	SD	Mean	SD	Mean	t	p
L	45	7.7	47	9.0	+2	−2.0	.05
F	68	17	62	17	−6	2.8	.01
K	50	9.7	51	9.0	+1	− .85	n.s.
Hs	61	13	54	10	−7	4.0	<.001
D	69	17	61	14	−8	4.2	<.001
Hy	64	12	59	9.7	−5	3.1	<.003
Pd	72	15	67	14	−5	2.8	<.01
Mf	59	14	56	14	−3	1.3	n.s.
Pa	66	14	61	13	−5	2.6	.01
Pt	70	16	62	13	−8	4.0	<.001
Sc	77	20	67	19	−10	4.7	<.001
Ma	68	14	63	15	−5	3.0	.005
Si	56	11	55	10	−1	1.4	n.s.

[a] Two-tailed probability estimate calculated with SPSS paired t-test; $df = 46$.

Table XI.5

COMPARISON OF FOLLOW-UP MMPI AVERAGE PROFILES WITH INITIAL MMPI
AVERAGE PROFILES FOR INDIVIDUALS WITH INCREASED IMPAIRMENT
RATING ON FOLLOW-UP (PAIRED SAMPLES, $N = 16$)

Scale	First MMPI Mean	SD	Follow-up MMPI Mean	SD	Differences Mean	Significance[a] t	p
L	46	7.3	53	12	7	−2.4	.05
F	74	18	80	15	6	−1.7	n.s.
K	49	6.4	48	6.3	−1	.3	n.s.
Hs	61	14	57	13	−4	1.9	n.s.
D	76	20	74	19	−2	.6	n.s.
Hy	65	10	61	11	−4	1.8	n.s.
Pd	74	14	78	11	4	− .9	n.s.
Mf	62	13	65	12	3	−1.2	n.s.
Pa	68	14	68	14	0	− .2	n.s.
Pt	77	20	73	20	−4	1.2	n.s.
Sc	83	21	82	23	−1	.4	n.s.
Ma	68	16	67	14	−1	.5	n.s.
Si	58	10	60	11	2	−1.4	n.s.

[a] Two-tailed probability calculated with SPSS paired t-test; $df = 15$.

take into consideration the weak, but possibly confounding effect of
psychological status, especially schizophrenia.

The general trend with polydrug patients at follow-up was improvement, whereas the impairment in schizophrenics was still present at
follow-up. The finding, even with this small group, suggests that neuropsychological testing may be of value in assessing impairment in schizophrenia.

Table XI.6

DIAGNOSIS BASED ON CLINICAL INTERVIEW BY GROUP MEMBERSHIP[a,b]

Group membership	Schizophrenia N (%)	Affective disorders N (%)	Personality disorders, neurosis, others N (%)
Psychiatric patient ($N = 48$)	22 (46)	18 (38)	8 (17)
Polydrug abuser ($N = 101$)	3 (3)	15 (15)	83 (82)

[a] $X^2 = 66.0$; $df = 2$; $p < .001$.
[b] Psychiatric diagnoses were available for 149 individuals.

Table XI.7

IMPAIRMENT BY CLINICAL DIAGNOSIS IN PSYCHIATRIC GROUP

				Impairment rating[a]			
Psychiatric diagnosis	Excellent N (%)	Normal N (%)	Borderline N (%)	Mild impairment N (%)	Moderate impairment N (%)	Severe impairment N (%)	Total N
Schizophrenia							
Initial testing	0 (0)	8 (37)	6 (27)	4 (18)	3 (14)	1 (5)	22
Follow-up testing	1 (6)	4 (22)	3 (17)	6 (33)	2 (11)	2 (11)	18
Affective disturbance							
Initial testing	2 (11)	15 (83)	0 (0)	1 (6)	0 (0)	0 (0)	18
Follow-up testing	3 (18)	12 (70)	1 (6)	0 (0)	1 (6)	0 (0)	17
Personality disorders							
Initial testing	0 (0)	3 (38)	3 (38)	2 (25)	0 (0)	0 (0)	8
Follow-up testing	0 (0)	6 (86)	1 (14)	0 (0)	0 (0)	0 (0)	7

[a] Chi square (χ^2) for initial testing, 20.1 ($df = 10$; $p < .05$); χ^2 for follow-up testing 20.3 ($df = 10$; $p < .05$).

ACKNOWLEDGMENTS

The authors thank Phil Erdberg, who provided consultation on early drafts of this paper, and Jay Danzig and Dianne Morgan who tested most of the psychiatric patients.

CHAPTER XII

Comparison of Results from Serially Collected Neuropsychological and EEG Data

Lewis L. Judd, Igor Grant,
Reginald G. Bickford, and William G. Lee

The threat of permanent "brain damage" from chronic abuse of one or more psychotropic chemicals has been with us since the dramatic epidemic rise in drug use during the late 1960s. This concern, in turn, has stimulated a need for more definitive information, and it is not surprising that a number of investigative efforts have concentrated on answering this question. To date there have been nearly 20 studies reported, using electroencephalogram (EEG) and/or assorted psychometric instruments, that have attempted to assess the effects of chronic substance abuse on cerebral function. While some of these investigations have focused on polydrug-abusing patient populations, the majority have studied the effects of cognition of individual substances such as alcohol, opiates, marijuana, and barbiturates.

Mendelson and Meyer (1972) administered a partial Halstead neuropsychological battery and other tests to two groups of experienced male marijuana users: 10 "heavy" users (daily for at least 1 year; mean age 22) and 10 "casual" users (monthly for at least 1 year; mean age 24). No evidence of cerebral impairment was discovered in either group. Grant *et*

273

Polydrug Abuse:
The Results of a
National Collaborative Study

al. (1973) in a study comparing 29 casual marijuana users (median 3 times per month for 4 years) with 29 nonusing controls (all medical students, mean age 23.3, matched on MCAT scores), were similarly unable to detect any cognitive impairment among the smokers using a partial Halstead battery and other psychometric and neurological measures. Rubin and Comitas (1972) studied 30 male Jamaican chronic ganja smokers (mean 18 gm daily, for a mean of 17.5 years; mean age 36.6 years), along with 30 demographically matched controls. Again, using the Halstead battery plus other psychometric tests, they found no indications of irreversible brain damage in the smokers, nor any consistent differences between groups. Miras and Fink (1972) recorded EEGs for 31 male long-term hashish smokers (mean: 3 gm per day for 28 years) in Greece, and no significant abnormalities were discovered.

Since the long-term central nervous system (CNS) effects of chronic alcohol abuse have been well documented, only the more recent and definitive studies will be mentioned here. Five different investigations (Fitzhugh *et al.*, 1960, 1965; Jones and Parsons, 1971, 1972; Goldstein and Shelly, 1973; overall mean age 44 ± 9 years, education 11 ± 3 years), have been reported since 1960, in which male alcoholic patients, matched normals (overall $N = 118$) and brain-damaged patient controls (overall $N = 92$), were studied. In each study, clear evidence of cognitive impairment in the alcoholic patients was obtained on the Halstead battery and related tests. Specific dysfunction was noted in abstracting abilities and visual-spatial cognition. Based on these and other findings, Tarter (1975), suggests that this evidence supports the view that alcoholics experience irreversible frontal-limbic-diencephalic impairment, which is consistent with Victor, Adams, and Collins' (1971) delineation of the Wernicke–Korsakoff syndrome.

Some evidence of CNS organic dysfunction related to long-term opiate addiction has been reported as well. Seyfeddinipur and Reiger (1975) reported that among 32 chronically addicted opium smokers (age 33–75 years; "up to 20 gm opium daily") in Iran, 10 cases were "strictly normal," 11 "borderline," and 11 "pathological." These ratings "correlated well" with an index of intensity and duration of addiction. Studies of patients undergoing methadone and LAAM (L-alpha-acetylmethodol) maintenance treatment have shown rates of EEG abnormality ranging from 32% to 63% in populations of young (mean age 27.6 years) male American addicts (Blacky, David, and Irwin, 1972; Savage, Karp, Curran, Hanlon, and McCabe, 1976). However, the presence of concurrent opiate addiction in the subjects of all these investigations obscures the question of reversible versus irreversible organicity. In 1955, Wikler *et al.* studied the recovery from experimental barbiturate intoxication (2–6 weeks) of 35 male "post-addict" patients (mean age 45 years). Of 30 EEGs obtained between 8 days and 3 months after cessation of barbiturate administration, 57.7% were "normal" and the rest characterized by "mild random abnormalities." However, no preexperimental EEGs were available for comparison.

Three studies of young polydrug-abusing populations have been reported in Europe. In one (Manoli, Presslich, Wessely, & Zwischenberger, 1974), 55 Austrian polydrug-using outpatients (67% male; mean age 20 years) were divided into opiate users (N = 25) and those who had never used opiates (N = 30). In the non-opiate-using group, 77% had normal EEGs; in the opiate group only 44% were classified as normal. The abnormalities were characterized by increased frontal theta-wave activity. Bruhn and Maage (1975) studied 87 male prisoners in Copenhagen, divided into four groups: non-users, cannabis–hallucinogen users, cannabis–hallucinogen–amphetamine users, and cannabis–hallucinogen–amphetamine–opiate users. No significant differences between groups were found on the Halstead Category Test. Wessely, Manoli, Presslich, and Zwischenberger (1975) studied 19 male Austrian polydrug users (mean age: 18.5 years) using standard EEGs: 2 to 3 weeks after detoxification, 7 EEGs were characterized as "normal," 11 as "moderately abnormal," and 1 "markedly abnormal." On later EEGs (mean 15 weeks; range 8–64 weeks), 13 were normal, 3 moderately abnormal, and 3 markedly abnormal.

In the United States, Grant et al. (1976) reported results of a complete Halstead–Reitan neuropsychological evaluation of 22 males (mean age 22 ± 3 years) admitted to a narcotic treatment facility. All subjects were free of clinical neuropathy, and most presented histories of multiple drug (including alcohol) abuse. The results, taken subsequent to narcotic detoxification, were compared against age-and-education-matched samples of (1) neurologically normal *medical* inpatients, and (2) *neurological* inpatients. Depending on the rater reviewing the protocols, 41% to 64% of polydrug users, as against 11% to 26% of medical patients and 84% to 89% of neurological patients, were diagnosed "definitely or probably abnormal–mild, generalized cerebral dysfunction." On refined statistical analysis, the Halstead Category Test and the WAIS Picture Completion and Object Assembly subscales yielded significant decrements for the polydrug users as compared to the medical patients; but the drug-using group was significantly superior to the neurological patient sample. In addition, numerous MMPI scales (*F, Pd, Mf, Pa, Sc, Ma*) were deviant for the drug users relative to the other groups, producing a mean Goldberg Psychotic Index of 68 versus 40 (medical patients) and 47 (neurological patients). There was no demonstrated association between impairment and use of any particular drug. Unfortunately, no neuropsychological indicators prior to drug use were available for comparison.

The full Halstead–Reitan battery was also administered to 50 chronic sedative abusers (62% male; 26 ± 9 years old; 11 ± 2 grades completed), all with histories of multiple drug abuse, shortly after admission to a poly-drug research project (Judd and Grant, 1975). Of these subject 50% were rated as impaired by a single rater. Statistical comparisons of the two index groups used in the previous study (i.e., medical and neurological patients) were performed. Again, these revealed significant decrements among the drug abusers on most of the Halstead–Reitan scales, relative to the medical patients; but they were significantly less impaired than the neuro-logical sample. The drug users' MMPI scales were deviant relative to both comparison groups, with a mean Goldberg Index of 60.

In a report preliminary to the current study (Grant and Judd, 1975), the results from serial EEGs and Halstead–Reitan batteries were reported for 66 polydrug users (55% male; 26 ± 9 years old; 12 ± 2 grades completed) shortly after their admission to a treatment program. Of these subjects 32% were independently rated as impaired on both the EEG and Halstead–Reitan measures, 43% were rated normal on both, while 25% were rated as impaired on one of these procedures. Impairment on both measures at initial testing was associated with heavier use of sedative–hypnotics and alcohol. Thus, there was 75% overall agreement between the EEG and the Halstead–Reitan ratings. Five-month follow-up data on a portion of the sample revealed that 20% were found to be impaired on both procedures, 65% normal on both, and 15% impaired on one proce-dure. This resulted in an overall concordance of 85% between the two procedures.

In summary, the findings reported in the literature to date indicate that irreversible neuropsychological damage appears to be specifically as-sociated with chronic alcoholism, while concurrent and short-term dec-rements can result from opiate and mixed substance (polydrug) abuse. The existence of some degree of irreversible organicity in a smaller proportion of the polydrug group is suggested by continued impairment in the Halstead–Reitan and abnormal EEGs after several months of relative drug abstinence.

One of our hypotheses prior to the initiation of the study was that polydrug-abusing patients, because of their indiscriminate and prolific use of psychoactive chemicals, would have significantly altered cognitive functioning on either a temporary or a permanent basis. This would result in difficulties in their comprehending or taking advantage of the traditional forms of interpersonal insight-oriented psychotherapy, the primary therapeutic modality offered by most treatment agencies. In addition, we hypothesized that at the very least, drug-induced cognitive deficits would be a salient factor in the core clinical syndrome manifested in these polydrug-abusing patients. To test these hypotheses and others a rather extensive testing assessment battery was designed, which included neuropsychological examination and electroencephalograms. In this regard we were curious as to the level of agreement present when these two independent assessment procedures, both of which focus upon potential cerebral deficits, are obtained concurrently in the same subject. To this end the results from a sophisticated clinical neuropsychological assessment procedure (Halstead–Reitan battery) and EEGs scored by both the Mayo system and a computerized compressed spectral array analysis technique, were compared. This was done to determine whether or not the information added in these two assessment procedures resulted in a fuller and more comprehensible picture of cognitive function in these patients.

METHODOLOGY

Subject Sample

Between November 1, 1973 and September 30, 1975 the San Diego Polydrug Study Unit admitted 170 patients for evaluation and treatment. Preliminary screening eliminated 19 individuals as being unsuitable for the research project prior to initial testing. These subjects, those with opiate addiction as their central problem, were referred to more appropriate treatment agencies. Substantially complete entry testing batteries (described in the following section on procedures) were administered to 117 of a possible 151 patients (77%). The remaining 23% (34 individuals), although acceptable at screening for the study, were for various reasons unable to complete enough of the initial testing battery to be included in the overall analysis. The reasons for incomplete test batteries included incarceration, moving away, and refusal of patients to participate, and inability of the study unit to maintain contact with patients despite rather aggressive outreach efforts.

The subject sample completing the entry assessment battery was made up of 65 men (56%) and 52 women (44%) ranging in age from 14 to 54 years (mean 25.5 ± 7.6 years) and in years of education completed from 7 to 19 years (mean 11.7 ± 2.0 years). Subjects' cumulative school grade point averaged ranged from 0.7 (D−) to 4.0 (A), with the vast majority of subjects falling within the C− to B grade categories (mean 2.25 ± 0.75). Subjects' Wechsler Adult Intelligence Scale IQ ranged from 75 to 138 (mean 103.8 ± 12.3). With very few exceptions (10.2%) all subjects fell into social categories ranging from class 4 to class 7 as determined by the

Hollingshead Two-Factor Index of Social Position: categories 4 and 5 (12% each), category 6 (10.2%), and category 7 (55.5%). These social class categories range from clerical and sales workers (category 4) down to unskilled, and/or unemployed for over 1 year (category 7). The drug experience of the subjects is summarized in Table XII.1. The vast majority of our subjects reported multisubstance experience (77% were frequent users of three or more substances). The most prevalent drugs of abuse (82% of the group) were in the sedative–hypnotic class which includes barbiturates, nonbarbiturate hypnotics, and minor tranquilizers (meprobamate, chlordiazepoxide, and diazepam). Daily use of these substances was reported by 59% of the subjects; 60% admitted to alcohol abuse (30% at daily levels), while 57% of the group were frequent users (36% at daily levels) of stimulant drugs (amphetamines). Frequent marijuana use was reported by 65% of this subject sample (37% at daily levels).

It is a known fact that severe drug-abusing individuals are unreliable and notoriously difficult to retain for treatment and follow-up purposes. Nevertheless, we were able, at 3 to 5 months postentry, to administer substantially complete identical retesting batteries to 66 of the initial 117 people tested (56%). With reference to this, it should be noted that the tables in this chapter will show varying total numbers, according to the particular test or evaluation procedure reported. We were unable to find any statistically significant differences with respect to initial neuro-

Table XII.1

DRUG USE PATTERNS BY HISTORY OF POLYDRUG SUBJECTS[a]

Substance	Percentage daily users	Percentage frequent users[b]
Sedatives, hypnotics, minor tranquilizers	59	82
Stimulants, including amphetamines, methylphenidate, and other anorexigenics	36	57
Marijuana	37	65
Narcotics, including codeine	17	26
Alcohol	30	60
Hallucinogens	0	25
Cocaine	6	14
Volatiles	0	2
Three or more of the above substances	41	77

[a] $N = 109$.

[b] Use = two or more times per week and includes daily users.

psychological findings between the group available for 3- to 5-month retesting and those who were not available. An 8-month follow-up on this population will be reported in a later publication.

Assessment Procedure

At the time of admission to the Polydrug Study Unit, an ambulatory facility in the downtown San Diego area, all subjects underwent an initial assessment which included a 25-page personal history questionnaire, a lifetime drug use inventory, a medical history, physical examination, and routine laboratory studies including blood and urine toxicology. Most subjects continued as outpatients, although a few (less than 10%) were admitted to an inpatient unit for detoxification from sedative, usually barbiturate, addiction. To allow acute drug effects and possible with-drawal symptoms to attenuate, subjects were monitored for 3 weeks before undergoing the neuropsychological evaluation and the EEG.

The neuropsychological examination consisted of the battery assembled by Reitan (1966) which includes seven Halstead tests, the Wechsler Adult Intelligence Scale (WAIS), the Trail Making Test, aphasia screening test, sensory perception examination, dominance examination, and the Minnesota Multiphasic Personality Inventory (MMPI). The testing took 4 to 5 hours to complete, and results were analyzed both quantitatively and clinically. The EEG was performed within 24 hours of neuropsychological assessment. Routine montage was employed. The examination included periods of activation by hyperventilation and photic stimulation. The results were scored clinically by an electroencephalographer using the Mayo system, and were also recorded on magnetic tape from which a computerized, compressed spectral array (CSA) and numerogram could be plotted.

Additional testing, requiring approximately 4 hours to complete, was obtained from all subjects and included the following: the California Psychological Inventory (CPI); the Zung Self-rating Depression Scale (SDS); the Profile of Mood States (POMS); the Psychiatric Evaluation Form (PEF); and the Global Assessment Scale (GAS).

All data were coded and placed into an SPSS (Statistical Package for the Social Science) computer file. For this report, a comprehensive statistical analysis was performed on initial and follow-up neuropsychological and EEG data using group t tests and chi-square analysis procedures. Only those statistical interactions significant at the .05 level or beyond are reported here. If interesting trends are reported they will be identified as such.

RESULTS

Assessment at Entry into Study

When possible, blood and urine toxicology screens were obtained on the days when the Halstead–Reitan and EEGs were run. Unfortunately, this was accomplished only 60% of the time. Of those urine and blood toxicology screens obtained, 85% were free of drugs at the time of testing.

Results from the clinical evaluations of the subjects' initial Halstead–Reitan battery are recorded in Table XII.2. It is apparent that an extraordinarily high proportion of this sample of polydrug abusers were neuropsychologically impaired: 58 individuals (51.8%) were psychometrically and clinically rated as functioning within the impaired range during their entry evaluation. Surprisingly, 28.6% were found to be functioning as moderately (16.1%) or severely (12.5%) impaired. This is of particular interest since impairment at these levels is often accompanied by or related to demonstrable behavioral changes.

The data from the EEGs recorded in Table XII.3 indicate also an increased incidence of EEG abnormalities among this population during their initial evaluation. By using the Mayo diagnostic criteria, it was found that nearly 40% had some abnormality. Approximately 10% of the sample had EEG abnormalities severe enough to warrant classification as dysrhythmia II or III, although the vast majority of the abnormal EEGs were those classed as dysrhythmia I. This is definitely elevated above that found in the population at large, in which 10–15% will have dysrhythmia I and less than 5% will have dysrhythmia II and III.

A more comprehensive categorization of the types of EEG abnormalities found in these subjects is described in Table XII.4. Of the 10 possible

Table XII.2

CLINICAL RATING OF THE RESULTS FROM THE SUBJECTS' HALSTEAD–REITAN NEUROPSYCHOLOGICAL BATTERY AT ENTRY INTO THE STUDY

Clinical rating	Number of subjects	Percentage of total group
Excellent	3	2.7
Average–normal	48	42.9
Borderline	3	2.7
Mild impairment	26	23.2
Moderate impairment	18	16.1
Severe impairment	14	12.5
	112	100

Table XII.3

MAYO DIAGNOSIS OF EEGs AT THE TIME OF THE SUBJECTS' ENTRY INTO
THE STUDY

Diagnosis	Number of subjects	Percentage of total group
Normal	33	29.5
Essentially normal	35	31.3
Dysrhythmia I	33	29.5
Dysrhythmia II	4	3.6
Dysrhythmia III	7	6.3
	112	100

diagnostic categories of EEG abnormalities, the following 4 stand out as
being more commonly manifested among this group of polydrug users:
beta activity, 44.6%; abnormal Mayo diagnosis, 39.3%; general slowing,
20.5%; and paroxysms (bursting), 15.2%. By far the most frequent
findings were excessive beta activity, most likely related to acute drug
intoxication, and abnormalities in the Mayo categorizations, also potentially similarly related.

To date few studies have focused on the relationship between clinical
information derived from the Halstead–Reitan battery and the EEG.
This is particularly surprising since each procedure, although based on
information from quite different sources, is concerned with the same end
point—namely the intactness of cerebral function. Therefore, we were

Table XII.4

NUMBER AND PERCENTAGE OF SUBJECTS WITH SPECIFIC EEG
ABNORMALITIES AT ENTRY TESTING

	Normal		Impaired	
	Number of subjects	Percentage	Number	Percentage
Mayo diagnosis	68	60.7	44	39.3
Localization	108	96.4	4	3.6
General slowing	89	79.5	23	20.5
Focal slowing	112	100.0	0	.0
Focal seizure	110	98.2	2	1.8
Generalized seizure discharge	105	93.8	7	6.2
Paroxysms (bursting)	95	84.8	17	15.2
Beta activity	62	55.4	50	44.6
Asymmetry	109	97.3	3	2.7
Background activity	96	86.5	16	13.5

interested not only in the documentation of whether chronic substance abuse was related to cerebral dysfunction but also in the level of agreement or disagreement between these two diagnostic procedures. Even more specifically, to what extent does the simultaneous acquisition of data from these two procedures result in a more comprehensive and accurate assessment of cerebral function?

The results in Table XII.5 indicate there is a statistically significant level of agreement between these two diagnostic techniques ($p < .01$): 41 individuals (36.6%) were normal on both procedures and 31 (27.7%) were abnormal on both EEG and Halstead–Reitan. Thus, the findings from these two independent assessment techniques, both reflecting CNS integrity, were in agreement in approximately 64% of the subject sample. The results from the remaining 36% of the subjects were in disagreement; that is, an abnormality was found in one procedure but not in the other. It is interesting that of this 36%, twice as many patients ($N = 27$, 24.1%) were found to have impaired performances on the Halstead–Reitan battery, but with normal EEG recordings, whereas only 13 patients (11.6%) had the reverse, that is, abnormal EEGs but normal results on the neuropsychological tests.

The reason for the discrepancy between the results of these two different procedures is in part clarified if those cases in which a disagreement occurs are examined more closely. The least frequent type of disagreement is that of an abnormal EEG with a normal performance on the Halstead–Reitan battery. As stated before, 13 individuals had this type of discrepancy and their EEG abnormalities were as follows: 6 had evidence of either focal or generalized seizure activity on their EEGs; 5 had excessive beta activity (dysrhythmia I); and 2 patients manifested paroxysms (bursting). Therefore, it would appear that those patients who are neuropsychologically normal, but with abnormal EEGs, are primarily

Table XII.5

LEVEL OF AGREEMENT BETWEEN THE RESULTS OF THE HALSTEAD–REITAN AND THE ELECTROENCEPHALOGRAM AT ENTRY[a]

	Entry EEG			
Entry Halstead	Normal	Abnormal	N	%
Normal	41	13	54	48.2
Impaired	27	31	58	51.8
N	68	44	112	
%	60.7	39.3		100

[a] Chi square (χ^2) = 8.92; $df = 1$; $p < .01$.

those patients with epileptic foci whose cognitive functioning is normal and those patients with drug-related fast activity, who are not sufficiently intoxicated to impair their neuropsychological functions.

The modal type of divergent pattern occurred in those patients who were judged to be abnormal on neuropsychological testing, but had normal EEGs. As previously stated, approximately 24% of the entire sample had this type of divergence between the two diagnostic techniques. Further, the level of severity of the Halstead–Reitan impairment was not related to an increased percentage of EEG abnormalities. Thus, it would appear that the neuropsychological battery demonstrates a better capacity to pick up more subtle functional cerebral deficits, which are not reflected in the electroencephalogram. On the other hand, the electroencephalogram can identify acute drug-related abnormalities (i.e., increased fast or slow activity) which are not robust enough to be manifested in abnormal performances on the Halstead–Reitan battery. Finally, the EEG does identify the type of seizure activity, which often is not related to demonstrable disturbance in cerebral abilities. In summary, it is clear that the two diagnostic procedures, while on the whole being concordant (64%) in their assessment of cerebral integrity, each elicit and assess different types of CNS dysfunction.

With respect to our initial hypothesis the data were analyzed by dividing the group into two subpopulations based upon the presence of impairment on the Halstead–Reitan battery. The question to be answered by this analysis was whether patients with cerebral dysfunction were noticeably different in their general characteristics and/or clinical picture from those patients who are not impaired. The two subsamples of patients (i.e., normal versus cognitively impaired) were compared using group t tests on clinical and drug use characteristics and on the scores from the various personality inventories. We were surprised to find that only a few demographic and drug use variables were significantly different between the groups. The impaired subjects as a group were older (27 years versus 24 years, $p = .026$), had less frequent use of marijuana ($p = .047$) and cocaine ($p = .037$), and used a fewer number of drugs ($p = .023$). There were no differences between the groups on the following variables: sex ratio, level of education completed, drop-out or expulsion from school, grade point average, arrest records, jail history, intravenous use of drugs, barbiturate use, tranquilizer use, alcohol use, amphetamine use, hallucinogen use, narcotics use, number of drugs used daily, having "streetwise" patterns of drug use, and time in treatment.

It was our hypothesis in advance of the statistical analysis that those individuals who were impaired on the Halstead–Reitan, and especially those who were severely impaired, would manifest distinctly different characteristics both clinically and in the scores from the various personality inventories. However, there were no statistically significant differences on the Global Assessment Scale (GAS) between the neuropsychologically impaired subjects and those who scored within the normal range. The results in Table XII.6 compare mean scores on the 20 scales from the Psychiatric Evaluation Form (PEF) which distinguish between polydrug-abusing groups with cerebral impairment and those without. There were 9 categories out of a possible 20 on the PEF which reached levels of significance at .05 or better. The PEF is a standardized rating instrument based upon a clinical empirical impression of the patient, on which the clinician rates 20 dimensions of social and psychological behavior. The group with cerebral dysfunction was seen by the clinicians as being much more severely disturbed and disordered ($p = .003$) in an overall sense than those polydrug users without impairment.

Table XII.6

CLINICAL RATINGS FROM THE PSYCHIATRIC EVALUATION FORM (PEF) COMPARING NORMAL AND NEUROLOGICALLY IMPAIRED SUBGROUPS

CAPPS Scale	Normal group			Impaired group			t Value	p Value[a]
	N	Mean	SD	N	Mean	SD		
Narcotics and drug use	56	3.80	1.03	57	4.07	.90	−1.46	n.s.
Agitation and excitement	56	2.14	1.33	56	2.46	1.20	1.34	n.s.
Suicide and self-mutilation	56	2.00	1.33	57	1.56	.94	2.01	.047−
Grandiosity	56	1.45	.83	57	1.93	1.18	−2.53	.013+
Somatic concerns	56	2.02	1.10	57	2.33	1.27	−1.41	n.s.
Antisocial attitude and acts	56	2.63	1.10	57	2.75	1.10	.62	n.s.
Speech disorganization	56	1.48	.87	57	1.61	1.08	− .71	n.s.
Hallucinations	55	1.11	.42	54	1.30	1.06	−1.21	n.s.
Social isolation	56	2.48	1.22	57	2.37	1.27	.49	n.s.
Belligerence and negativism	56	1.98	1.10	57	2.44	1.18	−2.12	.036−
Disorientation and memory	56	1.48	.91	57	1.93	1.24	−2.19	.031+
Alcohol abuse	56	2.14	1.07	57	2.65	1.55	−2.02	.046+
Anxiety	56	3.27	1.05	57	3.53	.93	−1.38	n.s.
Inappropriate	55	1.64	.95	57	1.81	1.08	− .89	n.s.
Suspicion and persecution feelings	56	1.93	1.02	57	2.42	1.18	−2.37	.019+
Daily routine and leisure time	56	2.52	1.25	57	3.02	1.11	−2.25	.027+
Denial of illness	56	2.25	1.15	57	2.88	1.47	−2.54	.013+
Depression	56	3.19	1.07	57	3.00	1.18	.93	n.s.
Retardation and lack of emotion	56	1.77	.99	57	1.64	.94	.65	n.s.
Overall severity of illness	55	3.67	.79	57	4.10	.70	−3.05	.003+

[a] Two-tail level of significance.

Apart from having less suicidal ideation (p = .047), all the other scales were in the direction of increased levels of psychopathology in the cerebrally dysfunctional group. Specifically, they manifested noticeably more grandiosity (p = .013) and belligerence and negativism (p = .036), had less insight into their illness through increased levels of denial (p = .013), and demonstrated more suspicion and feelings of persecution (p = .019). This latter cluster of symptoms and behavior is potentially indicative of a paranoid posture in this group of cerebrally impaired polydrug abusers. It is our speculation that this increased paranoid view of the world may result from the inability of this group cognitively to understand, order, and apprehend the worlds in which they live. Thus, they may feel consistently under threat and in a position of vulnerability. Further, the impaired group, as would be expected, had greater levels of disorientation and memory deficit (p = .031) and were functionally less able to establish, regularize, and maintain an acceptable daily routine. They were also unable to regulate their use of leisure time (p = .027). Finally, as we reported in a previous paper (Grant and Judd, 1976), the impaired group evidenced, by history, greater levels of alcohol *abuse* than the nonimpaired group (p = .046).

With regard to the other clinical and personality inventories that were obtained on the group at entry into the study, few variables distinguished between the impaired and the normal subgroups. Of the 18 scales on the California Psychological Inventory, only one scale (Achievement via Independence) distinguished between the two groups, with the impaired group scoring lower on this scale (nonimpaired = 47, impaired = 42, p = .012). Only one scale of 13 on the MMPI distinguished between the two groups. The cerebrally impaired group had a mean level of 76 on the Mania Scale (*Ma*) while the cognitively normal group scored 72 (p = .038). It should be noted, parenthetically, that the MMPI profile for the entire subject sample was very elevated, to such an extent that it would be very difficult for the cerebrally impaired subgroup to exceed systematically the scale scores of the group as a whole. Finally, there were no differences on the Zung Self-Rating Scale for Depression or the Profile of Mood State (POMS). Thus, the differences between the two subgroups were based primarily on the formalized clinical rating and assessment and were not reflected in personality inventories and other self-rating instruments.

A similar statistical analysis was performed with the group divided into those individuals with EEG abnormalities at initial testing and those with normal initial EEG tracings. Only two scale items revealed differences between the normal and abnormal EEG subgroups. Those with abnormal EEGs were more dysfunctional as rated on the Global Assessment

Scale (GAS) (p = .05), and had a lower score on the Psychiatric Evaluation Form (PEF) on retardation and lack of emotion (p = .05) than the normal group. It is obvious that this evidence is too sparse to justify any speculative conclusions.

Follow-up Assessment at 3 to 5 Months After Entry into the Study

Follow-up testing using both diagnostic techniques (EEG and Halstead–Reitan) was carried out between 3 and 5 months after the entry assessment battery. Of the 117 total individuals 66 persons (56.4%) completed the follow-up assessment batteries. Strenuous efforts were made by the research group to obtain testing on everyone in the sample. However, this type of chronic polydrug abuser is an exceedingly transient and unstable group. With only 56% completing the follow-up retest, this is still one of the higher percentages of follow-up assessment reported for this type of a clinical population.

Before more extensive statistical analysis of these follow-up cases was initiated, it was important to know whether those available for retest were a skewed sample in terms of the proportion of normal and impaired subjects. For example, it could be possible that only the initially non-cerebrally impaired individuals were available for retesting. As will be seen in Tables XII.7 and XII.8 this was not the case. The data presented in these tables reveal there are no statistically significant relationship differences between cerebral dysfunction or normal function, as demonstrated by Halstead–Reitan or EEG at entry, and whether or not the subject was available for retesting 3 to 5 months later.

The general movement seen when contrasting the neuropsychological assessment at entry with that at follow-up, is a trend to moderate im-

Table XII.7

COMPARISON OF HALSTEAD–REITAN RESULTS FROM SUBJECTS AVAILABLE FOR FOLLOW-UP RETEST VERSUS THOSE NOT AVAILABLE FOR RETEST[a]

	Retested	Not retested	Total	Percentage
Normal at entry	35	23	58	49.6
Impaired at entry	31	28	59	50.4
N	66	51	117	
%	56.4	43.6		100.

[a] Chi square (χ^2) = 0.44; df = 1; p = not significant.

Table XII.8

COMPARISON OF EEG-MAYO DIAGNOSES RESULTS FOR SUBJECTS
AVAILABLE FOR FOLLOW-UP RETEST VERSUS THOSE NOT AVAILABLE FOR
RETEST[a]

	Retested	Not retested	Total	Percentage
Normal at entry	35	41	76	60.8
Impaired at entry	25	24	49	39.2
N	60	57	125	
%	48.	52.		100.

[a] Chi square (χ^2) = 0.15; df = 1; p = not significant.

provement in neuropsychological performance. Specifically, at entry
over half (56%) of the sample scored in the impaired range, whereas at
retest 33% were found to have impaired functioning. The data as presented in Table XII.9 break down the Halstead clinical ratings into six
more refined categories of functioning. The majority of the subjects who
changed categories fall below the diagonal of the table, which indicates
improvement (i.e., movement to less severe categories of impairment) at
follow-up testing. Summarizing these categories (see Table XII.10), we
note that of the 31 subjects who were initially impaired at entry, 12 (39%)
improved to normal at follow-up. Only three of the initial 35 (9%)
individuals who were normal at entry testing demonstrated deterioration
by manifesting impaired performances at follow-up.

In Table XII.11 are recorded the data which contrast the initial EEG
diagnoses with those obtained at follow-up. Paralleling the neuropsychological data, there is a tendency for abnormal EEGs to improve at
follow-up testing. Of the 25 individuals who had abnormal EEGs at entry,
10 (40%) converted to normal at follow-up. However, 8 of 35 individuals
initially classified as normal (23%) moved in the opposite direction, in that
they had normal EEGs at entry and converted to abnormal EEGs at
follow-up. In an attempt to clarify the picture, the data were tabulated
using the more refined Mayo diagnostic categories rather than the normal
versus abnormal dichotomy. As can be seen in Table XII.12 the 8 individuals who changed from normal to abnormal were made up of 6 people
who moved from essentially normal to a dysrhythmia I classification,
which is a rather minor shift. Further, 4 of these 8 individuals had positive
urines for drugs at the time of the repeat EEG and this would account for
the shift to dysrhythmia I. Thus, that deterioration in EEG classification
which occurred at follow-up was never more extreme than a one-category
increase in severity of diagnosis. Of the 18 patients who were given a

Table XII.9

COMPARISON OF HALSTEAD–REITAN RESULTS AT ENTRY AND AT 3-TO 5-MONTH FOLLOW-UP

Initial testing	Follow-up testing							
	Excellent	Average-normal	Borderline	Mild impairment	Moderate impairment	Severe impairment	Total	%
Excellent	1	1	0	0	0	0	2	3.0
Average–normal	1	26	0	2	1	0	30	45.5
Borderline	0	1	2	0	0	0	3	4.5
Mild impairment	0	6	5	5	0	0	16	24.2
Moderate impairment	0	0	0	6	2	0	8	12.1
Severe impairment	0	0	1	0	3	3	7	10.6
N	2	34	8	13	6	3	66	
%	3.0	51.5	12.1	19.7	9.1	4.5		100.0

Table XII.10

INITIAL VERSUS FOLLOW-UP HALSTEAD–REITAN TESTING

| Testing at entry | 3-to 5-Month retest | | Total | Percentage |
	Normal	Impaired		
Normal	32	3	35	53.0
Impaired	12	19	31	47.0
N	44	22	66	
%	66.7	33.3		100.0

diagnosis of dysrhythmia I at entry, 6 remained in this category, 7 became normal or essentially normal, 4 advanced to dysrhythmia II, and 1 individual changed to asymmetry I at follow-up. Those individuals who had more severe abnormalities at entry, specifically those with dysrhythmia II or III, showed similar patterns. Of the 7 patients with dysrhythmia II or III at entry, 3 remained in this category and 4 improved at follow-up. Therefore, the tendency to improve on the repeat EEG is present, but is accompanied by converse trends as well. Individuals with abnormal initial EEGs are almost as likely to be diagnosed in the same category (40%), as they are to improve (44%), and less likely to be diagnosed as having a more severe dysrhythmia pattern (16%) at follow-up. As distinct from the Halstead follow-up, there is an increased tendency for some subjects to show deterioration on retest EEGs. Thus, the pattern seen in the serial EEG data in this population is more complex and less predictable than that obtained from the serially collected Halstead–Reitan data.

Table XII.11

INITIAL VERSUS FOLLOW-UP EEG–MAYO DIAGNOSES

| EEG–Mayo diagnoses at entry | EEG–Mayo diagnoses at follow-up | | Total | Percentage |
	Normal or essentially normal	Abnormal		
Normal or essentially normal	27	8	35	58.3
Abnormal	10	15	25	41.7
N	37	23	60	
%	61.7	38.3		100.0

Table XII.12

ENTRY EEG COMPARED TO RESULTS OF A FOLLOW-UP EEG USING MAYO CRITERIA

Entry Mayo diagnosis	Follow-up Mayo diagnosis						Total	Percentage
	Normal	Essentially normal	Dysrhythmia I	Dysrhythmia II	Dysrhythmia III	Asymmetry I		
Normal	7	6	1	0	0	0	14	23.3
Essentially normal	4	10	6	1	0	0	21	35.0
Dysrhythmia I	3	4	6	4	0	1	18	30.0
Dysrhythmia II	1	0	0	1	0	0	2	3.3
Dysrhythmia III	0	2	1	0	2	0	5	8.3
N	15	22	14	6	2	1	60	
%	25.0	36.7	23.3	10.0	3.3	1.7		100.0

COMPARISON OF HALSTEAD-REITAN
DATA WITH THAT OBTAINED BY
COMPRESSED SPECTRAL ANALYSIS OF
THE EEG

It is clear that the Halstead–Reitan battery represents what is currently the most sensitive and sophisticated assessment procedure evaluating neuropsychological functions. In this regard, we were curious whether the diagnostic power of the EEG, in relationship to the neuropsychological battery, could be improved by one of the more sophisticated techniques for analyzing the electroencephalograms, namely the computerized Compressed Spectral Array analysis, a technique in which one of the authors is a recognized pioneer. Therefore, computerized analyses resulting in both a Compressed Spectral Array and a numerogram were applied to a certain number of the EEGs obtained on these polydrug subjects. An example of an EEG analyzed by this method is graphically reproduced in Figure XII.1.

While the congruence from the results of these two advanced technologies was not as striking as we had anticipated there was nevertheless sufficient overlap to suggest considerable promise in the simultaneous use of these two diagnostic procedures, once a more formalized methodology for mutual interpretation is developed. Rather than present quantitative data, it seems best to depict the potential additive diagnostic power of the two techniques by a clinical example. In the example following, two clinical vignettes are presented on the same subject, each being derived at approximately the same time, independently from the other diagnostic procedure. The first is the clinical diagnostic impression based upon the Halstead–Reitan battery and the second from the Compressed Spectral Array and numerogram from the computer-analyzed EEG.

Subject identification number: 107
Age: 30
Sex: Female
Race: Indian–Mexican
Handedness: Right
Education completed: 9 years

Halstead–Reitan Neuropsychological Data

On initial testing the person identified as Subject 107 obtained an impairment index of .7 which is in the mildly to moderately abnormal

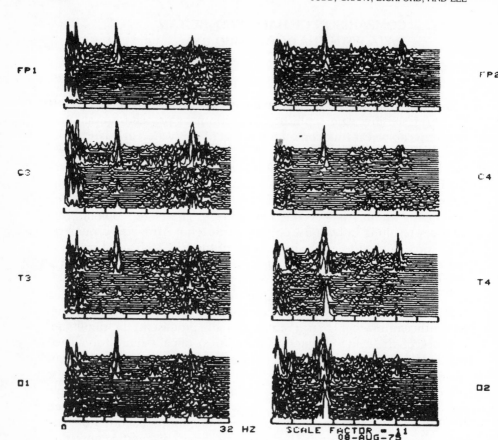

Figure XII.1. Example of compressed spectral array analysis of EEG recording.

range. It was noted that the total IQ score of 99 is probably an underestimate of this person's actual intelligence since the vocabulary subtest registered at 13. This probably means that there was a general reduction in IQ as a result of cerebral dysfunction at this testing period. The disturbance seems to be generalized with some impairment in abstracting ability, in perceptual motor skills, in remembering, and in certain language-related functions (dysnomia, dysgraphia).

Electroencephalograph Data, Compressed Spectral Analysis, and Numerogram

This is a report on Subject 107. Both the CSA and numerogram on this patient show a marked asymmetry with an alpha rhythm of considerably

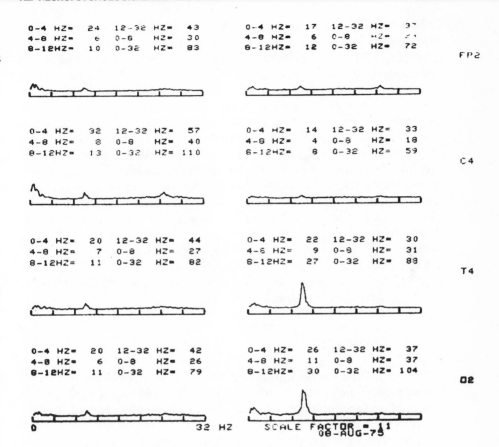

```
0-4 HZ=   24    12-32 HZ=   43        0-4 HZ=   17    12-32 HZ=   3
4-8 HZ=    6    0-6   HZ=   30        4-8 HZ=    6    0-8   HZ=
8-12HZ=   10    0-32  HZ=   83        8-12HZ=   12    0-32  HZ=   72
```
                                                                          FP2

```
0-4 HZ=   32    12-32 HZ=   57        0-4 HZ=   14    12-32 HZ=   33
4-8 HZ=    8    0-8   HZ=   40        4-8 HZ=    4    0-8   HZ=   18
8-12HZ=   13    0-32  HZ=  110        8-12HZ=    8    0-32  HZ=   59
```
                                                                          C4

```
0-4 HZ=   20    12-32 HZ=   44        0-4 HZ=   22    12-32 HZ=   30
4-8 HZ=    7    0-8   HZ=   27        4-8 HZ=    9    0-8   HZ=   31
8-12HZ=   11    0-32  HZ=   82        8-12HZ=   27    0-32  HZ=   89
```
                                                                          T4

```
0-4 HZ=   20    12-32 HZ=   42        0-4 HZ=   26    12-32 HZ=   37
4-8 HZ=    6    0-8   HZ=   26        4-8 HZ=   11    0-8   HZ=   37
8-12HZ=   11    0-32  HZ=   79        8-12HZ=   30    0-32  HZ=  104
```
                                                                          O2

```
0                            32 HZ     SCALE FACTOR = 1
                                          08-AUG-75
```

greater amplitude on the right in the occipital and parietal regions. On
the numerogram this reads 11 microvolts on the left and 30 microvolts on
the right. There is a considerable amount of fast activity. There is a rather
massive amount of fast activity most evident in the left hemisphere on the
numerogram. This reads, in the central regions, 57 microvolts on the left
and 33 microvolts on the right. In addition, the recording shows a mu
rhythm which is of somewhat greater amplitude on the left as compared
with the right. In the numerogram, in the central regions, the reading is 8
on the left and 4 on the right. If there is anything in the psychometrics
that corresponds to the diminished amplitude on the left of the alpha
rhythm it would be interesting. There is a moderate amount of slow wave
activity reading 20–30 microvolts throughout all areas. This also is not
clearly evident in the primary record. The slow wave activity is probably
accounted for on the basis of drowsiness.

In reviewing each of these impressions, it is clear that there are overlaps and congruences which are mutually supportive of both conclusions. For example, both the neuropsychological and EEG data implicate a generalized cerebral abnormality—so much so, at least in the neuropsychological data, that there was a generalized reduction in IQ secondary to an overall cerebral dysfunction. This corresponds with generalized increase in fast activity and some generalized slow wave activity found in the CSA and numerogram data. Of more interest is the implication from the CSA of a left-sided diminished amplitude of alpha rhythm. This may correlate with the specific delineation from the neuropsychological data of diminished language-related functions, specifically dysnomia and dysgraphia, which in this right-handed subject would indeed be located on the left side of the brain. It is our opinion that this combination of techniques is promising and well worth establishing a structured methodology for the mutual application of these diagnostic procedures. This is a promising direction of research, which will be pursued with other populations but which has had its initial start in the study of these polydrug abusing subjects.

COMMENT

It is clear from the data presented here, that in a relatively unselected population of polydrug abusers, evidence for central nervous system dysfunction is considerably elevated above that which would be encountered in the population at large. Over and above the small percentage of patients who were acutely intoxicated at the time of assessment, which would account for a certain number of patients exhibiting cerebral dysfunction, a rather high percentage had neuropsychological (51.8%) and EEG (40%) abnormalities at the time of intake into the study. These levels of abnormality are in approximate agreement with those reported elsewhere and specifically with those from the larger Collaborative Neuropsychological Study. This is not surprising, since our subject sample also makes up a considerable portion of the sample reported in the collaborative study. Thus, in addition to confirming our own preliminary data and the reports of others, the data described here also have potentially important ramifications which extend beyond that which has been previously reported.

The level of agreement, approximately 64%, between the results of these two independent diagnostic procedures assessing cerebral function, is worthy of noting. While this level of agreement should not be startling, nevertheless it is encouraging that the two techniques, so different in the data they generate, were in basic agreement. It was in those individual cases where discrepancies existed between the conclusions of the two procedures that the unique diagnostic contributions of each were more clearly highlighted. First, twice as many of our subjects were found to have abnormal Halstead–Reitan performances with normal electroencephalograms. A closer examination of these data has led us to conclude that the type of cerebral impairment evidenced by polydrug abusers is more amenable to identification through neuropsychological testing. The Halstead–Reitan battery appears to be more sensitive than the EEG in diagnosing subtle cerebral dysfunction. In addition, it appears to us, that apart from rather gross evidences of severe EEG abnormality, the EEG procedure itself is not capable of eliciting minor deficits in cognition. Thus, if one is interested in identifying cerebral deficits manifested by alterations in cognitive performance, the neuropsychological battery is more appropriate and successful in identifying and delineating this type of cerebral incapacity.

The less frequent type of discrepancy is seen in those disagreements in which patients had normal performances on the Halstead–Reitan and abnormal EEGs. Basically, those individuals found to have this type of disagreement, were individuals with either demonstrable drug intoxication or unsuspected seizure activity on the EEG. In the former instance, these individuals were not intoxicated enough to peform abnormally on the Halstead–Reitan, but drugs of the CNS depressant class did alter the EEG recordings. In the latter case, it is rare that the type of seizure activity evidenced by the EEGs of these subjects is correlated with demonstrable disorders in thinking.

In summary, although there is general agreement between the two procedures, each proves to be complimentary to the other when disagreement exists; namely, the Halstead–Reitan, designed to elicit functional thinking deficits, does accomplish this more reliably than the EEG. Individuals with neurological problems that do not classically present themselves with abnormalities in thinking, namely seizure activity, are much more reliably identified by the EEG. In addition, the EEG appears to be more sensitive to identifying states of drug intoxication, especially those induced by CNS depressants, which are not severe enough to alter cognition grossly.

The level of agreement between computerized Compressed Spectral Analysis of the EEG and the neuropsychological battery was such that it was promising but not definitive. Clearly, a methodology must be developed that can make use of data from these two more advanced technologies and allow it to be combined into a meaningful integrated conclusion. A clinical example was presented, and it is apparent that one of the major ways in which diagnostic powers are enhanced by combining the two techniques is through an improved capacity to localize the area of the cerebral deficit. We anticipate that the increased capacity to locate dysfunction more precisely anatomically may be one of the central advantages that will accrue to the simultaneous use of these two diagnostic techniques.

Despite the high degree of mobility and unreliability of this patient population, we were successful in obtaining follow-up assessment batteries in a little over half the population initially studied. The group available for follow-up, 3 to 5 months after entry into the study, was fully representative, at least in terms of neuropsychological and EEG abnormalities, of the total subject sample at entry. The follow-up data reveal that there is an overall trend which indicated that subjects tend to improve at follow-up both neuropsychologically and in their EEGs. Although at this time the data are incomplete, it is our impression that the basis for this improvement is the rehabilitative efforts of the project and the noticeable reduction in substance abuse secondary to the therapeutic program. Despite the overall trend to improvement, there are still significant numbers of patients with residual abnormalities in both the neuropsychological (33%) and the EEG (38.4%) data. Without prospectively gathered drug-free baseline data, it is impossible to say definitively that the residual evidences of cerebral dysfunction are specifically related to severe and chronic drug abuse. Nonetheless, it is our strong suspicion supported by these data, that continuous and excessive abuse of potent psychoactive substances is related to chronic cerebral impairment.

We were particularly interested to find that those individuals with demonstrable neuropsychological impairment were rated as being different on a number of clinical parameters by clinicians using the Psychiatric Evaluation Form (PEF). The fact that the cognitively impaired group demonstrated more grandiosity, belligerence, negativism, denial of their illness, suspicion, and feelings of persecution, was of interest. As previously stated, it was our impression that the psychological position of paranoia, which can be extrapolated from this cluster of signs and symptoms in the impaired group, may be a reflection of their cognitive incapacity to order and understand their hunan environments. Further, the impaired group were clinically judged to be so behaviorally dysfunctional that they were less able to regulate effectively their daily living patterns. It continues to be our hypothesis, now with some basis of support, that the cognitive impairment induced by continued and concurrent substance abuse is one of the central reasons for both the extraordinarily chaotic clinical picture which these patients present and for their recalcitrance to therapeutic intervention. Further, it seems to us, that this spectrum of chaotic behavior due to the cerebral impairment, must be addressed by more simple and direct methods of therapy. Specifically, for at least half of this population (i.e., those who are impaired) a day-care type of program, focusing upon very simple changes in life-style and upon teaching the patients to reorganize and reorder their lives, is necessary. Thus, the more abstract and sophisticated of the psychotherapeutic intervention techniques so commonly used in treatment agencies, address these individuals at levels of cognitive function far beyond that of which they are capable. Failure to acknowledge this may in part be responsible for the high level of treatment failure reported by most groups when dealing with this patient population.

ACKNOWLEDGMENTS

The authors wish to express their appreciation for superb technical help and assistance in every phase of the study by Dean R. Gerstein, Richard Avery, L. Dee Jacobson, and Winifred B. Riney.

This investigation was supported by the National Institute of Drug Abuse (ADAMHA), through a Polydrug Demonstration and Research Project No. 1H81-DA01467 (Friends of Psychiatric Research of San Diego).

CHAPTER XIII

Sleep Patterns of Abusers during Titration and Withdrawal from Methaqualone or Secobarbital

I. Karacan, M. Okawa,
P. J. Salis, R. L. Williams,
A. M. Anch, E. G. Comstock,
B. S. Comstock, and C. A. Moore

The modern era of sleep research began in 1935, when Loomis, Harvey, and Hobart (1935) described four patterns of electroencephalographic (EEG) activity observable during sleep. The first significant breakthrough in the field occurred when Aserinsky and Kleitman (1953) discovered a fifth stage, one characterized by conjugate rapid eye movements [REMs, as measured by electrooculography (EOG)], physiological activation, and a close association with dreaming. It became apparent that sleep, rather than being a unitary state of quiescence, is in fact at least two states. It is composed of both activated REM sleep and more quiescent non-REM (NREM) sleep. Moreover, NREM sleep consists of four distinct stages (stages 1–4) which are characterized by increasing EEG synchronization. Brief periods of wakefulness (stage 0) are typically interspersed among the sleep stages during a night of sleep. Although the function of the various stages of sleep remains unclear, the body seems to need REM and slow-wave (stages 3 and 4) sleep, because deprivation of them is followed by compensatory increases in their amounts on recovery nights (Dement, 1960; Agnew, Webb, & Williams, 1964).

299

Polydrug Abuse:
The Results of a
National Collaborative Study

To many sleep researchers, sleep laboratory technology has seemed to offer an especially promising method of evaluating the effects of drugs on the central nervous system. A primary advantage of the sleep EEG–EOG over the clinical EEG is the fact that the effects of external stimulation on brain activity are dampened during sleep. In addition, by the nature of brain activity during sleep, there is the possibility of assessing drug effects on a variety of patterns at differing levels of specificity: the most global patterns that differentiate wakefulness from sleep; the more specific patterns of REM sleep and each of the four NREM sleep stages; and the most specific patterns, the individual EEG–EOG waveforms themselves (i.e., alpha, beta, delta, spindle, K-complex, and eye-movement activity), which, in various combinations, define the sleep stages.

Until very recently, drug effects on the sleep EEG–EOG were described primarily in terms of rather global descriptors such as total sleep time, sleep latency, number of awakenings, and individual stage amounts. These parameters had proved to be useful and informative in experimental and clinical studies of other variables, they represented a reasonable degree of quantification for visual analysis of the massive amount of data generated in all-night EEG–EOG studies, and normative values had gradually been accumulated for them (Agnew, Webb, & Williams, 1967; Kohler, Coddington, & Agnew, 1968; Ross, Agnew, Williams, & Webb, 1968; Williams, Agnew, & Webb, 1964; 1966; Williams, Karacan, & Hursch, 1974; Williams, Karacan, Hursch, & Davis, 1972a; Williams, Karacan, Thornby, & Salis, 1972). Within the last 10 years, however, a number of investigators have developed automated systems for analyzing sleep EEG–EOG activity (Gaillard & Tissot, 1973; Martin, Johnson, Viglione, Naiton, Joseph, & Moses, 1972; Smith & Karacan, 1971). These systems seem most promising because they will allow automated quantification of the characteristics of the various EEG–EOG waveforms. Thus, even the most subtle effects of drugs on brain activity will be detectable and quantifiable (Johnson, Hanson, & Bickford, 1976; Smith & Karacan, 1973). Fortunately, normative data on the waveform characteristics are also being accumulated (Smith, Karacan, Funke, & Yang, in press).

Virtually all classes of drugs have been examined in sleep laboratory studies (Kay, Blackburn, Buckingham, & Karacan, 1976; Williams & Karacan, 1976). It appears that REM sleep is the most sensitive of the sleep stages to drug effects: most drugs reduce REM sleep amount and density of REMs and increase the time between sleep onset and the first period of REM sleep. Many drugs also reduce the amount of stages 3 and 4 sleep. Although some attempts have been made to discriminate among classes of drugs using sleep EEG–EOG effects, success has generally been elusive. Aside from the fact that the crucial discriminating parameters may not yet have been identified, this work has certainly been hampered by the nature of the research itself. A vast majority of sleep laboratory studies have involved normal subjects. Rarely has the drug administration period been longer than a week. The number of subjects has often been less than five. Problems of interpretation of results have sometimes been introduced by failure to include a placebo condition, use of an insufficiently long interval between drug or dosage administrations in crossover designs, and inadequate statistical analyses of the data; and, until recently, few parameters other than those describing REM sleep were included in published reports.

If such problems are common in experimental studies of drugs in the sleep laboratory, they, or equally severe ones, are inherent in clinical studies. Although some degree of control over the patients and their treatment is often possible, the situation is never ideal. Nevertheless, clinical studies have an important place in a research area because they may be the only source of certain types of information. Studies of patients with drug abuse problems fall into this category. The patients are extremely difficult to manage. If they are in a treatment program, their clinical condition often requires hour-by-hour changes in the treatment protocol, and this wreaks havoc on any systematic study design. On the other hand, the patients may offer a unique opportunity for the examination of the effects of drug doses exceeding the therapeutic maximum. Although the data from studies of such patients must by necessity be interpreted cautiously because of the lack of adequate control in the study situation, they may nevertheless provide potentially enlightening information on the nature of drug–brain interactions and mechanisms.

There have been six systematic sleep laboratory studies of methaqualone (Table XIII.1). From 4 to 12 subjects per study have been evaluated. The doses examined have ranged from 150 to 300 mg. The greatest number of drug nights per study has been 3. Normal volunteers who received methaqualone, 150 mg on 3 consecutive nights (Kales, Kales, Scharf, & Tan, 1970; Rechtschaffen, Robinson & Winocor, 1970), exhibited no significant changes in REM or NREM sleep stages or in awake time; but in one of the studies (Rechtschaffen et al., 1970) there was a significant decrease in the density of REMs during drug administration. When methaqualone (250 mg) was administered on single nights, there was a significant increase in stage 2 percentage; other stage percentages were not changed significantly (Risberg, Risberg, Elmqvist, & Ingvar, 1975). When it was administered for 3 consecutive nights, there were no

Table XIII.1

CHARACTERISTICS OF SLEEP LABORATORY STUDIES OF METHAQUALONE

Reference	Number and type of subjects	Dose (mg)	Time of administration	Number of nights of drug
Kales et al., 1970	5 Normal	150	Bedtime	3 Consecutive
Rechtschaffen et al., 1970	6 Normal	150	?	3 Consecutive
Risberg et al., 1975	6 Normal	250	Bedtime	2 Nonconsecutive
	4 Normal	250	Bedtime	3 Consecutive
Williams and Agnew, 1969	9 Normal	300	15 Minutes before bedtime	1
Itil et al., 1974	12 Normal	300	Bedtime	1
Kales et al., 1970	5 Normal	300	Bedtime	3 Consecutive
Goldstein et al., 1970, 1971	10 Insomniac	300	Bedtime	3 Consecutive

significant changes in any stage percentages (Risberg *et al.*, 1975). One sample of subjects who received single administrations of methaqualone (300 mg) exhibited no significant changes in stage percentages (Williams & Agnew, 1969). Another (Itil, Saletu, & Marasa, 1974) exhibited a significant increase in amount of stage 1 sleep and significant decreases in amounts of stages 2 and 4 sleep. In addition, although a number of REM sleep parameters remained unchanged, there were significantly fewer REM bursts on the drug nights; analyses of the EEG activity revealed that the drug reduced slow-wave activity, the average absolute amplitude, and amplitude variability, but increased fast activity, average frequency, and frequency deviation.

The studies of normal subjects have generally not revealed any significant changes in parameters describing wakefulness, perhaps primarily because there is little room for improvement in normal subjects. Insomniacs who received methaqualone (300 mg) on 3 consecutive nights (Goldstein, Graedon, Willard, Goldstein, & Smith, 1970; Goldstein, Stolzfus, & Smith 1971) exhibited a significant reduction in awake time and in a measure of sleep latency. However, the number and duration of awakenings were not significantly changed. In addition, in these insomniacs there was a significant increase in minutes of stage 2 sleep and a decrease in minutes of stage 4 sleep. There were no significant changes in the several REM parameters examined. During the 4-night placebo recovery period the minutes of wakefulness and REM sleep were significantly increased and the minutes of stage 2 sleep were decreased, relative to the drug period; minutes of stage 4 sleep were decreased relative to the placebo baseline night.

Secobarbital has also been examined in several sleep laboratory studies of normal subjects (Table XIII.2); we are not aware of any studies involving insomniacs or other patients with sleep problems. On single nights, secobarbital (100 mg) tended (nonsignificant) to reduce average frequency of EEG activity (Lester, 1960); produced no significant changes in NREM stage amounts but provoked visible and apparently significant reductions in REM percentage and the duration of REM periods, and an increase in the time between REM periods (Lehmann & Ban, 1968); and, in subjects who retired early in the evening, significantly increased total sleep time and reduced sleep latency (in comparison to placebo and nondrug nights) and produced no significant changes in minutes of REM sleep or of stages 3 + 4 sleep (Allnutt & O'Connor, 1971). Secobarbital (200 mg) significantly reduced REM percentage (especially during the first half of the night) and increased stage 2 percentage and tended to reduce slow-wave sleep percentage (especially during the second half of the night) and wakefulness (Lester, Coulter, Cowden, & Williams, 1968).

Table XIII.2

CHARACTERISTICS OF SLEEP LABORATORY STUDIES OF SECOBARBITAL

Reference	Number and type of subjects	Dose (mg)	Time of administration	Number of nights of drug
Lester, 1960	5 Normal	100	30 Minutes before bedtime	1
Lehmann and Ban, 1968	10 Normal	100	Bedtime	1
Allnutt and O'Connor, 1971	8 Normal	100	1 Hour before bedtime at 8 P.M.	2 Nonconsecutive
Lester et al., 1968	14 Normal	200	30 Minutes before bedtime	1
Feinberg et al., 1974	4 Normal	100 or 200	?	8 Consecutive

Finally, in a study of REM suppression and recovery REM rebound (Feinberg, Hibi, Cavness, & March, 1974), secobarbital (100 mg or 200 mg) significantly reduced both REM percentage and eye-movement activity during the 8-night drug period; on the 3 recovery nights, REM percentage reattained baseline levels and eye-movement activity was somewhat higher than the baseline level (although not significantly so).

In the present report we will describe selected results from a study of patients admitted to a local Polydrug Treatment Unit for treatment of methaqualone or secobarbital abuse. We will emphasize the striking qualitative (i.e., waveform) changes in the patients' sleep EEG–EOGs as they underwent a titration and withdrawal procedure. The data are unique, as far as we know, for toxic doses of these two drugs have never been studied with sleep EEG–EOG methodology.

METHOD

Patients

A total of 11 patients were studied during their titration with and withdrawal from methaqualone or secobarbital. The methaqualone group consisted of five males, ages 15 to 44 (mean 27 years), and three females, ages 16 to 27 (mean 23 years). The secobarbital group included three males, ages 16 to 21 (mean 18 years). On admission to the Polydrug Treatment Unit most patients gave histories of multiple drug use. The drug used in the titration and withdrawal procedures was determined by the drug preference revealed in a current drug history taken on admission to the Unit. Patients selected for study were those who agreed to permit our recordings.

Admission Procedures

Besides providing a current drug history, on admission each patient received a physical examination, chest X-ray, and EKG. Blood and urine specimens were collected for analysis of drug types and levels, CBC, serology, SMA-12, and routine urinalysis. Patients without current diseases, such as acute hepatitis, were scheduled for titration the following morning. In the meantime, each received the preferred drug in doses that were determined by the history of current use and adjusted as required by his response to each dose.

Titration and Withdrawal Procedures

The patient's diet was restricted to clear liquids after the midnight before titration was scheduled to begin. The first dose of drug was typically administered between 9 and 10 AM. Table XIII.3 shows the titration dosage times and amounts for each patient. A Unit staff member monitored the patient continuously during the titration procedure and noted vital signs. Before each hourly dose, the presence or absence of slurred speech, drowsiness, ataxia, and horizontal and vertical nystagmus was assessed and recorded. If all these signs were not present, the next dose was administered; if all were present, the titration procedure was considered completed and drug administration was terminated. All drugs were taken by mouth. Blood specimens for determination of drug levels were obtained before the first titration dose, at the time the titration procedure was completed, 30 minutes later, and then hourly until the patient would no longer tolerate abstinence. After the titration procedure, patients were allowed to sleep under supervision.

Controlled drug withdrawal was typically initiated within 4 to 12 hours following the final dose in the titration procedure. The total amount of drug administered during the titration procedure was calculated. The dose for the first 24 hours of controlled withdrawal was scheduled to be about 70% of the total titration dose, but in actuality it ranged between 50% and 104%. The treatment plan called for a reduction in the 24-hour drug amount of 10% each day thereafter, so that the patient would be drug free after 10 days. Two factors sometimes operated to modify the scheduled reduction in the daily drug amount: (1) occasionally the patient's clinical condition necessitated a slower or faster than scheduled reduction; (2) some patients declined to take one or more of the scheduled doses and thus accelerated the withdrawal process. Throughout the withdrawal procedure, the total amount of drug for a 24-hour period was administered in divided doses. After they were drug free, patients remained in the Unit until they were judged to be sufficiently adjusted for discharge.

Data Collection Procedures

All-night sleep EEG–EOG patterns were monitored on most nights during the withdrawal phase and on selected nights during the subsequent abstinence period. EEG–EOG recording and scoring procedures have been described elsewhere (Williams et al., 1974). For eight of the patients, blood samples for determination of growth hormone levels were taken (1) either on the titration night or on the night following it; (2) on a night roughly midway through the withdrawal period, if withdrawal took longer than several days; (3) on a night early in the abstinence period; and (4) if possible before the patient's discharge from the Unit, approximately 1 week following the first drug-free day. On each of these nights, 4-ml blood samples were drawn every 20 minutes throughout the night via an indwelling venous catheter. The drawing of blood was controlled from outside the patient's room so as to minimize sleep disturbance. Table XIII.4 shows the daily methaqualone or secobarbital intake of the patients and the nights on which EEG–EOG recordings were made and growth hormone was sampled.

During the study, each patient slept alone in his bedroom in the Unit. He was prevented from taking daytime naps. As far as possible, the patient's times of retiring at night and arising in the morning conformed to his usual schedule at home. Medications other than the drugs of interest were kept to a minimum. Nevertheless, the following drugs were administered to at least one patient on at least one occasion: aspirin, codeine, Empirin, Lomotil, Mylanta, Robaxin, Robitussin, Tylenol, Valium, and Varidase.

RESULTS

In this report our focus will be the dramatic changes in the quality of the EEG–EOG tracings of the patients after toxic doses of the two drugs. These changes were clearly observable by visual analysis. In future reports we will present the results of automated analyses of the waveform data, and of analyses of conventional sleep-stage data (scoring of sleep stages was often difficult or impossible because of the qualitative waveform changes).

Figure XIII.1 shows the tracings characterizing each of the five sleep stages and waking stage 0 in a healthy young-adult male. Wakefulness is dominated by 8- to 12-Hz alpha activity. In stage 1, or light sleep, the alpha activity disappears. EEG activity in stage 1 REM sleep is similar to that in stage 1 sleep, but eye movements appear in EOG channels. Stage 2 sleep is signaled by the occurrence of well-defined 11- to 14-Hz spindles and/or K-complexes. Stages 3 and 4 sleep are characterized by 1- to 3-Hz slow delta waves. In stage 3 sleep they occupy less than half the time, while in stage 4 sleep they predominate. Although 18- to 26-Hz beta activity is not used as a classification criterion for sleep stages, it is reasonably common during stages 0, 1, and 1 REM in normal subjects.

Changes in the sleep EEG–EOG tracings of our patients after drug

Table XIII.3

TITRATION DOSAGE TIMES AND AMOUNTS (mg) FOR METHAQUALONE AND SECOBARBITAL ABUSERS

Methaqualone patients[a]

Dosage number	M1(M,15) Time	Amount	M2(M,16) Time	Amount	M3(M,25) Time	Amount	M4(M,35) Time	Amount	M5(M,44) Time	Amount
1	9A.M.	600	10A.M.	600	9A.M.	600	9A.M.	600	10A.M.	600
2	10A.M.	300					10A.M.	300	11A.M.	300
3	11A.M.	300					11A.M.	300	12M.	300
4							12M.	300	1P.M.	300
5							1P.M.	300	2P.M.	300
6									3P.M.	300
7									4P.M.	300
8										
9										
10										
Total dosage (mg)	1200		600		600		1800		2400	

	Methaqualone patients[a]						Secobarbital patients[a]					
	M6(F,16)		M7(F,25)		M8(F,27)		S1(M,16)		S2(M,17)		S3(M,21)	
Dosage number	Time	Amount	Time	Amount	Time	Amount	Time	Amount	Time	Amount	Time	Amount
1	10A.M.	300	9A.M.	600	2P.M.	600	9A.M.	200	10A.M.	200	9A.M.	200
2	11A.M.	300	10A.M.	300	3P.M.	300	10A.M.	100	11A.M.	100	10A.M.	100
3	12M.	300	11A.M.	300	4P.M.	300	11A.M.	100			11A.M.	100
4	1P.M.	300	12M.	300	5P.M.	600					12M.	100
5	2P.M.	300	1P.M.	300	6P.M.	600					1P.M.	100
6	3P.M.	300	2P.M.	300	7P.M.	600					2P.M.	100
7	4P.M.	300									3P.M.	100
8	5P.M.	300										
9	6P.M.	300										
10	7P.M.	300										
Total dosage (mg)		3000		2100		3000		400		300		800

[a] Letters and numbers in parentheses indicate sex and ages of patients.

Table XIII.4

TWENTY-FOUR-HOUR DRUG INTAKE (mg) AND SCHEDULE OF SLEEP EEG–EOG RECORDINGS AND GROWTH HORMONE SAMPLING FOR METHAQUALONE AND SECOBARBITAL ABUSERS

	Methaqualone patients								Secobarbital patients		
	M1	M2	M3	M4	M5	M6	M7	M8	S1	S2	S3
	T dose										
	1200	600	600	1800	2400	3000	2100	3000	400	300	800
Day	24-Hour intake										
T	1200[b]	900[b]	1200[b]	2100[b,c]	2400	3300[b]	2400[b]	3300[b]	500[b]	350[b,c]	1000[b,c]
T + 1	750[b]	450[b,c]	300[b,c]	1875[b]	1500[b,c]	1500	1500[b,c]	2100[b]	300[b,c]	200[b]	400[b]
T + 2	750[b]	300[b]	600[b]	1800[b]	900[b]	1800	1500[b]	1500[b]	250[b]	150[b]	500[b]
T + 3	600[b]	0[b,c]	450[b]	1650[b]	600[b]	1500	1200[b]	1200[b]	200[b]	50[b]	400[b]
T + 4	450[b]	0[b]	450[b]	1350[b,c]	300[b,c]	2100	900[b]	900[b]	150[b,c]	0[b]	300[b]
T + 5	300[b]	0[b,c]	150[b]	1350[b]	300[b]	2250	600[b,c]	600[b]	0[b]	0[b]	200[b,c]
T + 6	0[b]	0[b]	0[b,c]	1200[b]	0[b]	1350	300[b]	0[b]	0[b,c]	0[b,c]	100[b]
T + 7	0	0[b]	0	1050[b]	0[b,c]	1350	150[b]	0[b]	0[b,c]	0[b]	0[b]
T + 8	0	0[b]	0	600[b]	0	1800	0[b]	D/C	0[b]	0[b]	0[b,c]
T + 9	0	0	0	600[b]	0	1650	0[b,c]		0[b]	0[b]	0[b]
T + 10	0	0	0	300[b]	0	1200	0[b]		0[b]	0[b]	0
T + 11	0	0[b,c]	0[b]	0[b,c]	0	750[b]	0[b]		0[b,c]	0[b,c]	0
T + 12	0	0[b]	0[b,c]	0[b]	0[b]	600[b]	0[b]		0[b]	0[b]	0
T + 13	0	D/C	0[b]	0[b]	0[b,c]	1050[b]	D/C ?[b]		0[b]	D/C	0[b]
T + 14	D/C		0	0	0	300[b]	?[b]		0		0[b,c]
T + 15			0	D/C	D/C	300[b]			0		0[b]
T + 16			0	?		300[b]			0		0[b]
T + 17			D/C	?		D/C ?[b]			0		0
T + 18				?		0[b]			0		0

T + 19	?	0^b	0	0
T + 20	?	0^b	D/C	0
T + 21	?	0^b		0
T + 22	?	$?^b$		D/C
.	.			
.	.			
.	.			
T + 27	$?^b$			
T + 28	$?^b$			
T + 29	$?^{b,c}$			

[a] Key to symbols:
  T = titration
  D/C = discharged from the Polydrug Treatment Unit
  ? = drug intake unknown or drug screen indicated the presence of one or more drugs
[b] EEC–EOG recording made.
[c] Growth hormone sampled.

311

312

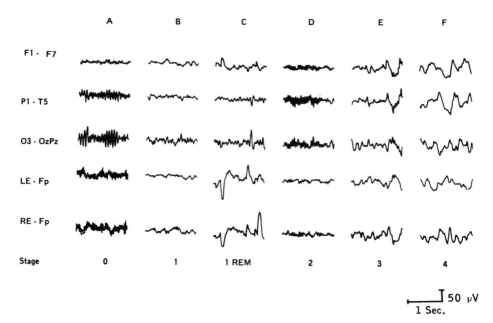

Figure XIII.1. EEG–EOG activity characterizing wakefulness (stage 0) and the five sleep stages in a normal young adult. Note alpha (8- to 12-Hz) activity in stage 0; low-voltage, mixed-frequency activity in stage 1; rapid eye movements (channels LE-Fp and RE-Fp) in stage 1 REM; spindle (11- to 14-Hz) activity in stage 2; some delta (1- to 3-Hz) activity in stage 3; and predominant delta activity in stage 4.

intoxication and during the immediate withdrawal period, when daily drug intake levels were still very high, were the following:

1. Increase in and distortion of spindle activity
2. Increase in beta activity
3. Distortion of alpha activity
4. Intermingling of alpha, beta, spindle, and delta activities
5. Distortion or disappearance of K-complexes

The remaining figures illustrate these findings and show the evolution of the changes during the withdrawal and abstinence periods.

Figures XIII.2–XIII.6 are samples from the records of patient M7 on selected nights during the withdrawal and abstinence periods. For each figure, the samples are from tracings made on the following nights: T (methaqualone 2400 mg), T + 2 (1500 mg), T + 5 (600mg), T + 7 (150 mg), T + 8 (0 mg), and T + 12 (0 mg). The changes illustrated were exhibited to a greater or lesser extent by all the other patients in the methaqualone group.

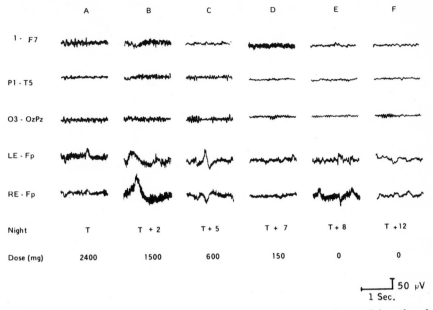

Figure XIII.2. Stage 0 for patient M7 on 6 nights during controlled withdrawal and abstinence from methaqualone. T = night after daytime titration.

Figure XIII.2 shows samples for stage 0. On night T (Figure XIII.2A), alpha activity was absent and beta activity was much in evidence. All activity was of high amplitude. On night T + 2 (Figure XIII.2B), alpha activity was present but quite disorganized and of unusually high amplitude; beta activity was still virtually continuous. By night T + 5 (Figure XIII.2C), alpha activity had assumed a more normal appearance, but its amplitude continued to be high; beta activity was still present in abundance. On nights T + 7, T + 8, and T + 12 (Figures XIII.2D–2F), alpha activity became increasingly more normal in appearance, its amplitude lessened, and beta activity became less and less apparent.

Stage 1 sleep on night T was characterized by much high-amplitude beta activity. On successive nights, the EEG amplitude gradually decreased and beta activity gradually disappeared. By the final recording, stage 1 activity was essentially normal in appearance.

On night T, REM sleep (Figure XIII.3A) also contained large amounts of beta activity; eye movements appeared to occur with normal incidence. On nights T + 2 and T + 5 (Figures XIII.3B and 3C), beta activity progressively decreased and the number of eye movements continued to appear normal. From night T + 7 on (Figures XIII.3D–3F), beta activity had disappeared altogether and REM sleep was entirely normalized.

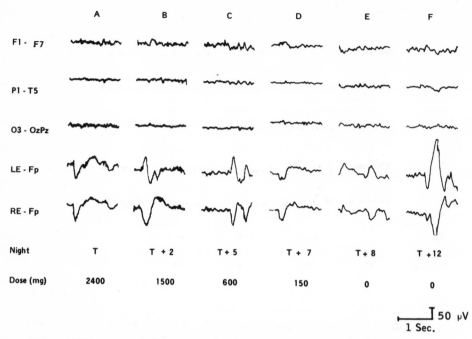

Figure XIII.3. Stage 1 REM for patient M7 on 6 nights during controlled withdrawal and abstinence from methaqualone. T = night after daytime titration.

High doses of methaqualone caused a distortion of spindle activity which we have called spindloid activity. This activity was generally sharper and of higher amplitude (over 100 μV) than normal spindle activity. The envelope of the normal spindle burst was distorted, and bursts of spindloid activity were of longer duration than normal spindle bursts. Figure XIII.4 shows the waveform changes in stage 2 sleep. On night T (Figure XIII.4A), spindloid activity dominated the tracing. It continued to do so on night T + 2 (Figure XIII.4B), when it appeared to be even higher in amplitude. By night T+ 5 (Figure XIII.4C), spindloid activity had occasionally given way to spindle bursts of more normal appearance. On nights T + 7 and T + 8 (Figures XIII.4D and XIII.4E), it had lessened considerably, but spindles had become unusually long and frequent in occurrence. By night T + 12 (Figure XIII.4F), spindles were essentially normal in appearance and incidence.

Another effect of high doses of methaqualone was the distortion of K-complexes during stage 2 sleep. On night T, K-complexes were rare. When they did occur, their amplitude was low and they were unusual in that they were not trailed by spindle activity. These distortions continued

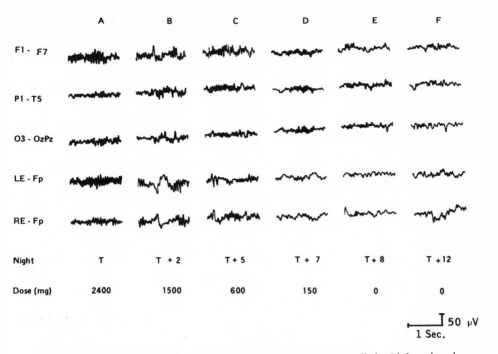

Figure XIII.4. Stage 2 for patient M7 on 6 nights during controlled withdrawal and abstinence from methaqualone. T = night after daytime titration.

to be apparent on night T + 2. From night T + 5 on, K-complexes assumed an essentially normal appearance and incidence.

The major effects of methaqualone on slow-wave sleep were a reduction in the amount of delta activity and an intermingling of spindloid and delta activity. On night T there was no stage 4 sleep. The delta waves in stage 3 sleep (Figure XIII.5A) had "riding" spindloid activity. By night T + 2 and on night T + 5 (Figures XIII.5B and XIII.5C), stage 4 sleep had returned but spindloid activity continued to ride on the delta waves. From night T + 7 on (Figures XIII.5D–XIII.5F), the delta waves appeared to be normal.

High doses of secobarbital produced similar changes in EEG–EOG waveforms, but the pattern and degree of change were somewhat different. Figures XIII.6–XIII.9 show samples from the records of patient S3. Like those for the methaqualone patient, the samples on a figure are arranged chronologically; they were taken from tracings made on nights T (secobarbital 1000 mg), T + 2 (500 mg), T + 5 (200 mg), T + 6 (100 mg), T + 7 (0 mg), and T + 15 (0 mg).

On night T, stage 0 (Figure XIII.6A) was characterized by rare and

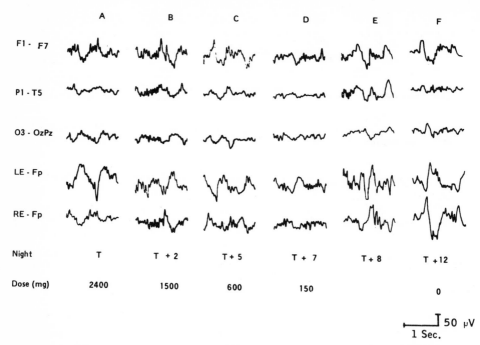

Figure XIII.5. Stages 3 (sample A) and 4 (samples B–F) for patient M7 on 6 nights during controlled withdrawal and abstinence from methaqualone. T = night after daytime titration.

disorganized alpha activity and heavy beta activity; the amplitude of all activity was quite high. On nights T + 2 and T + 5 (Figures XIII.6B and XIII.6C), alpha activity continued to be somewhat disorganized and beta activity remained pronounced; amplitude progressively lessened. By night T + 6 (Figure XIII.6D), alpha activity was definitely more normally organized and pronounced and beta activity had disappeared. From night T + 7 on (Figures XIII.6E and XIII.6F), stage 0 appeared quite normal.

Stage 1 sleep on night T showed little beta activity, but high-amplitude spindloid activity dominated the tracing sufficiently to make it difficult to distinguish stage 1 from stage 0 and stage 2. By night T + 2, some beta activity had appeared but low-amplitude spindloid activity still predominated. On night T + 5, beta activity was pronounced. The amplitude of the tracings had increased by night T + 6, and beta activity had become rare. From night T + 7 on, tracings for stage 1 sleep appeared normal.

There were virtually no eye movements during REM sleep on night T (Figure XIII.7A); spindloid and beta activity intermingled, but there was no alpha activity. Eye movements continued to be rare on night T+ 2 (Figure XIII.7B), and beta activity had increased. Night T+ 5 (Figure

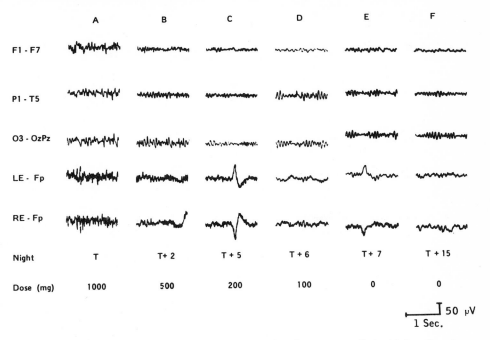

Figure XIII.6. Stage 0 for patient S3 on 6 nights during controlled withdrawal and abstinence from secobarbital. T = night after daytime titration.

XIII.7C) was characterized by the fewest eye movements and the most beta activity. On night T + 6 (Figure XIII.7D), eye movements were still rare but beta activity was less prominent. Eye movements were much more frequent on night T + 7 (Figure XIII.7E), and beta activity had almost completely disappeared. REM sleep had returned to normal by night T + 15 (Figure XIII.7F).

As with methaqualone, stage 2 sleep with high doses of secobarbital was dominated by spindloid activity. On night T this activity either completely obscured all other activity or was mixed with high-amplitude beta activity (Figure XIII.8A). On night T + 2 (Figure XIII.8B), the mixture of beta and spindloid activity continued but beta activity was less in evidence; trains of spindloid activity were longer and tended to obscure all background activity. By night T + 5 (Figure XIII.8C), recognizable spindles had appeared; they were, however, of unusually high amplitude, long duration, and high incidence. On nights T + 6 and T + 7 (Figures XIII.8D and 8E), the amplitude, duration, and incidence of spindles gradually lessened. By night T + 15 (Figure XIII.8F), stage 2 sleep and its spindles had normalized.

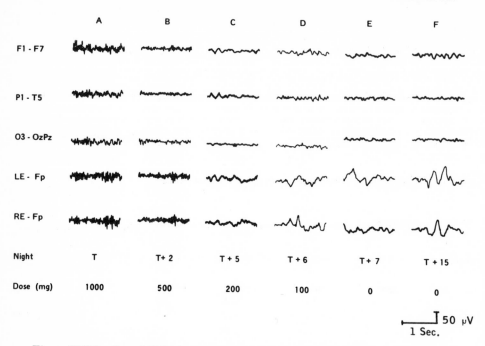

Figure XIII.7. Stage 1 REM for patient S3 on 6 nights during controlled withdrawal and abstinence from secobarbital. T = night after daytime titration.

Again as with methaqualone, the disappearance or distortion of K-complexes in stage 2 sleep was observed with high doses of secobarbital. After the toxic dose, on night T, no normal K-complexes were apparent, although waveforms resembling them sometimes occurred in conjunction with the dominant spindloid activity. On night T + 2, K-complexes of more normal appearance appeared in some channels but not in all, and spindloid activity was still predominant. By night T + 5, K-complexes had become exaggerated in amplitude and duration and were trailed by long trains of spindloid activity. On nights T + 6 and T + 7, K-complexes retained their high amplitude and long duration, but more normal spindle activity had begun to appear. By night T + 15, K-complexes were essentially normal.

Unlike methaqualone, secobarbital did not completely eliminate stage 4 slow-wave sleep. It did, however, produce the same mixture of delta and riding spindloid activity. This was apparent especially on nights T and T+ 2 (Figure XIII.9A and 9B). It continued to a lesser extent on night T+ 5 (Figure XIII.9C). On nights T+ 6 and T+ 7 (Figure XIII.9D and 9E), the amplitude of delta waves had increased somewhat but the waves were still

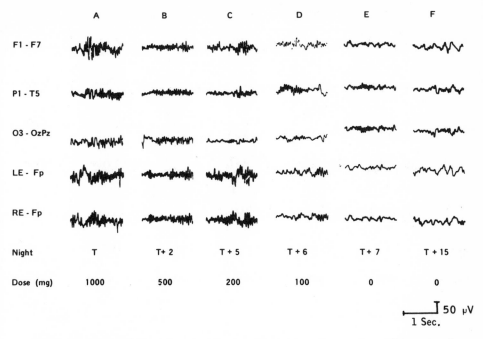

Figure XIII.8. Stage 2 for patient S3 on 6 nights during controlled withdrawal and abstinence from secobarbital. T = night after daytime titration.

occasionally intermingled with spindloid activity. By night T + 15 (Figure XIII.9F), slow-wave sleep had a normal appearance.

DISCUSSION

The most pervasive changes induced in the qualitative aspects of sleep EEG–EOG activity by toxic doses of methaqualone and secobarbital were (1) the distortion of spindle activity into spindloid activity, (2) the dominance of many of the tracings by spindloid activity, and (3) the abnormally high amount of beta activity. Also apparent with both drugs were the disappearance and/or distortion of K-complexes. Our visual inspection of the tracings suggested that toxic doses of methaqualone produced less spindloid activity and beta activity than toxic doses of secobarbital. It also appeared that methaqualone suppressed delta activity more than did secobarbital, while secobarbital had a considerably greater effect on the incidence of eye movements during REM sleep. We are investigating these drug differences more systematically by submitting the

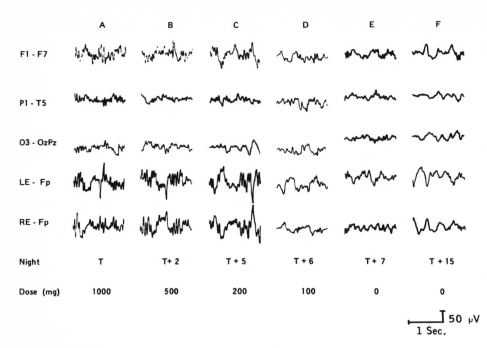

Figure XIII.9. Stage 4 for patient S3 on 6 nights during controlled withdrawal and abstinence from secobarbital. T = night after daytime titration.

data to quantitative analyses of waveform characteristics by our Sleep Analyzing Hybrid Computer (Smith & Karacan, 1971).

The evolution of changes in spindloid and spindle activity over the course of the withdrawal and abstinence periods was especially interesting. At high drug levels, spindloid activity was dominant and only very rarely were recognizable spindles visible. As the withdrawal period progressed, the spindloid activity gradually gave way at times to spindle activity, which nevertheless occurred in bursts of unusually long duration. The incidence of these long spindle bursts slowly increased until they entirely supplanted the spindloid activity. Then the spindles gradually developed more normal duration and incidence. We have observed similar patterns of change in several other patients undergoing the same type of controlled withdrawal from amobarbital, amobarbital–secobarbital, pentobarbital, phenobarbital, or diazepam. This suggests that very high doses of psychoactive agents, whatever the type, produce in certain brain areas a kind of "stress reaction" which consists of the breakdown of mechanisms controlling the organization of brain activity into discrete burst patterns.

Previous studies of waveform characteristics in normal subjects taking acute therapeutic doses of methaqualone indicated that the drug reduced slow-wave activity and increased fast activity (Itil *et al.*, 1974) and suppressed eye-movement activity (Rechtschaffen *et al.*, 1970; Risberg *et al.*, 1975). Our findings with abusers of the drug who received toxic doses would seem to support the results of Itil *et al.*, but our visual inspection of the data did not reveal a major suppression of eye movements. Other studies have shown that in normal subjects acute therapeutic doses of secobarbital reduce average EEG frequency (Lester, 1960); reduce theta (3–7 Hz) and riding "alphoid" (7–11 Hz) activity in all stages, and spindle activity in stage 2, and increase alpha activity in all stages and precentral beta activity in REM sleep (Lester *et al.*, 1968); and decrease eye-movement activity in REM sleep (Feinberg *et al.*, 1974). Our data indicate that toxic doses also increase beta activity and suppress eye movements. Toxic doses may, however, contrast with therapeutic doses, particularly by increasing spindle (or spindloid) activity. The most likely reasons for the divergent findings are the differences between studies in subject type and drug dose. If parts of the brain do respond to toxic doses of drug with a "stress reaction," then it would not be surprising to discover that therapeutic and toxic doses of a drug produce different effects on sleep EEG–EOG waveforms.

In conclusion, we have presented unique data on the effects of toxic doses of methaqualone and secobarbital on the qualitative aspects of sleep EEG–EOG activity. The normalization of the EEG–EOG activity has been examined during periods of controlled withdrawal and abstinence from the drugs. Both drugs produced dramatic changes in several waveforms and especially in spindle activity. The data suggest several effects common to toxic doses of psychoactive agents, but the two drugs under study appeared to differ in the degree to which they produced certain of these effects. If there is a common drug intoxication effect, then the waveform distortions associated with it may prove to be useful in a clinical setting where identification of general classes of intoxicating agents is of interest. On the other hand, the apparent differences in the degree of this effect may be helpful in the application of sleep EEG–EOG data to drug classification. Our finding that most effects slowly lessened as drug dose decreased would also indicate that the waveforms we examined should be considered as standard practice in dose-response studies of drugs.

ACKNOWLEDGMENT

This study was supported by grants from the National Institute on Drug Abuse, the Houston Veterans Administration Hospital, and Sleep Research, Inc.

PART 4

Impact of Polydrug Abuse on Nondrug Abuse Health Delivery System

EDITORS' INTRODUCTION

The majority of treatment contacts with polydrug problems occur in agencies not specifically geared to provide drug abuse treatment services. The role drug abuse played in initiating or confounding the treatment errors varies greatly depending upon the circumstances in which the intervention occurs. Sometimes the drug abuse element is never recognized; sometimes it is actively ignored, and sometimes well-intentioned, but inappropriate, treatment is used. Without question, it is the exception when drug abuse is correctly diagnosed and appropriate referral or definitive treatment initiated.

The authors of the next two chapters focus on the impact of polydrug abusers on alcohol and mental health programs and on the attitudinal responses of physicians to treating drug problems. The heterogeniety of responses described by these authors help us appreciate the multitude of attitudinal and programmatic barriers to definitive treatment.

CHAPTER XIV

Physician Attitudes Concerning Drug Abuse Treatment

David E. Smith and Donald R. Wesson

Since the passage of the Harrison Narcotic Act of 1914, physicians have been actively discouraged from treating opiate abuse problems, except in specialized clinics and hospitals. Until the past 10 years, the treatment of the opiate addict had been almost completely relegated to the criminal justice system.

Although policy for treatment of opiate dependency is clear, the role of the physicians in providing treatment to polydrug-dependent patients has been less subject to legislative control and left largely to the discretion of the physician. Most physicians, however, prefer not to treat drug abusers or at least to confine their involvement to treating the acute medical or surgical complications of drug abuse.

In our early work with polydrug-using patients, we became aware of two factions of drug abusers who were approached very differently by physicians. The first group of patients, whom we later termed "nonstreetwise" (see Chapter V in this volume for discussion and definitions of this terminology) fit well into the office medical practice of

Polydrug Abuse:
The Results of a
National Collaborative Study

many physicians. Addiction problems of the nonstreetwise group were primarily the result of self-medication for pain, insomnia, depression, or anxiety. This group of patients contrasted sharply with the "streetwise" patients, composed primarily of youthful, drug users who took drugs primarily for recreational purposes, although some streetwise individuals used drugs primarily to self-medicate symptoms.

Nonstreetwise patients did not find the storefront drug abuse clinic, designed for youthful, drug abusers, acceptable for their treatment needs. They preferred treatment via traditional medical channels, and, indeed, such individuals generally indicated an extensive medical treatment history. For patients who were ultimately treated in the polydrug projects, the drug problem had either been ignored (or undiagnosed) in past treatment efforts, and the treatment was ineffective in managing the underlying medical or psychiatric disorder.

Since the nonstreetwise individuals were already receiving most of their treatment through traditional medical channels, and the streetwise individuals had episodic contact with emergency room personnel and other private physicians for treatment of drug abuse complications, delineation of physician's attitudes toward their drug-abusing patients is important. In addition, the trend toward using third party payment mechanisms to fund drug abuse treatment may have the result that many individuals who are now treated in drug abuse clinics will be treated by physicians who are not drug abuse specialists.

Federal efforts to engage the physician in more active treatment of drug and alcohol abuse have been made, through the development of a Career Teacher Program sponsored by the National Institute on Drug Abuse (NIDA) and the National Institute on Alcohol and Alcoholism Abuse (NIAAA), in an effort to incorporate more information concerning diagnosis and treatment of drug abuse into the framework of medical school curricula. In addition, resource training materials, regional training centers, etc., were developed in an attempt to engage the attention of practicing physicians. As a substudy of the San Francisco Polydrug Project, we studied, in postgraduate, practicing physicians, attitudes that were perceived as obstacles to the treatment of alcohol and drug abuse patients. Our approach was twofold. The first approach involved informal interviews and case consultations with physicians about drug abuse problems that surfaced in their practice. Second, we administered a Physician Opinion Survey to as many physicians as possible. This chapter summarizes the findings of that survey with regard to attitudes affecting drug abuse and is amplified by our field observations and case consultations.

SOME FIELD OBSERVATIONS

In defining the characteristics of the nonstreetwise polydrug population, Wesson *et al.* (1975) noted that this large patient pool was "hidden" only in the sense that they did not go to existing drug abuse treatment programs. However, it was learned that they did receive treatment within the health care delivery system, including emergency rooms, hospitals, and the private practicing physician's office. Rarely was the purpose of entry into treatment for substance abuse per se, but rather a result of complications of drug use, such as falls and overdose.

Therefore, despite the reluctance of many physicians to treat patients for alcohol and drug abuse, physicians are nevertheless frequently exposed to the complications of these addictive disorders. While physicians may treat the complications adequately, their responses to the primary drug problem can be categorized into three categories: (1) a few experts in the field who provide state-of-the-art medical treatment to the substance abuser; (2) a group of physicians who devote some percentage of their time to problems of drug abuse with the intentions of trying to be helpful but contribute to the problem out of misinformation and poor training; (3) a substantial number of physicians who actively avoid the substance abuser. However, physicians in this latter category are frequently, although unwillingly, exposed to the substance abuse patient in a variety of ways, such as having a patient go into withdrawal while on the medical or surgical floor while being treated for an illness or injury not associated with drug abuse; medical emergencies associated with substance abuse; having pregnant women enter into the obstetrical–gynecological office with a drug or alcohol problem; or seeing a psychiatric disorder in a private psychiatrist's office masked, altered, and sometimes aggravated by substance abuse. It is virtually impossible for the practicing physician, no matter what his specialty, to avoid being exposed to the substance-abusing patient.

PHYSICIAN OPINION SURVEY

In order to quantify physician's attitudes, a questionnaire was developed which consisted of 15 statements concerning alcohol and drug abuse, in addition to statements concerning physicians' needs for additional resources. Parallel questions were asked concerning alcohol and drug abuse. The physicians were asked to respond to "obstacle questions" on a scale of: (1) not important obstacle, (2) present, not serious, (3) serious obstacle, or (4) not applicable to my practice. During 1975 to 1976, the physician opinion survey was completed by 277 practicing physicians. Primary specialty areas represented were general and family practice, 23%; general surgery and surgical subspecialties, 18%; internal medicine and medical subspecialties, 35%; psychiatry, 21%; with the remainder scattered across other subspecialties. Of the physicians surveyed, 89% listed their time involvement with drug abuse as being less than 30%. The number of years in practice ranged from less than one year to 47 years; 75% were from California and the remainder from other states. No state, other than California, accounted for more than 2% of the sample, however.

The questionnaire was passed out at county medical society meetings, the NIDA sponsored Career Teachers meeting in New Orleans in 1976, and to consultants who worked in the drug abuse area in California.

DATA ANALYSIS

While analysis of the data showed some interesting trends, the data should not be projected to all physicians as the representivity of the physicians sampled cannot be determined. For purposes of analysis, physicians were divided into four specialties including: (1) general and family practice physicians; (2) medical and medical subspecialties; (3) surgery and surgical subspecialties; (4) psychiatry.

Individuals who responded either "not applicable," or left blank more than 2 of the 15 items, were dropped from the analysis. While this dropped the total sample size to 147, these remaining individuals were probably paying serious attention to the questionnaire and were physicians who did see some drug or alcohol abusers in their practice.

Table XIV.1 tabulates response items for drug abuse.

THERAPEUTIC PESSIMISM SCALE

The item responses to the 15 questions allowed the development of an ordinal level scale of therapeutic pessimism computed by summing the responses on the 15 items counting "present, not serious" as one point, and "serious obstacle" as two points. As with the previous analysis, individuals who responded either "not applicable," or left blank more than 2 of the 15 items, were dropped from the analysis. The scale thus derived has a range of 0 to 30. The median response was 9. The distribution of scores is shown in Figure XIV.1.

Table XIV.1

PHYSICIAN'S DRUG ABUSE RESPONSES DISPLAYED BY SPECIALTY AREA FOR THOSE WHO RATED THE STATEMENT AS A "SERIOUS OBSTACLE." THIS TABULATION ELIMINATES PHYSICIANS WHO LEFT MORE THAN TWO RESPONSES BLANK OR WHO MARKED MORE THAN TWO STATEMENTS "NOT APPLICABLE TO MY PRACTICE."

| Statement | Physician's specialty | | | | | | | | Total number responding to item | p computed by chi square $df = 6$ |
| | General and family practice ($N = 47$) | | Surgery and surgery subspecialties ($N = 16$) | | Internal medicine and medical subspecialties ($N = 50$) | | Psychiatry ($N = 34$) | | | |
	N	(%)	N	(%)	N	(%)	N	(%)		
They don't pay their bills.	12	(27)	6	(38)	9	(20)	5	(16)	138	n.s.
They don't keep appointments.	13	(28)	9	(56)	22	(44)	9	(26)	147	n.s.
They are not appreciative.	10	(22)	3	(19)	6	(12)	3	(9)	146	n.s.
They don't get well.	26	(57)	6	(38)	13	(27)	4	(12)	143	<.05
I don't know what to do for them.	20	(44)	6	(38)	16	(33)	4	(12)	145	<.05
They take too much time.	17	(37)	3	(19)	9	(18)	3	(9)	145	<.05
They demand attention at odd hours.	15	(32)	4	(25)	9	(18)	5	(15)	146	n.s.
They are unpleasant.	5	(11)	2	(13)	5	(10)	1	(3)	147	n.s.
I don't want my other patients subjected to their unpleasantness.	7	(15)	2	(13)	7	(14)	1	(3)	145	n.s.
I don't want my staff subjected to their unpleasantness.	7	(15)	2	(13)	5	(10)	2	(6)	144	n.s.
I don't have follow-up services I can refer them to.	17	(36)	5	(31)	8	(17)	7	(21)	145	n.s.
I don't want the medical–legal problems involved.	14	(30)	2	(13)	7	(14)	2	(6)	147	<.05
I have trouble getting them into the hospital.	15	(32)	1	(7)	8	(17)	7	(21)	144	n.s.
Difficulty in collecting fees from insurance.	11	(26)	1	(6)	5	(10)	2	(6)	140	<.05
I don't want the poor professional image in the eyes of other physicians.	5	(11)	0	(0)	3	(6)	1	(3)	143	n.s.

329

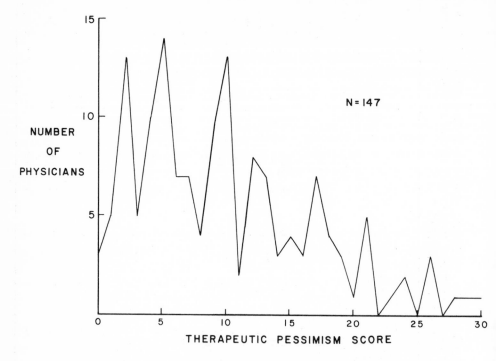

Figure XIV.1. Distribution of therapeutic pessimism sources. (N = 147.)

Table XIV.2

PHYSICIAN'S SCORES ON THERAPEUTIC PESSIMISM BY SPECIALTY (INCLUDES ONLY PHYSICIAN'S RESPONSES WHO LEFT LESS THAN TWO BLANK, OR WHO MARKED LESS THAN 3 RESPONSES "NOT APPLICABLE TO MY PRACTICE" (N = 147)

| | Therapeutic Pessimism[a] | | | |
| | High | | Low | |
Physician's specialty	N	(%)	N	(%)
General and family practice	30	(64)	17	(36)
Surgery and surgical subspecialties	13	(81)	3	(19)
Internal medicine and medical subspecialties	18	(36)	32	(64)
Psychiatry	8	(23)	26	(79)

[a] $\chi^2 = 22.8$; $df = 3$; $p < .001$.

Physicians scoring 10 to 30, were assigned to the category of high therapeutic pessimism and physicians responding 0 to 9 (the median score and below) were grouped into a category of low therapeutic pessimism. Using this dichotomous variable, the data were further cross-tabulated by age, sex, specialty, percentage of time working in drug abuse, and the role with drug abuse patients. There was no difference by age or sex. However, there were highly significant differences ($p < .001$) between specialty areas (Table XIV.2).

However, one of the difficulties in the interpretation of these data is the possibility that physicians who initially have a more positive attitude toward the treatment of drug abuse patients enter particular specialties. Thus, it is an association but does not necessarily infer causality.

Although sample size was small for physicians who spent greater than 31% of their time in treating drug abuse, physicians who spent the most time working in drug abuse were the least pessimistic regarding treatment (Table XIV.3).

The physician's perception of his role was also significant. Physicians who reported treating patients for *both* drug problems and other health problems were less therapeutically pessimistic (Table XIV.4).

In addition to our work with medical societies and case consultation with the practicing physician, we were able to do some prospective studies of the change in physicians' attitudes and information base as a result of special training and consultation efforts. Although this work must be viewed as preliminary, it nevertheless does aid in interpreting the data reported in the previous section. The analysis of this longitudinal clinical

Table XIV.3

PHYSICIANS SCORING HIGH AND LOW ON THERAPEUTIC PESSIMISM AS A FUNCTION OF PERCENTAGE OF TIME SPENT IN PROVIDING DRUG ABUSE TREATMENT SERVICES ($N = 146$)

	Therapeutic pessimism[a]			
	High		Low	
Percentage of time spent providing drug abuse treatment services	N	(%)	N	(%)
0–30	68	(100)	60	(77)
31–60	0	(0)	12	(15)
61–100	0	(0)	6	(8)

[a] $\chi^2 = 17.9$; $df = 2$; $p < .001$.

Table XIV.4

PERCENTAGE OF PHYSICIANS SCORING HIGH AND LOW IN THERAPEUTIC
PESSIMISM BY ROLE IN DRUG ABUSE TREATMENT

| | Therapeutic pessimism[a] | | | |
| | High | | Low | |
Physician's usual role with drug abuse patient	N	(%)	N	(%)
Treat both their drug problem and other				
health problems	38	(37)	63	(62.4)
Treat them for medical (or surgical)				
problems, but not their drug problem	27	(66)	14	(34)
I do not see drug patients in my practice	3	(75)	1	(—)

[a] $(\chi^2) = 10.6;\ df = 2;\ p < .005.$

experience and interaction with collaborative investigators such as the
Career Teacher programs with medical students, indicates that negative
attitude and therapeutic pessimism are correlated with poor training and
lack of clinical experience in the alcohol and drug abuse area. Further, it
appears that with improved medical school training and improved alcohol
and drug abuse training in the traditional medical specialties of family
practice, surgery, internal medicine, and psychiatry, one can increase
diagnostic and treatment skills and develop a more optimistic attitude
about the usefulness of therapy with drug populations.

Chappel and Schnoll (1976) stressed that "physician attitudes influence
all aspects of the management of the chemically dependent patient."
They posed a series of questions as to attitudes which enhance the quality
of treatment that can be developed during medical and postgraduate
medical education, stressing that modification of attitude is far more
difficult than transmitting information or developing technical skills.
Rexler (1974) concluded that the effects of training which foster a positive
orientation to patients' social and emotional problems declined. At least 2
years were spent consolidating these attitudes. Reynolds and Bice (1971)
emphasized the difficulty in altering attitudes that were supported by the
medical peer culture. For example, they described 5 months of vigorous
attempts to improve the attitudes of medical interns toward long-term
patients through alterations of the intern–patient relationship, informal
talks, discussion, teaching rounds, and other mechanisms, and concluded that "despite efforts to change them, the attitudes of the interns
appeared remarkably stable over the period of time studied," if the peer
support system was also not modified. It is apparent then, that medical

school and postgraduate negative attitudes toward the alcohol- and drug-dependent patient are reinforced by the broader negative attitudes manifested in the medical community and thus provide a resistance and counterbalance to training efforts to improve these attitudes. However, Chappel, using Mogar's (Mogar, Helm, Snedker, Snedker, & Wilson, 1969) premise, that experience is a more powerful determinant of attitude and persuasion, found that negative attitudes of medical students toward chemically dependent patients can be reversed (Chappel, Jordan, Tread-way, & Miller, 1976). They instituted a week-long course involving 28 instruction hours for second-year medical students, with the goal of developing positive attitudes toward the treatment of chemically dependent patients. Active student participation was encouraged through the use of clinical problem solving, small group discussions, and field trips to treatment programs. At the end of the course medical students reported significant decreases in feelings of upset and disgust while treating chemically dependent patients, seeing a more positive role for the physician and being more optimistic about job counseling, family involvement, individual counseling, and chemotherapy as treatment modalities.

Our case consultation indicates that postgraduate physician attitudes toward the chemically dependent patient can also be modified, after years of practice. For example, during one of our medical society lectures on the treatment of the alcohol and drug abuse patient, a psychiatrist in private practice indicated that he would not see drug abuse patients in his private practice because he was pessimistic about their prognosis and he felt unsure about his ability to manage them properly. At the time of the discussion, he had been approached by a middle-class nonstreetwise, female barbiturate abuser, who was seeking hospitalization for detoxification from her barbiturate dependence. We discussed the case using our case consultation model and provided him with a clinically oriented manual, which we developed especially for physicians, entitled "The Diagnosis and Treatment of Adverse Reactions to Sedative—Hypnotics." This manual outlines in simplified and precise fashion, the approach to detoxification of the barbiturate-dependent individual. As a result of this consultation the psychiatrist hospitalized the patient and detoxified her using the phenobarbital substitution withdrawal method (Smith & Wesson, 1971) and achieved a positive therapeutic outcome. Subsequently, as the physician became more confident of his ability to treat drug abusers and acquired more information in this area, his attitude became more therapeutically optimistic and he increased the percentage of his practice devoted to drug abuse treatment from zero to 15%. Periodically, he would request case consultation on a particularly difficult patient individual, but as his skills developed and his knowledge of the drug literature increased, he needed case consultation backup less frequently.

NEEDS IN DRUG ABUSE AS PERCEIVED BY PHYSICIANS

In addition to rating the obstacles to drug abuse treatment, physicians were asked on the questionnaire to rate a variety of "needs" on a scale ranging from 1 to 4, with 1= not needed, to 4= very much needed. The responses were cross-tabulated by speciality but no significant differences were found. In order to rank the perceived needs, the responses were recoded with not needed = 0, 1, for sometimes helpful, 2, for generally useful, and by 3, for very much needed, and adding the results together. The individual scores on each item were summed and the resulting values tabulated in Table XIV.5.

Table XIV.5

PHYSICIAN'S PERCEIVED NEEDS IN IMPROVING DRUG ABUSE SERVICES

Need	Score
More treatment units	250
Public education on drug abuse	248
Develop treatment and diagnosis standards	237
Physician hot line	208
M.D. assistance program in drug abuse	204
Increased understanding	201
Internship with drug abuse rotation	195
Residency in drug abuse	190
Continuing education credits	183
Consultants in drug abuse	171
Higher fees	147

Physicians ranked as most important the need for more treatment units and the need for public education on drug abuse.

DISCUSSION AND SUMMARY

Chappel (1973) as well as Fox (1973) and Tennant (1976) indicate that some substance-abusing patients can be treated within the mainstream of medicine and that some primary care physicians can provide effective early and long-term treatment for the alcohol and drug abuser. Even if the physician is not personally able to provide treatment, he can assume an important role in raising diagnostic issues early and in making an informed referral to an appropriate treatment source.

Our data indicate that physicians cannot be viewed as a homogeneous group with regard to attitudes concerning drug abuse. Psychiatrists, for example, report being the most optimistic regarding treatment, and report viewing the drug abuse patient with less aversion than physicians in other specialties.

CHAPTER XV

Response of Traditional Health Care Agencies to Nonopiate Abusers

Lewis L. Judd, Paul A. Attewell, Winifred B. Riney, and Richard F. Avery

Although specialized polydrug programs were set up in some cities, there was no reason to expect that *all* or even a significant portion of polydrug abusers would come to the programs for treatment. It was recognized that many polydrug abusers would continue to utilize existing drug, alcohol, and mental health treatment systems. Therefore, it was concluded that it would be useful to attempt a small-scale survey in different localities to elucidate certain facts about polydrug abusers who apply for treatment in "traditional" drug, alcohol, and mental health programs.

Specifically, we were interested in answering the following types of questions about polydrug abusers who appear for intake at traditional treatment agencies:

What kinds of agencies are treating polydrug abusers and in what numbers?

What patterns of drug use emerge?

What are the traditional treatment agencies' attitudes toward polydrug-abusing clients?

How do these agencies treat polydrug clients?

337

Polydrug Abuse:
The Results of a
National Collaborative Study

At the completion of the survey, we received the following rather surprising answers to these specific questions:

1. Polydrug abusers constitute a considerable proportion of patients seeking help at traditional treatment agencies. Of clients with substance abuse problems carried in the case loads of these agencies, the following percentages are polydrug abusers: in alcohol treatment agencies, 13%; in narcotics treatment agencies, 48%; in mixed-substance abuse treatment agencies, 40%; and in mental health agencies, a startling 71%.

2. The two modal patterns of polydrug abuse are as follows: alcohol use combined with nonopiate use, and narcotic (opiate) use mixed with nonopiate drug use. The former pattern of drug abuse constitutes about 11% of alcohol treatment program intakes, the latter about 32% of narcotics program intakes. But both of these figures are probably low estimates, as will be explained later.

3. In many alcoholism, narcotic, and mental health treatment agencies, polydrug abuse per se is seen as rather inconsequential or at best as a complicating adjunctive problem which is secondary to the "primary" problem. That is, if the agency defines itself as specializing in treating one type of patient, it tends to relegate the patient's "other problem" to a minor role.

4. In most cases, polydrug patients seem to be treated in the same way as the non-polydrug-abusing clients served by these agencies. That is, comparatively little or no special treatment is provided to clients with polydrug abuse problems.

The latter two points indicate that many treatment agencies are too specialized and exclusive in their perception and treatment of clients. For example, agencies specializing in alcoholism treatment tend to focus exclusively upon alcohol abuse and related problems. This type of self-defined exclusivity by treatment agencies may well hamper a comprehensive approach to the client and unconsciously narrow the focus by not taking into consideration the full spectrum of presenting problems which are plaguing the client. Thus, treatment agencies appear specialized and focused in their approach to client problems while the clients themselves often present a complex mixture of abuse patterns and problems.

METHODOLOGY

Sampling

Six cities in the United States participated in our survey of the response of traditional health-care delivery systems to polydrug abuse. They were:

Boston, Massachusetts; Richmond, Virginia; New York, New York; Minneapolis, Minnesota; Detroit, Michigan; and San Diego, California.

For each city the local NIDA Polydrug Project was asked to pick a sample of 12 to 24 of the largest treatment agencies in that city. Quotas were set up for 4 types of agencies (alcohol treatment, narcotics treatment, mixed-substance abuse treatment, and mental health), and for inpatient and outpatient agencies. Emergency rooms were not surveyed.

The resulting protocols were received:

Institutions Interviewed

	Mental health	Narcotics agencies	Mixed drug	Alcohol agency	Other	Total
Richmond, Virginia	7	1	6	4	—	18
Minneapolis, Minnesota	5	3	16	7	1	32
Detroit, Michigan	2	6	2	4	—	14
Boston, Massachusetts	2	4	8	5	—	19
New York, New York	6	6	6	6	—	24
San Diego, California	9	5	4	6	—	24
						131

Data Collection

Each agency sampled was telephoned, and an interview of approximately 30 minutes was arranged with the person in the agency who had the best practical knowledge of the agency's intake process. In some cases this person was a physician, but often it was a social worker, clinical therapist, or psychiatric nurse.

Each interview involved the use of a multiple choice questionnaire which asked questions concerning mainly the intake aspect of that agency's treatment process: "What kinds of persons do you see, what kinds of persons do you accept into treatment, what kinds of treatment are offered?" etc.

Screening Phase

This phase of the research involved a review of all questionnaire protocols, both visually and computer scanning. Missing data, unclear responses, and internal inconsistencies were identified. (By internal inconsistencies we mean percentages adding to less than 100%, "alcohol" agencies reporting few alcohol clients due to mislabeling, etc.) These errors were corrected by recontacting the relevant agencies by phone. Many such calls were made to check and correct data.

"Qualitative Data"

Several of the agencies were contacted for more detailed questioning. Our aim in this was to elaborate on the rather limited information gained from the questionnaire and to gain a more qualitative sense of the phenomena with which we were dealing.

Data Analysis and Evaluation of Accuracy and Representativeness

Since the interviews were, whenever possible, carried out with the head intake worker, it was felt that we could ask for numbers of weekly intakes at each agency and numbers of cases accepted into treatment. These figures concern a fairly routine part of clinic life, and none interviewed indicated any difficulty in giving them. These variables represent the initial "filter" in entry to treatment.

The second type of quantitative data requested was a breakdown, by pattern of drug use, of persons presenting at the agency. We asked for the best estimate from the person in the institution most likely to be knowledgeable. *It should also be stressed that we wanted these data as an agency's perception of its clientele (i.e., attitudinal), not necessarily as an objective truth.* These data were processed only for those agencies which had previously answered that they did question new clients about specific types of drug and alcohol use.

Finally, we asked for a breakdown of new clients by percentages of males and females and percentages of minors. Most agencies provided this information without difficulty, but where agency staff indicated that they didn't know, we coded it as missing data. (Occasional disparities between number of new patients per week and the total males plus females, for any given city, result from this fact.)

The use of these quantitative data to express the types of drug abusers entering the treatment network is most complete for San Diego and Minneapolis, because in both cities the vast majority of agencies in the treatment network included in the sample were interviewed and reinterviewed. Thus, the data for these two regions are the most fully sampled and accurate.

In other cities, the *accuracy* of the data is believed to be good. The investigators checked by phone with the larger agencies, and as many other agencies as possible. On the issue of representativeness of the sample of agencies, however, the other cities may not be as comprehensive in covering local agencies as are two case studies (Minneapolis and San Diego). Detroit, in particular, indicated an inability to sample state-run centers owing to large-scale staff and funding cutbacks at those agencies. The New York sample is based primarily on the large metropolitan hospital treatment centers, and the findings should be understood in that light. However, Richmond and Boston have good representative samples.

RESULTS

Users Solely of Nonopiates

This nonopiate category consists of anyone who abuses a single nonopiate, or a polydrug mixture of nonopiates, but not nonopiates with any other class of substances (e.g., with narcotics or alcohol). Pure nonopiate category accounted for approximately 2% of intakes into the total treatment network (see Table XV.1). These figures varied somewhat from city to city, from a high of 8% (Richmond) to a low of less than 1% (Minneapolis).

The Mixed-Substance Abuse Problem Involving Nonopiates and Other Substances

Agencies report large proportions of their clientele are abusing nonopiates concurrently with alcohol or opiates. Almost 17% of total intakes in the national sample derived from this study are joint alcohol and nonopiate abusers, and an additional 8% are joint narcotics and nonopiate abusers (see Table XV.1). Thus, in considering the total population entering treatment in all our samples, 27% are abusing nonopiates either alone or concomitantly with other substances. Thus, this pattern of substance abuse (i.e., nonopiate plus other drugs and/or alcohol), constitutes a very significant proportion of clients entering treatment. There were regional variations: 44% of San Diego's treatment cases abused nonopiates in some combination, whereas 14% were recorded for New York (see Table XV.1). Overall mixed-substance abuse problems were present in 25% of persons seeking treatment. This is considered to be a *conservative* estimate, however, because intake clinicians at many specialized alcohol, drug, and mental health agencies, have a bias against identifying the full extent of the mixed substance abuse in their clientele.

What Kinds of Agencies Are Nonopiate Abusers Entering?

We had expected that nonopiate abusers, of both the pure and the mixed type, would be heavily concentrated in mixed-substance abuse

Table XV.1

PERCENTAGE OF WEEKLY INTAKE OF DRUGS BY USERS IN VARIOUS CITIES

City	Number of agencies	Weekly intake by drug users						Breakdown of users		
		Solely alcohol (%)	Solely narcotics (%)	Narcotics with alcohol (%)	Narcotics with nonopiate drugs (%)	Alcohol with nonopiate drugs (%)	Solely nonopiate drugs (%)	Males (%)	Females (%)	Minors (%)
Boston	19	27	27	15	13	8	5	72	28	1
Detroit	14	33	21	15	32	4	3	66	34	10
Minneapolis	30	67	2	2	4	25	<1	83	17	5
New York	24	54	24	7	8	6	<1	78	22	13
Richmond	18	49	10	47	10	20	8	76	24	15
San Diego	20	49	6	2	5	36	3	79	21	5
All cities	131	51	16	6	8	17	2	77	23	9

agencies, and be seen sparsely elsewhere. This proved not to be the case. Fully 32% of persons entering the narcotics agencies in the national sample were joint abusers of narcotics and nonopiates (see Table XV.2). Perhaps even more important, 11% of persons entering *alcohol* agencies in our sample were described as having concomitant alcohol and nonopiate abuse problems.

This finding of high proportions of nonopiate polydrug abusers in the so-called specialized agencies is one of the strongest and most consistent findings.

If the extent of nonopiate abuse in specialized agencies was unexpectedly high, the client composition of the so-called "mixed-substance agencies" was equally surprising (see Table XV.2). First, it is clear that "mixed-substance agency" is not simply a synonym for an agency which deals with nonopiate abusers. In fact, in our sample, pure nonopiate abusers constitute only ~5% of persons entering these agencies. Polydrug abusers who combine (or substitute) both nonopiates and narcotics or alcohol *are* a sizable proportion of the clientele of mixed-substance abuse agencies, but are still a minority. Across the whole sample, the alcohol–nonopiate abusers accounted for ~21% of mixed-substance agency intakes, and narcotics-nonopiate abusers, ~7%.

In the nationwide sample, ~37% of intakes to mixed-substance agencies were reported as solely alcohol abusers, and ~22% as solely narcotics abusers. There was, however, considerable regional variation. Minneapolis mixed-substance agencies treated a very high proportion of solely alcohol abusers, and the New York mixed-substance agencies treated a high proportion of solely narcotics abusers. This indicates, nevertheless, that mixed-substance agencies are by no means solely, or even primarily, oriented toward the nonopiate users. Most mixed-substance agencies treat the whole spectrum of drug abusers in any given area. But frequently they are remarkably similar in client composition to the other specialized agencies in their city. Mixed-substance agencies in New York, for example, treat a high proportion of narcotics abusers, and in Minneapolis, they treat alcohol abusers and so on. They appear to provide an "overflow" resource for the more specialized agencies. It seems that whatever the regional differences in drug abuse, they are reflected by increased numbers of clients with that pattern being treated in *all* of the programs in that area, whether those programs are specialized or not.

Thus mixed-substance agencies are not solely nonopiate agencies, nor are they solely polydrug agencies. They are "mixed" in the sense that they treat many types of single- and multiple-substance abusers.

The mental health agencies constitute an important part of any sub-

Table XV.2

WEEKLY DRUG INTAKE OF ABUSERS ENTERING VARIOUS TYPES OF AGENCIES

Agency type	Number of agencies	Weekly intake of drugs						Total numbers entering agencies per week		
		Solely alcohol (%)	Solely narcotics (%)	Narcotics with alcohol (%)	Narcotics with nonopiate drugs (%)	Alcohol with nonopiate drugs (%)	Solely nonopiate drugs (%)	Males (%)	Females (%)	Minors (%)
Narcotics agencies	25	0	52	16	32	0	0	67	33	21
Alcohol agencies	32	87	0	2	0	11	0	89	11	3
Mixed-substance agencies	42	37	22	7	7	21	5	77	23	12
Mental health agencies	31	20	9	3	8	55	5	54	46	8

stance abuse treatment network. Unfortunately, our data on these agencies are relatively sparse, and probably less representative than for other types of agencies. Not being primarily involved in drug or alcohol treatment, mental health agencies are less likely to keep figures on which types of abuse patterns they see most. In addition, community mental health agencies are frequently so large that no one individual can have a good sense of the numbers and types of intakes. For this reason, we consider our data about mental health agencies to be of lower reliability than the data on other agencies.

In most areas mental health agencies do treat drug-related cases. Although there is substantial regional variation, overall 10–20% of patients entering mental health agencies have identifiable drug abuse problems. Of the persons who present at mental health agencies with substance abuse problems, 55% have the abuse patterns which involve both alcohol and nonopiate drugs. The next largest percentage of abuse is alcohol alone (~20%). Narcotics alone or in some combination constitute an additional 20%.

Treatment of Nonopiate Abusers in Other Institutions

It was stated by 47% of the alcohol agencies, by 28% of the narcotics agencies, and by 14% of the mixed-substance agencies that they referred polydrug abusers elsewhere. This in itself would not necessarily be noteworthy if the referrals were to agencies better equipped to treat polydrug abuse. However, many of the agencies who reportedly referred polysubstance-abusing clients elsewhere also reported that very high proportions of persons *presenting* at their agency were persons with polydrug abuse patterns. In numerous cases, moreover, these selfsame agencies reported .that they accepted nearly 100% of presenting persons into treatment. This appeared contradictory. Thus, we found agencies which reported 30% of presenting cases were polysubstance-abusing and which stated that their policy was to refer polydrug abusers elsewhere. In many cases, we phoned those agencies to verify our data. The agencies' descriptions of proportions of various kinds of substance abusers and polysubstance abusers seen remained consistent when they were phoned again later. When we asked what proportion of intakes were referred elsewhere, we found that the numbers referred were *insufficient* to account for the referral of all of the presenting polysubstance population.

We conclude therefore that perceived policy and actual behavior in some of these agencies are conflicting. Many polydrug abusers *are* entering these specialized treatment agencies, which claim they provide no special treatment for polydrug abusers and which claim to refer polydrug abusers to more appropriate agencies.

An additional feature, which should be mentioned here because it provides the underlying explanation of how this happens, concerns the distinctions between addiction and abuse, and primary versus secondary drugs of abuse. On numerous occasions, agencies reported that they referred elsewhere nonopiate polydrug abusers if they either were addicted to the nonopiate or were primarily nonopiate abusers. What this amounts to is the fact that nonopiate abuse is only referred elsewhere by many alcohol (and some narcotics) agencies if it is so acute as to indicate addiction clearly, or at least to overshadow the substance abuse in which the agency specializes.

We suspect that the identification of a nonopiate abuser as "addicted" or as "primarily a nonopiate abuser" is likely to be made only in extreme cases. Nonopiate abusers who do not appear to be addicted or whose nonopiate problem is not clearly primary, are *not* referred elsewhere. Instead they are given the standard treatment regimen of the agency, e.g., standard treatment for an alcoholic or standard treatment for a narcotics abuser. The dangers of this are apparent.

An additional 10% of alcohol agencies and 16% of narcotics agencies indicated that they would treat a client who had polydrug problems with emphasis only upon the drug of agency specialization (i.e., alcohol in an alcohol agency, narcotics in a narcotics agency; see Table XV.3). The agencies, many of whom have sizable polydrug intakes, essentially treat only one aspect of the polydrug habit, leaving the other in a state of "benign neglect."

About 40–45% of narcotics and alcohol agencies stated they they would treat a polydrug client with an emphasis on all drug (or alcohol) problems. These were, in several cases, agencies with broad ranges of modalities.

Finally, a low percentage of agencies took a primarily psychiatric approach, in which drug abuse was seen as secondary to or symptomatic of underlying psycho- or sociopathology. None of the narcotics agencies, 3% of alcohol agencies, and 17% of mixed-substance agencies adhere to this therapeutic philosophy.

Men and Women in Treatment

Differences appeared with respect to the ways in which men and women entered the treatment network. In Minneapolis and San Diego, the two cities which we chose for detailed analysis, women appeared in different concentrations in the treatment network than did men. In the

Table XV.3

PERCENTAGE OF RESPONSE TYPES TO MULTIPLE DRUG ABUSE

Response	Community mental health agencies (%)	Mixed-substance agencies (%)
Refer elsewhere	46	14
Treat as a problem of general drug abuse	4	33
Treat with regard to specific drugs abused	8	36
Treat psychiatrically regardless of type of abuse	38	17
Other	4	0

Response	Alcohol agencies (%)	Narcotic agencies (%)
Refer elsewhere	47	28
Treat with emphasis on only drug of agency specialization	10	16
Treat with emphasis on all drug problems	40	44
Treat psychiatrically, without particular regard to drug abuse	3	0
Other	0	12

Minneapolis sample, women appeared disproportionately frequently in both the non-county-funded agencies (i.e., the "alternative" agency network), and in its case-finding referral agency. While our data are not sufficiently sophisticated to enable us to control for potential age effects, it seems possible that these data do represent a true difference in behavior between men and women. Furthermore, the absolute number of women reportedly seen and referred by the case-finding–referral network each week was greater than the total reportedly entering treatment each week. We attempted to check the relevant numbers with the agencies concerned and to the best of our knowledge the result is not spurious. There does appear to be a marked attrition process between referral and treatment facilities.

In San Diego, the situation was somewhat different in the absence of a formalized referral-case-finding service. The women drug abusers in San Diego are disproportionately treated in the mental health agencies.

We interpret these data to suggest that women are more likely to enter alternative mental health and case-finding–referral agencies. Perhaps subpopulations of the female drug-abusing group exist who are reluctant to enter agencies where they are clearly labeled as drug abusers and who prefer to approach less "stigmatic" institutions for treatment.

Demands Made upon Patients

Both overt and covert expectations or demands are placed upon patients when they enter treatment programs. Some programs demand abstinence immediately upon entry, with treatment contingent upon continued abstinence. Others allow for a short period of time either for detoxification to occur or to allow a patient to "clean up his act" but subsequently demand a drug-free state as a condition of continued treatment. Yet other agencies, while perhaps encouraging a cutback in drug use, do not withdraw treatment if drug use continues.

We originally collected information on this issue because clinicians in charge of referral indicated that this was an important factor in deciding whether a patient would "fit" in a given agency (or vice versa). However, this also appears to be one of the more central philosophical or attitudinal boundaries within treatment agencies. For certain types of agencies, for example, many narcotics agencies and inpatient agencies, abstinence is a crucial demand upon the client. For some narcotics agencies, abstinence appears to be more of an outcome measure: that treatment was not achieving anything and that the patient was not taking treatment seriously if he or she continued drug use. In part, this is a reflection of state and federal regulations, especially with regard to methadone maintenance.

Some 84% of the narcotics agencies nationwide reported either that a client "must be drug free at time of entry" or that a client "will be detoxified or given some time to clean up, but will have to stop drug use." These same demands were made by 80% of mixed-substance agencies, 66% of alcohol agencies, and 52% of mental health agencies (Table XV.4).

There are regional variations. Agencies in New York and Minneapolis are more abstinence-oriented compared, for example, to those in San Diego.

While it would be misleading to suggest that the nonabstinence agencies all share a common philosophical orientation, there was an attitude expressed by a few agencies which gave a therapeutic rationale for *not* demanding abstinence as a condition of treatment. In particular, this rationale usually is seen in those utilizing psychiatrically based treatment approaches. It is clearly the belief of some agencies in this field that psychiatric syndromes underlie drug abuse in a significant proportion of cases. Polydrug abusers, particularly those involved in various forms of nonopiate abuse (nonopiates alone, nonopiates with alcohol, nonopiates with narcotics) have been seen as manifesting a high proportion of characterological disorders, as well as other forms of psychopathology.

Table XV.4

AGENCIES' DEMANDS ON CLIENTS REGARDING ABSTINENCE FROM DRUG USE AS A CONDITION OF (NATIONAL SAMPLE) REMAINING IN TREATMENT

Agency's requirement	Alcohol agencies (%)	Mental health agencies (%)	Mixed-substance agencies (%)	Narcotics agencies (%)
"Client must be drug free from time he or she enters agency."	35	35	43	12
"Client will be detoxified or given some time to clean up, but will have to stop drug use."	31	17	37	72
"Agency will allow continued use of drugs while treatment continues."	35	48	20	16

One theory which has gained credence in several of the NIDA Polydrug Projects has been that some polydrug abusers are using nonopiates as a form of *self-medication*. That is, the abuse of nonopiates and/or alcohol enables them to control, cope with, or modulate existing psycho-pathology. This is seen as being specifically so for mood and affect disorders which seemingly are modified and controlled through this self-medication process.

To the extent that self-medication is a valid model of the nonopiate abuse of many patients, requiring abstinence of a patient in the earlier stages of treatment is counterindicated. While psychiatrically oriented therapy is under way, if there is to be a serious hope of success it is unwise to demand that a client give up one of his or her major coping mecha-nisms as a first stage of treatment. To do so can precipitate major psychiatric crises at the very earliest stages of treatment and invite high dropout rates, etc.

Until specific treatment responses, particularly involving the careful medical management of chemotherapeutic regimens, are developed for the various types of pychopathologies met in this population, psy-chotherapy should be initiated before changes in drug use patterns are anticipated, and abstinence should be a longer term therapeutic goal initiated cautiously after sufficient progress as been made in treatment.

Modalities and Treatment Approaches

We attempted to elicit three types of information on modes of treat-ment. We wanted to know whether treatment was oriented psychiatri-cally, without particular regard to drug abuse, *or* with an emphasis on the drug problem as a whole, *or* with an emphasis on one or more specific drugs (e.g., the substance of the agency specialization). In addition, we asked whether modalities of detoxification, crisis intervention, counsel-ing, psychodynamically oriented therapy, group therapy, etc., were avail-able. Finally, we wanted to know if chemotherapy was used and, if so, what drugs were prescribed and for what purposes.

The psychiatric perspective was taken most often by mental health agencies. Of mixed-substance agencies, 17% are psychiatrically oriented. Some 12% of narcotics agencies, and 0% of alcohol agencies indicated this approach (see Table XV.3).

The remaining agencies indicated a treatment emphasis either on patients' general drug abuse problems *or* with regard to the *specific* drugs abused. Although these two categories seemed theoretically distinct, in practice we found that state-of-the-art in drug treatment makes them less meaningful. Where specific chemotherapies exist, treatment *is* geared to specific types of drugs abused. Thus, in detoxification modalities, and in methadone maintenance and antabuse modalities a specific type of drug abuse is specifically treated. Elsewhere, however, there are not different ongoing treatments for, say, an amphetamine user versus a barbiturate addict, according to our phone inquiries. In this regard, we replicated the findings of the Wynne Associates (Wynne, 1974, pp. 91–93).[1]

As Table XV.5 indicates, individual counseling appears to be the most frequent type of therapy. Remarkably high proportions of agencies in all

Table XV.5

ALL TREATMENT AGENCIES BY TYPE (MODALITIES)

	Alcohol agencies (%)	CMHs (%)	Mixed-substance agencies (%)	Narcotics agencies (%)
Treatment modalities provided				
Immediate crisis intervention	40	75	53	60
Detoxification	63	33	53	68
Individual counseling	93	71	92	92
Individual psychodynamically oriented therapy	10	71	42	36
Group therapy	80	88	89	80
Family therapy	70	83	69	60
Couple therapy (marital)	50	67	61	52
Vocational rehabilitation	37	25	47	52
Other (specify)	20	25	19	12
Percentage prescribing medications	66	88	56	72
Medications prescribed				
Antabuse	53	25	19	4
Methadone	0	13	33	52
Major and minor tranquilizers	33	79	42	44

categories reported *regularly* using family therapy (60–80%), couple or marital therapy (50–67%), and vocational rehabilitation (25–52%). All of these figures seem high, particularly the data on vocational rehabilitation. We can only suspect that some agencies included modalities that they did not offer themselves but to which they had access via referral.

Crisis intervention was available most often in mental health agencies (75%) and was available in only 40% of alcohol agencies and 60% of

---

[1] The state of the art in the treatment of non-opiate abuse. Vol. 1 of the Final Report to Contract HSM-42-73-231 (ND) Wynne Associates, 1974, Washington, D.C. 20015

narcotics agencies. Detoxification modalities occurred in between 53% and 78% of the nonmental health agencies, but these figures included large numbers of nonchemotherapy detoxifications. Minneapolis, in particular, tended to have agencies of this latter type.

Most agencies provided some form of chemotherapy, i.e., medications other than for purely medical complaints (see Table XV.5). About 66% of alcohol agencies, 88% of mental health agencies, 56% of mixed-substance abuse agencies, and 72% of narcotics agencies reported that they used medications. Antabuse was reportedly available at 53% of alcohol agencies, 25% of mental health agencies, 19% of mixed-substance agencies, and at one narcotics agency. Methadone was reported as available at 52% of the narcotics agencies, 33% of the mixed-substance agencies, and 13% of mental health agencies and none of the alcohol agencies. (These figures do not distinguish between the use of methadone for detoxification versus its use for maintenance.)

Finally, 33% of the alcohol agencies utilized minor tranquilizers (e.g., Valium and Librium), as did 79% of mental health agencies, 42% of mixed agencies, 44% of narcotics agencies. Most frequently tranquilizers are used to counteract muscle spasms and related withdrawal symptoms in detoxification centers. Some agencies did, however, indicate use of minor tranquilizers in nondetoxification setting to alleviate tension and depression, and to make the client more receptive to counseling modalities.

DISCUSSION

There are methodological problems which are apparent in surveys of this type, and the reader should be aware that these problems in design do influence the definitiveness with which these data should be viewed. It has been acknowledged that the agencies that were sampled are not a representative sample of all the agencies in the four classes of specialized treatment systems in which we were interested. An obvious example is that of New York City, where the treatment agencies that were contacted represented only a small percentage of the total number of treatment agencies in this large metropolitan area. The investigators are more satisfied with and sure of the representativeness of the Minneapolis and San Diego data and it is upon these data that the more detailed case studies were based.

It is clear that all types of surveys have certain biases built into them and, therefore, the potential for collecting inaccurate or skewed data. The methodology selected for this survey was chosen in the interest of time and to improve the certainty of the data over that of information which is acquired solely by mail questionnaire. The use of the telephone, while it is generally considered to be not as effective a medium as a direct interview, certainly improves both the level and quality of data acquisition over that of a questionnaire technique. Several cross-checks were made in order to assess the consistency and reliability of the information that was gathered. In each case, we were quite impressed with the internal consistency and stability of the data as evidenced by the reliability techniques utilized.

Despite the methodological problems involved, there are some interesting findings that have emanated from the study which deserve to be highlighted and discussed. It was of interest to us to find that the major pattern of drug abuse among many individuals abusing drugs was a pattern of mixed-substance abuse. There has been a rather common clinical stereotype that the "polydrug abuser" was an individual who abused single or multiple substances within the nonopiate classes of drugs. Our data reveal that this "classical" abuse pattern of the polydrug abuser was comparatively rare, accounting for about 2% of all the drug abusers who present for intake at traditional treatment agencies.

The data from this study showed that the "polydrug abuser" more frequently mixes a wide variety of compounds, using them both in combination and interchangeably. Of particular interest is the fact that alcohol use often plays a major role in the substance abuse patterns of these individuals. Further, it is not uncommon among this group of drug abusers for them to utilize narcotic analgesics as well. Thus, the modal polydrug abuse pattern is that of an individual who uses nonopiates, alcohol, and narcotic drugs in various combinations. This type of substance abuse accounts for at least 25% of polydrug abusers who present for treatment.

It was surprising to find that polydrug users in general did not necessarily find their way to treatment agencies which specialize in the treatment of mixed-substance abuse. Rather, polydrug users of the type previously referred to found their way to all types of treatment agencies regardless of what client population the agency had defined itself as specializing in treating. For example, it was found that more than one-third of the individuals entering all narcotics agencies were concomitant abusers of nonopiates and/or alcohol. Although less significant in terms of percentage, but possibly more significant in terms of effectiveness of treatment, approximately 11% of those individuals presenting for treatment at agencies specializing in alcoholism also had concomitant and significant amounts of nonopiate drug abuse.

Whereas it is clear that narcotic treatment and alcoholism treatment agencies are treating significant numbers of mixed-substance abusers, it is equally clear that those agencies specializing in the treatment of the mixed-substance abuser are also treating large numbers of clients who abused solely alcohol (37%) or narcotics (22%). In this regard there were regional differences as well. In Minneapolis, the mixed-substance-abuse agencies were treating a high proportion of purely alcohol abusers whereas the same type of treatment agencies in New York City were treating a high proportion of purely heroin abusers. Thus, it seems logical to conclude that whatever the differences in abuse patterns might be on a regional basis, this is reflected in increased numbers of clients with that specific abuse pattern being treated in all of the treatment programs regardless of their self-defined treatment specialization.

As might be anticipated, there was a rather distinct philosophical difference in terms of therapeutic approaches when one compared treatment agencies specializing in the treatment of any kind of substance abuse (i.e., narcotic, alcohol, or mixed-substance) with mental health treatment agencies. In the former case, their treatment approaches were focused on the elimination of the substance abuse behavior; whereas in the mental health agencies, substance abuse was viewed as a secondary symptom underlying psychological abnormalities. In the mental health agencies, the focus was on the amelioration of the psychological abnormality, with the feeling being that once solved, all the secondary symptoms (i.e., substance abuse, etc.) would be alleviated.

The majority of the treatment agencies which defined themselves as specializing in the treatment of one form of substance abuse as compared to another gave the distinct impression that they were uncomfortable in dealing with clients whose abuse patterns were not consistent with the self-definition of the treatment agency. That is, alcohol treatment programs, while admitting that they might treat individuals who had concomitant polydrug abuse, nevertheless indicated they preferred to treat pure alcohol abusers and would attempt to refer clients who were concomitantly using other substances. Even when clients were included in the case load of the treatment agency, the therapeutic intervention focused primarily upon that substance abuse problem which was consonant with the agency's specialization, which often resulted in an ignoring of the client's other substance abuse problems. This relegation of "other" substance abuse to a secondary and less important role in the treatment of the client in all likelihood compromises to some degree a comprehensive approach to the client. The most striking overall finding which emerged was that treatment agencies are generally too specialized in their treatment approaches. It does appear that substance abuse patterns are generally more mixed in nature than was previously believed, yet the exclusivity of focus of a number of the agencies treating substance abuse is arbitrary and not based upon client need or characteristics. Thus, for example, the identification of the treatment institution as specializing in the treatment of narcotic–dependent people may have strong reinforcing sociological roots in terms of institutional self-definition. However, when this self-definition is applied in an exclusive sense to clients who present for treatment, significant numbers of individuals are redefined as not possessing a polydrug problem. This presumably results in either a certain amount of shifting of patients from agency to agency until a proper match between institutional definition of expertness and patient problem has been achieved, or in situations where clients remain in agencies that focus their treatment on only one aspect of the clients' overall problems. Obviously, based on these findings treatment institutions should be encouraged to be flexible enough to develop treatment methods and approaches that are shaped by the needs and characteristics of their clients rather than by institutional need for role definition.

Paradoxically, accompanying this rigid specialization in self-definition, and the resulting lack of attention to polydrug problems, is a comparative lack of specialization in treatment technique. Outside of detoxification and chemotherapeutic modalities, neither specific nor wholistic approaches appear to exist for the treatment of these drug abusers. What exists is a fairly standardized constellation of counseling procedures: individual, family, and group therapies, which are brought to bear on the substance-abusing person whether he or she be a polydrug abuser or an alcoholic, or a narcotics addict, etc. Based on conversations with knowledgeable therapists, it is believed that treatment of drug abusers, except for detoxification, etc., is relatively uninfluenced by theoretical guidelines as to both the causes of drug-abusing behavior and the preconditions of successful treatment outcome. What this means to us is that the field is still searching for definitive models of abuse patterns, valid typologies of abusers, and appropriately specialized methods of treatment.

This corroborates and generalizes Wynne's finding (1974, p. 91) for specifically nonopiate agencies, that "By and large, the modalities we saw were adaptations of approaches used with heroin abusers and, indeed, with a great variety of persons with mental health-related problems. Few, if any, had been developed especially to deal with problems presented by nonopiate abusers, *per se.*"

It appears then that the agencies in the field are using the arsenal of the mental health field without an underlying nosology or theoretical base. Elsewhere in this volume are the reports of the various psychometric and psychiatric evaluations of polydrug patients of the NIDA polydrug agencies. They indicate a high degree of psychopathology and disturbance in this group, compared even to other groups of drug abusers. In our opinion, such persons are best treated within a mental health paradigm, and such a paradigm can best develop the typologies and specific treatments necessary. This would require an integration of previously specialized agencies, for example, alcoholism, narcotics, and mixed-substance agencies into nonspecific agencies within a community mental health framework. Until such time as this does occur, there is an urgent need to orient present traditional agencies toward the problem of polydrug abuse and the special needs of polydrug-abusing patients.

A final issue, unrelated to the preceding discussion, concerns the role of case-finding–referral and alternative agencies in polydrug abuse treatment. Some of our data suggest that women and, to some extent, minors are found in higher proportions in referral agencies, in so-called "alternative agencies," and mental health agencies, compared to traditional drug treatment agencies. These results must be considered as highly tentative, since they were based mainly on data from two cities. However, the possibility of differential access to treatment and to different types of treatment agencies by different demographic groups is of interest. We would recommend a more detailed study of this phenomenon, based upon several city case studies, to ascertain whether important demographic differentials are a general feature of entry into the drug abuse treatment network.

ACKNOWLEDGMENTS

The contributions of the participating Polydrug Projects are gratefully acknowledged:

Boston Polydrug: Vernon Patch, Principal Investigator; Gail Levine
Detroit Polydrug: Kenneth Schoof, Principal Investigator; Pam Page
Durham Polydrug: Hugh V. Angle, Principal Investigator
Houston Polydrug: B. Comstock, Principal Investigator; Thomas C. Welu
Minneapolis Polydrug: T. Siebold, Principal Investigator
New York Polydrug: Beny J. Primm, Principal Investigator; William Bright, Jr.
Richmond Polydrug: E. Gullick, Principal Investigator; S. Vignola

PART 5

Conclusions and
Recommendations

EDITORS' INTRODUCTION

Viewed in terms of the objectives Peter Bourne had in mind when he initiated the Polydrug Projects, the projects were highly successful. As is evidenced by the early history of the projects described in Chapter I, the projects were not initiated as major scientific inquiry but as a pragmatic step to investigate the demand for polydrug abuse treatment and to define the type of treatment that would be made available. Over time, investigators at several sites discovered overlapping interests among programs and lobbied for collection of additional data which was of common interest. Eventually a large collaborative study evolved which provided much of the data described in this volume.

The evolution from a dozen geographically scattered centers carrying out research of local interest to a collaborative study was not without waste of resources, time, frustration, and moments of high drama. This following chapter is intended as a user's manual for future collaborating investigators and hopefully will serve to guide them past many of the initial frustrations and difficulties confronted by the polydrug project. Careful adherence to the guidelines described by Kenneth Adams concerning collaborative data management would prevent much of the waste of research resources still rampant in drug abuse.

The final chapter, written by the editors, distills much of what was learned and adds to that our recommendations for future research.

CHAPTER XVI

Some Observations on Collaborative Data Management

Kenneth M. Adams

COLLABORATIVE RESEARCH PROJECTS

In attempting to investigate issues of national importance, both public and private agencies have identified the power and generalizability of combined samples as great advantages in drawing inferences from the data for policy decision.

The multi-center study also tackles the problem of "local" findings which others cannot replicate. A particular clinical research team may have continued trouble in gaining acceptance for a research finding because other centers do not find the same phenomenon. A close look at these types of situations usually shows subtle differences in instrumentation, analysis, and interpretation between centers. Where several centers are using highly comparable methods, direct comparisons can allow rational decisions concerning the existence and generalizability of findings.

359

Polydrug Abuse:
The Results of a
National Collaborative Study

SAMPLING CONSIDERATIONS

Careful planning must go into the selection and evaluation of prospective component centers for a collaborative project. The centers should be asked at the application phase to generate a predicted profile of what the basic parameters of their subject or client population might be in the study. Analysis of previous client statistics and/or comparison with census tract figures, may provide an early estimate of who the subjects are and how they might be representative of a particular geographic locale. Individual programs should produce a local "mini epidemiology" report, which can be used by funding agency officials to assess the program's capabilities as a collaborative project participant.

In turn, the integration of the selected component program's reports should be performed by a competent internal evaluation arm of the funding agency. Where this is not possible, the integration might be undertaken by a scientific (not business) contractor with broad social science and epidemiology experience. In any case, the role of the person or group writing a report on the representativeness of the total proposed collaborative sample should not be charged with the reports on the individual component programs. The ability of a particular program to generate such a report internally, or from local sources, is one indicator of how experienced, knowledgeable, and resourceful they are likely to be in researching the content area.

THE COLLABORATIVE GROUP PROCESS

The collaborative paradigm also seems to do an important service in bringing together workers with similar interests. In meetings of collaborative projects, representatives of constituent programs meet others doing the same job. The level of familiarity among program representatives is quite variable. Nevertheless, previous histories of cooperation, competition, or unfamiliarity in reference to previous work, are brought to a new situation where all participants must work together for the project to succeed.

The collaborative project representatives generally meet with funding agency representatives, at an early stage in such projects, to discuss the . aspects of the clinical research program that will be common to all centers. No less than any task-oriented group, it has a life and process of its own. Various participants have concerns, agendas, and personality characteristics that interact with more objective qualifications to define the roles they will play in relation to others in the project.

Typically, early meetings of such collaborative groups are long, and quite exhausting, as the group process evolves. In many ways, there is no way around this work, and resolution of certain personal power and leadership issues is a necessary condition before the project may proceed. The practical values of closure on the essential "who will do what" issues for the group are the creation of tangible agreements and the chance to identify potential sources of resistance to group objectives.

In most collaborative efforts, the various participating centers are concerned with the magnitude of their role in the study. At early meetings some centers will employ methods designed to ensure leadership in the project. One such method involves a mass attendance at the collaborative meetings by all members of the project—whether essential for business or not. This may be supplemented by local luminaries whose attendance is designed mainly to demonstrate the prominence of a particular group.

Associated with this, another problem can occur. At organizational meetings, agency officials will typically wish to develop certain schedules of work for various objectives. Another possible problem is the group which volunteers to do too much to gain control or ensure future support as an essential component of the study.

Capacity to deliver products and performance realistically must be demonstrated early and often. This does not mean very brief time periods to complete advanced goals, but it does mean the imposition of tasks designed to assess efficiency and competence of various contributors.

STEP FUNDING

It is the perceived need for this kind of groundwork, and the recognition of its inevitability in the collaborative paradigm, that has led to the "step-funding" recommendations. It is obviously wasteful to have full clinical complements and facilities "on line" while project officials are meeting elsewhere to analyze what should be done. Thus, a "start-up phase" is recommended which saves dollars by funding projects at a partial rate for specific planning functions. When agreements are reached at a national level, individual programs proceed to a second "clinical phase" at approximately the same time, with many planning functions complete.

DATA-RELATED ISSUES

It is not within the scope of this discussion to delineate or evaluate the majority of the issues which arise in planning collaborative studies. Of interest here are certain data concerns which must have closure if the project is to succeed. The manner in which the collaborative group handles these issues may indicate, as well as anything, their ability to solve problems and work together.

The first, and most formidable objective for the collaborative group, is the selection and definition of the variables to be measured. It is particularly difficult for a number of representatives to decide on a few key variables for which all the projects have the capability and which they desire to use. A particular danger here is that the group will agree to use too many variables to effect the needed compromise on the measures. Many clinical research programs have particular methods and interests which they would like to have represented. A more satisfactory solution usually involves an agreement on the part of the collaborative group to measure a limited number of common variables (which can be measured *well and uniformly*), with the understanding that extra measures of local interest may be collected in excess of the agreed collaborative data base.

This usually brings up a second issue. Even under optimal conditions of negotiation, the collaborative group may have difficulty determining the amount of data to be collected. Program representatives who are particularly sensitive to clinical issues, may be quick to point out that intensive data collection represents a burden for clients who have presented themselves for treatment. Arguments in favor of somewhat less ambitious data collection schedules are often well advised and based on experience. Yet it is also true that clients in clinical research projects may be receiving a very high level of clinical care, largely in exchange for their participation in the program. The collaborative participants, then, must determine the most appropriate balance between the clinical objectives of demonstration projects and the basic research and demonstration purposes.

Another concern that should be addressed is the ownership of the collaborative research data. This problem may be seen as embedded in the group process which occurs in the negotiation phase of the collaborative project. Principal investigators (PIs) and other representatives from collaborative projects, frequently have important concerns with respect to their contribution of data to a national pool. Often these personnel have academic appointments and are participating in the demonstration project research in the hope that they will eventually have the opportunity to present their findings to their colleagues in the field in some form. In most competitive academic environments, the productivity of the demonstration project is crucial to continued good standing and advancement in their institutions.

The collaborative project representatives thus have an important stake in the decision regarding the data. No investigators want to feel that the results of their work are being taken from them without a chance to exercise some control in regard to how the data will be used. In the Polydrug Project it was learned that certain standards were necessary in this very sensitive area. First, the contract and responsibility for the processing of a national data pool should not be vested in one of the collaborative projects if it can be avoided. This would prevent the feeling on the part of some workers that the data are somehow being "scooped" by another program. Principal investigators are not likely to feel comfortable with the prospect of surrendering the results of their work to a colleague. Certainly, there will be some groups that will be comfortable and/or confident in the capacity of a particular constituent project to execute the data acquisition and analysis. However, this seems to be the exception; and the most palatable solution is to have an external group assume primary responsibility for the basic organization and data management tasks. Some guidelines for the selection and regulation of these data-processing organizations will be described later in this chapter.

It is not enough merely to select an external data-processing organization. The collaborative project participants must have ongoing close interaction with the organization that does the data processing and analysis. Some organizational structures can be established to facilitate this kind of interaction. First, a "principal investigator for data analysis" should be designated to represent the data-handling organization. This person would have the ultimate responsibility for the quality, accuracy, and flow of data to and from the programs, as well as to the funding agency. The authority to complete this task must match the responsibility. From the programs, a "data advisory board" should be formed, which should consist of a few especially skilled members from the collaborative group as well as the principal investigator for data analysis. The data advisory board would represent the programs in negotiation with the principal investigator for data analysis. It would be the job of the board to ensure that the needs and wishes of the programs are communicated and implemented as much as possible. In this way, the programs continue to have input to a group that will represent their interests in the building of the data base.

There are other commitments that should be made. Each of the collaborative centers should periodically receive its own data back from the national pool. The important point here is that the projects should receive their contributed data as a minimum; and the collaborative group may ultimately feel comfortable with the distribution of the entire pool data base to all participating centers. Beyond the distribution of actual contributed data, the centers should receive response from the data acquisition and analysis organization in an appropriate manner to be detailed later in this chapter.

It is important that the data ownership issue be addressed early and openly. The pooled data base represent a shared clinical and scientific experience from the projects, and the agreements regarding the flow and regulation of data are as important as anything to the success of the collaborative project. Data flow protocols which exclude this type of agreement, or vest authority for scientific information in agencies that are not accountable to the projects, are at risk for noncompliance, delay in data submission, or even sabotage of scientific input. Data flow must be bidirectional.

These issues are examples of the difficult problems that must be resolved in an early stage. In the Polydrug Project it was learned that a "planning" phase is essential if the questions are to be properly resolved in the interest of obtaining accurate and reliable data. This inevitably places the timetable of the collaborative project at odds with the need for information by decision makers who direct the funding agency. In a sense, many collaborative projects are conducted as mission-oriented endeavors designed to answer specific questions. Certainly, officials have reason to expect the most competent and rapid performance of research tasks. A plan can be designed into the collaborative study so that periodic reports may be issued to appropriate officials and participating programs on preliminary findings and likely trends in the project. This should be done with the understanding that early outputs from collaborative studies are first results and generally more subject to error than conclusions drawn from later data slices. The reason for this is that procedures and data flow are generally better at later stages in the project.

There is also a need to consider some individual issues raised in the collaborative project. These involve the creation and maintenance of forms, files, and other operational problems.

THE IMPORTANCE OF RECORD DESIGN

How many investigators design forms for data collection on a collaborative project? When all the difficulties of organizing and excuting a multi-center study are considered, this would seem to be one of the least troublesome at first glance. If we assume that the collaborative group has reached closure on the selection of variables to measure, the whole problem of records design would seem to be reduced to a low-level technical job which could well be subcontracted to an outside group.

This level of comfort, or the assumption that "things will get done for the computer" represents the first sign that the project leaders are about to make a mistake. The real difficulty here is that bad form design is often not identified in a project until the project is well underway. Every social scientist has been faced with the reality of data which have been "spoiled" by some error in research implementation or execution. On a collaborative study basis, the high cost per datum and the time limits for such studies to deliver needed answers make the existence of "bad cases" in the data file a tragedy.

The steps to design and implement forms that will do what the collaborative project wants are ones which require absolute attention to detail. Three basic steps must be accomplished in the creation of data forms for collaborative study use. These involve the complete specification of what is to be measured, the provision for all logical occurrences of the data points, and a highly energetic effort to ensure proper coding and auditing of information placed on forms. For each collaborative study, the data organization should maintain a manual that reflects current forms, interpretations, and procedures. This document should exist from the first data collection and be under constant development.

THE MASTER FILE

The master file is a collection (usually on computer tape) of all valid responses and scores from each subject or patient in a collaborative study. It represents the complete record of the project, which is available for use even after the close of the study. In general, the standards for the file should be as follows:

1. It may reside on any computer-readable medium. Choices include tape, cards, disk pack, data cell, etc. The important consideration should be the "usability" of the selected medium at each of the collaborative centers. Since most users—both during and after the project—will have the use of tape drives, magnetic tape (9 track, 800 or 1600 B.P.I.) will be the usual choice.

2. Entry of each datum point must be verified. Audits should be conducted both before and after the keypunched records (which have already been desk-checked or manually audited) are transferred to tape.

3. Data from each center are included, except where of doubtful validity. Projects may wish to assign "confidence ratings" to particular records and analyze data later by "levels of confidence" in the observer or in the collecting agency itself.

4. The file must be in "fixed-length" format. This means that each record in the master file must be of the same length—even if almost all of the record is missing. This must be done so that the data tape may be used readily by prepared or "canned" statistical processing programs. Variable

length records, and records with "free field" formats must be avoided for the final tape. These formats may be gainfully used, however, in intermediate steps to be described.

5. Missing data are handled in a uniform way (see tabulation). A special code (i.e., − 999) is used for each *true* missing observation. A true missing observation is one where no attempt was made to collect the datum, or the subject was unavailable. This is different from the missing observation where the *subject was observed*, but could not, or would not, report. This, in turn, is different from the situation where the subject is observed and reports "no," "none," or "not applicable" to the item. In this case, the datum is *not* missing and should be assigned a true zero. The fourth case is the usual one—where a codable response is given and the entry properly recorded. Thus we have several options.

Type	Code	Status
a. True missing data	−999	Missing
b. Missing data	−99	Missing
c. True zero	0	Nonmissing
d. Valid data	(as per code book)	Nonmissing

6. Full documentation is available on the following points concerning the file:

a. Number of records in total
b. Number of records per case
c. Length of records
d. The name and general description of each variable, and its range
e. The length of the variable fields (and card location)
f. The code (numeric or alphanumeric) type for the variable
g. Missing data conventions used
h. Any deviations from the coding handbook used for the project (i.e., recodes or pooling of codes for variables, etc.)

Attaining these final standards requires review and discussion of the process used in designing the project data flow. Now that the final product has been presented, the routes by which it may be attained will be explored.

MASTER FILE PLANNING

The work on the master file should be in at the earliest stage in the collaborative project. Where possible, agreement should be obtained on a master variable list, which each center will collect and submit to the national data pool. This should not prevent the individual centers from collecting other data in excess of core national data requirements, but care must be taken that additional data collection *is* in excess of—and not in lieu of—core data. Further, extra measures should not disrupt or contaminate the flow of the national design.

The agreement to measure certain subject or patient variables is critical. The value of constancy, and care in the collection of data, must be imparted to each member of the center's data-handling staff.

In general, some conventions in item planning collection are suggested:

1. Items should be included which are checks of factual or obvious information. These should be repeated later in the forms for comparisons of patient and reporter accuracy.
2. Items should be scaled in a uniform direction—(i.e., more pathological, greater intensity, larger magnitude, etc., gets a higher rating).
3. Items should not be mixed in terms of number–letter combinations (i.e., use one or the other).
4. Codes for variables should be larger in range, since it is generally possible to pool and combine codes to a smaller code system. It is not possible to recover information going from a smaller to a larger code.
5. Missing data conventions must be specified and observed.
6. The use of open-ended or closed questions must be specified to the computer forms designer and programmer. This has been reviewed in a previous section.

THE DATA FLOW

In general, collaborative projects may require one of two types of file systems. We will describe these here, with the options involved.

The first system assumes that there will be relatively few "updates" in the patient's data. That is, all the data for the study will be finished in a time frame that will allow completion of a "code book" containing all (or almost all) measures. In this case, relatively few update runs must be made to merge the existing information with new data. To put this in other terms, the number of "transactions" on a subject is low. Forms are collected until a feedback run is needed, and then the forms are audited, keypunched, audited, put on tape, audited, and then run with the appropriate programs.

The advantage of this kind of system is that relatively little handling of the data is required. Code books are held until complete, or nearly complete, and then sent for processing. This eliminates an update or bookkeeping step where data loss is possible. It is a most feasible system, where an original study and a follow-up are done. Here the process may require few analyses and computer runs.

One of the disadvantages of such a system is time when the life of the study is long or many updates are required. Many times it is not possible to "hold" records until all data are complete, and the need for feedback is great. In these cases, the first system would be taxed, since the same data would have to be compiled and run many times. An even greater disadvantage occurs when many "updates" to case records are required. The first system is almost always oriented around canned or prepared statistical programs which do not have convenient "edit" capabilities. A study that required frequent follow-ups or corrections to the original data file would be cumbersome with this first system. A similar problem would be encountered where multiple code books were submitted at various intervals for each patient.

A second type of system uses an additional step to handle projects that have many "transactions" per case or have some of the attributes previously described which pose problems for the one-stage method.

The second system uses a file-maintenance system to handle a variable format record file which is maintained for each subject. In other words, a special system is designed which is oriented around a rapid and flexible access to each patient's file. The core of this type of system is the "sort and merge" routine. The sort and merge program is designed to quickly find, update, and restore a patient record. This means that adding, correcting, or deleting variables is fast and flexible. It should be noted that the sort–merge type of file maintenance system doesn't necessarily mean variable-length records are required, but this is the usual way in which this is handled.

Other references have recently appeared in which these issues are discussed in some detail. In fact, the file-maintenance system is the mode in business applications, and current systems in wide use (such as Mark IV) use this basic plan.

These flexible systems tend to be business-oriented. Tasks such as inventory, payroll, and client file maintenance, are familiar to many data-processing workers. To the degree to which updating research files has common characteristics, business-oriented systems can handle the special problems of collaborative studies with high data transmission and needs for change in the data base.

Yet most collaborative projects do not have data flow requirements that demand this kind of system. Some features of business systems—such as edit and range checks—are essential for scientific systems.

The problem encountered in the polydrug project was not the use of business-oriented data techniques, but rather the unfamiliarity, on the part of the contracting firms, with data practices, needs, and conventions of scientists.

In collaborative projects, a data contractor must have familiarity with the *content* of the data in addition to being adept at the *process* of its handling. This is an unusual requirement in the data-processing world. Usually, the data-processing organization focuses its attention on the operations involved in supervising the flow of information. In some ways it is an advantage to be unaware of the content or meaning of the data.

This is an unacceptable position, though, for health science research. The data flow must not only provide checks for accuracy of registration—the data must make sense. The contractor should have the capability to monitor the data base and do analyses that test basic characteristics—validity and reliability. More than that, the data organization must have the capability to know whether the data make basic sense.

Before final award of any data management contract, the contractor should be required to demonstrate actual data-processing capability. An inspection by representatives of the collaborative project, qualified experts, and granting agency officials of the proposed facilities and personnel is essential. In addition, the contractor should be given an experimental tape and required to perform a number of sophisticated analyses and provide reports in a manner similar to the actual study.

While these steps may appear to be costly and time consuming, it is clear that the data must be competently handled if the results of proposed collaborative projects are to have scientific validity.

STATISTICAL PACKAGES AND DATA EXCHANGE

An important point to be negotiated between the collaborative centers and the main data center is the exchange of data for local analysis. While data requests may be handled by the national center initially, many of the local sites may develop the interest and capability to do special analyses on certain issues. Thus, certain collaborative centers may wish to develop technical specifications for tapes (density, labels, etc.) and other media for exchange with the national center.

Selection of statistical packages or programs for analysis of data slices

depends upon a combination of factors. Availability, programmer preferences, and the structure of the data, often determine the selection. One
advantage of an agreement by all centers to use a common program set
(such as BMD or SPSS) is that control cards and technical advice become
interchangeable. In the Polydrug Project it was found that routines to do
variable and typology computation could easily be exchanged and implemented when a common program set was used. This left only
hardware differences (IBM versus CDC versus Burroughs, etc.) and job
control language to be reconciled.

IN CLOSING

Lessons from the Polydrug Project and other collaborative efforts are
outlined in this chapter. The conditions surrounding each of the projects
may be different but certain processes seem to be required. It is hoped
that these experiences will lead others to make more effective use of the
collaborative paradigm in the future.

Many researchers have realized that sequential research on individual
drugs on a univariate basis is inappropriate to the clinical world. In an
analogous way, it is hoped that individual investigators will more readily
participate in collaborative networks in an ad hoc or on more permanent
research basis. Successful collaboration produces de facto a working
relationship between investigators who will continue to produce together
long after a particular project has ended.

Quality of collaborative data management is certain to improve as the
multicenter research modality matures. Increasing sophistication by
working drug abuse professionals will increase the effectiveness of quantification efforts and reduce dependence on others for data processing.

CHAPTER XVII

Conclusions and Recommendations for Future Research

**Albert S. Carlin, Kenneth M. Adams,
George Beschner, and Donald R. Wesson**

The polydrug programs were successful in locating and treating a broad heterogeneous population of polydrug abusers. By and large, these individuals were not "hidden" but surfaced in a variety of treatment systems and the criminal justice system. It is impossible to speak meaningfully of *"the* polydrug problem" or of *"the* polydrug abuser." In retrospect, this should not be surprising since "polydrug" is a definition derived pharmacologically through exclusion, i.e., a definition based on what drugs are used or not used by an individual. Such definitions of drug abuse, while logically valid, fail to take into account the multiplicity of functions served by consumption of psychoactive drugs and the variations in individuals abusing drugs.

Whereas the sample of patients examined was broad and diverse, the sample of patients seen by the polydrug research projects is probably not truly representative of the population of polydrug abuse. For example, the referral source for the patient is associated with many patient characteristics and conclusions about the polydrug problem must take into account this possible nonrepresentativeness of sampling.

371

Polydrug Abuse:
The Results of a
National Collaborative Study

The study of nonpatients provided evidence that information gathered on polydrug abusers seeking treatment cannot be generalized to polydrug abusers in general. Some users do not seek or require treatment. Thus, drug use, per se is not an indicator of psychopathology or of drug abuse problems, while entry into drug abuse treatment is more likely to be associated with psychological disturbance.

Even when a more homogeneous subgroup, women, were considered, they could not be taken as a unitary group. Women are the major recipients of prescription psychoactive drugs, and not surprisingly the polydrug treatment programs saw a far greater percentage of women than typically is seen in most treatment programs. However, when compared to the sex ratio seen in the DAWN data, it appears that women may have been underrepresented in the polydrug programs. Those women seen by the programs were not representatives of the hidden population but, for the most part, had previous contact with hospitals and mental health and social welfare agencies.

The heterogeneity of the polydrug patient sample did not preclude construction of homogeneous subgroups through utilization of several typologies. Each of the several groupings generated was of value in helping to explore and delineate different patterns of polydrug abuse. The varying demographic, socioeconomic and psychological characteristics associated with each subgroup underlines the observations that nonopiate drugs are used for a variety of reasons by a variety of persons. Further, drug preference patterns seem to be dictated not by the pharmacological activity of the substance, but by a complex of economic, social, and drug availability variables.

In examining personality patterns and differences among polydrug patients no association was found between choice or preference of pharmacological agent and MMPI code types. In addition, examination of MMPI code types underlined the heterogeneity of polydrug abusers and failed to support the concept of an "addictive personality," at least as measured by the MMPI.

Despite the apparent utility of the subtypes generated, it is important to remember that no single classification scheme has universal value. Each emphasizes variables most relevant to that typology and ignores others which may be important for other typologies. In order to prevent any typology from becoming a Procrustean bed, the questions asked and the information required should dictate the typology rather than vice versa.

Although the polydrug programs identified a substantial number of persons whose dysfunctional life was associated with polydrug abuse, the absolute magnitude of the problem remains speculative. Indeed the very heterogeneity observed among the study patients also confounds generalization of incidence data. Variations in local incidence rates raise questions about the concept of a national epidemic of drug abuse and suggest that it would be more appropriate to conduct epidemiology and ethnographic studies in different localities and within different populations rather than attempting to make national projections.

Attempts to understand the magnitude of the polydrug problems are further confounded by the prevalence of polydrug abuse among clients seen and treated, but not recognized as drug abusers, by mental health, alcoholism treatment agencies, and other health treatment delivery systems.

Misuse of prescription or licit drugs interfaces heavily with medicine and mental health, whereas misuse of illicit substances is more likely to interface with the criminal justice system. Currently, most drug treatment is focused on the illicit behavior associated with drug use, and the treatment strategy in these cases is abstinence, methadone maintenance, and the reduction of criminal activity.

Patients who overuse drugs that were prescribed for the treatment of medical conditions may develop one of two patterns: (1) the patient takes increasingly larger amounts of the drug in order to control symptoms, such as insomnia or pain; or (2) the patient discovers the drug has desirable effects not related to the condition for which it was originally prescribed. For example, the individual taking barbiturates for sleep may discover that they can produce disinhibition euphoria.

Such patients frequently do not identify their problem as drug related and do not seek treatment in drug abuse treatment centers. Their problem is not likely to be defined as drug abuse by treating professionals.

Chronic and intensive use of psychoactive drugs is disruptive to many psychological functions. In this book we focused on the impact of drugs on central nervous system functions. Evidence has accumulated from sleep research that sedative withdrawal may disrupt sleep patterns and produce EEG changes.

Increased use of opiates and depressants was associated with impairment of critical cognitive and perceptual motor skills, while surprisingly amphetamines were not associated with these effects. These deficits can be related to EEG measure of brain function. Although a clear-cut dose–effect relationship is yet to be established and although social and personality variables are also implicated, a clear association between use of certain drugs and central nervous system deficits in function exists.

Not only were the polydrug users found to be a heterogeneous population, differences among treatment agencies contacting polydrug users was substantial. Differences among physicians (in different specialties) toward drug problems and treatment are substantial. The impact of differences in physicians' attitudes on *quality* of care is yet to be assessed, but provision must be made for these additional differences in training, treatment planning, and implementation of health care policy.

Each of the chapters which describes research efforts and findings has, if it has succeeded, partially answered the questions addressed and raised even more questions than it has answered. The complexity of polydrug abuse as a behavior problem, as a medical problem, and as a societal problem precludes easy or ready solutions. Future efforts at reaching an understanding of this phenomenon must take into account the heterogeneity of polydrug abuse and avoid obvious, but useless, pharmacological definitions. It must also be recognized that many aspects of polydrug abuse do not fit the traditional view of drug abusers primarily as socially deviant, and that further exploration should focus on the many medical and psychological needs of the population. Simply put, there are no villains; physicians are not massively overprescribing and are not creating an iatrogenic epidemic of drug abuse and patients are not deviant dope fiends. Future efforts should be aimed at further definition and articulation of subtypes. More definitive statements can now be made about some of the health consequences of polydrug abuse. However, social cost and health consequences can be and need to be further explored in conjunction with exploration of subtypes and not as global questions. The association of sedative and opiate drugs with central nervous system impairment is also an important observation requiring further exploration.

References

Aaronson, B. S. Age and sex influences on MMPI profile peak distributions in an abnormal population. *Journal of Consulting Psychology*, 1958, 22, 203–206.

Abelson, H. I., & Fishburne, P. *Non-medical Use of Psychoactive Substances*. Princeton: Response Analysis Corporation, 1976.

Abelson, H. I., Fishburne, P. M., & Cisin, I. *National Survey on Drug Abuse: 1977*. Washington, D.C.: DHEW Publication # (ADM) 78–618, 1978.

Acord, L. D. Hallucinogenic drugs and brain damage. *Military Medicine*, 1972, 137, 18–19.

Acord, L. D. & Barker, D. D. Hallucinogenic drugs and cerebral deficit, *Journal of Nervous and Mental Disease*, 1973, 156, 281–283.

Adams, K. M.; Rennick, P. M.; Schooff, K. G., & Keegan, J. F. Neuropsychological measurement of drug effects: Polydrug research. *The Journal of Psychedelic Drugs*, 1975, 7, 151–160.

Agnew, H. W., Jr.; Webb, W. B., & Williams, R. L. The effects of stage four sleep deprivation. *Electroencephalography and Clinical Neurophysiology*, 1964, 17, 68–70.

Agnew, H. W., Jr.; Webb, W. B., & Williams, R. L. Sleep patterns in late middle age males: An EEG study. *Electroencephalography and Clinical Neurophysiology* 1967, 23, 168–171.

Allnutt, M. F. & O'Connor, P. J. Comparison of the encephalographic, behavioral and subjective correlates of natural and drug-induced sleep at atypical hours. *Aerospace Medicine* 1971, 42, 1006–1010.

Anderson, O. & Feldman, J. *Family Medical Costs and Voluntary Health Insurance: A National Survey*. New York: McGraw Hill, 1956.

Aserinsky, E. & Kleitman, N. Regularly occurring periods of eye motility and concomitant phenomena, during sleep. *Science*, 1953, 118 273–274.

Ballard, R. G. The interelatedness of alcoholism and between marital conflict: III: The interaction between marital conflict and alcoholism as seen through MMPI's of marriage partners. *American Journal of Orthopsychiatry*, 1959, 29, 528–546.

Balter, M. & Levine, J. Nature and extent of psychotropic drug usage in the United States. *Psychopharmacology Bulletin*, 1969, 5, 3–14.

Bardwick, J. *The Psychology of Women: A Study of Bio-Cultural Conflicts.* New York: Harper & Row, 1971.

Barnes, Gerald W., & Lucas, George J. Cerebral dysfunction vs. psychogenesis in Halstead-Reitan tests. *The Journal of Nervous and Mental Disease*, 1974, 158, 50–60.

Barron, F. An ego-strength scale which predicts response to psychotherapy. *Journal of Consulting Psychology*, 1953, 17, 327–333.

Belleville, R. E. MMPI score changes induced by lysergic acid diethylamide (LSD-25). *Journal of Clinical Psychology*, 1956, 12, 279–282.

Bennett, A. E.; Mowery, G. L. & Fort, J. L. Brain damage from chronic alcoholism: The diagnosis of an intermedicate stage of alcoholic brain disease. *American Journal of Psychiatry*, 1960, 116, 705–711.

Bentler, P. M. & Eichberg, R. H. A social psychological approach to substance abuse construct validity: Prediction of adolescent drug use from independent data sources. In D. J. Lettieri (Ed.), *Predicting adolescent drug abuse: A review of issues, methods and correlates.* (National Institute on Drug Abuse, Research Series No. 11, DHEW Publication No. ADM 76-249.) Washington, D.C.: U.S. Government Printing Office, 1966.

Benvenuto, J. & Bourne, P. The federal polydrug abuse project: Initial report. *Journal of Psychedelic Drugs*, 1975, 7, 115–120.

Berzins, J. E., Ross, W. F. & Monroe, J. J. A multivariate study of the personality characteristics of hospitalized narcotic addicts on the MMPI. *Journal of Clinical Psychology*, 1971, 27, 174–181.

Berzins, J. I., Ross, W. F., English, G. E., & Haley, J. V. Subgroups among opiate addicts: A typological investigation. *Journal of Abnormal Psychology*, 1974, 83, 65–73.

Bickford, R. G., Brimm, J., Berger, L., & Aung, M. Application of compressed spectral array in clinical EEG. In Kellaway & Peterson (Eds.), *Automation of Clinical Electroencephalography.* New York: Raven Press, 1973. Pp. 55–64.

Blachly, P. H., David, N. A., & Irwin, S. l-alpha-acetylmenthadol (LAAM): Comparison of laboratory findings, electroencephalogram, and Cornell Medical Index of patients on LAAM with those on methodone. *Proceedings of the 4th National Conference on Methadone Treatment*, 1972, 203–206.

Blacker, K. H., Jones, R. T., Stone, G. C., & Pfefferbaum, D. Chronic users of LSD: The "acidheads." *American Journal of Psychiatry*, 1968, 125, 97–107.

Blum, R. H. *Students and drugs; drugs II: College and high school observations.* San Francisco: Jossey-Bass, 1969.

Blum, Richard H. & Associates. *Society and Drugs Drugs I: Social and Cultural Observations.* San Francisco, Calif. Jossey-Bass, Inc., 1969.

Braucht, G. N. A psychosocial typology of adolescent alcohol and drug users. In M. H. Chafetz (Ed.), *Proceedings of the Third Annual Alcoholism Conference of the National Institute on Alcohol Abuse and Alcoholism* (DHEW Publication No. ADM 75-137). Washington, D.C.: U.S. Government Printing Office, 1974.

Braucht, G. N., Brakarsh, W. D., Follingstad, D., & Berry, K. L. Deviant drug use in adolescence: A review of psychosocial correlates. *Psychological Bulletin*, 1973, 79, 92–106.

Brehm, M. L. & Back, K. W. Self image and attitudes toward drugs. *Journal of Personality*, 1968, 36, 299–314.

Brill, N., Crumptom, E. & Grayson, H. M. Personality factors in marijuana use. *Archives of General Psychiatry*, 1971, *24*, 163–165.

Brodsky, C. M. The pharmacotherapy system. *Psychosomatics*. 1971, *11*, 24–30.

Broverman, I. K.; Broverman, D. M.; Clarkson, F. E.; Rosenkrantz, P. S.; & Vogel, S. R. Sex role stereotypes and clinical judgments of mental health. *Journal of Consulting and Clinical Psychology*, 1970, *34*, 1–7.

Brown, R. R. & Partington, J. E. A psychometric comparison of narcotics addicts with hospital attendants. *Journal of General Psychology*. 1942, *27*, 71–79.

Bruhn, P. & Maage, N. Intellectual and neuropsychological functions in young men with heavy and long-term patterns of drug abuse. *American Journal of Psychiatry*, 1975, *132*, 397–401.

Burke, E. L. & Eichberg, R. H. Personality characteristics of adolescents of dangerous drugs as indicated by the MMPI. *Journal of Nervous and Mental Disease*, 1972, *154*, 291–301.

Buss, A. H. & Durkee, A. An inventory for assessing different kinds of hostility. *Journal of Consulting Psychology*, 1957, *21*(4), 343–349.

Button, A. D. A study of alcoholics with the MMPI. *Quarterly Journal of Studies on Alcohol*, 1956, *17*, 263–281.

Cahalan, D.; Cisin, I. H., & Crossley, H. M. *American Drinking Practices*, New Brunswick, N.J.: Rutgers Center of Alcohol Studies, 1969.

Calden, G., & Hokanson, J. E. The influence of age on MMPI responses. *Journal of Clinical Psychology*, 1959, *15*, 194–195.

Campbell, R. S. & Freeland, J. B. The hippie turns junkie: The emergence of a type. *The International Journal of the Addictions*, 1974, *9*, 719–730.

Carlin, A. S. & Post, R. D. Patterns of drug use among marihuana smokers. *Journal of the American Medical Association*, 1971, *218*, 867–868.

Carlin, A. S.; Post, R. D.; Bakker, C. B., & Halpern, L. M. The role of modeling and previous experience in the facilitation of marijuana intoxication. *Journal of Nervous and Mental Disease*, 1974, *159*, 275–281.

Carlin, A. S. & Trupin, E. W.: The effects of long-term chronic marijuana use of neuro-psychological functioning. *International Journal of the Addictions*, 1977, *12*, 617–624.

Carruthers, B. Young multi-drug users replace old style addicts. *The Journal*, 1973, *2*, 2.

Carson, R. C. Interpretative manual to the MMPI. In: J. N. Butcher, (ed.) *MMPI: Research Developments and Clinical Applications*. New York: McGraw-Hill, 1969.

Chambers, C. D. Barbiturate-sedative abuse: A study of prevalence among narcotic abusers. *The International Journal of the Addictions*, 1969, *4*, 45–57.

Chambers, C. D. Narcotic addiction in females: a race comparison. *International Journal of the Addictions*, 1970, *5*, 257–278.

Chambers, C. D., & Brill, L. Some considerations for the treatment of non-narcotic drug abusers. *Industrial Medicine*, 1971, *40*, 29–38.

Chambers, C. D., & Griffey, M. S. Use of legal substances within the general population: the sex and age variables. *Addictive Diseases*, 1975, *2*, 7–79.

Chambers, C. D., & Moldestad, M. The evolution of concurrent opiate and sedative addictions. In: Ball and Chambers (Eds.), *The epidemiology of opiate addiction in the United States*, pp. 130–146. Springfield: Charles C. Thomas, 1970.

Chambers, C. D., & Schultz, D. Women and drugs. A startling journal survey. *Ladies Home Journal*, 88(November, 1971a):130–131, 191–194.

Chambers, C. D., & Schultz, D. Housewives and the drug habit. What they take—and why. *Ladies Home Journal*, (December, 1971b). 88:66–70, 138.

Chambers, C. D., & Schultz, D. Working women and drugs. *Ladies Home Journal*, March, 1972, 89(3):60, 62, 64, 119.

Chapman, L. F., & Wolff, H. G. The cerebral himispheres and the highest integrative functions of man. *Archives of Neurology*, 1959, *1*, 357–424.

Chappel, J. N. Attitudinal barriers to physician involvement with drug abusers. *Journal of the American Medical Association*, 1973, 224, 1011–1013.

Chappel, J. N.; Jordan, R. D.; Treadway, B. J. & Miller, P. R. Substance abuse attitude changes in medical students. Presented at the American Psychiatric Association Meeting, Miami, 1976.

Chappel, J. N., & Schnoll, S. H. The effect of physicians' attitudes on the treatment of chemically dependent patients. Presented at the Annual Meeting of the California Medical Association, 1976.

Chesler, P. *Women and Madness*. New York: Avon Books, 1972.

Chiappa, K. J.; Brimm, J. E.; Allen, B. A.; Leibig, B. E.; Rossiter, V. S.; Stockard, J. J.; Burchiel, K. J., & Bickford, R. G. Computing in EEG and epilepsy—evolution of CEARS (comprehensive EEG analysis and reporting system). *Proceedings of the Conference on Quantitative Analytic Studies in Epilepsy*, Baylor/Methodist Hospital, October 1–4, 1975. Amsterdam: Elsevier, 1975.

Christie, R. L., & Caldwell, A. B. Illicit drug use vs. MMPI code types: code-specific use patterns, motives, and treatment implications in a chronic marijuana-using population. Presented at the Ninth Annual MMPI Symposium, Los Angeles, February, 1974.

Cisin, I. H. Community studies of drinking behavior. *Annals of the New York Acadamey of Science*, 1963, *107*, 607–612.

Citron, B. P.; Halpern, M., & McCarron, M., Necrotizing angitis associated with drug abuse. *New England Journal of Medicine*, 1970, 283, 1003–1011.

Cohen, S., & Edwards, A. E. LSD and organic brain impairment. *Drug Dependence*, 1969, 2, 1–4.

Comstock, B. S., Dammann, G., *Referral Strategies for Polydrug Abusers*. National Institute on Drug Abuse Services Research Monograph Series. Rockville, Maryland, 1977.

Cooperstock, R. Sex differences in the use of mood-modifying drugs: An explanatory model. *Journal of Health and Social Behavior*, September 1971, *12*:238–244.

Cox, C. & Smart, R. G. Social and psychological aspects of speed use: a study of types of speed users in Toronto. *International Journal of the Addictions*, 1972, 7, 201–217.

Curlee, J. A comparison of male and female patients at an alcoholism treatment center. *Journal of Psychology*, 1970, 74, 239–247.

Dahlstrom, W. G.; Welsh, G. S., & Dahlstrom, L. E. *An MMPI Handbook, Volume I: Clinical Interpretation*. Minneapolis: University of Minnosota Press, 1972.

Dahlstrom, W. G.; Welsh, G. S., & Dahlstrom, L. E. *An MMPI Handbook, Volume II: Research Applications*. Minneapolis: University of Minnesota Press, 1975.

Davis, R. & Munoz, L. Heads and freaks: patterns and meanings of drug use among hippies. *Journal of Health and Social Behavior*, 1968, 9, 156–164.

Dement, W. The effect of dream deprivation. Science, 1960, *131*, 1705–1707.

Devenyi, P. & Wilson, M. Abuse of barbiturates in an alcoholic population. *Canadian Medical Association Journal*, 1971, *104*, 219–221.

Devenyi, P. & Wilson, M. Barbiturate abuse and addiction and their relationship to alcohol and alcoholism. *Canadian Medical Association Journal*, 1971, *104*, 215–218.b

DeWolfe, A. S. Differentiation of schizophrenia and brain damage with the WAIS. *Journal of Clinical Psychology*, 1971, 27, 209–211.

Diagnostic and statistical Manual of Mental Disorders (DSM-II): American Psychiatric Association. Washington, D. C., 1968.

Domestic Council Drug Abuse Task Force. *White paper on drug abuse: September 1975.* Washington, D. C.: U. S. Government Printing Office, 1975.

Drug Enforcement Administration, *DAWN 2 Analysis*, Washington, D.C., 1975.

Duncan, D. F. The acquisition, maintenance and treatment of polydrug dependence: A public health model. *Journal of Psychedelic Drugs*, 1975, 7, 209–213.

Dunlap, N. G. Alcoholism in women: some antecedents and correlates of remission in middle-class members of Alcoholics Anonymous. (Doctoral Dissertation, University of Texas, 1961). *Dissertation Abstracts International*, 1961, 22, 1904. (University Microfilms, N. 61-4688).

Dunnette, M. D. Individualized prediction as a strategy for discovering demographic and interpersonal/psychological correlates of drug resistance and abuse. In D. J. Lettieri (Ed.), *Predicting adolescent drug abuse: A review of issues, methods and correlates.* (National Institute on Drug Abuse, Research Series No. 11, DHEW Publication No. ADM-76-240.) Washington, D.C.: U.S. Government Printing Office, 1966.

Edwards, A. L. *Experimental Design in Psychological Research*. New York: Holt, Rinehart & Winston, 1960.

Efron, V., Keller, M., & Girioli, C. *Statistics on the Consumption of Alcohol and Alcoholism*, 1974 edition. New Brunswick, N.J.: Publications Division, Rutgers Center of Alcohol Studies, 1974.

Ellingwood, E. H. Amphetamine psychosis: I, Description of the individuals and process. *Journal of Nervous and Mental Disease*, 1967, 144, 273–283.

Ellinwood, E. H. & Cohen, S. Amphetamine Abuse. *Science*, 1971, 171, 420–421.

Endicott, J., & Spitzer, R. L. Current and Past Psychopathology Scales (CAPPS): Rationale, reliability, and validity. *Archives of General Psychiatry*, 1972, 27: 678–687.

Feinberg, I., Hibi, S., Cavness, C., & March, J. Absence of REM rebound after barbiturate withdrawal. *Science*, 1974, 185, 534–535.

Fidell, L. S. Put her down on drugs: prescribed drug usage in women. Presented at the Western Psychological Association Meeting, Anaheim, California, April, 1973.

Fidell, L. S. & Pratner, J. E. The housewife syndrome: fact or fiction. In press

Fields, F. R. J. & Fullerton, J. R. The influence of heroin addiction on neuropsychological functioning. In: *Newsletter for Research in Mental Health and Behavioral Science*, Washington, D.C. Dept. of Medicine and Surgery, Veterans Administration, 1974.

Fisher, G. & Brickman, H. R. Multiple drug use of marihuana users. *Diseases of the Nervous System*, 1973, 34, 40–43.

Fitzhugh, L. C., Fitzhugh, K. B., & Reitan, R. M. Adaptive abilities and intellectual functioning of hospitalized alcoholics. *Quarterly Journal of Studies in Alcoholism*, 1960, 21, 414–423.

Fox, R. Treatment of the problem drinker by the private practitioner. In: Bourne, P. G. and Fox, R. (Eds). *Alcoholism: Progress in Research and Treatment*. New York: Academic Press, 1973.

Freed, E. X. Drug abuse by alcoholics: a review. *International Journal of the Addictions*, 1973, 8, 415–473.

Freedman, E. X. Implications for research. *Journal of the American Medical Association*, 1968, 206, 1280–1284.

Gaillard, J. M. & Tissot, R. Principles of automatic analysis of sleep records with a hybrid system. *Computors in Biomedical Research* 1973, 6, 1–13.

Gay, A. & Gay, G. Haight-Ashbury: evolution of a drug culture in a decade of mendacity. *Journal of Psychedelic Drugs*, 1971, 4, 81–90.

Gendreau, P. & Gendreau, L. P. The "addiction-prone" personality: A study of Canadian heroin addicts. *Canadian Journal of Behavioral Science*, 1970, 2, 18–25.

Gendreau, P. & Gendreau, L. P. Research design and narcotic addiction proneness. *Canadian Psychiatric Association Journal*, 1971, 16, 265–267.

Gendreau, P. & Gendreau, L. P. A theoretical note on personality characteristics of heroin addicts. *Journal of Abnormal Psychology*, 1973, 82, 139–140.

Gilbert, J. G. & Lombardi, D. N. Personality characteristics of young male narcotic addicts. *Journal of Consulting Psychology*, 1967, 31, 536–538.

Glaser, F. B. Narcotic addiction in the pain-prone female patient. I. A comparison with addict controls. *International Journal of the Addictions*, 1966, 1, 47–59.

Glaser, F. B. Narcotic addiction in the pain-prone female patient. II. Some factors in the doctor-patient relationship. *International Journal of the Addictions*, 1968, 3, 149–161.

Glenn, W. A. & Richards, L. G. Recent surveys of nonmedical drug use: a compendium of abstracts. National Institute on Drug Abuse, 1974.

Goldstein, G. & Shelly, C. H. Field dependence and cognitive, perceptual and motor skills in alcoholics: a factor analytic study. *Quarterly Journal of Studies on Alcoholism*, 1971, 32, 29–40.

Goldstein, L., Stolzfus, N. W., & Smith, R. R. An analysis of the effects of methaqualone and glutethimide on sleep in insomniac subjects. *Research Communications in Chemical Pathology and Pharmacology*, 1971, 2, 927–933.

Goldstein, J. W., Korn, J. H., Abel, W. H., & Morgan, R. M. The social psychology and epidemiology of student drug use: report on Phase One. ED 057 398, Educational Resources Information Center, Office of Education, Bethesda, MD, 1972.

Goldstein, L., Graedon, J., Willard, D., Goldstein, F., & Smith, R. R. A comparative study of the effects of methaqualone and glutethimide on sleep in male chronic insomniacs. *Journal of Clinical Pharmacology*, 1970, 10, 258–268.

Gorsuch, R. L. & Butler, M. C. Initial drug abuse: A review of predisposing social psychological factors. *Psychological Bulletin*, 1976, 83 (1), 1920–1937.

Goss, A. & Morosko, T. E.: Alcoholism and clinical symptoms. *Journal of Abnormal Psychology*, 1969, 74, 682–684.

Gove, W. & Tudor, J. Adult sex roles and mental illness. *American Journal of Sociology*, 1973, 78, 812–835.

Grant, I., Adams, K. M., Carlin, A. S., & Rennick, P. M. Neuropsychological deficit in polydrug users. *Drug and Alcohol Dependence*. 1977, 2, 91–108.

Grant, I., Adams, K. M., Carlin, A. S., Rennick, P. M., Judd, L. L., Schooff, K., & Reed, R., Organic impairment in polydrug users: Risk factors. *American Journal of Psychiatry*, 1978, 135, 179–184.

Grant, I. & Judd, L. L. Neuropsychological and EEG disturbances in polydrug users. *American Journal of Psychiatry*, 1976, 33, 973–978.

Grant, I., Mohns, L., & Miller, M., A neuropsychological study of polydrug users, *Archives of General Psychiatry*, 1976, 33, 973–978.

Grant, I., Rochford, J., Fleming, T., & Stunkard, A. A neuropsychological assessment of the effects of moderate marijuana use. *The Journal of Nervous and Mental Disease*, 1973, 156, 278–280.

Greaves, G. MMPI correlates and chronic drug abuse in hospitalized adolescents. *Psychological Reports*. 1971, 29, 1222.

Green, M. H. Report on the use of psychoactive substances in association with negative life events. SAODAP, July 1974.

Groves, W. E. Patterns of college student drug use and lifestyles. In E. Josephson & E. Carroll (Eds.), *Drug use: Epidemiological and social approaches*. New York: Wiley, 1974.

Gynther, M. D. White norms and black MMPI's: a prescription for discrimination? *Psychological Bulletin*, 1972, 78, 386–402.

Gynther, M. D., Altman, H., & Sletten, S. W. Replicated correlates of MMPI to-point code types: the Missouri actuarial system. *Journal of Clinical Psychology*, 1973, 29, 263–289. Special Monograph Supplement.

Gynther, M. D., Altman, H., Warbin, R. W., & Sletten, I. W. A new actuarial system for MMPI interpretation: rationale and methodology. *Journal of Clinical Psychology*, 1972, 28, 173–179.

Gynther, M. D., & Shimkunas, A. M. More data on MMPI F > 16 scores. *Journal of Clinical Psychology*, 1965, 21, 275–277.

Halstead, W. C. *Brain and Intelligence: A Quantitative Study of the Frontal Lobes*, Chicago: University Press 1947.

Hall, J. H. & Karp, H. R. Acute progressive ventral pontine disease in heroin abuse. *Neurology*, 1973, 23, 6–7.

Hamburger, E. Barbiturate use in narcotic addicts. *Journal of the American Medical Association*, 1964, 189, 366–368.

Hampton, P. J. The development of a personality questionnaire for drinkers. *Genetic Psychology Monographs*, 1953, 48, 55–115.

Harmatz, J. S., Shader, R. I., & Saltzman, C. Marijuana users and nonusers. Personality test differences. *Archives of General Psychiatry*, 1972, 26, 108–112.

Hathaway, S. R. & Briggs, P. F. Some normative data on new MMPI scales. *Journal of Clinical Psychology*, 1957, 13, 364–368.

Hays, W. L. *Statistics for the Social Sciences*. New York: Holt, 1973.

Hekimian, L. J. & Gershon, S. Characteristics of drug abusers admitted to a psychiatric hospital. *The Journal of the American Medical Association*, 1968, 205, 125–130.

Heller, M. E. & Mordkoff, A. M. Personality attributes of the young, non-addicted drug user. *International Journal of the Addictions*, 1972, 7, 65–72.

Henriques, E., Arsenian, J., Cutter, H., & Saraweera, A. B. Personality characteristics and drug of choice. *The International Journal of the Addictions*, 1972, 7, 73–76.

Hewitt, C. C. A personality study of alcohol addiction. *Quarterly Journal of Studies on Alcohol*, 1943, 4, 368–386.

Hill, H. E. & Belville, R. E. Effects of chronic barbiturate intoxication on motivation and muscular coordination. *Archives Neurology and Psychiatry*, 1953, 70, 180–188.

Hill, H. E., Haertzen, C. A., & Davis, H. An MMPI factor analytic study of alcoholics, narcotic addicts and criminals. *Quarterly Journal of Studies on Alcohol*, 1962, 23, 411–431.

Hill, H. E., Haertzen, C. A., & Glaser, R. Personality characteristics of narcotic addicts as indicated by the MMPI. *Journal of General Psychology*, 1960, 63, 127–139.

Hill, H. E., Haertzen, C. A. & Yamahiro, R. S. The addict physician: An MMPI study of the interaction of personality characteristics and availability of narcotics. In A. Winkler, (Ed.) *The Addictive States*. Baltimore: Association for Research in Nervous and Mental Disease, 1968.

Hodo, G. & Fowler, R. Frequency of MMPI two-point codes in a large alcoholic sample. *Journal of Clinical Psychology*, 1976, 32, 487–489.

Hoffman, H. MMPI changes for a male alcoholic state hospital population—1959 to 1972. *Psychological Reports*, 1973, 33, 139–142.

Hoffman, H., Jansen, D. G., & Wefring, L. R. Relationships between admission variables and MMPI scale scores of hospitalized alcoholics. *Psychological Reports*, 1972, 31, 659–662.

Hoffmann, H. & Nelson, P. C. Personality characteristics of alcoholics in relation to age and intelligence. *Psychological Reports*, 1971, 29, 143–146.

Holmes, T. H. & Rahe, R. H. The social readjustment rating scale. *Journal of Psychosomatic Research*, 1967, 11, 213–218.

Hoyt, D. P. & Sedlacek, G. M. Differentation alcoholics from normals and abnormals with the MMPI. *Journal of Clinical Psychology*, 1958, 14, 69–74.

Hughes, P., Crawford, G., & Jaffe, J. Heroin epidemics in Chicago. Proceedings of the World Congress of Psychiatry, Mexico City, 1971.

Hunt, L. *Heroin Epidemics: A Quantitative Study of Current Empirical Data*, Washington, D.C., Drug Abuse Council, 1973.

Hunt, L. *Recent Spread of Heroin Use in the United States: Unanswered Questions*, Washington, D.C., Drug Abuse Council, 1974a.

Hunt, L. *Drug Incidence Analysis*, Washington, D.C., Government Printing Office, 1974b (Special Action Office for Drug Abuse Prevention Monograph A-3).

Hunt, L. *The Assessment of Local Drug Abuse*, Lexington, Massachusetts, Lexington Books, 1977.

Hunt, L. & Chambers, C. *Pilot Test of an Epidemiological Technique for Detecting Abused Substances in Drug Using Populations*, Washington, D.C., RPC Foundation, 1976a (Final Report of Drug Enforcement Administration Contract No. DEA - 76 - 4).

Hunt, L. & Chambers, C. *The Heroin Epidemics*, Spectrum Publications, New York, 1976b.

Isbell, H., Altschul, S., Kornetsky, C. H. Chronic barbiturate intoxication: an experimental study, *Archives Neurology and Psychiatry*, 1950, 64, 1–28.

Isbell, H., Altschul, S., Kornetsky, C. H., Eiseman, A. J., Flanery, H. G., & Fraser, H. F. Chronic barbiturate intoxication: An experimental study. *Archives Neurology and Psychiatry*, 1950, 64, 1–28.

Itil, T. M., Saletu, B., & Marasa, J. Determination of drug-induced changes in sleep quality based on digital computer "sleep prints". *Pharmakopsychiatrie. Neuropsychopharmakologie*, 1974, 7, 265–280.

Jaffe, J. H. Drug addiction and drug abuse. In L. S. Goodman & A. Gilman (Eds.) *The Pharmacological Basis of Therapeutics*, fifth edition. New York: Macmillan, 1975.

Jansen, D. G. & H. Hoffman, H. Demographic and MMPI characteristics of male and female state hospital alcoholic patients. *Psychological Reports*, 1973, 33, 561–562.

Jessor, R. Predicting time of onset of marijuana use: A developmental study of high school youth. *Journal of Consulting and Clinical Psychology*, 1976, 44 (1), 125–134.

Jessor, R., Collins, M. I. & Jessor, S. L. On becoming a drinker: Social psychological aspects of an adolescent transition. In F. A. Seixas (Ed.), *Nature and nurture in alcoholism*. New York: Annals of the New York Academy of Sciences, 1972.

Jessor, E., Graves, T. D., Hanson, R. C. & Jessor, S. L. *Society, personality and deviant behavior: A study of a tri-ethnic community*. New York: Holt, Rinehart & Winston, 1968.

Jessor, R. & Jessor, S. L. Adolescent development and the onset of drinking: A longitudinal study. *Journal of Studies on Alcohol*, 1975, 36, 27–51.

Jessor, R., Jessor, S. L. & Finney, J. A social psychology of marijuana use: Longitudinal studies of high school and college youth. *Journal of Personality and Social Psychology*, 1973, 26, 1–15.

Jessor, S. L. & Jessor, R. Maternal ideology and adolescent problem behavior. *Developmental Psychology*, 1974, 10, 246–254.

Johnson, L. C., Hanson, K., & Bickford, R. G. Effect of flurazepam on sleep spindles and K-complexes. *Electroencephalography and Clinical Neurophysiology*, 1976, 40, 67–77.

Johnston, L. *Drugs and American youth*. Ann Arbor: Institute for Social Research, 1973.

Jones, B. M. Verbal and spatial intelligence in short and long-term alcoholics. *Journal of Nervous and Mental Disease*, 1971, *153*, 292–297.

Jones, B. & Parsons, O. A. Impaired abstracting ability in chronic alcoholics. *Archives of General Psychiatry*, 1971, *24*, 71–75.

Jones, B. & Parsons, O. A. Specific versus generalized deficits of abstracting ability in chronic alcoholics. *Archives of General Psychiatry*, 1972, *26*, 380–384.

Judd, L. L. & Grant, I. Brain dysfunction in chronic sedative users. *Journal of Psychedelic Drugs*, 1975, *7*, 143–149.

Kales, A., Kales, J. D., Scharf, M. B., & Tan, T. L. Hypnotics and altered sleep-dream patterns. II. All-night EEG studies of chloral hydrate, flurazepam, and methaqualone. *Archives of General Psychiatry*, 1970, *23*, 219–225.

Kammeier, M. T., Hoffmann, H., & Loper, R. G. Personality characteristics of alcoholics as college freshman and at time of treatment. *Quarterly Journal of Studies on Alcohol*, 1973, *34*, 390–399.

Kandel, D. B. Stages in adolescent involvement in drug use. *Science*, 1975, *190*, 912–914.

Kandel, D. B. & Faust, R. Sequence and stages in patterns of adolescent drug use. *Archives of General Psychiatry*, 1975, *32*, 923–932.

Kay, D. C., Blackburn, A. B., Buckingham, J. A., & Karacan, I. Human pharmacology of sleep. In Williams, R. L., & Karacan, I. (eds.) *Pharmacology of Sleep*. New York: Wiley, 1976 (in press).

Keller, J., & Redfering, D. L. Comparison between the personality of LSD users and nonusers as measured by the MMPI. *Journal of Nervous and Mental Disease*, 1973, *156*, 271–277.

Kendall, R. F. & Pittel, S. M. Three portraits of the young drug user: Comparison of MMPI group profiles. *Journal of Psychedelic Drugs*, 1971, *3*, 63–66.

Kessler, R. C., Paton, S. M., & Kandel, D. B. Reconciling unidimensional and multidimensional models of drug use. *Journal of Studies on Alcohol*, 1976, *37*, 632–647.

Kirby, M. W. & Berry, G. J. Selected descriptive characteristics of polydrug abusers. *Journal of Psychedelic Drugs*, 1975, *7*, 161–167.

Klonoff, H., Fibiger, C. H., & Hutton, G. H. Neuropsychological patterns in chronic schizophrenia. *Journal of Nervous and Mental Disease*, 1970, *150*, 291–300.

Klove, H. The relationship between neuropsychologic test performance and neuropsychologic status. Paper presented at the meeting of the American Academy of Neurology, Minneapolis, Minnesota, 1963.

Klove, H. Validation studies in adult clinical neuropsychology. In R. M. Reitan and L. A. Davison (eds.) *Clinical Neuropsychology: Current Status and Applications*, Washington, D.C.: Winston and Sons, pp. 211–237, 1974.

Kohler, W. C., Coddington, R. D., & Angew, H. W., Jr. Sleep patterns in 2-year-old children. *Journal of Pediatrics*, 1968, *72*, 228–233.

Kolanski, H. & Moore, W. T. Effects of marihuana on adolescent young adults. *Journal of the American Medical Association*. 1971

Kolb, D., Neil, R. L., & Gunderson, E. K. E. Differences in family characteristics of heroin injectors and inhalers. *The Journal of Nervous and Mental Disease*, 1974, *158*, 446–449.

Kornetsky, C. H. Psychological effects of chronic barbiturate intoxication, *Archives of Neurology and Psychiatry*, 1951, *65*, 557–567.

Kraft, T. & Wijeshinghe, B. Systematic densensitization of social anxiety in the treatment of alcoholism: A psychometric evaluation of change. *British Journal of Psychiatry*, 1970, *117*, 443–444.

Kristianson, P. A. Comparative study of two alcoholic groups and a control group. *British Journal of Medical Psychology*, 1970, *43*, 161–175.

Kurland, A. A., Unger, S., Shaffer, J. W., & Savage, C. Psychedelic therapy utilizing LSD in the treatment of the alcoholic patient—a preliminary report. *American Journal of Psychiatry*, 1967, *123*, 1202–1209.

Lachar, D. Accuracy and generalizability of an automated MMPI interpretation system. *Journal of Consulting and Clinical Psychology*, 1974a, *42*, 267–273.

Lachar, D. *The MMPI: Clinical assessment and automated interpretation*. Los Angeles: Western Psychological Services 1974b.

Lachar, D., Berman, W., Grisell, G., & Schooff, K. Objective personality traits of alcoholics, heroin addicts and polydrug abusers compared to matched psychiatric controls. Proceedings presented at the meeting of the Scientific Forum on Substance Abuse, East Lansing Michigan, October, 1975.

Lachar, D., Klinge, V., & Grisell, J. L. Relative accuracy of automated MMPI narratives generated from adult norm and adolescent norm profiles. *Journal of Consulting and Clinical Psychology*, 1976, *44*, 10–24.

Lacks, P. M., Colbert, J., Harrow, M., & Levine, J. Further evidence concerning the diagnostic accuracy of the Halstead organic test battery. *Journal of Clinical Psychology*, 1970, *26*, 480–481.

Ladner, R. A., Russe, B. R., & Weppner, R. S. Acute and chronic drug problems responsible for emergency hospital admissions. *Journal of Psychedelic Drugs*, 1975, *7*, 215–228.

Lanyon, R. I., Primo, R. V., Terrel, F., & Wenar, A. An aversion-desensitization treatment for alcoholism. *Journal of Consulting and Clinical Psychology*, 1972, *38*, 394–398.

Legislative History of the Drug Abuse Office and Treatment Act of 1972, Washington, D.C., U.S. Government Printing Office, 1972.

Lehmann, H. E. & Ban, T. A. The effect of hypnotics on rapid eye movement (REM). *International Journal of Clinical Pharmacology, Therpeutics, and Toxicology*, 1968, *7*, 424–427.

Lester, D. A new method for the determination of the effectiveness of sleep-inducing agents in humans. *Comprehensive Psychiatry*, 1960, *1*, 301–307.

Lester, B. K., Coulter, J. D., Cowden, L. C., & Williams, H. L. Secobarbital and nocturnal physiological patterns. *Psychopharmacologia*, 1968, *13*, 275–286.

Letteieri, D. J. (Ed.). *Predicting adolescent drug abuse: A review of issues, methods and correlates*. (National Institute on Drug Abuse, Research Series No. 11, DHEW Publication No. ADM 76-249.) Washington, D.C.: U.S. Government Printing Office, 1966.

Levine, D. G. "Needle freaks": Compulsive self-infection by drug user. *American Journal of Psychiatry*, 1974, *131*, 297–300.

Levine, J. & Feirstein, A. Differences in test performance between brain-damaged, schizophrenic, and medical patients. *Journal of Consulting and Clinical Psychology*, 1972, *39*, 508–511.

Levine, S. & Stephens, R. C. Types of narcotic addicts. In: R. E. Hardy, & J. G. Cull (Eds.) *Drug Dependence and Rehabilitation Approaches*, Springfield, Illinois: C. C. Thomas, 1972.

Levy, S. & Doyle, K. Attitudes toward women in a drug abuse treatment program. *Journal of Drug Issues*, 1974, *4*, 428–434.

Linn, L. Physician characteristics and attitudes toward legitimate use of psychotherapeutic drugs. *Journal of Health and Social Behavior*, 1971, *12*, 132–140.

Loomis, A. L., Harvey, E. N., & Hobart, G. Further observations on the potential rhythms of the cerebral cortex during sleep. *Science*, 1935, *82*, 198–200.

Loper, R. G., Kammeier, M. L., & Hoffmann, H. MMPI characteristics of college freshman males who later became alcoholics. *Journal of Abnormal Psychology*, 1973, *82*, 159–162.

Lucas, W. C., Grupp, S. E., & Schmitt, R. L. Single and multiple drug opiate users: addicts or nonaddicts. *HSMHA Health Reports*, 1972, *87*, 185–192.

Ludwig, A. M. & Levine, J. Patterns of hallucinogenic drug abuse. *Journal of American Medical Association*, 1965, *191*, 104–108.

Lynch, W. J. The performance of LSD users on certain neuropsychological tests. (Doctoral dissertation, University of Tennessee, 1970). *Dissertation Abstracts International*, 1971, *31*, 5630 B. (University Microfilms No. 71-7651).

MacAndrew, C. The differentiation of male alcoholic outpatients from non-alcoholic psychiatric patients by means of the MMPI. *Quarterly Journal of Studies on Alcohol*, 1965, *26*, 238–246.

Maccoby, E. E. & Jacklin, C. N. *The Psychology of Sex Differences*. Stanford: Stanford University Press, 1976.

Maier, L. R. & Abidin, R. R. Validation attempt of hovey's five-item MMPI index for CNS disorders. *Journal of Consulting Psychology*, 31, 542, 1967.

Manoli, B., Presslich, O., Wessely, P., & Zwischenberger, H. EEG-untersuchungen sei drogenmissblauch. *Wien Klin Wschr*, 1974, *86*, 287–289.

Martin, W. B., Johnson, L. C., Viglione, S. S., Naitoh, P., Joseph, R. D., & Moses, J. D. Pattern recognition of EEG-EOG as a technique for all-night sleep stage scoring. *Electroencephalography and Clinical Neurophysiology*, 1972, *32*, 417–427.

Mascia, G. V. A study of the prediction of alcoholics responsiveness to treatment. (Doctoral Dissertation, University of Kansas, 1969). *Dissertation Abstracts International*, 1969, *30*, 2912 B. (University Microfilms, No. 69-21, 549).

Mathias, R. E. S. An experimental investigation of the personality structure of chronic alcoholics, Alcoholics Anonymous, neurotic and normal groups. (Doctoral Dissertation, University of Buffalo, 1955). *Dissertation Abstracts International*, 1956, *16*, 156. (University Microfilms, No. 13, 748).

Matarazzo, J. D., Wiens, A. N., & Matarazzo, R. G., Psychometric and clinical test-retest reliability of the Halstead Impairment Index in a sample of healthy young, normal men. *Journal of Nervous and Mental Disease*, 1974, *158*, 37–49.

Matthews, C. G. Application of neuropsychological test methods in mentally retarded subjects. In R. M. Reitan and L. A. Davison (eds.) *Clinical Neuropsychology: Current Status and Applications*, Washington, D.C.: Winston and Sons, Pp. 267–287, 1974.

Matthews, C. G. & Booker, H. E. Pneumoencephalographic measurements and neuro-psychological test performance in human adults, *Cortex*, 1972, *8*, 69–92.

McAree, C. P., Steffenhagen, R. A., & Zheutlin, L. S. Personality factors in college drug users. *International Journal of Social Psychiatry*, 1969, *15*, 102–106.

McAree, C. P,, Steffenhagen, R. A., & Zheutlin, L. S. Personality factors and patterns of drug usage in college students. *American Journal of Psychiatry*, 1972, *128*, 890–893.

McGinnis, C. A. & Ryan, C. W. The influence of age on MMPI scores of chronic alcoholics. *Journal of Clinical Psychology*, 1965, 21, 271–272.

McGlothin, W. H. Drug use and abuse. *Annual Review of Psychology*, 1975, 26, 45–64.

McGlothlin, W. H., Arnold, D. O., & Freedman, D. X. Organicity measures following repeated LSD ingestion. *Archives of General Psychiatry*, 1969, *21*, 704–709.

McGuire, J. S. & Megargee, E. I. Personality correlates of marijuana use among youthful offenders. *Journal of Consulting and Clinical Psychology*, 1974, *42*, 124–133.

McLachlan, J. F. C. Classification of alcoholics by an MMPI actuarial system. *Journal of Clinical Psychology*, 1975, *31*, 145–147.

Mellinger, G., Balter, M., & Manheimer, D. Patterns of psychotherapeutic drug use among adults in San Francisco. *Archives of General Psychiatry*, 1971, *25*, 385–394.

Mendelson, J. H., & Meyer, R. E. Behavioral and sociological concomitants of chronic marijuana smoking by heavy and casual users. In *Technical Papers of the First Report of the National Commission on Marijuana and Drug Abuse*. Washington, D.C., USGPO 1972, 68–246.

Milkman, H. & Frosch, W. A. On the preferential abuse of heroin and amphetamine. *The Journal of Nervous and Mental Disease*, 1973, *156*, 242–248.

Miller, B., Pokorny, A. D., & Hanson, P. G. A study of dropouts in an in-patient alcoholism treatment program. *Diseases of the Nervous System*, 1968, *29*, 91–99.

Miras, C. N., Fink, M., *et al*. Investigation of very heavy, very long-term cannabis users: Greece. In *Technical Papers of the First Report of the National Commission on Marijuana and Drug Abuse*. Washington,D.C., USGOP 1972, 53–55.

Miskimins, R. W. & Braucht, G. N. *Description of the self*. Ft. Collins, Colorado: Rocky Mountain Behavioral Science Institute, 1971.

Mogar, R. E., Helm, S. T., Snedeker, M. R., Snedeker, M. H., & Wilson, W. M. Staff attitudes toward the alcoholic patient. *Archives General Psychiatry*, 1969, *21*, 449–454.

Mosher, D. L. The development and multitrait-multimethod matrix analysis of three aspects of guilt. *Journal of Consulting Psychology*, 1966, *30*, 25–29.

Muller, C. The overmedicated society: forces in the marketplace for medical care. *Science*, 1972, *17*, 288–292.

Murtaugh, T. L. Perceptual isolation, drug, drug addiction and adaptation phenomena. Masters Dissertation, Temple University, 1971. Cited in M. Zuckerman, Manual and Research Report for the Sensation Seeking Scale (SSS), March, 1975, p. 52.

National Commission on Marijuana and Drug Abuse. *Drug Use in America: Problem in Perspective*. Second Report of the National Commission on Marijuana and Drug Abuse. Washington, D.C.: U.S. Government Printing Offices, 1973.

Nie, N. H., Hull, C. H., Jenkins, J. G., Steinbrenner, K., & Bent, D. H. SPSS *Statistical Package for the Social Sciences* (2nd Edition), New York: McGraw-Hill, 1975.

O'Donnell, J. A., Voss, H. C., Clayton, R. R., Slafin, G. T., & Room, R. G. Young men and drugs—a nationwide survey. Rockville, Maryland: National Institute on Drug Abuse, 1976.

Olson, R. W. MMPI sex differences in narcotic addicts. *Journal of General Psychology*, 1964, *71*, 257–266.

Overall, J. E. MMPI personality patterns of alcoholics and narcotic addicts. *Quarterly Journal of Studies on Alcohol*, 1973, *34*, 104–111.

Parry, H. L., Balter, M. B., Mellinger, G. D., Cisin, I. H., & Manheimer, D. I. National patterns of psychotherapeutic drug use. *Archives of General Psychiatry*, 1973, *28*, 769–783.

Petersen, D. Acute drug reactions (overdoses) among females: a race comparison. *Addictive Diseases*, 1974, *34*, 58–72.

Pfeffer, A. Z. & Ruble, D. C. Chronic psychosis and addiction to morphine, *Archives Neurology Psychiatry*, 1948, *56*, 665–672.

Phillips, D. L. & Segal, B. E. Sexual status and psychiatric symptoms. *American Sociological Review*, 1969, *34*, 58–72.

Physician Visits: Volume and Interval Since Last Visit, United States, 1969. DHEW Publication #72-1064, 1972.

Pittel, S. Psychological aspects of heroin and other drug dependence. *Journal of Psychedelic Drugs*, 1971, *4*, 40–45.

Pittel, S. M. & Hoffer, R. The transition to amphetamine abuse. In D. E. Smith and D. R. Wesson (Eds.), *Uppers and downers*. Englewood Cliffs, New Jersey: Prentice-Hall, 1973.

Pollack, D. Experimental intoxication of alcoholics and normals: Some psychological changes. (Doctoral dissertation, University of California, (L.A.), 1965). *Dissertation Abstracts International*, 1965, *25*, 7383. *University Microfilms No. 65-5707).

Prather, J. & Fidell, L. S. Put her down and drug her up. Presented at the American Sociology Association, New Orleans, August, 1972.

Prigatano, G. P. & Parsons, O. A. Relationship of age and education to Halstead test performance in different patient populations, *Journal of Consulting Clinical Psychology*, 1976, *44*, 527–533.

Rae, J. B. The influence of the wives on the treatment outcome of alcoholics: A follow-up study at two years. *British Journal of Psychiatry*, 1972, *120*, 601–613.

Rae, J. B. & Forbes, A. R. Clinical and psychometric characteristics of the wives of alcoholics. *British Journal of Psychiatry*, 1966, *112*, 197–200.

Rechtschaffen, A., Robinson, T. M., & Winocor, M. Z. The effect of methaqualone on nocturnal sleep. *Psychophysiology*, 1970, 7, 346, (abstract).

Redick, R. W. "Addition Rate to Federally Funded Community Mental Health Centers, U.S. 1973", Statistical Note #126. Department of Health, Education, and Welfare— PHS. ADAMHA-NIMH-DBE. Survey Reports Branch, 1973.

Reed, H. B. C. Cognitive effects of marijuana. In: *The Use of Marijuana: A Psychological and Physiological Inquiry*, New York: Plenum Press, pp. 107–114, 1974.

Reitan, R. M. An investigation of the validity of Halstead's measures of biological intelligence. *Archives of Neurology Psychiatry*, 1955, 73, 28–35.

Reitan, R. M. A research program on the psychological effects of brain lesions in human beings. Ellis, N. R. (Ed.): *International Review of Research in Mental Retardation*. New York: Academic Press, 1966, Volume 1, pp. 153–218.

Reitan, R. M., & Boll, T. J. Neuropsychological correlates of minimal brain dysfunction, *Annals of the New York Academy of Science*, 1973, *205*, 65–88.

Reitan, R. M. & Davison, L. A. (Eds.). *Clinical Neuropsychology: Current Status and Applications*, Washington, D.C.: Winson & Sons, 1974.

Regal, L. H. Personality patterns of narcotic addiction. (Doctoral Dissertation, University of California (L.A.), 1963). *Dissertation Abstracts International*, 1963, *23*, 3982. (University Microfilms, No. 63-2950).

Rexler, A. G. Attitude changes during medical school: a review of the literature. *Journal of Medical Education*, 1974, 49, 1023–1030.

Reynolds, R. E. & Bice, T. W. Attitudes of medical interns toward patients and health professionals. *Journal of Health and Social Behavior*, 1971, *12*, 307–311.

Richman, A. & Abbey, H. Pseudoepidemics. Paper presented at the Annual Meeting, American Public Health Association, Statistics Section, Miami, October, 1976.

Risberg, A. M., Risberg, J., Elmqvist, D., & Ingvar, D. H. Effects of dyxyrazine and methaqualone on the sleep pattern in normal man. *European Journal of Clinical Pharmacology*, 1975, 8, 227–231.

Robbins, T. Characteristics of amphetamine addicts. *The International Journal of the Addictions*, 1970, 5, 183–193.

Rohan, W. P. MMPI changes in hospitalized alcoholics a second study. *Quarterly Journal of Studies on Alcohol*, 1972, 33, 65–76.

Rohan, W. P., Tatro, R. L., & Rotman, S. R. MMPI changes in alcoholics during hospitalization. *Quarterly Journal of Studies on Alcohol*, 1969, 30, 389–400.

Rosecrans, C. J. & Brignet, H. P. Comparative personality profiles of young drug abusers and non-users. *Alabama Journal of Medical Science*, 1972, 9, 397–402.

Rosen, A. C. A comparative study of alcoholic and psychiatric patients with the MMPI. *Quarterly Journal of Studies on Alcohol*, 1960, 21, 253–266.

Rosenkrantz, P., Vogel, S., Bee, H., Broverman, I. & Broverman, D. Sex role stereotypes and self-conceptions in college students. *Journal of Consulting and Clinical Psychology*, 32(3):287–295, 1968.

Ross, J. J., Agnew, H. W., Jr., Williams, R. L., & Webb, W. B. Sleep patterns in pre-adolescent children: An EEG-EOG study. *Pediatrics*, 1968, 42, 324–335.

Ross, W. F. & Berzins, J. I. Personality characteristics of female narcotic addicts on the MMPI. *Psychological Reports*, 1974, 35, 779–784.

Rozynko, V. & Stein, K. B. Typology of drug abusers. National Institute of Mental Health, Grant # MH 17647-01, 1972.

Rubin, V. & Comitas, L. Effects of chronic smoking of cannabis in Jamaica. A Report by the Research Institute for the Study of Man to the Center for Studies of Narcotic and Drug Abuse, NIMH Contract, #HSM-42-70-97, 1972.

Rubin, V. & Comitas, L. *Genja in Jamaica: A Medical and Anthropological Study of Chronic Marijuana Use*, Mouton: The Hague, 1975.

Rumbaugh, C. L., Bergeron, R. T., & Scanlan, R. L., Cerebral vascular changes secondary to amphetamine abuse in the experimental animal. *Radiology*, 1971, 101, 345–351.

Russell, E. W. Validation of a brain-damage vs schizophrenia MMPI key. *Journal of Clinical Psychology*, 1975, 31, 659–661.

Russell, E. W.; Neuringer, C. & Goldstein, G. *Assessment of Brain Damage: A Neuropsychological Key Approach*, Irving B. Weiner, (Ed.), New York: Wiley-Interscience, 1970.

Sadava, S. W. Research approaches in illicit drug use: A critical review. *Genetic Psychology Monographs*, 1975, 3–59.

Sanborn, D. E.; Casey, T. M. and Niswander, G. D. Drug abusers, suicide attempters, and the MMPI. *Diseases of the Nervous System*, 1971, 32, 183–187.

SAODAP #DA RG006 (Robert Cohen). A Quantitative Assessment of Non-Opiate Drug Abuse. Institute for Defense Analysis (IDA), 1974.

Savage, C., Karp, E. G., Curran, S. F., Hanlon, T. E., & McCabe, O. L. Methadone-LAAM maintenance: a comparison study. *Comprehensive Psychiatry*, 1976, 17, 415–424.

Schooff, K. G. & Keegan, J. F. Profiles of prescription medication abusers. National Academy of Sciences; Proceedings of the Annual Scientific Meeting Committee on Problems of Drug Dependence. Washington, D.C., May 1975.

Schoolar, J. C., White, E. H. & Cohen, C. P. Drug abusers and their clinic-patient counterparts: a comparison of personality dimensions. *Journal of Consulting and Clinical Psychology*, 1972, 39, 9–14.

Seidenberg, R. Drug advertising and the perception of mental illness. *Mental Higiene*, 1971, 55, 21–31.

Seyfeddinipur, N. & Rieger, H. EEG observations in chronic opium smoking. *Electroencephalography and Clinical Neurophysiology*, 1975, 39, 438–531.

Shaffer, J. W., Hanlon, T. E., Wold, S., Foxwell, N. H., & Kurland, A. A. Nailamide in the treatment of alcoholism. *Journal of Nervous and Mental Disease*, 1962, 135, 222–232.

Sharoff, R. L. Character problems and their relationship to drug abuse. *American Journal of Psychoanalysis*, 1969, 29, 186–193.

Sheppard, C., Ricca, E., Fracchia, J., & Merlis, S. Personality characteristics of urban and suburban heroin abusers: more data and another reply to Sutker and Allain. *Psychological Reports*, 1973, 33, 999–1008.

Shick, J. F. E., Smith, D. E., & Wesson, D. R. An analysis of amphetamine toxicity and patterns of use. *Journal of Psychedelic Drugs*, 1972, 5, 113–130.

Shrader, Binstock, & Scott. Subjective determinants of drug prescription: a study of therapists attitudes. *Hospital and Community Psychiatry*, 1968, 19, 384–387.

Simpson, D. D. & Sells, S. B. Patterns of multiple drug abuse: 1969–1971. *International Journal of the Addictions*, 1974, 9, 301–314.

Single, E., Kandel, D. B. & Faust, R. Patterns of multiple drug use in high school. *Journal of Health and Social Behavior*, 1974, *15*, 344–357.

Sinnett, E. R. The prediction of irregular discharge among alcoholic patients. *Journal of Social Psychology*, 1961, *55*, 231–235.

Smart, R. G. & Fejer, D. Illicit LSD users: Their social backgrounds, drug use and psychopathology. *Journal of Health and Social Behavior*, 1969, *10*, 297–308.

Smart, R. G. & Jones, D. Illicit LSD users: Their personality characteristics and psychopathology. *Journal of Abnormal Psychology*, 1970, *75*, 286–292.

Smart, R. G. & Whitehead, P. C. A typology of high school drug use: Medicinal usage, mood-modification, and tripping. *The International Journal of the Addictions*, 1972, *7*, 735–738.

Smith, A. Neuropsychological testing in neurological disorders. In: Walter J. Friedlander (ed.) *Advances in Neurology Volume 7: Current Reviews of Higher Nervous System Dysfunction*, New York: Raven Press Pp. 49–110, 1975.

Smith, D. E. & Gay, G. R. (Eds.) *It's So Good, Don't Even Try It Once. Heroin in Perspective*. Englewood Cliffs, New Jersey: Prentice-Hall, 1972.

Smith, D. E. & Wesson, D. R. (Eds.), *Uppers and downers*. Englewood Cliffs, New Jersey: Prentice-Hall, 1973.

Smith, D. E. & Wesson, D. R. Editors' note. *Journal of Psychedelic Drugs*, 6(2):129–133, April–June, 1974a.

Smith, D. E. & Wesson, D. R. Phenobarbital technique for treatment of barbiturate dependence. *Archives of General Psychiatry*, 1971, *24*, 56–60.

Smith, D. E. & Wesson, D. R. Diagnosis and Treatment of Adverse Reactions to Sedative-Hypnotics. (DHEW Publication No. (ADM) 75-144). Washington, D.C.: U.S. Government Printing Office, 1974b.

Smith, D. E. & Wesson, D. R. Editors' note. *Journal of Psychedelic Drugs*, 1975, *7*, 111–120.

Smith, J. R., Karacan, I., Funke, W. F., & Yang, M. Automated analysis of the human sleep EEG. *Electroencephalography and Clinical Neurophysiology*, in press.

Smith, J. R. & Karacan, I. EEG sleep stage scoring by an automatic hybrid system. *Electroencephalography Clinical Neurophysiology*, 1971, *31*, 231–237.

Smith, J. R. & Karacan, I. Quantification of the effects of a hypnoticlike drug on slow-wave sleep. In Koella, W. P., and Levin, P. (Eds.) *Sleep. Physiology, Biochemistry, Psychology, Pharmacology, Clinical Implications*. Basel: Karger, 1973, pp. 504–508.

Smith, J. W. & Layden, T. A. Changes in psychological performance and blood chemistry in alcoholics during and after hospital treatment. *Quarterly Journal of Studies in Alcoholism*, 1972, *33*, 379–394.

Sonquist, J. A. *Multivariate Model Building*. Michigan: Survey Research Center, The University of Michigan, 1970.

Sonquist, J. A., Baker, E. L. & Morgan, J. N. *Searching for Structure*. Survey Research Center, The University of Michigan, 1973.

Soskin, R. A. Personality and attitude change after two alcoholism treatment programs: comparative contributions of lysergide and human relations training. *Quarterly Journal of Studies on Alcohol*, 1970, *31*, 920–931.

Stauss, F. F., Ousley, N. R., & Carlin, A. S. Outreach for the middle-class drug user. *Drug Issues* (In press, 1978).

Stein, K. B. & Rozynko, V. Psychological and social variables and personality patterns of drug abusers. *The International Journal of the Addictions*, 1974, *9*, 431–446.

Stephens, R. C. & Slatin, G. J. The street addict role: toward the definition of a type. *Drug Forum*, 1974, *3*, 375–389.

Stoffer, S. S., Sapira, J. D., & Meketon, B. F. Behavior of ex-addict female prisoners participating in a research study. *Comprehensive Psychiatry*, 1969, *10*, 224–232.

Sutker, P. B. Personality differences and sociopathy in heroin addicts and non-addict prisoners. *Journal of Abnormal Psychology*, 1971, *78*, 247–251.

Sutker, P. B. & Allain, A. N. Incarcerated and street heroin addicts: a personality comparison. *Psychological Reports*, 1973, *32*, 243–246.

Sutker, P. B., & Moan, C. E. Personality characteristics of socially deviant women: incarcerated heroin addicts, street addicts and non-addicted prisoners. In: *Drug Addiction: Clinical and Social-legal Aspects. Vol II*, Mt. Kisco, N.Y.: Futura, 1972.

Swenson, W. M., Pearson, J. S., & Osborne, D. *An MMPI Source Book: Basic Item, Scale and Pattern Data on 50,000 Medical Patients*. Minneapolis: University of Minnesota Press, 1973.

Tarter, R. E. Psychological defects in chronic alcoholics: a review. *International Journal of the Addictions*, 1975, *10*, 327–368.

Tennant, F. Should a doctor treat heroin addicts in private practice? Newsletter, California Society for the Treatment of Alcoholism and Other Drug Dependencies, 1976 3(1):6–7, January.

Tinklenberg, J. R. & Berger, P. A. Treatment of Abusers of Nonaddictive Drugs. In (Eds.) Barchas, J. D., Berger, P. A., Ciarenello, R., & Elliott, G. R. *Psychopharmacology: From Theory to Practice*. Oxford University Press, New York, 1977.

Tomsovic, M. Hospitalized alcoholic patients: I, a two-year study of medical, social and psychological characteristics of hospitalized alcoholic patients. *Hospital and Community Psychiatry*, 1968, *19*, 197–203.

Toomey, T. C. Personality and demographic characteristics of two subtypes of drug abusers. *British Journal of Addictions*, 1974, *69*, 155–158.

Tryon, R. C. & Bailey, D. E. *Cluster Analysis*. McGraw-Hill, New York, 1970.

Ungerleider, J. T., Fisher, D. D., Fuller, M., & Caldwell, A. The "bad trip"—the etiology of the adverse LSD reaction. *American Journal of Psychiatry*, 1968, *124*, 1483–1490.

Users manual for the drug abuse treatment referral system—(DATRA). Berkeley: Berkeley Center for Drug Studies, 1973.

Vega, A. Cross-validation of four MMPI scales for alcoholism. *Quarterly Journal of Studies on Alcohol*, 1971, *32*, 791–797.

Vega, A. & Parsons, O. A. Cross-validation of the Halstead-Reitan tests for brain damage. *Journal of Consulting and Clinical Psychology*, 1967, *31*, 619–625.

Victor, M., Adams, R. D., & Collins, G. H. *The Wernicke-Korsakoff Syndrome*. Philadelphia: Davis, 1971.

VonZerssen, D., Fliege, K., & Wolf, M. Cerebral atrophy in drug addicts. *The Lancet*, 1970, 313, (letter to the editor).

Walizer, D. G. The need for standardized, scientific criteria for describing drug-using behavior. *International Journal of the Addictions*, 1975, *10*, 927–936.

Watson, C. G. An MMPI scale to separate brain-damaged from schizophrenic men. *Journal of Consulting and Clinical Psychology*, 1971, *36*, 121–125.

Watson, C. G. The separation of np hospital organics from schizophrenics with three visual motor screening tests. *Journal of Clinical Psychology*, 1968, *24*, 412–414.

Watson, C. G., Thomas, R. W., Andersen, D., & Felling, J. Differentiation of organics from schizophrenics at two chronicity levels by use of the Halstead-Reitan organic test battery. *Journal of Consulting and Clinical Psychology*, 1968, *32*, 679–684.

Weiner, I. B. *Psychodiagnosis in Schizophrenia*. New York: Wiley, 1966.

Webb, J. T. The relation of MMPI two-point codes to age, sex and education level in a representative nationwide sample of psychiatric outpatients. Unpublished paper presented at the Southwestern Psychological Association, 1970.

Welsh, G. S. MMPI profiles and factor scales A and R. *Journal of Clinical Psychology*, 1965, *21*, 43–47.

Wessely, P., Manoli, B., Presslich, O., & Zwischenberger, J. EEG Untersuchungen in Langsschnitt Sei der Entwohnung von Jugenlichen Polytoxikomanen. Psychiatrica clin 8: Pp. 212–221, 1975.

Wesson, D. R. & Smith, D. E. Barbiturate toxicity and the treatment of barbiturate dependence. In: D. E. Smith & D. R. Wesson, (Eds.) *Uppers and Downers*. Englewood Cliffs, New Jersey: Prentice-Hall, 1973.

Wesson, D. R., Smith, D. E. & Lerner, S. E. Streetwise and nonstreetwise polydrug typology: myth or reality. *Journal of Psychedelic Drugs*, 1975, *7*, 121–134.

Wesson, D. R. & Jacoby, J. E., *Medical Treatment for Complications of Polydrug Abuse*. National Institute on Drug Abuse Services Research Monograph Series. Rockville, Maryland, 1977.

Wheeler, L., Burke, C. J., & Reitan, R. M. An application of discriminant functions to the problems of predicting brain damage using behavioral variables. *Perceptual and Motor Skills*, 1963, *16*, 417–440.

Whitehead, P. E. & Smart, R. Alcohol and other drugs: perspectives on use, abuse, treatment and prevention. *Candian Journal of Criminology and Corrections*, 1972, *14*, 1.

Wiggins, J. S. Substantive dimensions of self-report in the MMPI item pool. *Psychological Monographs*, 1966, *80*, 22 (whole no. 630).

Wikler, A., Fraser, H. F., Isbell, H., & Pescor, F. T. Electro-encephalograms during cycles of addiction to barbiturates in man. *Electroencephalography and Clinical Neurophysiology*, 1955, *7*, 1–13.

Wilkinson, A. E., Prado, W. M., Williams, W. O., & Schnadt, F. W. Psychological test characteristics and length of stay in alcoholism treatment. *Quarterly Journal of Studies on Alcohol*, 1971, *32*, 60–65.

Williams, R. L. & Agnew, H. W., Jr. The effects of drugs on the EEG sleep patterns of normal humans. *Experimental Medicine and Surgery*, 1969, *27*, 53–64.

Williams, R. L. & Karacan, I. (Eds.). *Pharmacology of Sleep*. New York: Wiley, 1976.

Williams, R. L., Agnew, H. W., Jr., & Webb, W. B. Sleep patterns in young adults: An EEG study. *Electroencephalography Clinical Neurophysiology*, 1964, *17*, 376–381.

Williams, R. L., Agnew, H. W., Jr., & Webb, W. B. Sleep patterns in the young adult female: An EEG study. *Electroencephalography and Clinical Neurophysiology*, 1966, *20*, 264–266.

Williams, R. L., Karacan, I., & Hursch, C. J. *Electroencephalography (EEG) of Human Sleep: Clinical Applications*. New York: Wiley, 1974.

Williams, R. L., Karacan, I., Hursch, C. J., & Davis, C. E. Sleep patterns of pubertal males. *Pediatric Research*, 1972a, *6*, 643–648.

Williams, R. L., Karacan, I., Thornby, J. I., & Salis, P. J. The electroencephalogram sleep patterns of middle-aged males. *Journal of Nervous and Mental Disease*, 1972b, *154*, 22–30.

Winer, B. J. *Statistical principles in experimental design*. New York: McGraw-Hill, 1962.

Wright, M. & Hogan, T. P. Repeated LSD ingestion and performance on neuropsychological tests. *Journal of Nervous and Mental Disease*, 1972, *154*, 432–438.

Zelen, S. L., Fox, J., Gould, E., & Olson, R. W. Sex-contingent differences between male and female alcoholics. *Journal of Clinical Psychology*, 1966, *22*, 160–165.

Zuckerman, M. Drug usage as one manifestation of a "sensation seeking" trait. In: Keup (Ed.). *Drug Abuse–Current Concepts and Research*. Springfield, Ill.: Charles C. Thomas, 1972, chapt. 18, Pp. 154–170.

Zuckerman, M., Sola, S., Masterson, J., & Angelone, J. V. MMPI patterns in drug abusers before and after treatment in therapeutic communities. *Journal of Consulting and Clinical Psychology*, 1975, 43, 286–296.

Subject Index

A 8
B 9
C 0
D 1
E 2
F 3
G 4
H 5
I 6
J 7